Russia

From the reviews of the First Edition:

'Beautifully written and organised with admirable clarity. The argument is taut throughout, and the level of generalisation high and yet brought to life by vivid details and buttressed by sufficient supporting evidence succinctly presented. ...An excellent book which is a first-rate guide to anyone embarking on a study of Russian history or the Soviet Union. It is finely produced and well illustrated.'

John Morison, *Journal of Russian Studies*

'The great strength of the work lies in its resolutely analytical framework ... a lucid, yet succinct, summary and judicious evaluation of the various possible historical explanations of the developments described. From the point of view of the general reader or university undergraduate Dr Acton most usefully summarises the large volume of new research, both in the Soviet Union and the west, which has appeared in recent years. His acquaintance with and understanding of this vast mass of scholarship over a wide variety of topics is indeed impressive, as is his ability to present complicated material in a brief, yet comprehensible, form.'

Robert B. McKean, *History* (UK)

'The series of which this briskly written book is a part aims at providing the historical background for a proper understanding of the contemporary world, and to do so by illuminating political, economic, social and cultural structures through a study of their past. Acton does a good job at fulfilling the series goals.' Mark Raeff *History Today*

'Numerous maps and illustrations strengthen this tour of the Russian-Soviet past, as does an interesting epilogue and a fine index. The publisher deserves praise for an unusually attractive book... It should be acquired by every library.' ...mann, *History* (USA)

THE PRESENT AND THE PAST
Founding Editors: Michael Crowder and Juliet Gardiner

These books provide the historical background necessary for a proper understanding of the major nations and regions of the contemporary world. Each contributor illuminates the present political, social, cultural and economic structures of his nation or region through the study of its past. The books, which are fully illustrated with maps and photographs, are written for students, teachers and general readers; and will appeal not only to historians but also to political scientists, economists and sociologists who seek to set their own studies of a particular nation or region in historical perspective.

Titles already published

Australia: A Cultural History (Second Editon)   *John Rickard*

Modern China: A History (Second Edition)   *Edwin E. Moise*

Russia: The Tsarist and Soviet Legacy (Second Edition)   *Edward Acton*

Italy Since 1800: A Nation in the Balance   *Roger Absalom*

THE PRESENT AND THE PAST............................

Russia

The Tsarist and Soviet Legacy

Second Edition

Edward Acton

An imprint of **Pearson Education**

Harlow, England · London · New York · Reading, Massachusetts · San Francisco · Toronto · Don Mills, Ontario · Sydney
Tokyo · Singapore · Hong Kong · Seoul · Taipei · Cape Town · Madrid · Mexico City · Amsterdam · Munich · Paris · Milan

Pearson Education Limited
Edinburgh Gate
Harlow, Essex CM20 2JE, England
and Associated Companies throughout the world.

Visit us on the World Wide Web at:
http://www.pearsoneduc.com

First published 1986
Second edition 1995

ISBN 0 582 089158 CSD
ISBN 0 582 089220 PPR

British Library Cataloguing-in-Publication Data

A catalogue record for this book is
available from the British Library

Library of Congress Cataloging-in-Publication Data

Acton, Edward.
    Russia / Edward Acton.—2nd ed.
        p.   cm. —(The Present and the past)
    Includes bibliographical references and index.
    ISBN 0–582–08915–8 (csd).— ISBN 0–582–08922–0 (ppr)
    1. Russia—History.   2. Soviet Union—History.   I. Title.
II. Series.
DK40.A25   1995
947—dc20   94–11457
                                                                   CIP

Set by 8 in 10/12 Sabon
Produced by Pearson Education Asia Pte Ltd.
Printed in Singapore (MPM)

10   9   8   7
04   03   02

Contents

List of Maps

List of Illustrations

List of Tables

Acknowledgements

Among the many friends and relations to whom I am indebted for help in writing this book I would like particularly to thank Philip Bell, Michael de Cossart, Roy Davison, Geoffrey Hosking, Genia and Nick Lampert, Brian Pearce, Christopher Ryan, and Tom Scott for the time and trouble they took to read the manuscript of the first edition, and in some cases parts of the second, and for their invaluable critical comments. The blemishes that remain are no fault of theirs. I am grateful to the British Council for financing a research visit to Moscow and to the British Academy for supporting my research within Britain. Finally, I would like to mention Helen and Natalie, without whose moral support I would have taken much less pleasure in writing the second edition, and Stella, without whom it would not have been written at all.

E.D.J.L.D.A. *The University of East Anglia*

Illustrations were taken from the following publications: plate 2.3 from Sigismund von Herberstein: *Travels in Muscovy*, 1560 and plate 3.4 from Gustave Doré's *Histoire pittoresque, dramatique et caricaturale de la Sainte Russie*, 1854.

To my parents

Prologue

There is much in Russia to puzzle the western mind. Ever since the English 'discovered' Muscovy in the sixteenth century, foreigners have been expressing astonishment at things Russian. It is not only Russian tastes – be it for female obesity and interminable church services in the early modern period, for mushroom-picking and chess today, or for untold quantities of vodka throughout the ages – which have seemed bizarre. So too has the basic social, political and ideological make-up of Muscovy, the Russian Empire, the Soviet Union and, in turn, today's troubled Federation. The purpose of this book is to provide an introduction to contemporary Russia by examining her past. So rapid has the pace of change been, so far removed is the Russia of the 1990s from that of the Tsar, the revolution, or even Stalin that a historical approach might seem superfluous. Yet it is as true of Russian society as of any other that an assessment of the present which is not rooted in a knowledge of the past is liable to be shallow and distorted.

The value of a historical approach is not difficult to demonstrate where developments since the revolutionary upheaval of 1917 are concerned. The political instability and institutional turmoil of today can only be understood against the background of the Soviet political system which arose from the revolution. The nature of the social tension which confronts the post-Soviet leadership can only be understood in the light of the social transformation which the revolution inaugurated. Neither the current devastation of the Russian economy, nor its longer-term potential, can be appreciated unless set against the background of the industrialization drive undertaken by the Communist regime. Russia's relations with her immediate neighbours make little sense without reference to the hegemony Communist Moscow exercised over the other Soviet and eastern European republics. More generally, her international posture is conditioned by the experience of the Soviet years: the decades of isolation which followed the revolution; the carnage and trauma of Hitler's invasion; the paradoxical combination of economic desolation and massively increased military-diplomatic weight bequeathed by the Red Army's victory in 1945; and the nuclear superpower status attained by the USSR. By the same token, however hungrily pre-Soviet and Western currents of thought are now being imbibed, however furiously Soviet ideology, values, art and literature are now repudiated, it is only against the background of that heritage that today's cultural explosion can be understood. Every facet of contemporary Russia bears the imprint of the three-quarters of a century of Communist rule that began with the Bolshevik Revolution in 1917.

But if 1917 is rightly seen to mark a caesura in the country's development, it is equally true that neither the Bolshevik Revolution nor the direction taken by the post-revolutionary Bolshevik regime can be understood without reference to what went before. The victory of the far Left in 1917 was no fluke. It was not the handiwork of a few rogue intellectuals but the product of acute social polarization. Nor, once in power, did the Bolsheviks act on a *tabula rasa*: Russia provided no passive, insulated social laboratory within which the dreams of Europe's socialist tradition could be put to scientific test; to its last day every aspect of Soviet 'socialism' reflected the legacy of Imperial Russia. To appreciate that legacy it is essential to grasp the nature of the socioeconomic changes, generated by both international and domestic pressures, which began to destabilize the Empire from the mid-nineteenth century. This, in turn, requires an understanding of the traditional society upon which these changes impinged, the political, social, economic, and cultural composition of Imperial Russia in its prime. The point of departure must be an examination of the manner in which the Empire took shape.

To attempt an analytical history of Russia designed to illuminate the present is an exhilarating but perilous enterprise. It involves weighing and passing summary judgement upon a mass of painstaking research by scholars drawn from different nationalities and conflicting ideological persuasions. In one sense the task is easier than when I undertook the first edition a decade ago. Then, with Russia encased in a seemingly stable Soviet system, the major danger appeared to be the risk of presenting a bogus 'whig' view of the past which ignored the 'losers', disregarded the countless crossroads when various outcomes had been possible, and portrayed all roads leading inexorably to the Soviet denouement. Since then, the contingent nature of Russia's development has been underscored in the most powerful manner possible by the upheaval that began with Gorbachev's accession in 1985. On the other hand, the constraints of space have become even more challenging. A second edition must not only incorporate an analysis of the momentous changes through which the country has passed since the mid-1980s; it must also refine and develop earlier sections of the book in the light of a wealth of fresh research, much of it drawing on recently opened archives. I have found it necessary to introduce new material into every chapter and to expand substantially each of those dealing with the late imperial and Soviet periods. To achieve a synthesis while still operating within the compass of one manageable volume involves a process of ruthless selection.

Specialists in every field may take offence at the balance I have struck between different periods and different topics: just two chapters covering the entire millennium before Peter the Great, no more than scattered references to the smaller ethnic minorities, a few lines on Pushkin. I have adhered to a chronological framework, but rather than spreading coverage evenly across the centuries I have deliberately dwelt upon those developments which cast most light on the present conjuncture. In particular, I have concentrated upon five themes which seem of central importance to an understanding of the Russia emerging from the ruins of the Soviet Union: how the writ of the Tsar and then of the Communist Party came to run over one-sixth of the earth's surface; the complex way in which the country's international setting has interacted with her sociopolitical development; why it was here, in the most backward of the Great Powers, that Europe's most radical socialist revolution took place; the profound impact which this backwardness has had upon political, economic, social and cultural developments since the revolution; and, finally, the process by which in the Soviet period the State came to mediate such a broad range of human activity. It is above all the legacy of this 'statization' of society which conditions the development of post-Soviet Russia. And it is the relationship between State and society, between the power – coercive, administrative, legal, cultural and economic – at the disposal of Tsar, Politburo or President and the social body at large, which provides the guiding thread of my analysis.

Chapter 1 ....

The origins of the Russian Empire

The pleasing simplicity with which it is possible to summarize Russian history has led historians of various persuasions to seek one key factor to explain all. Among the most plausible of these is the physical setting of the East European Plain in which Russian society evolved. Three points merit particular attention: the low yield of the land, the absence of natural barriers, and the network of major rivers.

At the end of the Soviet period, only just over one-tenth of the territory under Moscow's rule was actively cultivated, while two-thirds were unfit for farming of any kind, and over half was virtually uninhabitable. Even on the best land, agriculture is handicapped by adverse climatic conditions. The richest soil, that of the so-called 'black earth' region which stretches from the south-west into Siberia, suffers from recurrent drought during the growing season and yields are frequently further devastated by thunderstorms and hailstorms in the harvest season. Moreover, until the seventeenth century these fertile regions were dominated by livestock-rearing nomadic tribes. The low yield of the land available to the Russians made it difficult for their settled agricultural communities to generate the necessary resources to resist nomadic raids. What further delayed settled development was the lack of natural protection against such raids. Only the Urals interrupt the East European Plain, and this low range of scattered hills is little more than a notional boundary between Europe and Asia, presenting no substantial obstacle to migration and military advance. Once a settled community able to defend itself was established, on the other hand, little stood in the way of a rapid extension of its power over more primitive peoples. The unification of a vast region was further facilitated by the waterways which all but link the Baltic, White, Black, and Caspian Seas. It was the rivers which to a large extent dictated the lines of settlement, the main trade routes, and the location of power centres. And it was precisely in the central region of European Russia, from where the

Map 1 Kiev and Muscovy: rivers, seas and mountains

great rivers radiate outwards, that the state of Muscovy arose in the fif-teenth century.

The huge country which these natural conditions fostered, however, was at a relative disadvantage when compared to the West. The harshness of the Russian climate, from the ice of the winter freeze to the slush of the spring thaw, severely hampered transport between her far-flung regions, and until the eighteenth century she had no secure access to western seas. Russia's neighbours, on the other hand, not only enjoyed a generally higher grain-yield but also benefited from the rapid expansion of European, and especially overseas, commerce from the fifteenth century onwards. Economic advantage tended to place these states at a military advantage as well. That Russia should become involved in sustained conflict with them over land and resources was by no means geographically determined. But once she did so, the demands made upon her backward economy were nec-essarily heavy and the social repercussions profound. Unchanging physical conditions cannot, on their own, explain the development of social life, but Russia's history can only be understood in the context of her geopolitical environment.

It was in the ninth century that an independent Russian state emerged. The tribes who came to be known as Russians were East Slavs, one of the three branches of the Slavic-speaking peoples. They had been settled on the great steppe to the north of the Black Sea for centuries, probably since before the birth of Christ. But until now they had been dominated by a suc-cession of tribes from east and north – Cimmerians, Scythians, Sarmatians, Goths, Huns, Avars, and Khazars. The relatively stable conditions estab-lished by the last of these peoples in the eighth century fostered the development of viable urban trading centres dominated by a native aristoc-racy on which a state could be built. An important role in this process was played by merchant mercenaries from Scandinavia. Wave upon wave of Viking expeditions made their way down the waterways, attracted by the lucrative trade with Constantinople in the south, and willing to serve native chieftains. The precise relationship between these 'Varangians', as the Russian chronicles call them, and the Slav tribes has been the subject of fierce controversy since the mid-eighteenth century. Russian national pride has taken offence at the notion that the first Russian state, centred on the city of Kiev, and the very name 'Rus' should have been of Scandinavian ori-gin. Generations of Russian and Soviet historians, moreover, have been at pains to demonstrate the organic evolution of East Slav society towards statehood. The chronicles, however, on which historians depend for much of their knowledge of the period, speak of the warring Slavs inviting the Varangians 'to come and rule over us'. This has given rise to the view that the state of Kiev was the creation of the adventurers from the north. The Varangians appear, in fact, to have acted as a catalyst, accelerating commer-cial and political development. They provided Kiev with the ruling house of

3

Rurik, but his descendants and their retinue were rapidly assimilated by the native Slavs and made little cultural impact.

At its prime in the eleventh century the Grand Principality of Kiev asserted at least nominal control over a vast area extending from the Vistula in the west to the Don in the east, and from the city of Kiev itself in the south all the way to the Baltic. The great bulk of the population was engaged in agriculture, but the early princes derived their wealth from booty, tribute, and commerce. Basing themselves upon existing towns, they encouraged and participated in both local and international trade, exporting furs, honey, wax, and slaves. The city of Kiev and the great northern centre of Novgorod rivalled the leading cities of Europe in size, wealth, and architectural splendour. The Rurik dynasty intermarried with royalty from as far away as France and England and with families as august as that of the Byzantine Emperor. The Slav state became a considerable force in eastern Europe.

It was during the Kiev era that Russia was converted to Christianity. By the late tenth century her most important neighbours had each adopted one of the great monotheistic religions, and contacts with their adherents were growing. The inferiority of Kiev's paganism, in terms of spiritual vitality and sophistication, was becoming apparent. For the Prince, provided he could carry his retinue with him, the option of conversion provided a major diplomatic asset. Kiev's vital commercial ties with Constantinople encouraged and were powerfully reinforced by the choice of Byzantine Orthodoxy rather than Catholicism, Islam, or indeed Judaism, to which the Khazars had been converted. In 988 Vladimir I was baptized, married the Byzantine Emperor's sister, and proceeded to convert his people. The fact that there already existed written translations of the Scriptures and liturgy in Church Slavonic – intelligible to East and South Slavs alike – greatly assisted the process. The new religion spread out from the cities to the countryside and though pagan resistance and ritual lingered for centuries, especially in the north, evangelization was on the whole remarkably peaceful and swift.

For Russian culture, the conversion was decisive. All levels of society, from prince to slave, gradually learned to articulate their values and aspirations through the medium of Byzantine Christianity. Byzantium provided the model for art, architecture, and literature. It served, too, to reinforce patriarchal features of Russian society and the Russian family. Women's subordination in public and economic life was complemented by their inferior status in the eyes of the Orthodox Church. Canon law unreservedly upheld male authority to the point of sanctioning (limited) wife-beating. The Church, it is true, played an important role in developing legal codes which, compared to other patriarchal societies, provided a relatively dignified and humane system for upholding women's honour. From early in the Orthodox era, for example, rape within marriage was grounds for divorce, and from the fifteenth century a woman could divorce her husband for adultery. On the other hand, there was no equivalent of Western medieval

1.1 The twelfth-century Cathedral of St Dmitrii in Vladimir, a major centre of early Orthodox church-building. The massive scale and elaborate design reflect the wealth and influence of the Church.

literature of courtly love. Nor did either the Renaissance or the Reformation penetrate Russia, and it was not until the seventeenth century that Western influence made any significant impression on the Orthodox mould.

The ethos of the Orthodox faith strikes the non-Orthodox as markedly conservative and passive. Where Western theology was stimulated by classical philosophy and remained open to development, Russia inherited a body of doctrine settled for all time by the great Ecumenical Councils. Where the Latin Church sought to bolster faith with reason, to explain and rationalize dogma, the East was content with mystery. It was not by reason, sermons, or even direct reference to the Bible that Orthodoxy was sustained and expressed, but rather by the celebration of the liturgy. The emphasis on communal worship was reflected in the extravagant architecture of churches and cathedrals, and their lavish interior decoration, lined with mosaics, frescos, and icons and lit by candles burning in elaborate candelabra. The 'Kievan Primary Chronicle' has left an immortal account of the impression such a setting made upon Vladimir's envoys to Constantinople: 'They led us to the edifice where they worship their God, and we knew not whether we were in heaven or on earth. For on earth there is no such splendour or such beauty, and we are at a loss how to describe it.'[1] The drama of the service itself, led by ornately robed clergy and accompanied by the rich fragrance of incense, the chiming of church bells, and the moving sacred chant, was central to the faith. Here God was present. The aesthetic rather than intellectual tenor of Orthodoxy provided little encouragement to innovation and individualism. Despite an impressive tradition of saintly hermits and mystics, the hierarchy tended to emphasize ritualistic conformism. 'Man's own opinion,' said Joseph of Volokolamsk, an immensely influential abbot of the late fifteenth–early sixteenth century, 'is the mother of all passions. Man's own opinion is the second fall.'[2]

The sociopolitical impact of this ethos, however, should not be exaggerated. The philosophy inherited from Constantinople was sufficiently flexible and complex to permit different social groups in Russia to emphasize different facets, to imbibe and accentuate the ideas which spoke to their own predicament. As elsewhere, the secular power took full advantage of the respect for authority which the Church preached. But, equally, decade after decade, century after century, outbursts of peasant protest were justified with direct reference to Orthodox doctrine. For all its cultural importance, the Byzantine heritage is among the least plausible 'keys' with which to explain the distinctive features of Russian history.

It was as an institution that the Church did play a very substantial

---

[1] S. H. Cross & O. P. Sherbowitz-Wetzor, transl., *The Russian Primary Chronicle* (Cambridge, Mass. 1953), p. 111.
[2] As quoted in H. Brandenburg, *The Meek and the Mighty* (Oxford 1976), p. 8.

role in shaping the Russian state. A network of monasteries, bishoprics and parishes spread rapidly across Kievan Rus and the Church became a major landowner. With the clergy having a near monopoly upon literacy until the seventeenth century, the Church was able to develop an unrivalled administrative structure. It penetrated the countryside in a way that the rudimentary power of the princes could not hope to do. Moreover, this elaborate institution was under the unified jurisdiction of the Metropolitan of Kiev 'and all Rus', established soon after Vladimir's conversion. As such it constituted a formidable political force which the Metropolitan, supported and appointed (until the fall of Constantinople in 1453) by the Greek Patriarch, used to good effect. When Kiev broke up and the Russians came under the sway of stronger powers to east and west, the Church worked vigorously to maintain its own unity. In the process it nourished the ethnic consciousness of the East Slavs and greatly assisted their eventual political reunification.

Kiev's prime was short-lived. The commercial wealth of the south was undermined from the latter half of the eleventh century as constant incursions by the nomads of the south-east impeded trade with Constantinople. During the twelfth century the Crusades hastened a permanent shift in the trading pattern of the region, the overland route between East and West being supplanted by the Mediterranean route. Political decisions accelerated Kiev's decline. In 1054 the most impressive of Kiev's rulers, Yaroslav the Wise, divided his patrimony among his five sons. His heirs did not practise primogeniture so that by 1100 there were a dozen principalities and the number grew during the next century. Despite the enormous prestige enjoyed by Grand Prince Vladimir Monomakh early in the twelfth century, and the enduring sense of Russian unity bequeathed by Kiev, the old capital's effective authority evaporated. In the north-west, where commerce continued to flourish, the leading cities were able to impose tight restrictions on the power of their local princes. In Novgorod the princely office became effectively elective and sovereignty came to reside in the vigorous *veche*, or city council, dominated by leading landowners and merchants. Elsewhere the growing number of princes and their retinue (*boyars*) turned to landownership and direct exploitation of the peasantry to supplement their dwindling profits from trade. Under these conditions the country became subject to constant civil war between rival princes, and increasingly vulnerable to incursions from Swedes and Germans to the north, Lithuanians, Poles, and Hungarians to the west, and above all Turkic tribes to the south. A major movement of population from the unstable south to the more secure centre and north-east further weakened the old capital, and by the second half of the twelfth century the new Grand Principality of Vladimir-Suz'dal had clearly surpassed Kiev. Incipient tendencies towards unification around this new power centre, however, were cut short by the invasion of the Mongols in the late 1230s. Politically divided and economically too backward to sustain an adequate army, the Russian principalities were

helpless in the face of the terrifying mounted warriors launched upon Russia by the Mongol Empire. In 1240 Kiev was razed to the ground, the principalities overrun, and the Russians subjected to the yoke of the Great Khan.

The invasion of the Mongols (or Tatars as the Russians called them) was horrendous. To subjugate the Slavs they swept through the region, butchering tens of thousands of victims, laying waste villages, towns, and cities, and carting away skilled craftsmen and artisans. Where the land was most fertile, in the south-east, they colonized it, thereby greatly accelerating the mass migration of Russians north-eastwards. From the rest of the country they exacted a heavy annual tribute which the shattered society could ill afford to pay.

The so-called 'Eurasian' school of historians, influential in the West since the 1920s, has depicted the Mongol invasion as the decisive event in Russian history. According to this view, the blow to the economy was matched by the Mongols' formative influence on the cultural and political life of the country. Russia was now cut off even from Byzantium and left to stagnate in an isolated backwater. Above all, she derived from the despotism of the Khan an arbitrary absolutism, extreme centralization, and disregard for individual property and liberty which marked her off from the rest of Europe. This interpretation, however, has been subjected to effective criticism. The Mongol Empire and the smaller khanates which succeeded it were neither culturally dynamic nor politically stable. They had little in the way of models and ideas to offer the heirs of Kiev. They did not destroy the property rights of the boyars, and they positively fostered the wealth and influence of the Church, making no attempt to interfere with the faith of their Christian subjects. It was not until a century after the Mongol yoke had been broken that the Russian government began to acquire the kind of powers that were to distinguish it from Western states. The distinctive features of Muscovite and Imperial Russia can be explained with minimal reference to the primitive institutions of the semi-nomadic and heathen Horde.

The impact of the Mongols on Russia's social and political development was limited by countervailing influences from the West and by the form that their rule took. In the north-west the great principality of Novgorod escaped invasion. She was governed at the time by Alexander Nevsky, who gained legendary stature by his success in repelling attacks from the west by Sweden (1240) and the Teutonic Knights (1242). To avoid onslaught from the Mongols, Novgorod accepted the Prince's advice and consented to pay tribute. Cultural and commercial exchanges with the

---

1.2 The Mongols sack Kiev, December 1240 (from an illustration in *Kazanskii letopisets*, a sixteenth-century historical account of the Khanate of Kazan). The old capital never recovered from the carnage and destruction of the assault.

Baltic states were thereby preserved, and the city flourished during the following two centuries. In the west and south-west Mongol rule was curtailed in the fourteenth century when the territory passed to the more tender mercies of Lithuania, then reaching the zenith of her power. The Russians incorporated into Lithuania, which was itself dynastically linked with Catholic Poland under a single king in 1386, came under very different influences, developing the distinct Belorussian (White Russian) and Ukrainian[3] (sometimes known as Little Russian) linguistic and ethnic types. These distinctions were destined to be reinforced when at the end of the sixteenth century (1596) the Polish government forced them into union with Rome, establishing the Uniate Church, which retained the Orthodox rite but accepted papal supremacy. By the time most of these territories were reunited under Russian rule during the course of the seventeenth and eighteenth centuries, the bases on which Ukrainian and Belorussian national self-consciousness would develop had been laid. It was the central and north-eastern principalities of the Great Russians which suffered most from the Mongols, only finally overthrowing them in 1480. But the Mongols' overriding concern was to collect tribute, and on occasion military recruits. After a brief period in which they imposed their own tribute collectors, they were content to leave even that to the Russian princes. Their rule was indirect and their interference in native custom and traditions relatively superficial.

Certain specific repercussions of Mongol rule do deserve emphasis. To apportion tribute, the Mongols carried out a crude census of the population, and in delegating responsibility for collection to the Grand Prince of Vladimir, they provided him with a powerful instrument to assert his authority. The lesser princes were to hand over their contributions to the Grand Prince, and he alone was to conduct relations with the Khan. Moreover, the urge to overthrow the yoke served to strengthen the desire for unity among the princes, even at the expense of acknowledging the suzerainty of the Grand Prince. But the basis for consolidation around the new focus of wealth and population in the north-east had been laid before the Mongols arrived, and the blow they dealt the economy outweighed any positive influence their intervention had on Russian political development.

During the first century of Mongol vassalage, with agriculture disrupted and urban life shattered, even the most powerful princes had difficulty in holding – let alone expanding – their principalities. By the first decades of the fourteenth century, however, the process of political fragmentation began gradually to be reversed. Various factors favoured the creation of a unified state. Boyars and lesser landowners stood to gain from the greater stability and more effective control over the peasantry which

---

[3] From 'Ukraina' ('borderland') as the south-western territories of what had been Kievan Rus became known.

unification would bring. The Church's centripetal influence increased along with the rapid growth in its wealth, which was facilitated by the immunity from tribute granted it by the Mongols, and in the number of new monasteries founded. Novgorod provided a major source of economic power for any prince who could gain control of it. Moreover, the Mongol Empire split up into separate khanates, and the Golden Horde of Sarai, which oversaw Russia, itself underwent internal upheaval. As a result the Mongols began to look more favourably on a native Russian ability to repel the growing threat from Lithuania in the west. True, the Golden Horde remained anxious to prevent any one prince becoming a real menace to its power, but as its military advantage declined the foremost Russian princes found more and more room for manoeuvre.

That it should have been the Principality of Moscow which provided the focal point for these centripetal forces was far from inevitable. The city itself, which is first mentioned in the chronicles in 1147 and became the centre of a separate principality in 1301, was well fortified and benefited from the buffer principalities of Tver and Ryazan to the west and south. It was, moreover, located near the centre of the north-eastern land- and water-routes and thus attracted merchants who in turn enriched the prince. However, when the Prince of Moscow first laid claim to the title of Grand Prince of Vladimir in the early fourteenth century, it was neighbouring Tver, with many similar advantages, which seemed a more likely focus for political unification. A bitter struggle between the two was settled in Moscow's favour in part because she seemed more pliable to the Mongols and less menacing to Novgorod. Tver also fatally alienated the Metropolitan, not least by her sinister contacts with the heretical West, and was further handicapped by the fertility of her princes whose sons each claimed a share of the principality. Once Moscow began to gain the upper hand, success bred success. Boyars, merchants, and peasants were drawn to the relative peace and prosperity she offered. By the 1370s the princes of Moscow claimed succession to the throne of Vladimir as part of their patrimony. In 1380 Moscow's ascendancy was demonstrated to all when Dmitrii led a Russian army drawn from several principalities against the Mongols, achieving the famous victory of Kulikovo.

The success was short-lived and the Mongols exacted harsh revenge, but the spell of their invincibility was broken. In the first quarter of the fifteenth century the process of reunification around Moscow gathered pace. Dmitrii's successors expanded the principality and undermined the political independence of the other princes. Novgorod found Muscovite merchants trespassing on her far-flung provinces and diverting her lucrative fur trade to Moscow. Between 1425 and 1450 Moscow's advance was checked as the energies of Basil II (1425–62) were focused upon winning the first major civil war fought over the succession to the principality. It was his successor, Ivan III – the Great (1462–1505) – who earned the sobriquet of 'gatherer of

the Russian lands'. He used Moscow's superior economic and military resources to absorb the weaker principalities, persuading their princes to
accept his authority or bequeath their possessions to him. He succeeded in
incorporating the appanages left to his own brothers with a minimum of
bloodshed. His most significant step was the abolition of Novgorod's independence. Despite her enormous wealth, the 'crowned republic' of the north
had long been in a precarious position. Worsening conflict between the
boyar-merchant oligarchy and the lower classes undermined the city from
within and vitiated her efforts to mount an effective military deterrent to
Ivan. Control of Novgorod's vital grain supplies gave Moscow powerful
leverage, and during the 1470s Ivan took advantage of her 'treasonable'
and unsuccessful attempts to gain help from the West, invaded the principality, destroyed her defences, and carted away the great symbol of her
independence, the *veche* bell.

The growing resources at his disposal enabled Ivan to make parallel
advances in Moscow's international position. The military balance swung
decisively against the Mongols, and when in 1480 Ivan renounced their
authority, they were unable to strike back. The smaller khanates into which
the Golden Horde had by now fragmented – those of Kazan in the east,
Astrakhan in the south-east, and the Crimea in the south – would never
again be able to destroy Moscow's independence. At the same time, the
ground was prepared for the gradual assertion of Muscovy's claims over the
Ukraine, the western lands which had come under Lithuanian rule. Enticing
the Crimean Tatars into alliance with him, Ivan prepared the way first for
border raids and then for open warfare with Lithuania. A significant number of princes and boyars – attracted by Moscow's evident military
advantage, and repelled by the Catholic pressure of the Polish-Lithuanian
regime – switched their allegiance to Ivan and he made considerable inroads
into the Ukraine. When peace with Lithuania was signed in 1503 there
seemed a real prospect that in time Moscow would make good her claims to
all the lands that had once belonged to Kiev.

Ivan's successor Basil III (1505–33) consolidated his achievement,
absorbing the remaining independent principalities. To prevent renewed
fragmentation he forbade his own brothers to marry until he himself had an
heir – an end he achieved after insisting, like his contemporary Henry VIII,
on a controversial divorce. By the middle of the sixteenth century the population had reached six million, and Ivan IV – the Terrible (1533–84) –
opened the way to further expansion to the east and south-east by destroying the khanates of Kazan (1552) and Astrakhan (1556). The pacification
and colonization of the vast territories now under Moscow's nominal control took decades, but east of the Urals local tribes could offer no effective
resistance. During the course of the seventeenth century settlers established
small towns across the thinly populated expanses of Siberia, reaching the
Pacific in mid-century. Events elsewhere, however, fully exposed the limits

THE
SWEDISH
EMPIRE

WHITE SEA

REPUBLIC OF NOVGOROD

GULF OF FINLAND

URALS

Ivangorod

Novgorod

• Riga

PSKOV

• Kazan

• Vilna

• Moscow

Smolensk

KAZAN
KHANATE

• Minsk

Kulikovo

WHITE
RUSSIA

• Sarai

• Chernigov

UKRAINE

ASTRAKHAN
KHANATE

LITHUANIA

Kiev •

Dnieper

CRIMEAN KHANATE

• Azov

Astrakhan
•

BLACK SEA

CASPIAN
SEA

Constantinople
•

THE OTTOMAN EMPIRE

The Principality of Moscow by 1462

0   200

The further expansion of Moscow by 1533

miles

Map 2   The expansion of Muscovy, 1462–1533

of Muscovy's strength. In the 1550s Ivan the Terrible made a fateful decision to try to gain access to the Baltic by attacking Livonia. In doing so he not only stimulated a Polish-Lithuanian-Scandinavian alliance for which Muscovy was no match, but also left his southern border unprotected. In 1571 the Crimean Tatars invaded, burned down the capital, slaughtered and carried into slavery hundreds of thousands of Muscovites and threatened to undo the work of Ivan the Great. Relief came from Austria's defeat of the Crimea's Turkish patron the following year. But the Livonian adventure was an unmitigated disaster. The war dragged on for a quarter of a century and drastically disrupted the economy of the western and central regions. Not only did it signal the end of Russian expansion north and south until the reign of Peter the Great (1682–1725), but it also marked a critical turning-point in Muscovy's domestic development.

Table 1.1 The emergence of Muscovy

880	Rurik dynasty establishes capital at Kiev
988	Baptism of Vladimir I
1054	Death of Yaroslav. Fragmentation of Kievan Russia begins
1237-40	Mongol invasion
1380	Dmitrii of Moscow defeats Mongols at Battle of Kulikovo
1480	Ivan III – the Great – renounces Mongol yoke
1547	Ivan IV – the Terrible – crowned Tsar of All the Russias
1552, 1556	Conquest of Kazan and Astrakhan
1598-1613	Time of Troubles
1648	Siberian settlers reach the Pacific
1667	Treaty of Andrusovo

The economic havoc wreaked by Ivan the Terrible's reckless foreign and domestic policies issued in the tumultuous Time of Troubles (1598–1613). In a fit of rage Ivan had killed his eldest son with his own hands, and since his younger son and successor, Fyodor (1584–98) had no surviving children, the Rurik dynasty died out. Fyodor's brother-in-law, Boris Godunov (1598–1605), was crowned Tsar but his efforts to stabilize the country were undermined by appalling famines between 1601 and 1603. After his death in 1605 acute social tension found expression in a prolonged struggle over the throne and opened the way for sustained efforts by Poland and Sweden to take advantage of Muscovy's weakness. The confusion and strife of the period enabled a succession of dubious figures to claim the throne. The most absurd case was that of the Second False Dmitrii. The true Dmitrii, who was Ivan's youngest son by his seventh wife and whose claim was dubious since his parents' marriage was canonically illegal, had died in mysterious circumstances as long ago as 1591. A Polish-sponsored pretender claiming to be Dmitrii fought his way to the throne in 1605 and was duly acknowledged by the true Dmitrii's mother as her long-lost son. In a matter of months he was assassinated, only to be followed by the Second

Map 3   The expansion of Muscovy, 1533–98

The following labels appear on the map:

SIBERIA

THE
SWEDISH
EMPIRE

Archangel

Dvina

Ob

Tobolsk

URALS

BALTIC SEA

LIVONIA

Novgorod

Volga

Pskov

Kazan

LITHUANIA

Moscow

Smolensk

UKRAINE

Chernigov

THE
NOGAI
HORDE

Kiev

CRIMEAN KHANATE

Volga

Astrakhan

ARAL
SEA

BLACK SEA

CASPIAN SEA

CAUCASUS

THE OTTOMAN EMPIRE

Russia in 1533

Russian conquests by 1598

0   300
miles

False Dmitrii. This time credence was lent to his claim by the wife of the First False Dmitrii who went to the lengths of bearing the second pretender a son. By 1610, however, the urge to restore order and drive out the Poles was sufficiently strong among all sections of the population for a triumphant Russian army to be raised. In 1613 the boyar Michael Romanov was elected Tsar by the *Zemsky sobor* (Assembly of the Land), a semi-representative body which acquired real political significance during the Time of Troubles. Michael ruled until 1645. The centripetal forces in Muscovy had held her together through what had appeared a terminal illness.

During the seventeenth century the tide gradually turned against both Poland–Lithuania in the west and the Crimean Tatars in the south. Despite her own handicaps, Muscovy proved better equipped than oligarchic Poland or the semi-nomadic Tatars to make use of innovations in military technique and technology. In the Ukraine, she found an unruly but invaluable ally in the Cossacks, free warriors whose independent communities had emerged during the fifteenth and sixteenth centuries as discontented elements fled to the south and south-east. Cossack loyalty to Orthodoxy intensified their violent resistance to Polish rule. In 1654 Tsar Alexis (1645–76) acceded to Cossack requests that he extend his protection over the Ukraine. After a prolonged struggle, Poland finally admitted defeat over the issue and ceded the eastern Ukraine under the Treaty of Andrusovo in 1667. In the same period an effective line of fortifications was built to protect the southern frontier. The Regent Sophia, who governed from 1682 to 1689 on behalf of her sickly brother Ivan V (co-Tsar 1682–96) and their under-age half-brother Peter, failed in her efforts to crush the Tatars. But the balance now favoured the Russians. Although by the time Peter came of age the coveted access to the Baltic and the Black Seas was still lacking, the area under Moscow's rule was approaching that of today's Russian Federation. A vast empire was taking shape.

Chapter 2

The genesis of Russian 'absolutism'

Numerous labels have been attached to the political system which Ivan the Great bequeathed to Muscovy at the beginning of the sixteenth century – oriental despotism (Plekhanov, Szamuely), patrimonial monarchy (Pipes), estate-representative monarchy (favoured by Soviet historians). In part this variety reflects the poorly defined vocabulary available to historians seeking to distinguish various traditional authoritarian regimes. But it also derives from sharply differing interpretations of the nature of the Muscovite system. The central issue at stake is simple and crucial to an understanding of Russian history. How far was the State – the power concentrated in the hands of the Grand Prince – representative of and responsive to privileged groups or interests within society? Was the ruler's freedom of action significantly limited by independent institutions and social pressure or was he in a position to subject every social stratum to his own will?

In a famous description of Basil III, the Imperial Ambassador Sigismund von Herberstein described him as the most despotic sovereign on earth. 'He has power over both secular and clerical individuals and freely, according to his will, disposes of the life and property of all. Among the counsellors whom he has, none enjoys such importance that he would dare to contradict him in anything or be of another opinion.'[1] Unification under Moscow had been accompanied by the creation of a powerful centralized monarchy. All appointments to military and administrative posts were in the gift of the Grand Prince. It was in his name that taxes were collected, the law enforced, war waged and treaties signed. His realm was bound together by an increasingly standardized legal code, gradually extended over newly incorporated areas, a rudimentary postal system, and uniform coinage, weights, and measures. Executive, legislative, and judicial authority flowed from him and there were no legal limitations to his power.

---

[1] S. Herberstein, *Zapiski o moskovskikh delakh* (St Petersburg 1908), p. 28.

2.1 The small state seal of Ivan IV (1569). The twin-headed eagle, inherited from Byzantium, was to remain the royal emblem until the fall of the monarchy – and was to be revived by the Russian Federation after the collapse of the Soviet Union.

Muscovite ceremony and rhetoric – the messianic claim, after the fall of Constantinople (1453), that it was Moscow's destiny to be the 'Third Rome', and the adoption of the twin-headed eagle, the Imperial emblem inherited from Byzantium – surrounded the person of the Grand Prince with an ever more glorious halo, emphasizing the slavish subjection of all to his semi-divine authority.

Yet the Grand Prince's position was in fact more complex than Herberstein's influential picture suggests. Ivan III and Basil III were not despots on the Asiatic model. The Grand Prince lacked a sizeable military apparatus directly responsive to his will. With the money economy spreading extremely slowly, he could only centralize very limited financial resources. The central bureaucracy was embryonic and his provincial officials were spread wafer-thin and proved very difficult to supervise. In these conditions he was in no position to ride rough-shod over the interests of either the Church or the nobility, and in the mid-sixteenth century there were momentary signs that the wealthier commoners were gaining a modicum of political leverage. On the other hand, Muscovy's social elites did suffer from weaknesses which made them much less independent and their property much less secure than elsewhere in Europe. With the eclipse of the Greek Patriarch, there was no rival foreign ecclesiastical authority comparable to that exercised by Rome in Catholic Europe; the Grand Prince faced neither *parlements*, nor Magna Charta and individual landowners who fell foul of the monarch enjoyed no legal protection. Equally important, the peasantry at the bottom of the social pyramid were acutely vulnerable to royal power. The great mass of them, those living on the lands unoccupied by nobility or Church (the so-called 'black' lands – not to be confused with the fertile 'black earth' region), owed allegiance only to the Grand Prince. And during the sixteenth century the Crown exploited this massive reservoir of land and labour to effect a major increase in state power.

The most significant institution outside the State itself was the Church. The favour shown it by the Mongols had enabled it to consolidate its position across Russia long before the Muscovite State managed to do so. Culturally dominant and playing a pervasive role in the everyday life of elite and masses alike, it wielded enormous influence. Enjoying immunities from various forms of taxation and from administrative interference by the State, the monasteries were at a distinct advantage in accumulating land and retaining scarce peasant labour, and they benefited from a flow of bequests by repentant sons of the Church. The non-celibate parish clergy were little better off than their peasant flock, but in the early sixteenth century over 25 per cent of all cultivated land was in clerical hands.

The combination of spiritual, cultural, and economic influence at its disposal made the Russian Church in some ways better placed than its Western counterparts to resist the ambitions of the newly centralized State. When Ivan III manoeuvred to undermine the security of monastic property – before most of his Western peers embarked on the same road – he found himself unable to do so. His method was to patronize the so-called 'Nonpossessor' reformist current within the Church, which urged the clergy to shed material wealth and pursue their spiritual mission unencumbered. The hierarchy, however, mounted stiff resistance and publicly denounced any attack on ecclesiastical privileges and property. This conservative response, led by the fiery Abbot Joseph of Volokolamsk, carried the day, and Ivan's successors were unable even to halt effectively the further growth of ecclesiastical landholding.

Yet the Josephite victory presaged no broader attempt to circumscribe royal power. The challenge from the Nonpossessors, viewed sympathetically as it was by the land-hungry Grand Prince and aristocracy alike, had frightened the Josephites too much for that. They feared that to alienate the Grand Prince, who had a wide measure of control over appointments to the hierarchy, would leave them vulnerable to the intellectual vigour of the 'heresy'. To crush their rivals, therefore, they sought not to limit the power of the Grand Prince, but to gain influence over him by identifying themselves with the elevation of his personal authority. It was the Josephite hierarchy who orchestrated the remarkable development of monarchic ideology which so impressed Herberstein. It was the Metropolitan Makarii who nurtured Ivan the Terrible's hugely inflated notion of his office, and who prepared the dramatic ceremony which saw him crowned in 1547, not as mere Grand Prince but as unfettered 'Tsar' (derived from 'Caesar'). Rather than checking the power of the State, the Church thus augmented it, ensuring

19

only that the Tsar would launch no wholesale attack on monastic property. The Church drew ever closer to the State but became a distinctly junior partner.

At the top of the social pyramid was the aristocracy, large landowners whose families had long served Moscow (the boyars) and ex-appanage princes who had gradually been drawn to the metropolis. They provided the high command in wartime, bringing their own retinue to serve in the royal army, and the senior personnel for enforcing order in the countryside. It was they who surrounded the monarch and provided most of his advisers. From the sixteenth century, they developed new customs which reflected their elevated status as a social and political elite bound together by kinship ties. Within their homes, for example, separate living quarters, the so-called *terem*, were set aside for their womenfolk, who ceased to socialize with men and outside the home travelled in closed or curtained carriages shielding them from public gaze. The Boyars' *Duma* (Council) might lack closely defined rights, but by custom the Tsar legislated and acted in consultation with it. Even if individually neither their lives nor their property were secure, collectively they constituted an interest group with whom the Grand Prince was intimately bound up.

What limited the boyars' political weight, however, was the fragile nature of their landed wealth. In contrast to much of western Europe, primogeniture was not practised in Russia: a father's property was divided among his heirs. Very quickly the greatest fortune tended to be dissipated among innumerable descendants. This process prevented even the most distinguished families from establishing the kind of firm territorial base which underpinned the political influence of Western aristocracies. Instead of seeking to contain royal power they were preoccupied with gaining the favour of the Grand Prince, or control of the government when the monarch was personally weak or a minor. For apart from the unique case of the Stroganov family, who built an immense entrepreneurial empire, the only way to replenish the family fortunes lay in service to the State. The Grand Prince could confer lucrative posts in the army and provincial government as well as new grants of land confiscated, unoccupied, or held by mere peasants. The competition for senior posts in the royal service became formalized in the so-called *mestnichestvo* system, whereby precedence was based on the rank achieved by a boyar's most eminent forebears. The system posed some obstacles to the monarch's freedom of appointment, but it reflected above all the nobles' concern to benefit from rather than to limit the power of the State.

Groups further down the social scale were in a much weaker position

---

2.2 Ivan the Terrible, by Vasnetsov. The artist's impression of Ivan's majestic features and lavish robes captures the awe inspired by the first Grand Prince to be crowned 'Tsar'.

than the boyars or the Church to press their interests upon the Grand Prince. The Prince looked upon the towns as part of his patrimony and those townsmen not on monastic or boyar land as his tenants. With a few exceptions, sixteenth-century towns were in any case little more than glorified military and administrative headquarters, supplied by a small population of artisans and petty traders. The townsmen developed no organizational bases comparable to those of Western cities, no craft guilds or town councils. Ancient institutions representing the urban population had withered under the Mongol yoke. Where the *veche* had survived, in Novgorod and Pskov, the centralizing activity of Ivan III and Basil III had been deliberately designed to destroy it.

The political weakness of the commoners corresponded to their economic weakness. One of the features which most sharply distinguished Muscovy from western and much of central Europe was the relative backwardness of her commercial, manufacturing, and urban development. Kiev's flourishing trade had been undermined by inter-princely warfare, nomadic incursions, and the virtual severance of her commerce with Byzantium. The Mongol invasion had hit the urban centres particularly hard, and the tribute paid to the Golden Horde for over two centuries had made recovery difficult. It is arguable that Russia suffered more than her fair share of famine and plague, and her wooden cities were again and again ravaged by fire. Certainly the climate impeded the development of internal communications, thereby retarding the division of labour and the break-up of self-sufficient estates, villages, and indeed households. The critical handicap under which she laboured, however, appears to have been the low yield of the land. In the sixteenth and seventeenth centuries the yield ratio of her major crops was less than half that of western Europe and well below much of central Europe. With incomes pegged little above subsistence level, the domestic market remained very small, and what inter-regional trade did develop was generally in the hands of the boyars, the monasteries, and the Grand Prince. Since the overwhelming majority of the population were necessarily involved in tilling the soil, the supply of labour for handicraft and manufacture was restricted. Moreover, the struggle for control of what little surplus was produced gave rise to various forms of bonded labour which created further barriers to economic development.

Muscovy's commoners, of course, were not an undifferentiated mass. Despite its primitive agricultural methods, the peasantry was far from monolithic: above the significant numbers of outright slaves, beggars, and migrant workers, were the peasants on private and church lands suffering various degrees of bondage, military colonists on the frontiers, and peasants on the 'black' lands whose only obligations were to the State. Moreover, the early sixteenth century saw tentative signs of further differentiation. The reunification of Russia coincided with and helped to sustain a century of relative prosperity which lasted into the 1560s. In the richer agricultural regions the dues owed to the Grand Prince, or to lay and ecclesiastical land-owners, gradually began to be converted from payment in kind to money rents. More successful peasants began to elevate themselves above their fellows, to accumulate land and employ their own labourers. Local trade grew perceptibly and a thin stratum of relatively well-off artisans and merchants began to emerge.

It was partly in recognition of these tender sprouts of leadership among Russia's 'third estate' that during the 1550s Ivan the Terrible drew up a new legal code and made a number of important administrative reforms. He offered the leading commoners in most towns and regions the option of taking over their own administration and taxation. Under the existing system, royal governors entrusted with judicial and tax-collecting powers 'fed' upon the local population, using their very brief tenure of office to line their own pockets. For the State the system was unsatisfactory because so little revenue found its way to Moscow, yet fixed salaries were beyond the government's means. The major advantage of the new proposal, from Ivan's point of view, was the additional revenue it would bring to the central treasury, for his offer was conditional on a steep rise in the rate of taxation. But he was also responding to a mounting chorus of complaint about the system of 'feeding', which was disastrous for the local population. Tax burdens were arbitrary and unpredictable and the judicial verdicts of royal governors were blatantly dependent upon bribery. 'Fear not the law,' ran a popular proverb, 'fear the judge.' The relatively well off, the 'best people' of the provinces, therefore, welcomed Ivan's proposal and it appears to have been widely implemented. To prepare his reforms, Ivan summoned the first *Zemsky sobor* (1549), the consultative body destined to play an important, if erratic, role in the next century of Muscovite history. It established no right to be consulted, was dominated by the nobility and clergy, and such leading merchants as were included were appointed rather than elected. It was primarily a means for the Tsar to sound out the men in his service. Yet it also represented at least a first step towards an institutional framework for dialogue between State and commoners. The dialogue, however, was not destined to prosper. The 1560s marked the beginning of a period of economic dislocation and social upheaval which stunted the development of Muscovy's fragile 'proto bourgeoisie'.

This period of upheaval was to have an epoch-making impact upon the whole structure of Muscovite society. It saw two crucial and intimately connected social changes gather irresistible momentum: the creation of a new stratum of service landholders – the *pomeshchiki* – and the subsequent enserfment not only of those peasants already suffering *de facto* bondage, but of the entire Russian peasantry.

This dual process had begun in the late fifteenth century. Ivan III had established several thousand new landowners on the estates confiscated from the victims of his conquest of Novgorod in the 1470s. Small farms were assigned to sons of noblemen and promising warriors, on condition that they reported annually for military service. This conditional landholding – the *pomestie* – created the nucleus of a new service stratum dependent on the Prince in a way the boyars had never been. Under Ivan the Terrible the *pomestie* system was expanded in the most dramatic fashion possible. The rising prestige of Ivan's royal office went to the head of that gifted but vicious and unbalanced character. Encouraged by the Josephite hierarchy, who rightly suspected Nonpossessor sympathies among his closest advisers, the Tsar became increasingly impervious to advice. His conquest and annexation of the khanates of Kazan and Astrakhan further inflated his self-confidence. And in the midst of his fateful Livonian War (1558–83), he launched a bitter attack upon the treachery and corruption he claimed to detect among the boyars and clergy. In 1564 he abruptly withdrew from Moscow and threatened to abdicate. When begged to return, he relented only on condition he could carry out a remarkable experiment: the so-called *oprichnina*. Ivan designated something like one-third of the country, carved out of scattered towns and provinces, as his personal domain, and set up a new administration to subject it to his personal will. To sweep graft and treason from the land, he created a 6,000-strong army of oprichniks, a terrifying death squad, dressed in black, the regalia of each warrior including the skull of a dog and a symbolic broom. Whole families of suspect boyars were butchered and their lands confiscated. The terror became increasingly arbitrary, hitting out at lesser nobles, merchants and peasants. The Metropolitan was deposed and strangled, individual monasteries ransacked, and Novgorod, still the greatest city outside Moscow, was despoiled in a manner which made Ivan III's treatment of it a century earlier appear positively statesmanlike. Not until the shock of the Crimean invasion did Ivan abolish the *oprichnina*, and intermittent terror continued for the rest of his reign, swallowing up not a few of the oprichniks themselves.

Ivan's aims have left historians in a quandary. It is extremely difficult to discover any coherent pattern to the *oprichnina* and, although it is true many boyars suffered, sceptics have had great fun exploding successive attempts to explain Ivan's behaviour in terms of the class affiliations of the victims and beneficiaries. Whatever his motives, his experiment was made possible by the power he had to distribute land to the motley collection of individuals who would join him. In exercising this option he rapidly increased the number of pomeshchiks. By the end of the sixteenth century, in the central provinces little was left of the 'black' lands owned nominally by the State and inhabited by peasants owing dues only to the Crown. The pomeshchiks had become a substantial body and provided the military backbone of the State.

The rise of this new landholding stratum had a drastic impact upon the Russian peasantry. The pomeshchiks derived their livelihood in part from an irregular salary paid while on active service, but primarily from the

2.3   The heavily-clad pomeshchik cavalry of sixteenth-century Muscovy. Although the pomeshchiks proved difficult to train and discipline, they played a vital military role until the introduction of firearms and new-formation regiments in the seventeenth century. (Woodcut from Herberstein's *Gratiae Posteritati*, 1560.)

income they could extract from the peasants settled on their farms. On average they had only five or six peasant households at their disposal, and since they lacked the capital, the expertise, and the time to raise peasant productivity, the exactions they made were onerous. Life on their farms was distinctly less attractive to the peasantry than conditions on monastic and boyar estates, let alone in the new territory opened up by the conquest of Kazan and Astrakhan. Yet growing numbers of boyar and state peasants found themselves subjected to the harsh rule of small landowners.

To make matters worse, during the 1560s, 1570s, and 1580s the country suffered economic and demographic losses of catastrophic proportions. The combined impact of the Livonian War, the *oprichnina*, and the Crimean invasion of 1571, together with a steeply rising tax burden and

25

severe famine ravaged the central and western regions of Muscovy. Foreign visitors were appalled by the evidence of massive depopulation, by the sight of whole villages abandoned. Feeble recovery in the 1590s was cut short by the famines of 1601–03 and the prolonged disruption of the Time of Troubles. Those peasants who had not disappeared became ever more anxious to migrate, while the pomeshchiks became ever more anxious to tie them to the land. The classic conditions for enserfment were created: an abundance of land and a dearth of labourers. Unable to offer economic inducements, the pomeshchiks relied increasingly upon sheer force to keep their peasants, exploit their labour, drive them deeper and deeper into debt, and reduce them to servile status. And the government responded to their request that the repressive power of the State be mobilized in their support. The process of legal enserfment began. Ivan III had recognized the peasant's right to leave his lord, provided he settled his debts and paid a fee, laying down only that such movement should take place at the end of the harvest, during the fortnight surrounding St George's Day (an autumn as well as spring feast in the Orthodox calendar). This remained the law until the 1580s. Ivan IV then began the practice of temporarily halting any movement at all during a number of 'forbidden years'. In the 1590s landlords were permitted to recover fugitive peasants for up to five years after their flight. Under mounting pressure from the pomeshchiks, this period was gradually extended until, by the Code of Laws enacted in 1649, the peasants were permanently bound to the land and forbidden to move.

Table 2.1   The Muscovite succession

1462–1505	Ivan III – the Great
1505–1533	Basil III
1533–1584	Ivan IV – the Terrible
1584–1598	Fyodor I
1598–1613	Time of Troubles
1613–1645	Michael
1645–1676	Alexis
1676–1682	Fyodor III
1682–1689	Regent Sophia

The process which led to the entrenchment of serfdom in Russia – just when it was being undermined in the West – has been the subject of prolonged historiographical debate. Whereas in much of eastern Europe, which was moving in the same direction, enserfment seems to have been the response of a very powerful nobility to a labour shortage (made more acute in areas responding to the growing Western market for grain), in Russia the State clearly played a greater role. But was the State's action dictated by its own interests or those of the nobility? The Russian nobility were much less formidable than their counterparts elsewhere, they had not yet begun to export grain, and for the great landowners serfdom was not an unmitigated blessing: as long as there was still peasant mobility they were in a position to attract labour away from the estates of their weaker rivals. From the point of view of the State, too, there were drawbacks: although fettered peasants were easier to tax, their complete immobilization would impede the colonization of newly acquired lands in the south and east. What settled the issue was the rise of the pomeshchiks. As the State's military requirements increased and the number of pomeshchiks to be sustained multiplied, the demands made on the peasantry intensified. With the yield from the land at best stagnant and the available work-force actually contracting, only naked force could extract the required surplus from the peasantry. The needs of Muscovy's new military backbone could not be ignored. An alliance between the new landowners and the State enforced full-scale enserfment.

The consequences were profound both for countless generations of abased families and for the sociopolitical setting in which the Russian Empire took shape. On private land, the State made the pomeshchik responsible for the collection of taxes from his serfs and then left him to his own devices. The lord's power over his serfs became absolute. He was free to lay down what proportion of their produce was to be made over to him, and how many days in the week they were to work the fields he set aside

2.4 Muscovite peasants. The axe became symbolic both of peasant labour and of peasant revolt. (Seventeenth-century illustration from the *Voyages* of Olearius.)

for his own use. He was their final court of appeal and punished them as he saw fit. Gradually he established the right to separate them from the land, to buy and sell serfs like cattle. Males and females alike were subject to his whim. The relationship struck at the very roots of their human dignity.

Serfdom stifled both collective and individual initiative among the peasantry. Unlike outright slaves, they maintained themselves by cultivating the land conditionally allotted to them by their master. But there was little incentive to raise productivity when any increased surplus would simply be creamed off by State or landlord. In any case, the land and time left at their disposal was steadily reduced from the seventeenth century as pomeshchiks and monasteries expanded their demesne and exacted dues in labour (*barshchina*) rather than quit-rent (*obrok*). At the same time serfdom gave a profoundly negative twist to the levelling tendencies already present within most villages. There had long been a tradition whereby many of the resources of a village were owned in common. Explanations advanced for the prominence of these collective forms of ownership include the collective effort required to bring virgin soil under the plough and the harshness of a climate which rendered isolated homesteads extremely vulnerable. In any case, in the early modern period, land tenure by individual households co-existed in most parts of the country with a form of common ownership by the land commune, the institution which a group of households – usually those living in one village – established to represent and preside over it. While each household acquired hereditary rights over some of the land it cultivated, the commune as a whole owned other usable land, forests and ponds. Moreover, even the land over which a household did gain hereditary rights was itself owned not individually by the head of the household but jointly by its members. This in turn was connected to the tradition of partible inheritance: when families broke up, departing sons took with them an equal share in the household's land and assets. Under serfdom these levelling tendencies were reinforced and the social pressure of the commune harnessed to discipline peasants. The members of each commune were made collectively responsible for taxation and other dues owed to the State and the landlord. This made it imperative to ensure that each household had sufficient land to meet its share of the payments due. From the late seventeenth century the practice spread whereby the land was periodically redistributed among the villagers, each household being given a number of strips scattered between the desirable and less desirable fields. With minimal opportunity to hire labour, even the most thriving household had little incentive to accumulate or hold onto more land than it could work itself. The repartitional serf commune presented all but insuperable obstacles to the emergence of economically powerful peasants.

The additional duties taken on by the commune – redistributing land, apportioning obligations, and adjudicating the disputes these gave rise to – served to strengthen the primitive institution. The impact on peasant culture was complex. The assumption of collective responsibility clearly fostered collectivist aspects of peasant mentality, and over time the tradition of repartition was to nurture a deeply egalitarian ethos. The close interdependence of commune members encouraged mutual aid when a household was struck by fire, death or other disaster. For all its patriarchal character, the commune provided women with a relatively stable social environment and, although they could not even speak at meetings of the village assembly, widows in particular could wield considerable power when taking on the responsibilities of household heads. Arguably, too, the commune's rudimentary democratic structure, whereby male heads of household elected the village elders, made possible a minimum of collective bargaining in the face of landlord and official. But the solidarity it bred seldom extended beyond the limited horizons of the local village. It institutionalized the subordination of women to their husbands and fathers and placed a heavy burden of manual labour upon them – which contributed to the numbingly high rate of infant mortality among Russian peasants. The social discipline the commune imposed and the authoritarian family relations it upheld underpinned the wider political order. Since the majority in each commune stood to lose should any individual of either sex fail to play their part, meet their share of the payments due, or take to flight, it came to serve a major coercive function.

The predicament of peasants on state lands which had not been handed over to private landowners was marginally easier, but did not differ fundamentally from that of private serfs. The judicial and administrative functions left to the commune were somewhat broader, and in place of the pomeshchik stood a lowly government official. But here too the peasant was tied to the land, taxed ever more heavily, and confronted by the same obstacles to economic self-improvement.

The establishment of serfdom conditioned the way in which the relationship between State and society developed from the seventeenth century onwards. Where the serfs were concerned, of course, there could be no question of the legal expression of their interests. The only way the peasantry could exert political pressure was by flight or revolt. Peasant violence was generally localized and poorly organized, but there were serious risings in almost every decade of the seventeenth century. One dimension of the Time of Troubles was the outbreak of peasant resistance in every region of the country, and the revolt of 1606–07 led by an ex-slave named Ivan Bolotnikov attracted widespread peasant support. In 1670–71 the government briefly lost control of a vast area from the Don to the Volga as peasants rallied under the leadership of a Don Cossack named Stenka Razin. The government responded to such pressure not with concessions or negotiations but with outright repression. The uprisings in the early part of the century may have served temporarily to postpone formal enserfment, but they were powerless to prevent it.

Urban economic and political development suffered severely from the social and demographic upheaval set in train during Ivan IV's reign. The number of tax-paying urban households fell by no less than 45 per cent between the mid-sixteenth century and the 1620s, and recovery was protracted and uneven. The binding of the peasantry to the land severely restricted urban migration. With peasant income actually in decline during the seventeenth century, the domestic market grew painfully slowly. To make matters worse, even in their depleted condition the cities remained a vital source of income to the government. The Romanovs reimposed military governors and the townsmen were in no position to challenge the demands made upon them. The fact that the government had to rely on the townsmen themselves to apportion and gather the levies was therefore an additional burden rather than a basis for establishing municipal independence. Too weak to bargain over the State's impositions, the townsmen could do no more than try to spread the burden as thinly as possible. To this end they repeatedly urged the government to return fugitives to their cities, and to abolish the immunities enjoyed by church and noble land in and around the cities. Artisans and traders living on this privileged land escaped the tax and other service duties of townsmen. Although the State shared the townsmen's interest in broadening the urban tax base, the political influence of the Church and landowners delayed any decisive legislation. Matters were brought to a head by a series of urban riots in the late 1640s, triggered by resentment at tax increases and made particularly dangerous by the reluctance of the infantry, disaffected by their irregular receipt of pay, to defend unpopular officials and boyars. Most dramatic were the disturbances which broke out in Moscow itself in 1648. Having managed to quell the outbreak, the government summoned a *Zemsky sobor*. Under the Code of Laws which it enacted in 1649 (the same Code which entrenched serfdom), urban land enjoying immunities was confiscated and artisans and traders living there were included in the towns' tax-paying rolls. At the same time, all townsmen were forbidden to leave their home cities, and in future only townsmen were entitled to practise urban trades and crafts. Lacking economic dynamism and political weight, the townsmen aspired no higher than to become a closed caste heavily burdened by duties to the State.

In this hostile environment, there were few opportunities for townsmen to accumulate capital. During the seventeenth century, it is true, there were growth points in the economy. The State actively fostered foreign trade, notably with English and Dutch merchants in the west and Persia in the south, and fitfully encouraged the establishment of a number of large-scale manufacturing enterprises. Yet international trade and the major enterprises were generally in the hands either of the Tsar or of foreigners, and the privileges granted Western entrepreneurs were not withdrawn until late in the century. As a result only a thin stratum of wealthy native merchants developed. Their prosperity was directly dependent upon political favour: the government itself constituted the most valuable market, established monopolies in the most lucrative goods, disposed of much of the available credit, and had the legal power to advance or halt new ventures. Moreover, as with the rank-and-file townsmen, the State's bureaucratic weakness led it to impose crippling burdens on the leading merchants. The most eminent among them, headed by the so-called *gosti*, were saddled with the dubious honour of running the Tsar's own commercial interests, or collecting customs and excise dues. The system distracted them from their own businesses and led many of the richest families to ruin, punished for failure to fulfil the Tsar's expectations. Moreover, by turning the most prosperous commoners into semi-bureaucrats exempt from taxation, it alienated potential urban leaders from the mass of townsmen. Although prominent merchants were summoned to the meetings of the *Zemsky sobor* in the seventeenth century, their dependence on the Tsar left them little leverage. Thus, although the cities were fiscally too valuable for the government deliberately to stunt their economic and institutional development, its own needs led it to do just that. The 'service city' which evolved was firmly subordinated to the interests of the State.

What did constrain the seventeenth-century monarchy was the growing class of landowners. The privileges of the boyars, it is true, were steadily undermined. During moments of acute royal weakness they tried to re-establish their influence, but as a political force they were clearly in decline. Ivan the Terrible had not only decimated their ranks during the *oprichnina* but had eroded the distinction between their hereditary property (*votchina*) and the conditional terms of the *pomestie* by establishing a norm of military service to be borne by all estates. The Time of Troubles had further weakened their position, and as the Duma swelled in size from about 30 in the 1620s to almost 180 in the 1680s, the old families found themselves dissolving among the parvenus. The abolition of *mestnichestvo* in 1682 symbolized the decline of boyar pretensions and their fusion with the pomeshchiks.

But the relationship of the landowning class as a whole to the Crown was by no means one of abject subordination. For its part, the royal government was fully conscious of its dependence upon the pomeshchiks. There could be no thought of undermining the class which served as the first line of resistance to smouldering peasant insubordination. The new Romanov dynasty, elected to the throne in 1613, took care to cultivate their support. Between 1613 and 1622 the *Zemsky sobor*, in which the pomeshchiks predominated, was generally summoned at least once a year and it continued to play an important consultative role until 1653. The landowners were able to express their views on problems of internal security, foreign affairs, and taxation increases. Through the forum of the *Zemsky sobor* and through joint petitions they were able to exert considerable pressure upon state policy.

The position of the pomeshchiks certainly had its own weaknesses.

2.5 The Boyars' Duma in the seventeenth century. Tsar Alexis, attended by a formal sitting of the Boyars' Duma, receiving a foreign delegation.

They had no corporate institutions at the provincial level; they were divided by wide variations in wealth, education, and regional interest; their consciousness of sharing common interests was vague and little developed. Those best placed to influence government policy were also most dependent on state patronage to further their military and civil careers, while the police and tax functions delegated to serf-owners made the whole class in one sense a part of the machinery of government. But the fact that they did not impose formal constraints upon royal power reflected above all their overriding interest in the maintenance of a strong central State capable of holding the peasants in check. This was why, having secured the legal codification of serfdom in 1649, they showed little anxiety to consolidate an institutional mouthpiece at the centre and the *Zemsky sobor* faded away. The harmony that reigned between the partners was less than complete. From the mid-seventeenth century the proportion of the government's revenue coming from direct taxation of the peasantry began to rise steeply. Since the pomeshchiks depended on the same source – peasant produce – for their income, there was always a conflict of interest over the portion to be paid to the State. But the alliance between State and serf-owners was too close to generate formal dialogue let alone confrontation between them.

During the course of the century the limitations to government authority over the pomeshchiks were fully exposed. The pomeshchiks became more and more absorbed in their farms, and as these grew in size, military service for a minimal salary became less and less attractive. The government faced mounting problems in enforcing the service obligations which were supposed to accompany landownership. It found itself unable to prevent the pomeshchiks from buying and selling their estates and rapidly establishing *de facto* hereditary rights of ownership. The instrument of royal power which the *pomestie* system had been designed to create became increasingly unsatisfactory.

It was the military deficiencies of the pomeshchiks which gave the government the greatest grounds for concern. Even if they had been eager to serve, these landowners could be no more than part-time soldiers. Between campaigns they had of necessity to return to supervise their estates. In this they suffered from the same defects as the *streltsy*, the small force of regular infantry originally set up during Ivan the Terrible's reign. Unable to pay the rank and file an adequate salary, the government had been compelled to allow these semi-professional soldiers to engage in petty trade and handicraft and to farm a small plot of land. In the case of both pomeshchiks and *streltsy*, their need to support themselves during much of the year placed enormous obstacles in the way of training and disciplining them, or introducing them to new methods of warfare. By the seventeenth century the ill-organized cavalry of the pomeshchiks, still generally armed with bows and arrows rather than firearms, was becoming less and less effective. Even as a match for the Tatar warriors of the Crimea, who were similarly equipped, their value declined when in the 1630s and 1640s a strong line of fortifications was built in the south. Against western armies they were becoming distinctly anachronistic. Muscovy's major European rivals were investing in full-time professional infantry and modernized cavalry using firearms. By the time of the Smolensk War of 1632–34 against Poland the government had recognized the need for reform. Between 1630 and 1680, therefore, growing efforts were made to organize the Muscovite Army on a new basis. Foreign mercenaries were hired to officer new-formation regiments into which an increasing number of peasant recruits were drafted. The infantry replaced the cavalry as the army's mainstay, and the emphasis was placed on European-style firearms and artillery. By the 1680s the old-fashioned cavalry of the pomeshchiks had disappeared as an independent force, the *streltsy* were restricted to internal policing duties, and Muscovy had gone a long way towards establishing a professional army.

The heavy cost of military modernization generated major fiscal and administrative innovations. To increase direct tax revenue, liability was shifted from a land base (which had discouraged peasants from expanding the area they sowed) to a flat rate per peasant household. Various new indirect taxes were introduced, and in the late 1650s and early 1660s the coinage was debased. Popular resistance to these measures gave the government pause, but efforts to increase revenue continued. In administering the expanding army and the various forms of taxation, the central offices of the bureaucracy multiplied. By the 1680s there were over fifty chancelleries (*prikazi*) set up to deal with new tasks and newly incorporated areas. In retrospect their structure seems irrational, with no clear division between territorial and functional responsibilities. But the major chancelleries, concerned with finance, the army, and foreign affairs, do not appear to have operated inefficiently by contemporary standards, and their officials became steadily more specialized. Although revenue tripled in real terms during the seventeenth century the budget was not brought into balance. The Treasury was still unable to pay and supply the army adequately – despite the fact that over half the budget was devoted to military expenditure, even in peacetime. All too often the soldiers had to be allowed to supplement their income in a manner reminiscent of the *streltsy*. Nevertheless, the State's room for manoeuvre was increasing. The civil and military instruments which would provide Peter the Great with the leverage for a more forthright assertion of state interests were taking shape.

If the changes set in train in Ivan the Terrible's reign recast secular society, the impact upon the Church was no less momentous. On the face of it, the debilitated condition in which Ivan left the Crown, compounded as it was by the extinction of the Rurik line on the death of his son Fyodor in 1598, much enhanced the political stature of the Church. During the Time of Troubles the Patriarchate (established in 1589) became a vital focus of authority. The Church took the lead in rallying the forces which drove out the Poles and established the Romanovs on the throne. It was as Patriarch that Michael Romanov's father, Filaret, dominated the government between 1618 and 1633. In the 1650s Patriarch Nikon claimed for the Church an autonomy which exasperated Alexis I, the most pious and gentle of tsars. As late as the succession crisis of 1682 Patriarch Joachim played a critical role and even briefly acted as Regent. Yet in fact the Church's power was being eroded throughout the seventeenth century. Filaret owed his eminence less to his holy office than to his son's willingness to treat him as a co-ruler. The fact that Nikon overreached himself was clearly exposed when Tsar Alexis forced him to withdraw from public affairs and subsequently had him deposed and replaced by a more pliant successor. And Joachim was swiftly ousted when Sophia established her regency. Forceful individuals might use the prestige of the Patriarchate to wield political influence, but this only disguised the decline in the political weight of the Church.

In temporal terms, the Church suffered from the growing interest shown in ecclesiastical wealth by both pomeshchiks and the government. Pomeshchiks on small and medium-sized estates resented the privileges enjoyed by monasteries and looked hungrily at their lands, while the swelling needs of the Treasury drew the Tsar's attention to the resources of the Church. Repeated steps were taken to raise the Church's contribution to the state budget, to remove tax immunity from church land, and to prevent more land coming under clerical control. Though church property remained intact, it became progressively less secure.

More ominous still were the first serious cracks in the Church's spiritual hegemony. The absorption of a substantial Muslim population as Muscovy pushed east and south presented a relatively minor problem – although it underlined the Church's reliance on state support and fiscal sanctions to convert the heathens. Of much greater significance were contacts with western Christianity which increased markedly from the mid-sixteenth century along with closer military, diplomatic and commercial exchanges between Muscovy and central and western Europe. The Polish intervention during the Time of Troubles briefly raised the spectre of a Catholic Tsar in Moscow. The ensuing struggle to detach the Ukraine from Poland and bring it under Russian rule did nothing to weaken Western influence. Indeed the gradual incorporation of the eastern Ukraine into Muscovy between the 1640s and the 1670s actually aggravated the problem.

Once incorporated into Muscovy, the Ukraine radiated deeply unsettling currents of thought. While under Polish rule, the Orthodox hierarchy in the Ukraine had been able to resist the spread of Catholic influence only by adopting many of the methods and some of the ideas characteristic of the Counter-Reformation. There had been a determined attempt to root out abuses among the clergy and to raise their intellectual calibre. And now, even if the Muscovite hierarchy felt Ukrainian methods to be tinged with Latin heresy, they could no longer ignore the issues raised. Moreover, pressure for reform had already arisen within the Russian Church. This had found partial expression as early as 1589 when the government had persuaded Constantinople to raise the Metropolitan of Moscow to patriarchal status in order to strengthen Orthodoxy's defences. During the 1620s Patriarch Filaret had sanctioned cautious liturgical reform precisely to forestall foreign infection. In the reign of Alexis I the Ukrainian stimulus took full effect, and the Tsar himself eagerly supported a flurry of reforms aimed at intellectual and moral renovation. Accumulated errors were to be erased from the holy books, services were to be conducted in a more intelligible manner, sermons were to be encouraged, and scholarship was to be actively fostered in a number of monasteries; at the same time, new saints were canonized, clergy and laity alike urged to observe the prescribed fasts, and for a brief time the government even went to the lengths of closing the taverns. The result of these efforts to stiffen Orthodoxy's moral fibre, however, was to spark off a disastrous schism within the Church.

Much of the blame for the schism is generally attributed to Nikon, the overbearing prelate elevated to the Patriarchate in 1652. He pushed ahead with further reforms, insisting that Russian practice be brought into line with that of the Greek Mother Church. Relying upon authority rather than cultivating widespread support, he soon came up against resistance from those who detected a tampering with the basic fabric of Orthodoxy. The issues on which the schism turned have often seemed to Western scholars so insignificant as to be almost laughable. How could grown men and women risk excommunication, persecution, and even burn themselves to death rather than see the altar procession move from left to right, the number of alleluias cut from three to two, and the number of fingers used in making the sign of the cross raised from two to three? To Nikon's opponents, however, the changes not only smacked of foreign heresy but seemed to threaten the whole meaning of the liturgy, to break the link between the service and the faith. Although the reforms had the support of the Tsar and in 1667–68 a church council anathematized those who refused to conform, the attempt to impose the new liturgy by force proved unsuccessful. Resistance, concentrated among the peasantry but common among the urban population including the *streltsy*, was widespread and the Church found itself confronted with mass disobedience. The 'Old Believers', as the schismatics became known, attracted the support of no bishops and exhibited little intellectual vigour. However, their leader the Archpriest Avvakum, who was burned at the stake in 1681, wrote a vivid and fiery account of his own life and the privation he and his family suffered, which is regarded as the masterpiece of seventeenth-century Russian literature. Moreover, the protest of the Old Believers gave expression to more general social discontent and they contributed to popular revolts from that of Stenka Razin (1670–71) onwards. The Established Church was never able to stamp them out. The challenge to its authority increased its reliance upon the secular power, upon fines, torture, and execution. By the late seventeenth century, with its economic base vulnerable and its spiritual authority flouted, the Church was ill equipped to stand up to an increasingly dynamic State.

The general decline in the Church's influence was reflected in a degree of secularization in Russian culture. A narrow elite among the wealthier landowners and bureaucrats was developing tastes and interests which broke the Orthodox mould. Alexis I himself took several initiatives, setting up a court theatre and appointing tutors not only for his sons but for his daughter Sophia as well. Literacy among the children of noblemen was increasing and secular literature based on the spoken language of Muscovy began to rival the traditional fare of saints' lives written in Church Slavonic. Art and architecture reflected a new refinement, a new concern for luxury and symmetry, and even iconography placed more emphasis upon natural, realistic representation.

Traditionalist resistance, of course, remained strong. Change was popularly associated with the impious ways of foreign heretics. In 1652 Alexis was persuaded to establish a new 'foreign suburb' in Moscow to replace the one destroyed during the Time of Troubles. The expanding number of immigrant soldiers, merchants, architects, craftsmen, shipwrights, and doctors were to live apart from Orthodox Muscovites. Yet these efforts to preserve tradition by isolating society from Western influence were doomed to failure. On the one hand, growing diplomatic, military and commercial exchanges with the West inevitably involved increased intellectual contact. Equally important was the fact that various ideas and fashions developed in the West answered a native need for new forms of expression. Like much of the rest of the Continent, Muscovy was gradually drawing on the example of dynamic elements in the countries of the Atlantic seaboard. The speed of change should not be exaggerated. By the standards of the West's most sophisticated citizens, the life-style, the table manners, the long robes and flowing beards of Moscow's elite still seemed antiquated. The cosmopolitan ways of Prince Golitsyn, the Regent Sophia's favourite, stood out even at court. But the more closely historians examine the seventeenth century, the more precedents they find for the innovations associated with the name of Peter the Great.

The prime of the Empire

It was in the eighteenth century that Russia became a major European power. The most spectacular rise in her international status occurred in the reign of Peter the Great (1682–1725). His Great Northern War against Sweden, concluded by the Treaty of Nystadt in 1721, secured for Russia her 'window on the West'. Her acquisitions included the territories that became modern Estonia and parts of those which became modern Latvia. Peter founded the new capital of St Petersburg on the Gulf of Finland to demonstrate Russia's permanent footing on the Baltic. Embassies were rapidly established in the capitals of Europe and the Imperial title he accepted from the newly created Senate was gradually recognized by his fellow monarchs.

During the mid-eighteenth century, without making major territorial gains, Russia significantly increased her influence both in the Baltic and in central Europe. This was reflected in her growing ascendancy over Poland, and in the new-found respect with which the major continental powers treated her. The cornerstone of over a century of Russian diplomacy was laid with the signing of a formal alliance with Austria in 1726. Under Anne (1730–40) the two eastern monarchies defeated French sponsorship of a candidate for the Polish throne. Under Elizabeth (1741–61), south-eastern Finland was annexed following victory over Sweden (1743), and Russian support for Austria in the Seven Years' War (1756–63) brought Prussia to the brink of ruin: Frederick the Great was saved only by the death of Elizabeth. In the south, although French support for Turkey postponed any decisive reckoning, the military balance was clearly moving in Russia's favour.

The reign of Catherine the Great (1762–96) saw the largest territorial acquisitions since the sixteenth century. The Empire expanded across a broad band of territory running from the Baltic to the Black Sea, and down to the Caucasus. Most satisfactory for Russia were the gains made at the expense of Turkey. Until now Turkish protection of the Crimean Tatars had enabled them to launch repeated slave raids on Russian territory, prevented settled cultivation of wide areas of the Ukraine, and blocked Russian access to the Black Sea. The defeat of Turkey in the war of 1768–74, therefore, marked a major step in consolidating Russia's southern flank. By the Treaty of Kuchuk Kainardzhi Russia acquired a Black Sea coastline. In 1783 she proceeded to annex the nominally independent Crimea and to construct a large Black Sea fleet. Turkey's efforts to reverse the verdict between 1787 and 1791 were unavailing and by the Treaty of Jassy she was compelled to acknowledge Russian rule across the northern coast of the Black Sea.

The Empire's expansion in central Europe was a much more qualified blessing. Recurrent Polish resistance to Russian domination encouraged Catherine to destroy the buffer state altogether. Russia's prolonged struggle with Turkey gave Prussia and Austria the leverage to ensure that they should benefit from the dismantling of Polish independence. By the partitions of 1772, 1793, and 1795, therefore, Poland was carved up between the three powers and erased from the map. Russia's share included Lithuania, the remaining territories of modern Latvia, Belorussia, and the western Ukraine (with the exception of Galicia, which fell to Austria). Unlike the acquisition of the Black Sea coast, the Empire's new western border was marked by no natural barrier. Moreover, among the 7.5 million new subjects acquired were two national and religious minorities, Catholic Poles and Jews, who were destined for very different reasons to prove particularly disruptive to the Empire.

South of the Caucasus, Catherine had been invited to extend protection over the kingdom of Georgia, which was subject to encroachment by both Turkey and Persia. When at the end of his brief reign, Paul I (1796–1801) decided to annex the kingdom, Russia faced Georgian resistance and became involved in a long, if relatively untaxing, war with Persia (1804–13), which yielded most of eastern Transcaucasia. By Paul I's time, however, Russia's primary concern was with the destabilizing energy radiating from revolutionary France. Dissension among France's enemies broke up the Second Coalition, though not before Russia's most revered commander, Suvorov, had temporarily driven the French from northern Italy and conducted a legendary retreat through the Swiss Alps. Paul then allied briefly with Napoleon before he was assassinated in favour of his son, Alexander I (1801–25).

It fell to Alexander to bear the full brunt of Napoleon's ambition. Russian participation in the Third Coalition ended in disaster at Austerlitz (1805), but Alexander used the breathing-space afforded by the Treaty of Tilsit (1807) to good effect. He drastically lowered the price demanded from Turkey for an end to the war of 1806–12, accepting Bessarabia as adequate spoils, and having deprived Sweden of the remainder of Finland, he hastily concluded a treaty with her in 1812. That summer Napoleon assembled the

Grande Armée and in June invaded Russia through Poland. The Russians denied him the decisive pitched battle on which he had counted. The Armée's massive size proved a positive handicap to Napoleon as its supply problems became horrendous. By the time the French approached Moscow, General Kutuzov was ready to stand his ground. On 7 September[1] on the field of Borodino the Russians inflicted the worst savaging any army of Napoleon's had ever suffered, before withdrawing in good order. Moscow was abandoned, but Napoleon could make little use of its capture – especially since nine-tenths of the old capital was burned to the ground. As winter approached, Napoleon was unable to advance further, nor could he persuade the Tsar to negotiate. On 19 October the French Emperor turned for home. The retreating army was ravaged by hunger, cold, disease, and ever more audacious and vicious assaults by peasant partisans. Alexander insisted upon chasing the French all the way back to Paris. A relieved Russian establishment conferred upon him the title of 'the Blessed'. He had done what all Europe had failed to do: he had stopped Bonaparte.

Alexander extended Russia's borders further west than ever and they remained essentially unchanged until the First World War. Despite Allied opposition he reconstituted the much expanded Polish territory under his control as an independent kingdom linked to Russia through the person of the monarch. He created the Holy Alliance of Christian monarchs dedicated to peace and upholding the existing order, and in subsequent years urged Great Power intervention against revolutions in Spain, Piedmont, Naples and, with much less conviction, Orthodox Greece.

His brother Nicholas (1825–55) adopted an even more rigidly conservative approach towards the West. A fierce revolt in Poland in 1831 was crushed and the separate kingdom abolished. During the revolutions of 1848 he used his seemingly impregnable position to repress rebellion in Romania, to restore Habsburg control in Hungary, and to prevent constitutional change in Germany. Alexander the Blessed had been succeeded by 'the Gendarme of Europe'.

In fact, however, the Empire had passed its prime by Nicholas's time. Russia's armies were adequate to increase her influence in central Asia and to inflict further defeats on both Turkey and Persia, thereby extending Russian rule in the Caucasus, incorporating much of modern Armenia and Azerbaijan. They could deal with the ill-organized forces of eastern Europe's revolutionary outbursts. But their limitations were fully exposed in the course of the Crimean War (1853–56). Nicholas's government underrated the concern felt by Britain, France, and her traditional ally Austria over Russia's growing influence in the Balkans, and above all over the

---

[1] Between Peter I's calendar reform in 1699 and that of the Bolsheviks in 1918, Russia used the Julian calendar which was twelve days behind the West in the nineteenth century and thirteen in the twentieth.

Map 4 The western expansion of Russia under Peter I and Catherine II, 1689–1796

possibility that Constantinople might fall under her sway. Nicholas refused to back down from asserting his right to protect the Sultan's Orthodox subjects, Turkey declared war, and Britain and France came to her aid. In the ensuing conflict Russia was defeated at sea and humiliated on her own doorstep by the fall of her Crimean naval base at Sevastopol. She was compelled to sue for peace, and under the terms of the Treaty of Paris, was disarmed on the Black Sea.

In the century and a half before the Crimean War, however, the Empire had brought a rich array of peoples under her sway. Russian rule had been extended over most of the territory which would one day constitute ten of the fourteen 'Union Republics' united with Russia in the USSR: to the north, Estonia, Latvia and Lithuania; to the west, Belorussia, the Ukraine and Bessarabia (which would form the nucleus of the Moldavian Republic); in the Caucasus, Georgia, Armenia and Azerbaijan; and in the south, Kazakhstan.[2]

Table 3.1　The Imperial succession

1682–1725	Peter I – the Great
1725–1727	Catherine I
1727–1730	Peter II
1730–1740	Anne
1740–1741	Ivan VI
1741–1761	Elizabeth
1761–1762	Peter III
1762–1796	Catherine II – the Great
1796–1801	Paul
1801–1825	Alexander I
1825–1855	Nicholas I

How are this massive expansion and the remorseless rise in Russia's international prestige to be explained? A significant part of the answer lies in the social, economic, and political problems of her neighbours, and the pattern of their diplomatic manoeuvres. The remarkable ascent of Swedish power from a tiny base was doomed to retraction in the eighteenth century, and Russia was the natural beneficiary. Poland's collapse owed as much to the failure of her serf-owning nobility to cooperate behind a powerful central government and army as to the exertions of her neighbours. Social and economic stagnation ensured Turkey's decline (and to an even greater extent Persia's) compared to Europe's major powers. The rivalry between Austria and Prussia, and their involvement in the wars of the West, increased Russia's weight in central and eastern Europe.

---

[2] The territory that would constitute the other 4 Union Republics – the Central Asian Republics of Turkmenistan, Uzbekistan, Tadzhikistan and Kirgizia – was acquired in the latter part of the nineteenth century.

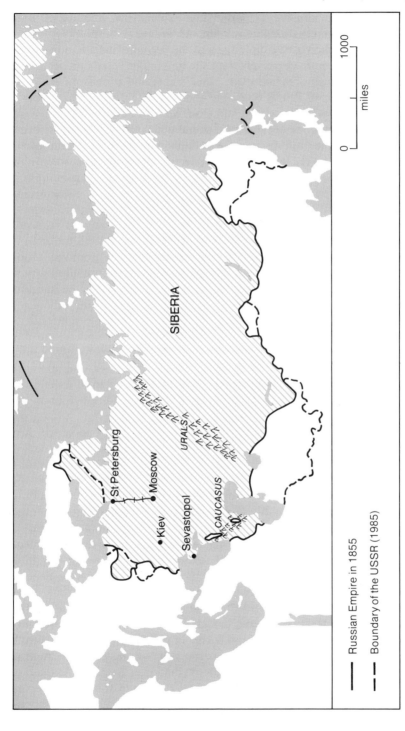

Map 5 The Russian Empire by 1855

Russian Empire in 1855

Boundary of the USSR (1985)

SIBERIA

URALS

CAUCASUS

St Petersburg

Moscow

Kiev

Sevastopol

0 ————— 1000

miles

Yet this provides only a part of the explanation. In order to benefit from favourable international developments, indeed in order to avoid falling victim herself to the volatile diplomacy of the period, Russia had to mobilize her resources far more effectively than she had under Peter's predecessors. It was his success in mobilizing men, arms, ships, and provisions which was most characteristic of Peter's reign. He abolished the *streltsy* and the old service cavalry altogether and, building on Muscovy's new-formation regiments, he completed the construction of a regular standing army. It became possible to instil the drill, discipline, and skills required to make the army an effective fighting force. It became possible to standardize the *matériel* and develop strategy in a way that had been beyond Muscovy's capabilities.

The Petrine military system remained unchanged in essentials until after the Crimean War. The rank and file were drawn from forced levies laid upon the tax-paying population. Service was for life: this was reduced to twenty-five years at the end of the eighteenth century, but all too often the difference was purely nominal. The officers were drawn from the nobility. Peter made service in the army or the civil administration compulsory and lifelong for all noblemen. The term of service was reduced by his successors and in 1762 it was made voluntary, but the great bulk of the officer corps continued to be staffed by hereditary noblemen. During the eighteenth century the irregular Cossack hosts were gradually brought under control and absorbed into the regular army. Although the government was cautious about enrolling men from newly incorporated minorities, the size of the army rose in line with the population – which increased from some 15 million under Peter to double that figure under Catherine II and reached about 67 million by the 1850s.

At the same time as Russia became a leading military power she began to develop a considerable naval capacity as well. Peter founded the navy out of virtually nothing, recruiting officers and sailors in the same way as for the army, and used it to good effect against the Swedes. Renewed progress was made, after a prolonged period of decline, when Catherine II's acquisition of the northern coast of the Black Sea initiated a major shipbuilding programme.

The shift from short-term mercenary troops, from unreliable feudal levies, and part-time forces expected to earn their own living was undertaken by most of the powers of early modern Europe. Success depended upon discovering ways to supply the standing army. In Russia, rank-and-file wages were kept very low, and throughout the period Russian regiments supplied many of their own needs, a high proportion of 'soldiers' serving as tailors, carpenters, cobblers, and so forth. In peacetime, regiments were billeted upon towns and villages. Nevertheless, it was necessary to raise and administer far more revenue than Muscovy had ever handled. At the centre Peter created a governing Senate to oversee all administration. He replaced the overlapping chancelleries with colleges in which efficiency was supposed to be ensured by the mutual responsibility of thirteen top officials in each, and which, at least in theory, had more clearly defined duties. Under Alexander I they were, in turn, replaced by distinctly more effective ministries. At the local level Peter left tax collection to the army, dealing through intermediaries chosen by the peasantry and townsmen themselves. From Catherine II's reign the local administration began to expand, and although the number of officials remained minuscule the system sufficed to meet the needs of the army.

Peter's reign saw the most dramatic leap in the revenue raised by the State. It is estimated that he trebled it in real terms – and this at a time when the population was stagnant. His most important innovation was the poll-tax in place of the household tax, which the peasantry had been able partially to evade by merging households. The poll-tax, a fixed annual levy placed on all tax-paying males regardless of age, together with the rent extracted from state peasants, formed the basis of state revenue for over a century. In addition Peter imposed an astonishing range of indirect taxes, on everything from beards to blue eyes, the most important being those on alcohol and salt. In the nineteenth century, as the pace of domestic and foreign commerce quickened, indirect taxes gradually yielded more than the poll-tax. Peter also greatly increased the subventions paid out of church revenue towards the needs of the State, a process which culminated in the secularization of church property in the 1760s. Peter himself achieved a balanced budget, but his successors found it necessary to supplement their income by resorting to ever larger foreign loans.

With the help of the army, then, Peter and his successors were able to squeeze more revenue from the population. But the State's increased income also reflected significant economic development from Peter's reign onwards. Forced labour was used to found metallurgical and textile industries, making Russia self-sufficient in arms and uniforms. The major step in agriculture was the opening-up of the rich lands of the Ukraine as Russian rule was consolidated against Turks, Crimean Tatars, and Cossacks, while the establishment of outlets to the Baltic and then to the Black Sea greatly expanded foreign trade.

Once the industrial and social changes which were transforming the West during the later eighteenth and early nineteenth centuries began to find military expression, of course, the limits of Russia's resources would be fully exposed. Handicapped by serfdom, primitive agricultural methods, and the far-flung, inconvenient location of her natural resources, it was impossible for her to keep pace. The most graphic illustration of her rapid relative industrial and technological decline is provided by figures for production of pig-iron. Whereas in the 1780s she produced twice as much as her closest competitor, Great Britain, by the end of the Crimean War she had been overtaken by Belgium, France was exceeding her output threefold, and Britain no less than fourteenfold. The army itself constituted a major drain

PETRUS PRIMUS
RUSSORUM IMPERATOR

on the economy. It numbered well over a million men by Nicholas's day. Annual recruitment had to be even heavier than this total suggests, since well into the nineteenth century a high percentage of recruits died before even reaching their regiments and disease took a heavy toll among established troops. Yet the government found it impossible to reduce the size of the army. The extended frontiers, the recurrent danger of resistance from national minorities, and the permanent threat of peasant disturbances necessitated a huge military presence. Nor could the standing army be cut by building up a reserve since trained men, automatically liberated when drafted, could hardly be returned to enserfed villages. Russia's defeat in the Crimean War certainly owed something to poor leadership and complacency at the top. But in an age of railways and steam-power it became increasingly difficult for her to compete. Her army and navy were becoming antiquated.

The State which organized the Empire's military effort is described in both Soviet and Western historiography as an 'absolute monarchy'. The label draws attention to three important developments which distinguish it from the early Romanov State. In the first place, the creation of a regular standing army marked a qualitative change in the authority of the monarchy. Whereas Muscovy's *streltsy* and pomeshchiks had proved thoroughly unreliable and resistant to central organization and discipline, Peter bequeathed a military machine responsive to hierarchical control. The last traces of independence within the military establishment were removed and the State's powers of coercion greatly enhanced.

The second major departure was the *coup de grâce* administered to the Church, the one institution outside the State with which Muscovite monarchs had been compelled to reckon. Peter firmly subjugated the Church to the State. The Patriarchate was abolished and ecclesiastical administration taken over by the Holy Synod (1721), a department of State headed by a layman. After the secularization of church lands, initiated during the brief reign of Peter III (1761–62) but completed by Catherine II, the clergy became salaried employees of the State. The political independence of the hierarchy was broken.

Finally, from the time of Peter the Great decision-making power was concentrated in undiluted form in the hands of the monarch. Peter ceased appointing his most trusted aides to the Boyars' Duma, the Duma's residual right to be consulted went by default, and the institution withered away. The *Zemsky sobor*, whose role in decision-making had never approached the status of a right, disappeared altogether. The nearest thing to a *Zemsky sobor* summoned by Peter's successors was Catherine II's Legislative Commission (1766–68). It helped make the government conscious of some

3.1 Peter the Great. A portrait celebrating the Imperial status conferred upon the Tsar by the Senate following his victory over Sweden.

of the preoccupations of nobility and townsmen, but when its proceedings were interrupted by the Turkish War, Catherine allowed the experiment to lapse. Nor did any of the projects for constitutional constraints upon the Tsar's discretion bear fruit. The only major attempt to impose terms on the Crown was made in 1730, when Peter's daughter, Anne, was offered the throne. The Supreme Privy Council, established during the reign of Peter's widow Catherine (1725–27), sought to establish the right to participation in, and an effective veto over, all major policy decisions. Although the Empress submitted momentarily, divisions within the nobility enabled her to tear up the councillors' terms. Both Catherine II and Alexander I were urged early in their reigns to make significant if less dramatic institutional reforms, but in neither case could the reformers mobilize strong pressure upon the monarchs to consent. The more sophisticated projects drawn up by Speransky in 1809 and Novosiltsev in 1819 were made at Alexander's instigation and fell to the ground the moment he lost enthusiasm. Thus no institutional check upon the Tsar was established. Even when the incumbent on the throne showed little inclination for active policy-making, those who acted for the Tsar owed their power solely to proximity to the throne.

These developments concentrated enormous power in the hands of the individual on the throne. His or her personality and judgement were of most significance in the fields of foreign and military affairs. There were of course major guidelines within which even the most idiosyncratic monarch would operate: security in the west, a steady probing towards outlets in the Baltic and the Black Sea, incremental expansion and pacification in the south-east. Yet major strategic decisions could depend very much upon the will of the monarch. The grim determination with which Peter the Great restored the army after the disaster at Narva (1700), and risked all in the decisive battle against the Swedes at Poltava (1709), reflected in large measure his own indomitable, exuberant, ruthless personality. Peter III was personally responsible for the abrupt cessation of hostilities against a prostrate Prussia in the midst of the Seven Years' War. Alexander I rebuffed repeated advice that he come to terms with Napoleon during the French invasion. The Crimean War was as much the product of Nicholas's own judgement – or misjudgement – as of any irresistible pressure upon him. There was plenty of room for sheer caprice: Paul I's order for an overland march across unmapped territory to wrest India from the British was only the most bizarre instance. Military organization, too, owed much to the whim of the Tsar. Virtually all the Romanovs from Peter's time took limitless pleasure in the glitter and order of parade-ground drill, thereby seriously diminishing the emphasis on combat training. Equally striking was Alexander I's experiment with 'military colonies', which was very much his own pet scheme. He envisaged combining farming and family life with military service in idyllic rural settlements. But the colonies were run on a shoe-string and generated explosive tensions; both officers and men loathed the system, and the attempt to make it pay by imposing the most detailed and humiliating regulations sparked off repeated risings. With over a third of the standing army enrolled in the colonies, the situation became dangerous and Nicholas phased them out.

For all the Tsar's power over the army, where domestic affairs are concerned the phrase 'absolute monarchy' may obscure as much as it reveals. It conjures up the picture of an omnipotent and independent sovereign – the image actively cultivated by the ideology of Tsarism. It was this image of the disinterested and all-powerful Tsar which so endeared the 'little father' to generations of Russian serfs. And the myth was sincerely believed by many of the monarchs themselves. Their personal responsibility for decision-making seemed to elevate them above the social struggle, to make them neutral arbiters between the competing interests of nobles, townsmen, and peasants. Paul I was the last Tsar who actually enjoyed his office. His successors were weighed down by the sense of duty. Nicholas wore himself out seeking to keep control over every conceivable decision in his own hands, so convinced was he that the sovereign alone could perceive the common good. This supposition informs much Imperial legislation and permeates many liberal treatments of the nature of state power. Yet the reality was different. Although the post-Petrine State was much more formidable than that of Muscovy, there remained very real constraints upon the options open to the Tsar. These were of two kinds: those deriving from the social structure on which the monarchy rested, and those implicit in the rudimentary nature of the administrative instruments at the Tsar's disposal.

In a society based on serfdom, order depended upon upholding the authority of the serf-owners. To subvert them would be to incite peasant revolts even more threatening than those which punctuated the eighteenth century. It was simply inconceivable for the monarchy to contemplate sweeping away the nobility. This is not to deny that the monarchs themselves became increasingly conscious of the social tension, economic stagnation, and moral evil implicit in serfdom. Tsar after tsar floated notions of at least ameliorating the virtual slavery of the peasantry. Alexander I refrained from reimposing serfdom in the Polish territory he acquired, and between 1816 and 1819 he gave to the peasants of the three Baltic provinces the doubtful blessing of landless emancipation. Nicholas set up no less than nine secret committees to consider the issue. Yet each tsar was advised against drastic action and each duly backed away. To tamper with serfdom was certain to arouse wild expectations among the peasantry and would require the most rigorous control. Should the nobility refuse to cooperate, the monarchy would be left high and dry and the monarch himself would be unlikely to survive. Nothing could be done without noble acquiescence.

The effective veto that the nobility exercised over this most central issue of social life was guaranteed by the whole structure of the State. The army, the Tsar's ultimate weapon, was commanded by noblemen. The influence this gave to the nobility was most clearly demonstrated in the role played by the elite Guards regiments in settling the succession struggles in the period between the reigns of Peter I and Catherine II. Should a wayward tsar stray too far from the path approved by the nobility, he or she could be replaced. Nor was noble influence brought to bear only in moments of crisis. In the eighteenth century the civil administration was overwhelmingly staffed by men of noble origin. Thereafter the proportion of commoners began to rise, but the upper reaches remained wholly dominated by the nobility: at Nicholas's death 70 per cent of the highest ranking bureaucrats were landowners, often possessing vast estates. Despite the arrival of occasional parvenus such as Speransky in the early decades of the nineteenth century, the Tsar was surrounded by military and civil advisers who were bound by the strongest bonds to the serf-owning nobility. And the royal family itself, despite intermarriage with foreign royalty and its unique treatment in law, lived and moved within the milieu of Russia's aristocracy.

It is in this context that the absence of any corporate forum through which the nobility could participate in decision-making should be understood. Various secondary explanations for the Russian nobility's failure to mount a *fronde* against the Crown can be adduced. Court politics were pursued within a context of competition between rival patronage groups. Senior officials inevitably tended to view any proposals for constitutional reform or institutional innovation according to the impact that would be made upon their own position and that of their clientele. This made it impossible for those who did advance reform proposals, such as Panin under Catherine II and Pahlen under Alexander I, to organize united pressure upon the Tsar to compromise royal authority. Moreover, outside Moscow and St Petersburg political consciousness among landowners remained weak. Not until Catherine II deliberately established permanent provincial assemblies of the nobility (1785) were there any estate institutions in which pressure upon the central government might gather momentum – and even then the assemblies remained passive and ill-attended. As in the seventeenth century, the development of political consciousness was inhibited by the low cultural level of provincial noblemen, and by the differences in outlook between noblemen of different regions and different degrees of wealth. In any case, the career patterns of service to the State and the rapid fragmentation of noble estates, divided among several heirs, continued to deprive them of strong local ties comparable with those of British and French noblemen. But the fundamental explanation for the absence of political confrontation between Crown and nobility remained the community of interest between them. The need both for foreign and domestic security was evident to all. It was royal troops who drove out Poles, Swedes, Turks, and Frenchmen; it was government forces which kept the serf in his place. The fate of Poland demonstrated the price to be paid for oligarchic fracturing of state power; the Pugachev rebellion (see below, pp. 58–9)

(1773–74) demonstrated all too brutally the need to buttress the Tsar's authority. Only when the Crown showed itself unable or unwilling to uphold their serf-owning authority would the nobility be motivated to question the Tsar's 'absolute' power.

Individually, the Russian nobleman continued into the eighteenth century to enjoy much less security under the law than his Western counterpart. The ruthless punishment meted out to senior officials who fell from favour reflected the general lack of legal safeguards for life and property. Yet, while bureaucratic power over commoners remained capricious right into the nineteenth century, steady progress was made in entrenching the individual rights of noblemen. From the mid-eighteenth century, in theory at least, they could not lose rank, estate, honour, or life without trial by their peers, and they became immune to corporal punishment. Catherine's Charter to the Nobility of 1785, which formally confirmed these rights, also recognized their absolute property rights and exemption from personal taxation and billeting obligations. Not the least of the offences which led to Paul's assassination in 1801 was his contemptuous treatment of courtiers. Noble sense of personal dignity had passed the point where such treatment was tolerable.

The constraints imposed upon the State by the interests of the nobility are sometimes overlooked because of its apparent collective vulnerability to state interference. Yet such interference was possible for only one ruler of Imperial Russia: Peter the Great. The creation of a regular army and somewhat more effective administrative apparatus enabled him briefly to force the pace of change in the face of widespread noble hostility. The astonishing range of innovations made by this tireless giant of a man gave contemporary noblemen – never mind humbler folk – the sense of being in the hands of some alien, elemental force. His most striking imposition on the nobility was the introduction of compulsory, lifelong service to the State. All noblemen over the age of 15 were to register for service and proceed through the fourteen grades of a carefully constructed Table of Ranks (1722) drawn up for military, civil, and court service. He succeeded in forcing several thousand nobles into service by threatening them with loss of status and land. No other eighteenth-century European elite was so ruthlessly dragooned.

Yet even Peter's ascendancy over the nobility must not be exaggerated. The most prominent families had no objection to service – it had long offered them the surest route to power, wealth, and prestige. Those who did object found various means of evasion, and in any case, within a very brief period, the initially reluctant provincial nobility became acclimatized. During the succession crisis of 1730 complaints against compulsory service were barely audible even among the lesser nobility. In 1736 the period of service was cut to twenty-five years, and in 1762 Peter III abolished compulsory service altogether. By the time of Catherine's Legislative Commission (1766–68), the predominant concern among the nobility was to exclude

commoners from the Table of Ranks. Even the middle-ranking provincial posts continued to attract humbler noblemen who often took them up after retiring from the army. Once they had acquired the taste, a service career became increasingly attractive to them. It offered wider horizons, higher status, an opportunity to wield power, and, above all, a valuable source of income. Through the fruits of office a significant proportion of the payments imposed on the taxable population flowed to the nobility. They made Peter's creation their own.

The symbiotic relationship between State and nobility limited the scope of state power and conditioned government policy. The most fundamental limitation concerned jurisdiction over private serfs. Provided the landlord ensured that his serfs' poll-tax did not fall too far into arrears, he was left to his own devices. During the eighteenth century the State acknowledged his right to punish to the point of death a serf who displeased him, to enrol him in the army, to exile him to Siberia, to trade and dispose of his human property as he pleased. Catherine explicitly denied the serf's right to appeal to the State against his master's treatment. Private serfs, some 46 per cent of the total peasant population at Nicholas's death and concentrated in the most fertile areas of the Empire, were beyond the reach of the State.

A large portion of the State's scarce resources was absorbed in upholding the serf-owners' authority and subsidizing their income. Throughout the eighteenth century peasant flight, resistance, murder, and revolt were endemic, and the incidence of peasant disturbance began to rise again soon after the Napoleonic Wars. Government forces had constantly to be at hand. Nor was government aid to the landlord restricted to armed assistance. Despite the opportunities opened out from the late eighteenth century by an expanding grain trade, a marked increase in the land available, and a steady rise in labour and money dues extracted from the peasantry, the nobility found it difficult to make ends meet. Through the agency of the Nobles' Bank established in 1754, and later the State Loan Bank, the State issued massive loans to sustain them. In 1762 commoners were forbidden to purchase serfs, thereby giving noble industrialists a temporary advantage since hired labour was still scarce. By steadily eroding the townsmen's monopoly over urban trade and craft, the State assisted not only serf entrepreneurs but also their noble masters who claimed much of their profit in the form of quit-rent. Since noble interests were not always uniform, deference to their wishes did not dictate all the Tsar's major decisions, but it did inform every sphere, including the fiscal, commercial, and, very often, the tariff policy of the State.

Dependence on the nobility was not the only constraint upon the

3.2 Catherine the Great. A nineteenth-century lithograph marking the centenary of Catherine's Legislative Commission (1766–68).

'absolute monarchy'. Even where noble interests constituted no barrier, the government's effective power was severely limited by the rudimentary nature of the bureaucratic apparatus available to it. The Tsarist Civil Service was small, ill-trained, and corrupt. Peter almost doubled Muscovy's few thousand administrative posts, but his successors cut the number so that in the mid-eighteenth century the total was still little over 10,000. Catherine II sharply increased the number, which reached about 38,000 by the end of the century, and in the nineteenth century steady expansion set in, bringing the total to some 114,000 by Nicholas I's death. Yet, although the number of officials for every 2,000 head of population rose from one in the 1750s to about four in the 1850s, the proportion was still incomparably lower than that prevailing in the West. Even in the towns, where officials were concentrated, the government had to rely right into the nineteenth century on reluctant elected townsmen to carry out a host of fiscal, economic, and general administrative functions. Although the government found the 'service city' far from satisfactory, it was not until Catherine II's reign that centrally appointed officials began to take over many of these functions. Some strata of the urban population were still apportioning and collecting their own tax dues in Nicholas I's reign. As for rural Russia, although local officials did begin to relieve landlords of some of their policing duties in the early nineteenth century, it remained palpably undergoverned.

Officials underwent no formal education in the eighteenth century, and in the early nineteenth the level of education in the provincial offices remained very low. Efforts by Alexander I's reforming minister, Speransky, to make promotion dependent upon examinations were frustrated by opposition from officials. Not until the end of the Napoleonic Wars did increased specialization effect a sharp drop in the number of transfers from military to civil service. The preference given to hereditary nobles, and the free exercise of patronage, retarded the establishment of administrative ability as the major criterion for promotion.

What aggravated the problem of developing a genuine bureaucracy was the paltry level of salaries. Catherine laid it down that every post should be paid, but the limited funds set aside by the government were rapidly eroded by inflation. The result was a level of corruption which became proverbial. Officials from the highest to the lowest subsidized themselves by creaming off state revenue and taking bribes – a modern version of Muscovy's 'feeding' system. In the absence of any clear division between administrative and judicial functions, even the humblest official enjoyed arbitrary power. The haphazard state of the law left bribery the only effective method by which individual commoners could cushion the action and demands of officials.

The result was a morass of confusion. It was impossible for the government to derive any clear picture of its own administrative apparatus, let alone of the distribution of resources in the Empire. When under

Nicholas the governor of each province was instructed to draw up an annual report, the information supplied was hopelessly vague and did nothing to identify the major weaknesses and problems of the administration. Nicholas frankly admitted that for the most part the reports were a pack of lies. As late as the 1850s local offices kept no regular accounts. Even where it was possible to draw up useful statistics, local officials were reluctant to forward information which might increase the demands made upon them by their superiors in St Petersburg.

Repeated attempts were made to rationalize the system. Building on Peter's efforts, Catherine II restructured local government (1775) by dividing the Empire into fifty tidy provinces, subdivided into districts, each with its own administrative centre. Admirable as such schemes seemed from St Petersburg, they looked very different on the ground: it was reported from one 'city' designated an administrative hub that no one had entered or left it for three months. At the centre some progress was made. Alexander's ministries, each with a clearly defined function and headed by a single official, represented a distinct improvement on the old colleges. Perhaps the most important achievement of Nicholas's reign was the codification of the laws: the publication of an authoritative digest in 1835 made it possible at least to begin to impose standard procedures on the bureaucracy. The institutes of higher education and jurisprudence established in the early nineteenth century began to train a small number of highly competent officials who consciously broke with the haphazard approach of the past.

Yet to the end of the period the central government expressed intense frustration at its inability to carry out its policies. Tsar after tsar resorted to officials outside the regular hierarchy or appointed 'watchdogs' – fiscals, procurators, inspectors, Nicholas's notorious police of the Third Section – to supervise and expose maladministration. One motive behind the efforts of both Peter and Catherine to enhance the role of elective institutions among nobility and townsmen was to discipline appointed officials. But the impossibility of relying upon orderly execution generated a mass of unproductive paper-work. Much of the bureaucracy's time was absorbed in checking and double-checking its own work.

Backed by the army, the administration was generally able to keep a semblance of order, to crush peasant insubordination, and to gather at least a proportion of the taxes decreed. But it could not begin to realize the grandiose schemes dreamed up in St Petersburg to establish schools, orphanages, hospitals, clinics, veterinary services, insurance funds, grain stores, and so forth. Viewed from the Winter Palace the much-vaunted power of the monarchy seemed distinctly overrated.

For Russia's commoners, of course, the frustration experienced by the central government did nothing to make the burdens imposed by the State any less onerous. In many ways the capricious and unconstructive nature of the administration made its demands weigh even more heavily. For the government gave so little in return: the roads remained abysmal, the judicial system tortuously slow and arbitrary, the educational and health facilities minimal. And the constant drain from the cities, in cash and service, retarded capital accumulation, technical advance, the development of independent urban culture, institutions, and political assertiveness.

It is true that despite her natural handicaps and the overriding barrier to mobility and enterprise represented by serfdom, Russia's non-agricultural economy did expand substantially in the period. The military-oriented industries founded by Peter on forced labour gradually gave way to more diversified manufacture based on hired labour (generally serfs still sending payments back to their villages). The domestic market grew as the demands by government and nobility for cash forced increasing numbers of peasants into handicraft production and petty commerce. The abolition of internal customs tolls in 1775 provided a major stimulus. Regional specialization developed, the major division of labour being between the grain-surplus areas of the south and the grain-deficit areas of the north and centre. Foreign trade responded to the opportunities opened up by the outlets to the Baltic and later the Black Sea, grain becoming the major export. The quickening pace of commerce increased the urban population: a mere 3 per cent of the population in 1700, it rose to about 8 per cent in 1800 and reached around 11 per cent by the 1850s.

But this urban growth was not matched by commensurate development of a bourgeoisie comparable to that of many parts of the West. Leadership might have been expected from the more substantial merchants, members of the elite merchant guilds established by Peter and reformed by Catherine. Instead their political energy was absorbed in enhancing the privileges of guild membership, seeking exemption from as many of the burdens of the 'service city' as possible, and distancing themselves from petty traders. In any case, during the eighteenth century the basic manufacturing sectors were dominated by noblemen, socially far removed from the merchants. The ravages of the Napoleonic Wars hit the merchant guilds particularly hard. And when their membership began to recover and expand, and the noble grip on industry to slip, the influx came largely from successful peasant entrepreneurs. Culturally deprived and still closely tied to the village, the latter did nothing to raise the level of sophistication or political consciousness of the proto-bourgeoisie.

The most dynamic economic growth took place on the periphery of the Empire – in Poland and the south – and here ethnic divisions and sheer distance from the political centre acted as further constraints. A high proportion of merchants in the textile-dominated Moscow region belonged to the inward-looking Old Believer tradition. Many of the most wealthy merchants and industrialists were to be found in St Petersburg, where Peter had done his best to concentrate commercial activity. It was here that in 1846 a revised version of Catherine's largely unsuccessful Charter to the Towns

(1785) created the first urban institutions capable of significantly improving local amenities. Yet the capital's merchants were made particularly conscious of their dependence upon government favour and contracts, and this inhibited any coherent assertion of non-noble interests. The one issue upon which the merchants felt most sure of their ground in petitioning the government concerned the stranglehold on foreign trade by foreign companies. Yet as late as the 1840s foreign entrepreneurs controlled 90 per cent of Russia's imports and 97 per cent of her exports, besides making considerable inroads into domestic commerce. Even here Russia's middle class could not mount a significant campaign. Their political weight remained minimal.

If the townsmen found difficulty in making their voice heard, unyielding resistance to pressure from the rural masses was the primary domestic function of the State. Worst off were the private serfs, whose numbers grew with the extension of serfdom to the Ukraine and the newly settled lands of the south. Since the State virtually abdicated all responsibility for their welfare, they were at the mercy of their masters. There was a remorseless rise in the demands made upon them, especially from the late eighteenth century. State peasants, who as a percentage of the rural population grew to about 54 per cent by the time of the Crimean War, fared little better. They continued to enjoy rather more autonomy in running their own affairs, but the state officials who dealt with them were scarcely less rapacious than landlords. Theoretically the government had greater leeway to introduce reforms to improve their conditions and increase their productivity. But the efforts in this direction of Nicholas's Minister for State Domains, Kiselev, foundered on the chronic inability of the central government to discipline its local officials.

Both government and landlords continued to uphold the peasant commune as a convenient instrument for apportioning tax, labour dues and, in many areas, allotments of land. As the tax burden rose and the shortage of land available to peasants worsened, the practice of land repartition became increasingly widespread and entrenched. The effect was to weaken further the peasant notion of household or any other form of private landownership, strengthen their egalitarianism, and deepen their resentment against the rights and property of landlords. The commune continued to provide some marginal bargaining power for the peasantry at the local level. It was in the landlord's interest not to press his demands beyond what his serfs considered tolerable: organized go-slows were expensive to overcome and the agents whom absentee landlords employed to supervise the peasantry were themselves notoriously unreliable. Concerted resistance by the commune and refusal to meet taxes and dues could be even more costly: neither landlord nor state official relished resorting to calling in the military, whose help would not be given gratis. But in conditions of serfdom, the group pressure exerted by the commune system also served to discipline individual peasants and it continued to act as a major obstacle to the emergence of any substantial stratum of better-off and potentially more assertive peasants. In the less fertile north and central regions, where peasant trade and crafts developed most rapidly, a measure of differentiation did develop as successful petty peasant entrepreneurs hired their fellows. In the 'black-earth' regions, however, the great majority remained close to the breadline. In the absence of any significant improvement in agricultural techniques the peasantry were acutely vulnerable to harvest failure, and living standards in many areas actually declined in the period.

The only method by which the peasantry could bring serious pressure to bear upon their masters was through flight or outright resistance. In the 1720s a government survey counted almost a quarter of a million fugitives, and the opening out of new lands to the south and east continued to attract desperate peasants throughout the eighteenth century. In Moscow province alone, between 1764 and 1769 some thirty noblemen were murdered by their serfs. Generally the government was able to contain such local outbreaks. But when endemic peasant resentment fused with numerous cross-currents of resistance, the situation could easily get out of hand. The most important rebellion was that of 1773–74, named after its Cossack leader Emilyan Pugachev. Beginning as a Cossack revolt against government encroachment on their traditional liberties, the uprising rapidly attracted support from Old Believers, minority nationalities trying to shake off Russian colonization (most notably the Bashkirs), serfs assigned to work in the mines and factories of the Urals, and tens of thousands of peasants. The rebellion spread across a vast stretch of eastern European Russia and severely shook the government and nobility alike. It was successfully repressed, and integration of the Cossacks into the regular army deprived subsequent risings of similar leadership. But soon after the Napoleonic Wars the incidence of peasant disturbances began to rise again: there was a serious outbreak in the Urals in 1835 and widespread violence in 1847.

The peasantry never became resigned to their condition. Government actions were repeatedly misinterpreted as portents of imminent relief. The abolition of compulsory service for the nobility (1762) appears to have been widely read as an indication that freedom for serfs would follow shortly. Countless rumours of noble treachery against the generous wishes of the Tsar, and an astonishing number of 'false tsars' believed to be coming to their aid, kept peasant hopes alive. Their trust in the Tsar himself remained unshaken: but it never entailed acceptance of their subordination to officialdom, the army, or the nobility. If anything, the gulf separating them from an outside world which uprooted families and whole villages for labour on distant farms, or worse still in factories and mines, which

---

3.3 Pugachev in chains. A contemporary portrayal of the rebel leader brought in a cage to Moscow where he was beheaded.

extracted taxes, recruits and grain, and which subjected them to constant brutality and humiliation, grew steadily wider.

The most striking new manifestation of the gulf between the villages and the outside world was cultural. While the peasantry remained loyal to traditional customs, dress, idiom, and primitive Orthodoxy, the nobility and officials underwent a cultural transformation. Peter the Great gave dramatic impetus to the westernization which had begun to affect Muscovy. He himself made an extended visit to the West at the outset of his reign and on his return he created consternation – and a legend – by his impatience to change the face of Russia. With his own hands he cut off the beards of leading courtiers and ordered all noblemen to abandon this ancient symbol of Orthodox manhood. Russia was to stop numbering the years on the calendar from the creation of the world; the elite were to adopt Western dress, to refine their manners, to refrain from belching, spitting, and picking their noses in public; and the traditional seclusion of noble women in the *terem* was to be abruptly terminated. Peter's efforts were epitomized by the new European-style capital of St Petersburg. He increased significantly the number of Russians travelling to the West and the number of skilled foreigners settling in Russia. Despite very limited success in establishing schools, he did his best to compel young noblemen to gain a basic education by making it a condition of securing a marriage certificate. He simplified the alphabet and gradually, as the everyday speech of the elite was given new literary form, Church Slavonic was displaced. The basis was laid for the flowering of secular literature in the late eighteenth and early nineteenth century. Under Elizabeth and Catherine the sumptuous, French-speaking court was the inspiration for westernization in architecture, furniture, art, music, dancing, theatre, and cuisine. In 1764 Catherine founded the first boarding school for girls of noble birth, the Smolnyi Institute in St Petersburg, and she took the first steps in providing public schools for a few lower-born girls. By degrees the new mores spread from St Petersburg and Moscow to the provincial cities and in time affected the humblest noble homes.

A mere fraction of the population shared in the cultural revolution. In 1801 students enrolled in schools of all kinds numbered no more than one in a thousand, and by Nicholas's death this figure had only risen to six. The government deliberately concentrated its efforts on higher education: by the 1850s there were six universities, with a total of some 3,500 students. For the autocracy the aim was not to spread general enlightenment but to improve the quality of the civil and military leadership, to train men capable of developing administrative, military, and technological skills. Both Peter and Catherine II were also consciously seeking to raise Russia's international prestige by bringing her court, her diplomatic corps, and the cultural life of her elite abreast of more refined rivals. In many ways the results were gratifying. The style of the elite was westernized, secularized, 'civilized' in an astonishingly brief period. A country that could boast the encyclopaedic knowledge of Lomonosov (1711–65), the elegance of Karamzin's (1766–1826) *History of the Russian State*, and above all the poetic genius of Pushkin (1799–1837) found its sense of cultural inferiority fading. Following the defeat of Napoleon in 1812, polite society gradually abandoned its eighteenth-century preference for French over Russian and there was a growing sense of national identity. But the autocracy paid a heavy price. For the sophistication which benefited the State also made possible the articulation of ever more intransigent criticism of the whole structure of Russian society.

The government did its best to stifle such criticism. Catherine reacted furiously to the first major attack on serfdom and autocracy, *Journey from Petersburg to Moscow* (1790) by A. D. Radishchev (1749–1802). Exiling the author to Siberia, she pronounced such sedition 'worse than Pugachev'. The upheaval of the French Revolution made her increasingly hostile to the ideas of the Enlightenment which earlier she had actively promoted in Russia. After the first decade of Alexander I's reign censorship became progressively more heavy-handed, and under Nicholas I travel to the West was curtailed and efforts made to prevent the import of seditious books. Nicholas's government mounted a counteroffensive, using press and pulpit to reinforce loyalty by propagating the doctrine of so-called 'official nationality', with its celebration of the supposed Russian national values of autocracy and Orthodoxy. During the 1830s and 1840s, encouraged by the Minister of Education, S. S. Uvarov, conservative professors sought to stimulate patriotism and identify it with the regime by glorying in Russian history, and in the country's military and cultural achievements. Yet these measures enjoyed no more than limited success. Effective censorship and monitoring of Western contacts was beyond the capability of the administration. And whatever attractions Church and throne may have had for the peasantry, their hold on educated society was being slowly eroded. The political subservience and intellectual torpor of the Church's hierarchy prevented Orthodoxy from rebuffing new currents of scepticism and secularization. Autocracy appeared the very linchpin of everything that offended a small but intellectually dynamic intelligentsia which was breaking away from the traditional values of the nobility.

To conservative opinion the emergence of a critical intelligentsia from within the womb of privileged society was puzzling. It was simply incomprehensible that some of these writers, teachers, students, and independently minded landowners should go beyond reformism to full-blown visions of social transformation. Yet the formation of the intelligentsia, that most elusive of Russian social phenomena, is explicable without attributing any peculiar, inborn extremism or heroism to Russia's educated youth. In a society rigidified by autocracy and serfdom, the educated could easily find their ambitions thwarted, and their sensibilities offended. The caprice and incompetence of the bureaucracy, the arbitrary administration of justice, the seemingly ubiquitous police could not fail to affront at least some among an elite increasingly conscious of their own dignity. Life as an officer in the army was barbaric, life as an official was corrupt, humiliating, and, in the words of the radical young Dostoevsky, 'as boring as potatoes'. The culturally conservative world of commerce and industry was hardly more attractive, and relatively few noblemen combined the capital, the ability, and the inclination to find satisfaction in serf-based farming.

It was upon serfdom that the critics of Tsarism rapidly came to focus their attention. Serfdom seemed to lie at the root of many of their own frustrations, to preclude progress, be it economic, social, or political. Even the most loyal officials found it increasingly difficult to defend serfdom on moral grounds. To the emergent intelligentsia the moral iniquity of 'baptized property' was intolerable. Acquaintance with social progress in the West highlighted what V. G. Belinsky (1811–48), the foremost literary critic of the 1840s, called 'cursed Russian reality', and added a sense of national humiliation to their indignation.

Yet this discontent was denied political or institutional expression. Aspirations which in many Western countries attached themselves to autonomous organizations, pressure groups, and even political parties found no outlet in Tsarist Russia. In the absence of a vigorous middle class the intelligentsia lacked any effective levers through which to bring about change. Deprived of other outlets, they brought all their compressed energy to bear on the world of literature and ideas. Hungrily devouring the latest fruits of

3.4 'Gambling for souls'. Gustave Doré's mid-nineteenth-century caricature depicts Russian landowners gambling not for money but for bundles of serfs. For the intelligentsia, the humiliating treatment of serfs symbolized the moral iniquity of the entire system.

Western thought – Romanticism, German philosophical idealism, French socialism – they adapted this intellectual harvest to express and grapple with their own problems. In doing so they invested Russian literature with a moral passion and intensity which remains breathtaking.

The most creative artists were by no means always preoccupied by social criticism. Much of Pushkin's poetry exuded an almost Renaissance delight in the richness and beauty of life. N. V. Gogol (1809–52), whose novel *Dead Souls* (1842) painted a devastating and influential picture of provincial life in Russia, discovered on reflection that his political views were distinctly reactionary. A favourite theme of early nineteenth-century literature was the personal ordeal of the 'superfluous man', the quest of the young, educated Russian for a meaningful role in life. Yet in Russia's polarized society neutrality was impossible. Even when no political or social statement was intended, the most abstruse philosophical inquiry, the most obscure historical research, the narrowest psychological study took on political meaning. And where a subversive message was intended, it was easily woven into any subject-matter. No amount of censorship could hold back the rise of a new social consciousness bursting to find expression.

Before Nicholas's death few of Russia's disaffected minority went beyond a loosely conceived commitment to liberty and justice and fewer still took their protest to the point of action. The major exceptions were the Decembrists. The march to Paris at the end of the Napoleonic Wars had stimulated the imagination of a significant number of Tsarist officers. Taking pride in the military feats which raised Russia's prestige, they aspired to erase the features which most disfigured their homeland: autocracy and serfdom. Six hundred men, some from the most distinguished aristocratic families, went on trial for the quixotic rising of December 1825. The affair was venerated by later revolutionaries as the opening round in their battle against the autocracy. More indicative of future trends than this rising from within the officer corps were the activities of the *Petrashevtsy* in the 1840s. Several overlapping circles of young officials, junior officers, teachers and students in St Petersburg began to take up French socialist ideas, particularly those of Charles Fourier. Before being struck by a wave of arrests in 1848, the most audacious among them – including the flamboyant M. V. Petrashevsky himself – were on the brink of establishing a radical organization.

For the most part, though, the energy of the first generation of intelligentsia was absorbed in the ideological quest which blossomed in the 1840s. The major division among the exceptionally gifted intellectuals of Russia's 'marvellous decade' (1838–48) was between the so-called Slavophiles and the Westerners. Their debates encompassed the whole range of problems which would preoccupy successive generations of the intelligentsia, from the legal and social status of women to the destiny of Russia. Both groups were predominantly drawn from the nobility and both were critical of serfdom and political oppression, but they looked to very different solutions. The Slavophiles, the most prominent of whom were leading and innovative landowners, sought a way forward which would draw on what they perceived as Russia's peculiar strengths: the social solidarity expressed in both the Orthodox faith and the traditional peasant commune. They regarded the reign of Peter the Great as a fateful rupture in Russia's organic development. It had introduced alien values into court and nobility and opened a cultural chasm between educated society and the timeless virtues of Orthodoxy and unique customs and folklore of the Russian peasantry. The Westerners, on the other hand, whose leading figures were men of letters rather than active farmers, envisaged progress towards civil liberty and economic justice along Western lines. They had greater respect for the progressive role of the State, for the rule of law, and for what the Slavophiles denounced as the vulgar western bourgeoisie. The most radical Westerners, following a path very close to that of the *Petrashevtsy*, aspired to something more than liberalism and embraced socialism. It was Alexander Herzen (1812–70) who, having emigrated to the West in 1847, began to give currency to what was to be the dominant theme of the revolutionary wing of the intelligentsia for the next four decades. He fused the dreams of western socialists with the egalitarian and democratic potential he saw in the peasant commune to create a unique brand of Russian socialism. The revolution, when it came, must be a peasant revolution, transforming autocratic, serf-ridden Russia into a land of autonomous and free village communes.

The immediate impact of the founding fathers of what came to be called revolutionary 'populism' was minimal. Lacking any organization and completely out of touch with the peasant masses in whose interests they sought to speak, they were easily dealt with. Yet the peasantry represented, at least potentially, a lever of social change which the more moderate intelligentsia lacked. The danger of a conjuncture between the heirs of Pugachev and those of Radishchev haunted the government and fired the desperate efforts of Nicholas's last years to silence all criticism.

Chapter 4 ....

The Great Reforms and the development of the revolutionary intelligentsia (1855–1881)

From the mid-nineteenth century the pace of change in Russia rapidly accelerated. The decade following the Crimean War saw the most dramatic social and institutional upheaval that the Empire had ever undergone. Central to the so-called 'Great Reforms' of the period was the abolition of serfdom. By the Statute of 1861 the 22 million serfs owned by private landlords were set free from personal bondage. The fundamental relationship upon which the economic, social, and political structure of the Empire had been based was to be dismantled.

So profound were the changes implicit in the statute that historians of all schools of thought have recognized its promulgation as an epoch-making event. In the Soviet view it marked off an entire millennium of 'feudalism' from the capitalist phase which it inaugurated. The long-term repercussions fully justify the significance attached to Emancipation. For the serfs themselves it brought to a close the degradation of chattel status and subordination to serf-owners' authority, and opened the way to the rehabilitation of human dignity. As Emancipation took effect it would loosen many of the constraints which handicapped the economy, accelerating the replacement of forced labour by wage labour and the spread of market relations. Conditions would become more conducive to entrepreneurial initiative, capital accumulation, the division of labour, technological innovation, and industrialization. In time the development of the market would speed up the rate of urbanization and reshape the social structure, thereby undermining the traditional dominance of the landowning nobility and the monarchy itself.

The immediate impact of the statute was much less dramatic than this longer-term picture might suggest, not least because of the economic terms and administrative arrangements under which the peasants were set free. These terms preserved, if in milder form, many of the obstacles to economic growth and social change characteristic of the pre-reform era. The principle of the statute was that the serfs should be emancipated with their household plots and an allotment of land, but that they should pay for this land. The amount of land made available to them to purchase should be approximately equivalent to the allotments they had been allowed to till for their own subsistence under serfdom. The government would compensate the nobility immediately and the peasantry would repay the government with annual redemption dues spread over a period of forty-nine years. In practice the peasantry emerged even worse off than these guidelines implied. The peasants' allotments were significantly smaller than those they had used before Emancipation; the 'cut-offs' withheld by landlords were particularly large in the fertile 'black-earth' regions and were a source of intense and lasting bitterness. The price the peasants paid was artificially inflated to compensate the nobility for the dues in labour and cash which they were losing. However unattractive the peasants found the terms of land redemption, they were compelled to transfer from the initial status of 'temporarily obligated' tenants to outright purchasers if their landlords insisted. On the other hand, where it suited the nobility to retain landownership, they could, until 1881, refuse to embark upon redemption at all.

In addition, to ensure discipline and orderly payment of taxes and redemption dues, the government adopted administrative arrangements which perpetuated the peasantry's position as a subordinate social estate. Except in the most westerly provinces, the land was redeemed not by individual peasants but by the land commune. The commune, saddled with responsibility for all peasant obligations, was empowered with a wide range of sanctions over its individual members. Under the crude tutelage of the rural police, the village was left to regulate its own affairs and to administer justice according to customary rather than state law.

The economic impact on the peasantry of the settlement and the powers entrusted to the post-emancipation commune is, as we shall see, a matter of fierce controversy. Clearly, the phasing out of traditional dues removed the spectre of increased production being creamed off by the landlord, while peasant security was increased by the opportunity to buy land. Peasants on crown lands and state peasants, liberated by the Statutes of 1863 and 1866 on broadly similar terms to those of private serfs, were able to buy rather more land on better terms. Despite the harshness of the terms of the settlement, the 1860s and 1870s did see the beginning of a prolonged period in which both the amount of land in peasant hands and the yield on peasant land gradually increased.

Yet the peasantry as a whole remained in a position of extreme economic and political weakness. Advantaged households might briefly establish a privileged position within their own commune and rent land from the nobility on their own behalf. But the continuing practice of periodic communal redistribution of the land, the heavy impositions of the State, the vulnerability of even the most successful household to the vagaries of the climate – all provided major obstacles to the emergence of sturdy yeomen. Most significant was the process by which peasants continued to divide the land of large households to set up new families in their own homes and merged plots which old age and death had rendered unviable. The overwhelming majority of peasants remained 'middle peasants' who, despite gradual integration into the market and a slow rise in literacy, remained in large measure set apart from and subordinate to the world outside. The other Great Reforms of the 1860s, affecting the judicial system, the press, and the universities, had little effect on the peasantry. They did gain a minority voice on the new local government bodies (the *zemstva*) set up in 1864, but they tended to view them as an additional burden rather than as a vehicle for the pursuit of their own interests. For the most part, their political leverage was still restricted to local instances of illegal resistance and the spectre of mass disturbances. Amidst the dislocation of the Crimean War and the uncertainty which followed it, rural unrest had made a significant impact on government policy. Peasant protest had reached a level which led Soviet historians to identify the period as Russia's first 'revolutionary situation'. Acute disappointment at being made to pay for the land they considered their own sparked widespread – and in places violent – protest between March and May 1861. But swift and drastic action by the government succeeded in crushing resistance. Although below the surface tension remained high in the countryside – at once reflected in and fed by repeated rumours of an imminent 'real' Emancipation – the number of disturbances tailed off.

Disappointing as the terms were from the peasant point of view, for the Imperial government to grasp the nettle of Emancipation at all was a remarkable departure. The step which for decades successive tsars had contemplated but abandoned in the face of noble opposition was taken at last.

That a measure apparently so contrary to noble interests was carried through has encouraged the view that, in the hands of a determined tsar, the Russian State was able to ride roughshod over every class. From the moment Alexander II (1855–81) took power, an image was built of the 'Tsar Liberator' as a resolute and liberally minded champion of progress who imposed his autocratic will over the objections of subservient nobles and bureaucrats. Yet as historians have examined the memoirs of those who knew Alexander, as they have combed through his letters, his marginal comments on state documents, and his private papers, what they have found has been uniformly disappointing. All witnesses concurred in one thing: Alexander was singularly irresolute. From boyhood he had been easily discouraged by obstacles in his path. As Tsar he was inclined to agree with the last person he had spoken to and to authorize wholly incompatible initiatives by different ministers. His impressive whiskers concealed a de-cidedly weak chin. Moreover, his values differed little from those of his unlamented father: he was committed to upholding autocracy, the nobility, and Russia's

4.1 Alexander II, the 'Tsar Liberator', in his study. Although Alexander's public image set him apart from his conservative father, Nicholas I, in fact the values of the two tsars differed little.

military might. He was by no means an inhumane individual; he was a loving father, he was faithful to his wife for many years and to his mistress until death. Like his father he recognized the evil in human bondage. But he left no unequivocal evidence of why he personally felt Emancipation necessary. His view of the world was thoroughly conservative. While the statute was being prepared he noticed the word 'progress' in an official document: 'What is progress?' he scribbled across it. 'I ask you not to use this word in official correspondence.' A stubbornly reactionary tsar might conceivably have delayed the measure, but the key to the decision to emancipate lies considerably deeper than the mind of Alexander.

The Tsar's support for emancipation must be understood within the broader context of the State's role in a serf-based society. That role involved two primary and overriding responsibilities: to guarantee domestic and foreign security. The head of the Third Section had explicitly warned Nicholas that friction between serf and master constituted a time-bomb which threatened the whole Empire. Peasant disturbances grew ominously in number and intensity as each decade passed, and outbreaks were overwhelmingly concentrated on private estates. Confronted by noble resistance and alarmed by foreign upheaval, Nicholas had shelved the issue and committed himself to upholding the status quo at home and abroad. It was the catastrophe of the Crimean War which rendered this commitment untenable. Humiliated on her own doorstep, Russia's ability to influence Western affairs was sharply curtailed. The whole framework within which Nicholas had viewed the options before him broke down. Moreover, the war rudely brought home the military cost of social and economic backwardness. The Treasury had run up a huge deficit. Russian forces had been incomparably less well armed than those of Britain and France. Supply problems during the war made it seem madness to postpone further the steps necessary to improve communications and construct strategic railways. The correlation between serfdom and economic backwardness was now conventional wisdom, vague though the economic analysis on which it was based might be. The case for following the Western example of reducing the costly standing army by building a reserve of trained men became incontrovertible. Yet as long as serfdom remained, so did the objection that it was not safe to return hundreds of thousands of trained men to the countryside. Serfdom was becoming a dire threat to both domestic and foreign security.

It is this conjuncture which explains why a State rooted in the social and economic dominance of the serf-owning nobility should have undertaken Emancipation. It also explains why the Tsar was able to secure the acquiescence of the nobility. The sense of urgency over the issue took time to spread. It was not at first shared by most serf-owners in the provinces, or indeed by most of the great landowners among senior officials. Individual noblemen had of course learned to their cost of both peasant fury and Russia's military decline. A minority, responding to a combination of moral conviction, economic incentive, frustration at the cost and difficulty of overcoming the inefficiency and petty insubordination of serf labour, and fear, might favour some form of Emancipation. But the vast majority preferred to live with the moral problem and forgo the reputed advantages of freely hired labour rather than contemplate the abolition of their traditional rights over their peasants. Yet should their own government, run by fellow noblemen and dedicated to their security, conclude that serfdom was too dangerous to perpetuate, they would bow to the inevitable. And it was this message which, haltingly, the Tsar and some of his ministers began to communicate. At a meeting of the Moscow nobility on 30 March 1856, while insisting that he had no immediate plans for Emancipation, Alexander delivered the famous warning: 'You yourselves know that the existing order of ruling over living souls cannot remain unchanged. It is better to abolish serfdom from above than to await the day when it will begin to abolish itself from below. I ask you, gentlemen, to consider how this is to be accomplished.'[1]

---

[1] S. S. Tatishchev, *Imperator Aleksandr II* (St Petersburg 1911), I, p. 278.

Understandably, the nobility dragged their feet. The Secret Committee which Alexander set up to consider the matter also played for time. The Tsar showed signs of lapsing into inertia. But the sense of urgency was becoming more and more widespread, enveloping the key Ministry involved, that of the Interior. The Minister, S. S. Lanskoy, elicited a proposal from the nobility of the Lithuanian provinces in the north-west that their peasants be emancipated without land as their neighbours in the Baltic provinces had been in Alexander I's reign. This was used as the basis for invitations, issued at the end of 1857, to the nobility of every province to form committees which would draw up projects for the emancipation of their peasants. Once the commitment was public, and peasant expectation soared, it rapidly became clear that the government could not backtrack without risking explosion from below. Though he showed no very clear signs that he realized it, the Tsar had crossed the Rubicon, carrying the nobility with him. Noble energy was directed into the debate over the precise terms, rather than the principle, of early Emancipation.

Many provincial nobles, as well as a majority on the Secret (now the 'Main') Committee, entertained the hope that the norm would be for peasants to be emancipated without any land. In the course of 1858, however, the government ruled out this option. For one thing, a brief period of looser censorship unleashed vigorous and open debate over the issue, strengthening the minority of officials and nobility – including the Tsar's aunt and brother – who actively favoured a more generous settlement. At the same time, during 1858 the potential drawbacks of a landless settlement were graphically illustrated by an alarming series of peasant disturbances in Estonia, where just such a settlement had been imposed in 1816–19. This made plain the potential threat to domestic stability. It underlined the arguments of those who warned that if rural unrest was to be contained, it was vital both to minimize disruption of current peasant agriculture and to keep the peasantry closely bound to the land, thereby avoiding the spectre of a restless, landless proletariat. The Tsar's own views appear to have been strongly affected when even some conservative officials, notably I. Rostovtsev, a long-standing friend and leading member of the Main Committee, became convinced that landless emancipation would be unviable. Hence the adoption of the general principle that ex-serfs were to be able to purchase an area of land roughly equivalent to the allotments they had tilled for their own subsistence under serfdom. Nevertheless, while the statute was taking shape the nobility were able to reduce both the quality and the size of peasant allotments and to extract various favourable amendments to the legislative proposals. In acquiescing, the government was well aware that the final terms would provoke peasant hostility, and took suitable precautions. In the capital the police told employers to work their men to the point of exhaustion the day before the terms were to be made known, in order to leave them too weary to protest. The statute was promulgated on the first day of Lent, in the hope that abstention would find the peasants in subdued mood. The military were fully alerted and when the village priest read out the details the police were in attendance to stifle the groans of disbelief with which they were met. Throughout, the Tsar had made abundantly clear his wish to damage the position of the nobility as little as was compatible with social order – and with the parlous condition of the State Treasury. In doing so he avoided confrontation: the State continued to be guided by a primary concern for the interests of the landed nobility.

Nevertheless, the crude and uncomplicated alliance between State and nobility which had characterized the heyday of Tsarism could never be the same again. Conservative though its aims were, in carrying through so fundamental a reform as Emancipation the government could not help but loosen the rigid framework of public life. The provincial committees of the nobility summoned to discuss the peasant question rapidly became involved in a wide-ranging dialogue with the government. The prospect of losing the traditional source of their wealth and authority induced among many

4.2   The terms of Emancipation are proclaimed on an estate in Moscow province in 1861. The authorities took care that the change in the status of the peasantry should upset neither their discipline nor their deference.

noblemen a reappraisal of their role which amounted almost to a crisis of identity. The attention of both reactionary and liberally inclined noblemen focused upon the need to establish a new basis for local government. In part they were motivated by concern to shore up the influence of their class over provincial affairs. But they were also seizing the opportunity to express their frustration with the caprice, incompetence, and sheer inadequacy of provincial administration and judicial procedures. Blemishes which had been accepted as part and parcel of a society based upon serfdom now lost their justification even in noble eyes.

At the same time as it stimulated political activity and consciousness among the provincial nobility, the process leading to Emancipation also speeded the emergence of more socially diverse public opinion. The government found it expedient to slacken the grip of censorship in order to encourage loyal expressions of support for the Emancipation programme. There was a dramatic flowering of public discussion and debate. Whereas under Nicholas I on average no more than eight new journals were founded annually, that number leaped to thirty-three in the early years of Alexander II's reign. The government's discomfiture during the Crimean War had aroused great expectations of major change, and Slavophiles and Westerners alike were privately circulating ambitious proposals even before Alexander had committed himself to Emancipation. Once that commitment became public, the non-government press mounted quite unprecedented pressure for reform in a whole range of different fields.

For a time the movement for reform even embraced demands for a Constitution. The most outspoken advocates of public participation in central government were a minority of activists among the provincial nobility. Their campaign reached its height in the winter of 1861–62 at a time when the anxieties of both reactionary and liberally inclined sections of the nobility were intense. The transition to the new order did not seem to be going smoothly. It appeared likely that the alarming peasant disturbances of the previous spring would be repeated, and there were many reports of peasants refusing to fulfil their 'temporary obligations' or to agree to the redemption terms envisaged in the Statute of Emancipation. Many landowners feared for their immediate financial position as well as their ultimate physical security. Some blamed the government for ineffective support for their interests and conceived of an oligarchic assembly in St Petersburg which would reinforce the bonds between Tsar and nobility. Others, led by the liberal nobility of Tver province, believed that security lay in a more radical break with the past and envisaged a broadly based assembly which would help reduce tension in the countryside. The overall tone of noble criticism remained moderate, yet political consciousness had taken a momentous leap since Nicholas's death.

Until 1862 the mood within the government was by no means unresponsive to pressure for reform. The abolition of the authority of serf-owners made inevitable significant administrative and judicial changes. Moreover, the process of organizing Emancipation had given the initiative within the central bureaucracy to a minority of officials who were enthusiastic about a broad programme of reform. When establishing the Editing Commissions responsible for drawing up the Statute of 1861, the Tsar had recognized the need to appoint men who not only could cope with the intricacies of the legislation involved but who positively favoured Emancipation, who were convinced in their hearts as well as their heads of its desirability. This brought together a powerful nucleus of 'enlightened' bureaucrats and strengthened the position of like-minded officials working for reform through various ministries, notably that of Justice. They tended to move in the same circles and share many of the same values as the liberal nobility and progressively minded public opinion articulated by journalists, writers, professors, and students. On some issues support for reform within officialdom was widespread. Even the least 'enlightened' senior officials in St Petersburg and governors in the provinces shared public frustration at the incompetence of the local bureaucracy. The severe straits in which the Treasury found itself after the Crimean War made it seem quite impractical to seek a solution which involved increasing the duties of officialdom. The idea of establishing elective councils outside the existing administration with responsibilities for some aspects of local government therefore made sense to ministers.

Official sympathy did not extend to pressure for constitutional change: 'enlightened' bureaucrats interpreted such pressure as the work of reactionary oligarchs, while most conservative officials saw behind it the machinations of radical members of the intelligentsia challenging the entire social structure. But within and outside the government support for legislation which would vastly increase civil liberty and the scope for political activity by reforming local government, the judicial system, censorship, and the universities gathered seemingly irresistible momentum.

Before these reforms were implemented, however, the prevailing mood of government, nobility, and a large section of the educated public underwent a sea-change. The confidence which marked the early years of the reign that major liberal reforms could be introduced without endangering the social and political order was severely shaken. An omen that more conservative counsels might yet prevail was given within weeks of the promulgation of the Emancipation Statute when the Tsar dismissed the officials most closely identified with reform, headed by Lanskoy and his deputy, Nicholas Miliutin. Lanskoy's successor as Minister of the Interior, P. A. Valuev, was a prickly character cast in a much more cautious mould. For the time being, many ministers continued to favour cultivating support among as wide a section of the educated public as possible. The government attitude towards protest among university students, towards press censorship, and the growing problem of unrest in Poland vacillated between firm repression and conciliation. But in the summer of 1862 anxiety began to get the upper hand.

A rash of illegally printed revolutionary pamphlets was followed in May 1862 by the outbreak of alarming fires in several cities, including the capital itself. The coincidence naturally accentuated suspicion even among officials more intrepid than Valuev, whose own chambers were scorched. Radical journalists headed by N. G. Chernyshevsky (1828–89), N. A. Serno-Solovievich (1834–66), and D. I. Pisarev (1840–68) were held morally responsible and arrested for sedition. The so-called Sunday School movement – a voluntary campaign launched in 1859 on a wave of public enthusiasm for providing basic literacy and numeracy for workers and their children, and staffed by students and minor officials – was condemned as a cover for dangerous propaganda and suppressed. Pessimists among the Tsar's ministers urged that the reform programme be curbed, and some of the more visionary proposals – such as those of the Shtakelberg Commission considering legislation to regulate the conditions of urban labour – forfeited essential support within the government.

At the same time the pressure for reform from the nobility abated sharply. Confirmation that ministers were drawing up plans for local government and judicial reform was enough to satisfy many. Moreover, the peasantry were proving more acquiescent than had been expected, and the government was responding to the financial concern of the nobility with a variety of measures, including plans to establish provincial banks. By the time of the St Petersburg fires both provincial nobility and the mainstream of public opinion in the cities were much more receptive to official appeals for loyal support. What finally transformed the situation was the outbreak of violent rebellion in Poland in April 1863. Until then there had been widespread sympathy for Polish aspirations for greater autonomy, and the government had moved cautiously in that direction. But news of the massacre of Russian troops stationed in Warsaw, combined with what seemed in Russia a serious threat of foreign intervention on the rebels' side, altered attitudes dramatically. Press and provincial assemblies hastened to proclaim solidarity with the Tsar. The initiative moved firmly back into the hands of more conservative forces within the government.

The Polish revolt, coming on top of evidence of underground activity by the radical wing of the intelligentsia, cast a suspicious light over all pressure for reform. Loyal and moderate as the noble constitutionalists seemed, any concessions to them might open the way to federalism, separatism and even more dangerous tendencies. Too much momentum had gathered behind several of the major reform proposals for them to be abandoned, but the final legislation reflected the government's intense concern that the new freedom should be carefully circumscribed.

The local government statute of early 1864 duly established the zemstvos, elective bodies at provincial and district level empowered to improve a range of local facilities from transport, credit, and insurance to health and education. But care was taken that the wealthier members of the nobility should dominate the minority of peasant and urban representatives, and peasants proved extremely reluctant to take any active part in debate. Moreover, zemstvo assemblies only met for a few days once a year, their budget and powers of taxation were strictly limited, and through the provincial governor and local police the government retained close supervisory powers. At the end of 1864 the legal system was reformed and the judiciary separated from the administrative bureaucracy, as reformers had long urged. Judges were to be irremovable, trials were to be held in public, juries were to adjudicate serious criminal cases, and elected justices of the peace were to hear minor criminal and civil cases. This was the most thorough-going and remarkable of all the reforms which followed Emancipation, promising a giant stride towards security under the law. Yet here too the new system was hedged in with clauses designed to preserve leeway for the authorities. An official accused of breaking the law could only be prosecuted with the consent of his superior, and the government reserved the right to deal with cases it considered politically dangerous through administrative action outside the control of the courts. Regulations laid down in 1865 made life significantly easier for the bulk of the press, reducing pre-publication censorship and committing the authorities to refer most alleged offences to the courts. But again the government retained extensive administrative powers to give it a free hand in dealing with radical writers and journalists. The same qualifications characterized the University Statute of 1863 which, while granting the universities greater autonomy, made clear that it was to be exercised within narrow guidelines.

As the new legislation came into force the government's concern to limit the scope for independent initiative was further intensified. In April 1866 an emotionally unstable radical student named D. V. Karakozov made an attempt on the Tsar's life. The incident played into the hands of advocates of harsher measures of control. The grimmer tone of government was set by the new head of the Third Section, P. A. Shuvalov: typical of the ministerial changes which took place was the replacement of A. V. Golovnin, the liberally minded Minister of Education, by the much more conservative Dmitrii Tolstoy. The leading radical journals were closed and Tolstoy instituted much closer supervision of university curricula and student activities. The rights of the zemstvos were curtailed and they were forbidden to communicate with each other even on the most mundane matters of common concern. Mounting pressure was brought upon judges to interpret the law as it suited the government, and when the courts refused to be cowed, the police resorted freely to administrative action. Every aspect of government policy was affected by the new mood. The efforts of the Minister of War, D. A. Miliutin, to take advantage of Emancipation and introduce universal conscription and a reserve army on the Western model were frustrated by conservative opposition. Only after Prussia's startling display of military efficiency against Austria (1866) and France (1870–71) would he be able to overcome this opposition. Earlier attempts to defuse the Polish problem, including a more generous form of Emancipation designed to detach the peasantry from the nationalist nobility, gave way to reliance on *force majeure* and an aggressive policy of Russification. Alarmed by the sense of losing control over the sprawling Empire, the government moved further and further away from the spirit of the 'enlightened' bureaucrats. Not until gripped by a severe crisis of confidence at the end of the 1870s would the authorities be driven again to blend repression with conciliation.

On the face of it, the regime's growing concern for security was paradoxical, since the number of peasant disturbances fell away sharply after 1863. Police reports suggested that the countryside was more quiescent than it had been for generations. In part this may have reflected the fact that the emancipation edict reduced – though it by no means removed – day-to-day friction between landlord and peasant. It is possible, too, that the peasantry found it marginally easier to postpone and evade reparation and taxation payments to the State than they had dues owed to their masters. Moreover, contrary to the long-established conventional view, these decades saw a measure of improvement in peasant agriculture. Traditionally, historians have emphasized the failures and inefficiencies of post-emancipation peasant farming, pointing above all to the fetters imposed by the peasant commune. Because land was not owned individually, was held in scattered strips, and was liable to be repartitioned periodically, so the argument went, individuals had little room or incentive to innovate or conserve and improve the quality of the land. Moreover, the commune has been blamed for exacerbating pressure on the land. The assumption has been made, on the one hand, that because its members were collectively responsible for payments due to the government, it used its extensive powers over its members to prevent them leaving and seeking work elsewhere, and on the other, that the prospect of land redistribution encouraged peasants to increase rather than to limit the size of their families. Against this, recent work has stressed that differential population increase in the various provinces of the Empire appears to have borne little relationship to the prevalence of the repartitional commune. It has also been pointed out that where land was short or of poor quality, the commune had a strong incentive to grant its members permission to seek work elsewhere, and while the commune naturally tried to compel departing workers to remit a large proportion of their earnings, the number of 'internal passports' issued to Russian peasants rose steeply from the 1860s. The major point made against traditional strictures on the inefficiency of the repartitional commune is that it does not appear to have prevented innovation and an increase in peasant output. It was not beyond the wit of communes to ensure that, at the time of a repartition, households which had improved their strips were rewarded appropriately. Equally, the collective decision-making served to compel innovation on reluctant minorities once the majority of households were persuaded of its merits. From the 1860s, many peasants made a range of improvements, albeit small-scale and unspectacular, and undertook a measure of specialization. They introduced new seed strains, crops and livestock breeds; they adopted improved methods of crop rotation, increased fertilizer, undertook swamp drainage, irrigation and land-clearing projects; they replaced wooden implements with iron; they began to make use of a host of mass-produced articles, from scythes to iron horseshoes. Yields on allotment land began to rise significantly and only marginally more slowly than those on privately-owned land. Together with expansion in the land cultivated, this made possible an average annual increase in net grain and potato output of 2 per cent between the 1860s and the 1890s.

This did not mean, however, that peasant living standards improved commensurately. With the population rising at an average rate of 1.5 per cent per annum, the increased output per head was extremely modest. Moreover, in few regions did peasants have the resources to cope with harvest failure, while individual households were acutely vulnerable to fire, chronic illness or disability. Beneath the surface, conditions remained tense in the countryside. Occasionally the calm was broken by serious outbreaks of disorder, most notably in Kiev province between 1875 and 1878, and the government found itself repeatedly denying peasant rumours that a sweeping redistribution of the nobility's land was being planned. The backdrop of rural discontent kept at a minimum the government's tolerance level for criticism and signs of independent organization in the cities. Yet not only was the urban population rapidly increasing, it was becoming ever more complex and articulate.

As we have seen, the stimulus given to the economy by Emancipation was at first limited. Agriculture was briefly disrupted and a manufacturing recession, aggravated by a drop in military orders after the Crimean War, a severe financial crisis in 1858, and a fall in cotton imports during the American Civil War, was only overcome in the mid-1860s. Thereafter, however, the economy expanded considerably. A minority of landlords commanded sufficient capital to adapt successfully to farming based on hired labour and greater mechanization, thus contributing to a very sharp rise in Russia's grain exports. Indirectly, this helped to stimulate industrial development. Moreover, for all its reluctance to see the emergence of a proletariat detached from the land, the government became more and more firmly convinced of the need to encourage manufacture. The lesson of the Crimean disaster, underlined by Prussia's triumphs, impelled officials in the Ministry of War to urge that Russia develop strategic railways and reduce her dependence on imported arms. The Ministry of Finance, headed from 1862 to 1878 by the liberal economist M. K. Reutern, became equally convinced that only by significant industrial expansion could the regime's chronic budgetary problems be solved. Reutern rationalized the administration of the Treasury, improved banking and credit facilities, and, breaking dramatically with the intensely cautious financial policy of Nicholas I's reign, made large loans available, particularly to industrialists willing to undertake railway construction. Russian industrialists were still largely dependent on foreign raw materials and machinery, but from the late 1860s they did enjoy a steep rise in orders. The metal and machine industries benefited most directly, while the stimulus spread to the textile and other light industries. The quickening pace of commercial life during the reign was reflected in a fivefold increase in joint-stock companies and a twenty-fold expansion of the railway network. This striking rate of growth should not obscure the fact that the absolute level of industrial activity was still extremely low. Russia's economy remained overwhelmingly agrarian, the peasantry were in no position to provide a strong market for industry, and not until the following reign would the State itself embark upon large-scale industrial investment. Nevertheless, the economic development achieved was sufficient to generate a degree of social change that alarmed the government.

Of immediate concern was the increase in the ranks of the urban poor. Despite the measures taken to bind the peasantry to the land, rural conditions drove a small percentage to the cities in search of work. Unskilled and impoverished, they found limited employment opportunities, were ill-paid and insecure, and urban health and housing conditions deteriorated sharply enough to arouse unease among the police. Moreover, reluctant though most educated Russians were to admit it, there were clear signs that the urban migrants' village ties provided no guarantee against the emergence of that Western curse, a restive urban working class. In May 1870 St Petersburg cotton spinners staged what was widely seen as Russia's first fully fledged strike: within days a report was on the desk of the Tsar himself. The newly established courts treated the offenders too lightly for the liking of the authorities, and the press gave the case unwelcome publicity. The government reacted by issuing instructions that future strikes should be dealt with outside the courts, and that press comment should be curtailed. But the number of strikes and disturbances grew during the 1870s, peaking at the end of the decade. Equally ominous was the illegal foundation in St Petersburg of the short-lived Northern Union of Russian Workers to improve the conditions of labour. As yet working-class protest was on too small a scale and too sporadic to pose a major challenge, but it contributed to official anxiety.

Direct pressure on the government from the business community remained distinctly limited. A minority of the more sophisticated industrialists, technical experts, academics, and publicists enthusiastic about Russia's industrialization did begin, with official support, to form organizations through which to voice the needs of industry. In 1870 they helped organize the first All-Russian Industrial Exhibition and the first All-Russian Congress of Manufacturers and People Interested in Native Industry. But this small avant-garde was by no means typical of the business community. On such matters as labour legislation, it tended to be very much more 'progressive' than most manufacturers, arguing the need to cultivate a self-respecting, educated, skilled, and sober working class. Moreover, even this articulate minority urged its views upon the government in extremely respectful tones, while the great majority of Russian industrialists and merchants remained politically obsequious, inhibited by cultural backwardness, ethnic divisions, and their sense of dependence upon the State.

The respect the government accorded them was correspondingly limited: it was significant that among the great civil reforms of the reign that of urban government should have been left until last, and that when enacted it should have concentrated power in the hands of a very narrow elite. Moreover, when in 1870 urban administrative councils (*dumy*) analogous to the rural zemstvos were established, even the most prominent commoners tended to defer to the minority of nobles represented on the councils. Far from taking municipal institutions as a platform for broader political participation, they dragged their feet even about using these bodies to improve urban facilities. Towards the end of the 1870s they did gradually become more outspoken in pressing the case for tariff protection and against any legislation which would interfere with their rights as employers. But the business community remained muted and far removed from the assertive bourgeoisie of Western Europe.

Nevertheless, the expansion of the urban economy – and of the education system – rapidly broadened the ranks of educated public opinion outside officialdom. Alongside the lawyers, doctors, and teachers appointed in the wake of the Great Reforms were now being added technological experts, economic statisticians, managers, engineers, and educated entrepreneurs. Together with the more refined landowners, they provided steadily widening scope for cultural, philanthropic, and professional organization and activity beyond the immediate control of the government. The expansion of the reading public called into being a commercially viable and increasingly sophisticated press, and provided the context for the masterpieces of Russia's golden age of literature. The political attitudes articulated by journalists and writers were by no means either homogeneous or uniformly hostile to the government. The political allegiance owed by the three greatest novelists of the period, for example, could hardly have had less in common: I. S. Turgenev (1818–83) was a moderate liberal, F. M. Dostoevsky (1821–81) preached his own brand of Orthodox conservatism, and L. N. Tolstoy (1828–1910) was to become a great prophet of non-violent protest against modern civilization. Their artistic genius – the exquisite delicacy of Turgenev, the psychological penetration of Dostoevsky, the panoramic vision of Tolstoy – illuminated the whole range of Russian

4.3 The cultural conservatism of Russia's merchants, many of whom were Old Believers, is captured in this late nineteenth-century photograph of merchants of Nizhni-Novgorod drinking tea.

intellectual, cultural, and social life and appealed to all shades of public opinion. There were times when large sections of the educated public rallied to the government. During the Polish revolt of 1863, M. N. Katkov (1818–87) established himself as the leading spokesman of an upsurge in nationalist fervour. In the late 1870s the government was almost embarrassed by the enthusiasm for a crusade against Turkey expressed by Panslavist publicists. Yet the predominant attitude of the educated public towards the regime was critical, and security-minded officials were made uneasy by 'society's' growing self-confidence. Moreover, as Alexander's reign proceeded the government was given cause for alarm by the most radical section of the educated public: the revolutionary wing of the intelligentsia.

The revolutionary intelligentsia were to assume an importance out of all proportion to their meagre numbers. They helped to bring about a severe crisis of authority at the end of Alexander's reign, they laid the foundations for the major radical parties of the twentieth century, including the Bolshevik Party, and they provided the country's leadership in the early

Soviet period. Accordingly, they have been the subject of intensive research and fierce controversy. What motivated them, whom did they represent, were they altruistic democrats or ambitious elitists? Soviet historians regarded the revolutionaries of Alexander's reign as the authentic, if Utopian, spokesmen of the peasantry, and their Bolshevik heirs as effectively fused with the proletariat. Western liberal historians tend to see them as alienated intellectuals, motivated not by the interests of any major section of society but by a host of heterogeneous ideas, romantic and modernizing, dictatorial and democratic. A third view treats them as the forerunners of a managerial class destined to impose its own oppressive rule upon peasants and workers.

Until the period of Emancipation, only a few isolated individuals had carried the dissent of the 'marvellous decade' to the point of revolutionary commitment. Herzen, the most gifted man of the 1840s, had in 1853 founded a Free Russian Press in London, smuggling his publications into Russia in the hope of stimulating pressure for the transformation of the Empire. From the late 1850s, however, a vigorous subculture, generating a series of revolutionary organizations, took root within Russia's privileged elite.

The major sources of recruitment to this subculture were the institutions of higher education. During the first decade of Alexander's reign university enrolments rose appreciably, while professional and technical colleges were expanded in line with the Great Reforms. It is true that even by the mid-1870s the total student body was little over 10,000 in a population of 75 million. And for those willing to serve the State there was no question of a graduate unemployment problem before the 1880s. Yet far from ensuring loyalty to the status quo, their elevated position made students receptive to radical ideas. Deliberately nurtured as an elite destined to man the upper reaches of the State, they developed a sense of their own importance and dignity which gave them the confidence to question the conventions of Tsarist society. Young, ebullient, and articulate, the student world was uniquely conducive to the free flow of new ideas and encouraged a disregard for differences in social origin, an egalitarian sense of solidarity quite unlike the stratified society outside. Students of noble origin predominated, but there was a marked increase in the number of sons of lower officials, urban commoners, and, especially during the 1870s, the clergy. Although these assorted commoners, or *raznochintsy*, remained a minority both within the student body and within its radical wing, they represented an important leaven whose underprivileged background and frequently severe poverty increased social awareness among their fellow students. In these conditions controversy over student fees or over interference by the authorities – be it with the freedom of speech of progressive professors, the content of the curriculum, or the right of students to form their own organizations – sparked lively protest. In the period of Emancipation, in the late 1860s, and again at the end of the reign the government faced major student disturbances. Moreover, disciplinary measures proved counterproductive. Individuals who were expelled for political activity or failure to meet the fees – or simply for poor examination results – were given additional grounds for grievance, while the punishment of an entire college tended to strengthen student *esprit de corps*.

In a highly charged political atmosphere it was a short step from dispute with the authorities over student issues to broader criticism of the sociopolitical structure. Student assemblies, cafeterias, and libraries provided a semi-institutional network within which radical ideas and literature could circulate. Though the great majority of students never became deeply involved in radical activity, those who did, together with pupils lower down the education ladder, made up over half the 7,000–8,000 political offenders of the 1860s and 1870s. Moreover, by providing a sustained source of recruits they brought into being the radical subculture which revolved around discussion circles, experimental communes, and avant-garde journals.

During the 1860s the energy of the radicals was absorbed for the most part in rebellion against the values and conventions of the educated world from which they sprang. 'What can be smashed, must be smashed,' wrote Pisarev, the most brilliant spokesman of the men of the 1860s. 'What withstands the blow is good; what smashes to smithereens is rubbish.'[2] Identifying with the 'nihilists' of Turgenev's *Fathers and Sons* (1862), and inspired by the heroic portrayal of the 'new people' in Chernyshevsky's immensely influential *What is to be Done?* (1863), they heaped scorn upon their elders. The moral niceties, the aesthetic sensibilities, the philosophical abstractions of even the most progressive wing of conventional public opinion were luxuries Russia could not afford. Progress depended upon an ascetic, unflinching commitment to 'realism'. Only that which was immediately useful had value. The most respected fields of study in the radical milieu were the natural and physical sciences. They scorned the authority of tradition, religion and the family. Several of the leading radical publicists of the 1870s made their name as champions of female emancipation. During the reform period women had gained permission to attend university lectures and played a prominent role in the Sunday School movement. Their opportunities for secondary education and skilled employment had broadened somewhat and from the 1870s a significant number or women began to train as teachers. The more active and visible this educated minority became, the fiercer radicals became in criticizing the value system imposed upon women by custom and Orthodoxy, the idealization of humility, submission and capacity for suffering. They attacked women's inferior legal status, the limitations upon their property rights, parental influence over

---

[2] D. I. Pisarev, *Sochineniia* (Moscow 1955), I, p. 135.

their choice of marriage partner, and their general subjection to fathers and husbands. The life-style, the communes, the language, the red peasant-style blouses, high leather boots, hair-styles, and blue-tinted wire-rimmed glasses of the men and women of the 1860s were designed to express their rejection of what they saw as the brazen hypocrisy of conventional society.

By the end of the decade, however, cultural revolt was being overlaid by concern for broader social problems. This was reflected in the literary diet on which the radical subculture fed. In addition to a steady flow of Western social, political, economic, and scientific works, contact was being made with Western radical organizations, including the First International, and an expanding body of Russian social criticism was becoming available. A number of short-lived clandestine presses were set up within Russia, and at the same time radical publicists took full advantage of periods of lighter censorship. Between 1857 and his arrest in 1862 Chernyshevsky, in collaboration with N. A. Dobroliubov (1836–61), made of *Sovremennik (The Contemporary)* the most outstanding legal vehicle for subversive propaganda. In the second half of the reign the most important radical thinkers included P. L. Lavrov (1823–1900), P. N. Tkachev (1844–86), and the rather more moderate N. K. Mikhailovsky (1842–1904). At the same time the enormous success enjoyed by Herzen's London-based *Kolokol (The Bell)* between 1857 and 1863 launched a tradition of *émigré* journals, whose number multiplied rapidly during the 1870s.

The dominant theme of this literature was concern for the well-being of the peasantry. The radical intelligentsia identified their own revolt against the status quo with the plight of the peasantry. This process of identification was crucial to the entire revolutionary ethos. At one level it is explicable in terms of their profound sense of guilt over their own privileges, cultural and material, for which the masses, as Lavrov wrote, had paid 'billions of lives, oceans of blood, incalculable suffering and the endless toil of generations'.[3] At the same time they saw a causal link between the predicament of the peasants and their own frustrations; the political, social, and cultural constrictions which impinged directly upon them seemed to be the product of a society based upon oppression of the masses. Moreover, peasant resistance appeared to be the only social force that could conceivably transform Russia. During the 1870s their sense of being at once indebted to and dependent on the masses generated a highly romanticized image of the simple virtue and integrity of peasant life.

In seeking a path forward for peasant Russia, therefore, they spurned the prescriptions of *laissez-faire* liberalism. Informed by Western socialism, they saw in capitalism a brutal form of exploitation. The Russian peasantry must not be condemned to the ordeal of the proletariat of Manchester or

---

[3] P. L. Lavrov, *Filosofiia i sotsiologiia: izbrannye proizvedeniia v dvukh tomakh* (Moscow 1965), II, pp. 80–1.

Birmingham. Nor did they see any future in piecemeal political reform of the autocracy. The parliamentary facade of Bismarck's Prussia, the French democracy which had crushed the revolution of 1848 and did the same to the Paris Commune in 1871, and even Britain's constitutional monarchy seemed merely to disguise flagrant injustice. By broadening the bases of support for the regime among the relatively privileged classes, constitutional reform might in fact make radical change harder to achieve. The revolutionaries' lack of interest in a programme of political reform and gradual extension of the rule of law did not imply indifference to individual liberty. Indeed their protest against restrictions on the individual was almost anarchist in tone. It was in this milieu that Peter Kropotkin (1842–1921) developed his ideas and, as we shall see, the works of the veteran anarchist Michael Bakunin (1814–1876) were to find an enthusiastic response among them. But even if the revolutionaries had been willing to settle for gradual extension of liberty, the middle classes appeared powerless to extract major concessions from the Tsarist regime. And in fact, the isolation and weakness of the radical milieu put a premium upon commitment to an unqualified Utopia. Compromise seemed to imply concern for their own privileges and betrayal of the masses.

The 'populist' ideology they developed, therefore, was socialist. Reacting both against existing conditions in Russia and against the prospect of capitalist development they built upon the specifically Russian socialism adumbrated by the *Petrashevtsy* and spelled out by Herzen. At its centre stood the peasant commune which, they believed, had preserved the peasantry from the corruption of private property. With its egalitarian traditions of periodic redistribution of the land it provided a basis on which Russia could bypass capitalism and make a direct transition from semi-feudalism to socialism. They rejected the liberal view that the commune was a barrier to economic progress. Relieved of the burdens imposed upon it by State and nobility the commune could flourish – especially once, as most of them envisaged, individual use of the land had given way to collective farming. Moreover, few believed that in avoiding capitalism Russia must forgo modern machinery and technology. An anti-industrial current was evident within populism, voiced most explicitly by Mikhailovsky, who deplored the dehumanizing effect of the ever narrower division of labour that industrialization involved. But, in so far as the subject was addressed, the dominant view was that, by integrating modern industry into the communal structure, Russia could enjoy its benefits without enduring proletarianization. The overriding concern of the populists, however, was to free the peasantry from poverty and to do so before Russia had irrevocably embarked upon capitalist development in agriculture and industry. They engaged in a passionate search for a 'science of society' which would demonstrate that Russia need not follow the Western path. The anxiety that she was on the point of doing so created a mounting sense of urgency during the 1870s.

It was these conditions that gave rise to the revolutionary movement of Alexander's reign. Euphoria over the government's commitment to Emancipation had created a short-lived hope that the Tsar might carry through a major redistribution of wealth 'from above'. But even before the Statute of 1861 was promulgated, radicals were abandoning these hopes and those who counselled patience came under fire. With the publication of the terms of Emancipation, inflammatory pamphlets began to call for a mass uprising. In 1861 'Land and Liberty', the first underground organization since the days of the Decembrists, was formed. It had no more than a skeletal structure and embraced liberals as well as socialists. The failure of the Warsaw uprising, where it had several adherents among the Russian officers of the garrison, dealt the organization a severe blow. It was liquidated in 1864 when it had become evident that the peasantry would not mount an immediate challenge to the Emancipation terms.

To would-be revolutionaries it was becoming abundantly clear that their central problem was lack of contact with the masses. During the 1860s a few isolated attempts to form close-knit organizations overlapped with more widespread efforts to develop educational circles for workers and to take up posts as village teachers or medical assistants in order to establish links with the peasants. Police surveillance made communication between different groups difficult, while separate circles and indeed individuals were acutely suspicious of submitting themselves to any centralized underground authority, even in the interests of 'the cause'. Their suspicions were heightened by the case of S. G. Nechaev (1847–82), an amoral firebrand who tried to build a rigidly disciplined organization by deliberate deception, and to assert his own authority by involving his fellow conspirators in the murder of one of their number. The trials of 1872 and 1873 which followed his exposure and the arrest of several dozen radicals whom he had deliberately implicated gave the case wide publicity, as did Dostoevsky's classic *The Devils* (1872), based upon it. Nechaev's dictatorial style highlighted an issue that had already begun to exercise the populists. A centralized revolutionary organization, created and directed by the intelligentsia, might 'run ahead' of the peasantry, or even develop ambitions contrary to those of the masses and subject them to a new form of oppression. A minority viewed such anxieties as veiled excuses for inaction, but the majority would endorse the warning Herzen had delivered in 1862 that the revolutionaries must not 'take the people for clay and ourselves for sculptors'.[4] The result was that when impatience to reach out to the peasantry boiled over into a significant movement in the early 1870s there was minimal planning and organization.

The 'mad summer' of 1874 saw some 2,000–3,000 young radicals leave the cities and 'go to the people'. Adopting peasant dress and a peasant

---

[4] Alexander Herzen, *My Past and Thoughts* (London 1968), IV, p. 1557.

craft, they sought to spread political consciousness with the help of revolutionary literature couched in peasant idiom. The euphoria of that summer gripped radicals of various persuasions: some sought merely to serve the peasantry, with no clear political goal; some hoped to lay the foundations for a conscious peasant socialist movement; others shared the hope of Bakunin that it would be possible to ignite immediate peasant rebellion. The experience was disillusioning. Not only did their numbers seem insignificant in the vast Russian countryside, not only were they rapidly overtaken by police arrests, but they found great difficulty in putting their ideas across to the peasantry. Peasants might share their longing to see the abolition of taxes and noble landownership, but they could make little of the more visionary socialist elements of the young radicals' propaganda, or indeed of their attacks on the revered Tsar. Moreover, in the absence of any evidence of impending upheaval, individual peasants were wary of risking involvement in seditious talk. Although there was another substantial missionary exodus in 1875 and some radicals settled semi-permanently in the villages, the euphoria evaporated.

The failure of 1874 helped to overcome radical reluctance to form centralized organizations. It also forcibly raised the question of the need for political change before substantial propaganda could be spread among the peasantry – a question shelved since the early 1860s amid general hostility to constitutional compromise. In 1876 the second 'Land and Liberty' was formed. While attention remained focused upon the peasantry, renewed emphasis was given to contact with urban workers. It was from 'Land and Liberty' that the populists' most effective organization evolved. In the south of Russia radicals had begun to combine ideological propaganda with 'propaganda by deed': terrorist attacks on officials. In 1878 a young revolutionary named Vera Zasulich (1851–1919), one of several prominent female populists, shot and wounded the Military Governor of St Petersburg, General Trepov. Her aim was to avenge the brutal treatment of comrades in police custody. But the impact of her deed both upon public opinion and upon the government directed revolutionary attention towards this form of political action. The turn to terror coincided with the renewed willingness on the part of some radicals to consider seeking constitutional concessions as a preliminary step to social change. Physical attacks on leading government figures might at least disorganize the regime enough to force it to accede to the appeals for political reform which were once again coming from more moderate sections of public opinion. In 1879 'Land and Liberty' split into two parties, the 'Black Repartition', which remained faithful to a programme of propaganda, and the 'People's Will', which concentrated its efforts on 'disorganization'. The 'Black Repartition' was stillborn but the 'People's Will' became the most highly centralized and coherent underground organization Russia had ever seen. It enrolled at most a few hundred members but attracted

4.4 'Going to the people'. An artist's impression of a young radical addressing a gathering of peasants in a village. The men sit at the front while the younger women stand at the back. Sympathetic local intelligentsia look on.

active support from up to 2,000 sympathizers. The Executive Committee pronounced a sentence of death on the Tsar himself and organized a whole series of attempts to assassinate him.

The terror campaign induced in the government something approaching panic. This was partly because it proved so difficult to crush or even to assess the strength of the 'People's Will'. But it was also because the overt challenge to the authority of the State highlighted the potential for much more widespread unrest. Peasant disturbances might be running at a low level, but evidence was mounting of severe discontent in the overpopulated 'black-earth' regions. Labour protest in the cities might pose no immediate security risk, but it had gathered pace ominously throughout the 1870s. Student demonstrations increased sharply at the end of the decade and, although the educated public in general dissociated themselves from the violent means and socialist ends of the revolutionaries, a large section of the press showed scant sympathy for the government. The major trials which followed the movement 'to the people' were used with great skill by the accused and their defence lawyers to expose the incompetence and brutality of the police, to draw attention to the plight of the peasantry, and to win sympathy for the wretched poverty of many students. A significant minority of the zemstvos joined in liberal demands that the government return to the spirit of the Great Reforms, respect the independence of the courts and the freedom under the law of the press, and provide some means for public participation in framing legislation.

The government's growing sense of isolation was heightened by the damaging outcome of the Turkish War of 1877–78. During most of Alexander's reign, the regime had carefully avoided all but minor military entanglements. The Caucasus had been steadily pacified and nominal Russian authority made effective. In central Asia local commanders had taken the initiative in extending the Empire over vast areas defended only by relatively weak local tribes. In the Far East substantial territory had been more or less peacefully wrested from the embattled Chinese Empire. This semi-colonial expansion took place without great enthusiasm in St Petersburg. The government was determined to avoid confrontation with any Great Power over peripheral areas where significant economic development was out of the question. St Petersburg's major diplomatic goal had been to nullify the clauses of the Treaty of Paris which had disarmed Russia on the Black Sea. This was achieved when Russia was rewarded for the benevolent neutrality she had maintained while Prussia redrew the map of central Europe: in 1870 she was able to renounce the clauses without risking diplomatic isolation. But in 1876 the protracted decline of Turkey's power in Europe provoked a crisis in the Balkans. When the Slav nations of the Ottoman Empire tried without success to overthrow Turkish authority, Russia gradually moved from diplomatic pressure in their favour to a declaration of war in April 1877. Intervention was strongly urged by a group of Panslavist publicists who portrayed it as a crusade for the liberty of fellow Slavs. The expanding popular press, newly equipped with communication by telegraph, provided colourful coverage of Russian feats of arms and the war aroused nationalist fervour among the educated public. After initial disappointments the Russian Army succeeded in forcing the Treaty of San Stefano upon Turkey in March 1878. Austria-Hungary, Britain and France, however, viewed with alarm the dramatic increase in Russian influence in the Balkans which the treaty implied. At the Congress of Berlin in July, Russia was compelled to accept revised peace terms. At home, this was felt to be a major humiliation, and the government found itself under fire from every direction. The widespread and open protest at the climb-down dealt a severe blow to the regime's prestige and self-confidence, and the passions inflamed by foreign affairs lent a certain leverage to domestic critics of the social, economic and political ills of the Empire. The autocracy was faced by the emergence of a markedly more vigorous and independent public opinion.

There was no consensus among senior officials on how to react to the complex of pressures bearing down upon the government. But the diplomatic débâcle strengthened the hands of ministers who urged that the fierce police measures taken against sedition during 1879 should be combined with efforts to conciliate less intransigent critics. An important factor swaying Alexander's own judgement in their favour was the way in which ministerial differences over policy were interwoven with differences over his irregular private life. Ever since 1864 he had spent as much time as possible with his mistress, Catherine Dolgorukaya. This increasingly public scandal had deeply affronted the Tsarevich, who took his mother's side, and the family rift divided high society. In 1880 when the Empress died, Alexander II hastily contracted a morganatic marriage with Catherine and installed her in the Winter Palace. Traditionalist hostility to Catherine forged a bond between her and more progressively-minded ministers who favoured a flexible response to anti-government critics. In failing health and with a growing sense of embattlement, Alexander II hesitantly sided with this alliance. For a brief interlude, political reform appeared on the government's agenda.

In January 1880 General M. T. Loris-Melikov, a hero of the Turkish War, took charge of the government, first as head of an emergency Special Administrative Commission and, from August, as Minister of Internal Affairs. He tried to broaden the base of support for the government: he relied as far as possible on legal processes in restraining the press and arresting suspects; he sacked the hated Minister of Education, Tolstoy, and he planned steps to alleviate the burden of redemption payments on the hardest-pressed peasants. In January 1881 he went so far as to recommend the involvement of zemstvo and municipal duma representatives in commissions appointed to consider reform of peasant affairs and local government. He even suggested that a few such representatives from outside the government might be co-opted onto the State Council, the supreme bureaucratic body beneath the Tsar. In themselves, the proposals amounted to very much less than a commitment to constitutional government. But the implication that unvarnished autocracy was no longer sustainable was clear to all, and both opponents and supporters of Loris-Melikov saw the issue as a momentous and possibly irrevocable step along the path trodden by western constitutional monarchies. Alexander himself hesitated: it was entirely characteristic that he marked Loris-Melikov's draft of the latter proposal with a question-mark. But on 1 March 1881 the Tsar did go as far as to accept the proposal for consultative commissions. That same day he fell victim to the 'People's Will'.

The assassination momentarily stunned the government, and the new Tsar, Alexander III (1881–94), fled to his country palace. 'When you are retiring, Your Majesty,' he was urged by K. P. Pobedonostsev, who had been his boyhood tutor and from 1880 to 1905 was Procurator of the Holy Synod, 'do shut the doors behind you not only in the bedroom but in all adjoining rooms, the hall included . . . check every evening underneath the furniture.'[5] Although throughout the crisis Alexander III had expressed his contempt for any concessions to appease the government's critics, for some two months after coming to the throne he hesitated to reverse official policy. Loris-Melikov continued to press significant innovations to strengthen public support for the government. Pobedonostsev, on the other hand, together with a minority of reactionary ministers, strongly urged the dismissal of Loris-Melikov and bold reaffirmation of the autocratic principle. At the end of April, having assessed the strength of the opposition, Alexander took Pobedonostsev's advice, issued an uncompromising manifesto and precipitated the resignation of Loris-Melikov and several other relatively liberal ministers. The reforms already set in train were either dropped immediately or gradually diluted, and from 1883 a period of intense reaction set in.

Alexander III's approach reflected his own predilections, but it was also based on a sound sense of the options open to him. Even if he had been so inclined it would have been extremely difficult to pursue reforms which posed a significant threat to the interests of the landed nobility. By rejecting reform, on the other hand, he won the enthusiastic support of the great majority of the nobility. Their social and economic pre-eminence was just beginning to seem more precarious and they wholeheartedly welcomed vigorous confirmation of the regime's commitment to the status quo. Moreover, the opposition seemed to wilt. The police rapidly destroyed the remnants of the 'People's Will' and successfully contained underground activity during the rest of the 1880s. 'Temporary' regulations of August 1881 – ultimately extended until the fall of the Empire – empowered the government to declare virtual martial law wherever and whenever it chose to do so. In the absence of a direct threat to order the public opinion which had caused Loris-Melikov such anxiety appeared powerless. During the 1880s there was no effective protest against increasing infringements of the independence of the courts, the press, the universities, and the zemstvos. Reaction seemed triumphant.

---

[5] *Pis'ma K. P. Pobedonostseva k Aleksandru III* (Moscow 1925–26), I, pp. 318–19.

4.5 The assassination of Alexander II, 1 March 1881. The 'People's Will' achieved their aim after at least six unsuccessful attempts. A first bomb failed to destroy the imperial carriage, and when the Tsar dismounted to investigate (above) a second bomb exploded at his feet (below).

Yet in the longer term a regime resting upon the narrowing social base of the landowning nobility was doomed. The discontent generated by the government's pursuit of a reactionary Utopia in defiance of rapidly accelerating social change was to explode in the revolutionary upheaval of 1905.

Chapter 5 ....

Industrialization and Revolution (1881–1905)

While Alexander III and his son Nicholas II (1894–1917) remained resolutely committed to unvarnished autocracy, Russia's traditional social structure passed through a process of profound transformation. Underlying much of this change was the rapid industrial development of the period. In large measure this was the result of the steady spread of market relations. The peasantry were being drawn into the money economy, thereby raising consumer demand. Both handicraft production – the great bulk of which was done by village peasants rather than urban artisans – and the major light industries, headed by textiles and sugar, expanded fast. Even more striking was the upsurge in heavy industry, and for this the State itself was primarily responsible. The focal point of the policy developed by the government was the construction of a railway network. A major stimulus in the industrialization of most European countries, railways held out particular promise to an economy uniquely handicapped by vast distances and poor communications. They would link the Empire's far-flung mineral resources with each other and with the centres of population; they would enormously increase the volume of both domestic and foreign trade; and their construction would create a massive new demand for coal, iron, steel, and manufactures.

It was in the 1880s that the Ministry of Finance began to coordinate its tariff, fiscal, and investment policies to extend the railway lines already laid. The major problem was the shortage of domestic capital. The aim, therefore, was to attract substantial foreign investment. This could only be achieved if foreigners could rely upon the stability of the rouble, which made it essential to maintain a favourable balance of payments and avoid a budget deficit. From 1881 the trade balance was kept positive with the help of high protective tariffs, culminating in a prohibitive tariff in 1891, and of positive steps to increase exports, especially of grain. The government's budget was strengthened by increased customs revenue and more particularly by a spectacular rise in indirect taxation. The results were gratifying. The rouble became progressively stronger and in 1897 foreign confidence was ensured by placing it on the gold standard. The conclusion of an alliance with France in 1894 had already contributed to the favourable publicity which Russian securities received in the West. With world interest rates low, investment in Russian state securities and direct investment in Russian industry became highly attractive. The government poured money into the railway programme, while subsidies and guarantees encouraged private capital to develop the supplying industries.

The full force of the policy was felt during the 1890s under the dynamic organization of S. Iu. Witte, Minister of Finance from 1892 to 1903. Annual railway construction more than trebled between the end of the 1880s and the boom years of the late 1890s. The production of leading minerals required by the railway programme – iron, coal, and oil – rose almost as fast between 1885 and 1900, and virtually every sector of industry benefited from the stimulus. Although light industry continued to exceed heavy industry in terms of value of output, the balance between the two shifted significantly. Russia, it is true, still lagged behind her major industrial competitors. She was highly vulnerable to sharp downturns in the economy and from 1900 to 1903 suffered particularly severely from an international depression. Her new heavy industries were concentrated in narrowly restricted areas. She remained an overwhelmingly agrarian country. Nevertheless, the economic development achieved by the turn of the century was sufficient to have a profound impact upon the social and political life of the Empire.

It was in a sense paradoxical that a regime for which the social repercussions accompanying industrial development in the West were anathema should have become actively committed to industrialization. Yet its motives are not difficult to see. In large measure it was responding to the rapid industrialization of Russia's Great Power rivals. Unless she could dispose of the same modern means of transport and production, the same machinery and armaments, Russia could not hope to uphold her political independence. The strategic necessity of railways, in particular, was becoming ever more pressing. Likewise, even conservative ministers felt the force of the argument, ably expounded by Witte, that the regime's domestic stability depended upon its financial strength – and this required sustained economic growth. In any case few statesmen grasped that there was a profound contradiction between the economic and the social policies being pursued by the government. This was in part because there was still no unified policy-making body, no cabinet. Each minister reported to the Tsar only about his particular field of responsibility, and the monarch's own gruelling routine of official audiences, requests, petitions, reports and ministerial visits minimized the chances that he would provide strategic coherence. The government, therefore, could pull in two opposite directions without fully realizing

Map 6   Railways in European Russia by 1900

that it was doing so. While the Ministry of Finance energetically fostered industrialization, the other ministries still pursued conservative social policies which ignored or even impeded economic change. This led to intense interdepartmental rivalry and antagonism, most clearly visible in repeated clashes between the Ministry of Finance and the Ministry of the Interior.

They adopted widely divergent approaches to almost every issue – from tariffs and taxation to the affairs of the nobility, the peasantry, and the working class. But the illusion was preserved, among conservative ministers as well as by Alexander III and Nicholas II themselves, that in Russia industrialization need not upset the traditional social structure, let alone undermine the authority of the throne.

In some respects, of course, greater economic and commercial activity did strengthen the regime. The resources at its disposal expanded. During the 1880s the poll-tax was abolished and indirect taxes – especially the liquor monopoly – became the major source of government revenue. They proved much easier to collect than direct taxes and made it possible for government revenue to keep pace with the swift rise in production. Although a proportion of this was absorbed in investment and servicing the growing national debt, the bulk financed a great expansion of the apparatus of the State. The bureaucracy developed fast – not only in terms of the proportion of officials to subjects, but also in terms of education and levels of pay. The police force grew, the political police (*Okhrana*) developing relatively sophisticated techniques of social control.

At the same time both the army and the navy became better equipped. This, together with closer economic ties with the West, added to the Empire's leverage in international affairs. The assumption underlying Bismarck's diplomacy in the 1880s, that given her conflict with Austria-Hungary over the Balkans, Russia would have to accept German terms to avoid diplomatic isolation, proved unfounded. When Germany raised high trade barriers against Russian grain and closed Russia's access to the German money market in the late 1880s, France was happy to come to Russia's aid. Paris became Russia's major source of foreign capital, while diplomatic and military negotiations culminated in the alliance of 1894. Successive finance ministers were adamant that Russia was in no position to risk war, and her Western policy was necessarily cautious. Nevertheless the steep decline which her diplomatic status had suffered since the Crimean War was arrested.

In one respect, too, the development of large-scale private enterprise increased the support within society on which the regime could count. For while the economic power of leading industrialists and businessmen grew enormously, they tended to remain as politically subservient as the traditional merchant community. They cooperated extremely closely with the Tsarist government. Three factors stand out in explaining this harmonious relationship.

In the first place, there was the range of benefits at the government's disposal – subsidies, credit, large contracts, tariff protection. Witte was particularly lavish with financial aid in times of crisis, and assisted in the formation of producer associations, thereby fostering the concentration of ownership in the hands of large banks and corporations. Major financiers and industrialists, notably those in St Petersburg, were made acutely conscious of their dependence on ministerial goodwill and it became increasingly common for senior officials to take up directorships on the boards of leading companies.

Equally important in retarding the political independence of the business community were the continuing divisions and antagonisms within it. The development of heavy industry intensified regional specialization, typified by the massive iron- and coal-mining enterprises of the Donets basin in the Ukraine, the oil industry in the Caucasus, and the textile-oriented Moscow region. This created significant differences of approach to a variety of policy issues from tariffs to labour problems. Moreover, a marked tension developed between the predominantly Great Russian businessmen of the centre and the variety of mutually divided ethnic minorities operating on the periphery – including Poles, Jews, Armenians, Greeks, and Tatars. Taken together with the very large percentage of investment in heavy industry held by foreign interests, this presented a formidable obstacle to the emergence of a politically powerful business lobby. Representative organizations were formed, but they remained under firm government tutelage and studiously avoided issues beyond a narrow range of business problems.

Perhaps the most fundamental factor drawing government and businessmen together was the common ground they shared in relation to labour. Large-scale employers could not fail to appreciate their dependence upon the regime for a cheap and docile work-force. In the interests of security the government refused to countenance labour organizations and strikes were a criminal offence. In a situation of massive rural underemployment and considerable urban unemployment this ensured that labour's bargaining power was minimal and that Russian wages were extremely low. It also meant that the police were immediately involved when serious disputes arose between labour and employers. Although government officials were often highly critical of the appalling working conditions for which employers were responsible, their overriding concern was to demonstrate to workers that organized protest could not pay. A rudimentary factory inspectorate was set up in 1882, but government intervention in labour relations was overwhelmingly favourable to employers. It was not surprising that leading industrialists and financiers found no more than minor fault with the Tsarist regime. Only in the upheaval of 1905, with labour protest running out of control, would they be moved to criticism.

Yet the very factors which inhibited the politicization of Russia's business classes also limited the political value of their support. Far from commanding respect they were the object of widespread disdain and, although a few magnates became major patrons of the arts, they were in general almost wholly lacking in cultural influence over the wider educated public.

The economically less powerful sections of the middle classes were growing fast, both in numbers and in political consciousness. Their ranks

97

were swelled not only by the general growth of the economy and steady expansion of secondary and higher education but also by the rapid development, especially during the 1890s, of services run under the aegis of the zemstvos and staffed by the so-called 'third element' – teachers, doctors, statisticians, veterinary surgeons, and agricultural experts of various kinds. Their political affiliation was by no means uniform. Russian intellectual and cultural life was becoming increasingly diverse. The turn of the century saw the birth of the so-called 'silver age' with its explicit rejection of art as a vehicle for social and political criticism. The flowering of Russian opera and ballet pointed in the same direction. It was symbolic that in 1902–03 a group of prominent and progressively-minded intellectuals opened a dialogue with the hierarchy of the Orthodox Church. Not since the Slavophiles of the 1840s would any self-respecting member of the intelligentsia have dreamed of such an enterprise. For all the socio-political criticism implicit in the drama of A. P. Chekhov (1860–1904), the paintings of I. Repin (1844–1930), and the music of P. I. Tchaikovsky (1840–93), it was less didactic than the work of their predecessors. Yet the prevailing mood of public opinion remained distinctly hostile both to the regime and to the profiteering and corruption widely associated with private capitalism. Opposition sentiment was galvanized by a catastrophic famine and cholera epidemic in 1891–92. Despite what in retrospect seem impressive efforts by the State to bring relief through a food loan scheme, the government was blamed and its tariff and trade policies came under fierce attack. It became ever more difficult to prevent discussion of political issues. One profession after another began to form organizations to discuss their common concerns and find ways of pressing upon the government the need for greater resources, and the removal of bureaucratic interference.

The increase in the size and self-confidence of educated public opinion was reflected in the flourishing commercial press. By the 1890s a variety of mass-circulation newspapers were offering a mixture of news, political and social comment, sport, fashion and gossip designed to appeal to a wide range of men and women – not unlike the contemporary press in the West. Although not all were overtly liberal in sentiment, even the most nationalistic and broadly loyalist newspapers tended constantly to expand the scope of public debate. As in the reign of Alexander II, repressive measures against outspoken journals and rebellious students tended to exacerbate rather than quell criticism. The demand for guaranteed civil liberties and public participation in state decision-making gathered pace. An important landmark was the foundation in 1902 of the *émigré* journal *Osvobozhdenie* (*Liberation*) edited by Peter Struve (1870–1944), a gifted political economist. The journal showed up the regime in the most clumsy, incompetent, and oppressive light. In 1903 a loosely structured organization, the Union of Liberation, was formed to unite all sections of the opposition. With growing assurance it mounted pressure for constitutional democracy based upon universal, equal, secret, and direct franchise.

On its own, enlightened public opinion had little more chance of shaking the regime than in the reign of Alexander II. But under Nicholas II, active discontent became increasingly evident among wide sections of society, both privileged and non-privileged. Most perplexing, from the point of view of Tsar and government, was the growing resentment expressed by the landowning nobility.

Even by Romanov standards, the last two tsars were not gifted statesmen. Their recorded remarks and their private diaries reveal a breathtaking insensitivity to the strains within the society over which they ruled. Yet neither was completely lacking in political sense. Although they faithfully echoed the time-honoured myth that the Tsarist government stood above social divisions and cared for the interests of all classes, they firmly grasped that the mainstay of the autocracy was in fact the landed nobility. Accordingly, they did all they could to protect the nobility's privileged position. In taking steps to tighten control over the peasantry and the zemstvos, the government saw itself consolidating the alliance between State and nobility. Wherever possible local landowners were chosen to fill the powerful post of land captain, established in 1889 to discipline the peasantry. The zemstvo reform of 1890 increased noble domination of the local assemblies. Both Alexander and Nicholas were also extremely concerned to perpetuate noble preponderance among senior civil and military officials. Sustained efforts made to limit educational opportunities for commoners were inspired in part by the hope that this would ensure that noblemen would provide the increasingly specialized and trained personnel required. Throughout the period the government made crystal clear its anxiety to shore up noble landownership. The Noble Land Bank established in 1885 became the source of low-interest loans to rescue insolvent estates and encourage landlords to secure their future by investing in and improving their land. The problem of conserving the noble land fund was the central preoccupation of a high-powered ministerial conference which Nicholas set up in 1897 to consider what further aid could be given to the nobility.

Yet, for all the goodwill of the government, the position of the nobility was gradually being eroded. The pressures which led many noblemen to sell their land were largely beyond the control of the State. Grain prices during the 1880s and 1890s, in Russia as elsewhere, were severely depressed, making it even more difficult for landowners accustomed to rely on serf labour to adapt to commercial farming. At the same time land prices soared in response to peasant land hunger, and the option of selling became increasingly attractive. Between Emancipation and 1905 the amount of land in noble hands fell by over a third.

The sympathy of the Tsar was of only marginally more help where state service, the other major bastion of noble power, was concerned. All the efforts of the Ministry of Education could not produce a sufficient flow of educated recruits from the landed nobility. Although social origins remained a crucial determinant of promotions, increasing professionalism within both army and bureaucracy tended to make ability ever more significant. By the end of the century the link between state service and landed wealth had become markedly weaker: even among the higher ranks of the Civil Service, over 70 per cent of the personnel were landless, and the proportion was greater still in the officer corps.

The nobility's landholdings remained formidable, and the dominant ethos among both officers and senior officials was still overwhelmingly sympathetic to noble privilege. Yet the symptoms of decline were tangible and created a growing sense of embattlement among middle-ranking landowners. Their resentment focused on the way industry seemed to be benefiting at their expense. Although reactionary journalists found difficulty in framing a coherent economic policy – and their spokesmen within the government were pulverized by Witte's expertise – they became increasingly critical. They attacked specific measures such as tariffs which forced up the price of agricultural machinery. And they blamed the Finance Ministry's favouritism towards industry for the plight – and the restiveness – of the peasantry. Although the Tsar heartily endorsed their values and aspirations, by the late 1890s they were becoming deeply embittered by what they took to be the government's inadequate concern for their well-being. Their anger began to take political form. This was visible not only in fierce complaint from reactionary newspapers but also, paradoxically enough, in the growth of the liberal zemstvo movement. The number of committed liberals among the middle-ranking landowners who dominated the zemstvo electorate was not large. But they commanded a stronger sense of political direction, a higher level of education, and greater willingness to take an active part in the zemstvos than the more conservative majority. Moreover, their criticism of the arbitrary nature of the bureaucracy and autocracy seemed to correspond to the widespread dissatisfaction among the provincial nobility. This enabled them to seize the initiative at the turn of the century and ally the zemstvos ever more closely with the broader liberal and constitutional movement.

The decline in noble landownership was accompanied by at best marginal and uneven improvements in the conditions of the peasantry. It is true that, in addition to land purchased from the nobility, a vast amount of unused land was brought under cultivation, and the incremental improvements in farming methods we have seen taking place in the 1860s and 1870s continued to bring a gradual rise in yields. Peasants were also able to cushion the impact of indirect taxes by falling back on barter and home products when necessary, and the number finding non-agricultural work and remitting part of their wage to the village continued to increase. Recent research suggests that average grain consumption per head in the village rose during the period. Generalizations about the trend in peasant living standards, however, are difficult to make. This is not because of any sustained differentiation between rich and poor peasants within a given village. Although tendencies in that direction are visible on the periphery of the Empire, to the west, the south and the south-east, in the Russian heartland the overwhelming majority remained 'middle' peasants, directly dependent on their own labour for their livelihood. But there were significant variations from year to year and between different regions. The grain-short areas of the north and south-east benefited from the low price of grain. Moreover, it was here that peasant incomes were most often supplemented by handicraft production and off-farm work, making them less directly dependent upon the vagaries of the harvest. Paradoxically, it was the grain-surplus areas which were most at risk of severe deprivation and even famine. It was in these areas that the depressed level of grain prices caused most hardship. Compelled to raise cash for payment of rent, redemption dues, taxes, and essential purchases, they were driven to sell as much grain as possible, retaining minimal reserves for subsistence and planting. This left them highly vulnerable to harvest failures. The central 'black-earth' and Volga regions suffered a series of very poor harvests between 1889 and 1892, including the disastrous drought of 1891. The drought and famine triggered a sharp decline in the number of horses and other livestock per head, and unlike the country as a whole these regions witnessed a long-term decline in per capita grain output. The evidence of acute poverty was widespread. Repeated commissions and zemstvo investigations drew a grim picture of peasant destitution and growing frustration. Arrears on direct taxes, including redemption dues, soared after the harvest failure of 1891 and the government responded with the harshest punitive measures, including flogging and property confiscation. Worst of all was the high incidence of malnutrition, chronic sickness, and epidemics.

The policies of the Ministry of Finance were widely blamed both for peasant misery and for the threat to social stability which it entailed. Reactionary, liberal and latter-day populist opinion alike tended to view the peasantry as the victim of the heavy industrialization programme. The rapid increase in indirect taxes, it was maintained, wiped out any relief to the peasantry from the abolition of the poll-tax and periodic cancellation of unpaid redemption dues. High protective tariffs penalized the peasant consumer. And at a time of frequent harvest failures and recurrent food shortage, exports of grain were being ruthlessly forced upwards. The peasantry, it seemed, were being squeezed in order to earn foreign exchange and uphold the value of the rouble. I. A. Vyshnegradsky, Witte's predecessor at the Ministry of Finance from 1887 to 1892, was credited with the heartless motto: 'We will go hungry, but we will export.'

The early stages of industrialization certainly brought precious little relief to the peasantry, and grain exports were undoubtedly vital to the

5.1   Famine. During the famine of 1891-92, there were reports of peasants being forced to strip the thatch from their barns and houses to feed their starving livestock. (Contemporary engraving from the *Illustrated London News*.)

'Witte system'. Yet the government's conversion to a policy of favouring industrialization did no more than exacerbate the peasant predicament. The proportion of government revenue directed into industry was a mere fraction of that devoted to the upkeep of the armed forces and administration. The main burden borne by the peasantry remained the upkeep of the State and the landed nobility. Government policy towards the village changed remarkably little during the period. The commitment to the commune, as the best means of taxing and policing the peasantry, was repeatedly reaffirmed. A proposed programme of resettlement from the most overpopulated areas was shelved for fear of raising peasant expectations and unleashing dangerous mass migration. The resources made available to the peasantry to purchase land through the Peasant Bank (1883) were niggardly compared to those available to the nobility, and accounted for a small proportion of the land the peasants managed to acquire. Minimal effort was made to assist peasants in improving their farming methods: the attempts in this direction of a few dynamic zemstvos only highlighted how little was being done in the Empire as a whole.

The State, in short, pursued a policy of neglect towards peasant agriculture. When asked in 1890 if a country like Russia should not have an independent Ministry of Agriculture, Vyshnegradsky was responsible for another *bon mot*: 'But the Minister of Agriculture will not have anything to do.'[1] Despite the overall rise in output per head, therefore, the predicament of most peasants remained dire. Pressure on the land mounted as the rural population swelled by some 25 per cent between 1877 and 1905. Although urban migration accelerated, it acted as a very inadequate safety valve: between 1880 and 1913 the proportion of the labour force working in agriculture only dropped from 74 to 72 per cent. Moreover, the increase in urbanization and industry made least impact in the 'black-earth' provinces where the peasantry had acquired least land at Emancipation. It was here that the shortage of land became most acute.

Accordingly, peasant aspirations remained firmly fixed on what seemed to them the supreme panacea: the land of the nobility. The very intensity of their land-hunger, however, forced up the cost of both renting and buying land to levels which were quite unrelated to the land's yield. At the same time overpopulation kept agricultural wages at pitiful rates. The result was intense resentment against noble exploitation. The whole peasant outlook precluded them from meekly submitting to the dictates of the market and the rights of private property. Deeply rooted in peasant culture and the whole commune tradition, as we have seen, was the belief that the land should belong to whoever worked it with his own hands. The inroads that modern culture was making into the village, moreover, tended to make them more assertive. The development of the railways and the spread of the market, as well as peasants seeking both temporary and long-term work in industry, increased village contact with urban life. The ideas propagated by young radicals and democratically-minded members of the 'third element', among whom village teachers had the most significant impact, found a readier reception than in the days of the movement 'to the people'. Above all, the period saw a slow but steady spread of literacy, as much by village schools set up on peasant demand as by zemstvo and church schools. Much of what was available to literate peasants to read was designed by Church and State to bolster discipline. But much, too, consisted of light entertainment and popular story books written specifically for them, usually by authors themselves of peasant origin, and sold by itinerant pedlars. The effect was to arouse curiosity, increase self-awareness, and widen horizons. The primers used in schools became increasingly secular and realistic, and access to the written word served to lessen the aura surrounding the Bible, and to reduce deference towards both village elders and the educated classes in general. Peasants showed greater resentment at contemptuous treatment by rural police and officialdom and more indignation at taxes imposed upon

---

[1] F. A. Rotshtein, ed., *Dnevnik V. N. Lamsdorfa, 1886–1890* (Moscow 1926), p. 350.

them, including those imposed by the noble-dominated zemstvos. At the same time the conservative and pacifying influence of the Orthodox Church began to weaken markedly. There is little evidence that peasant faith declined, but the authority of village priests was progressively undermined: in terms of culture and way of life they differed too little from the ordinary villagers to inspire much respect, and the miserly provision made for them by the State resulted in constant friction over money matters between priest and parishioner. The last decades of the century saw the flowering of numerous bizarre but intensely committed religious sects which often reflected disenchantment with both Church and State. Even the hallowed belief in the benevolence of the Tsar became less assured. The incidence of rent and labour strikes and land seizures from private landowners rose sharply during the 1890s. Serious crop failure in 1901 was followed in 1902 by peasant protest in the Volga area and Georgia and by alarming uprisings in the Ukrainian provinces of Poltava and Khar'kov. Any significant weakening in the authority or military resources of the government would run the risk of unleashing rural disturbances on an even greater scale.

If the government's support for the landowning nobility perpetuated its age-old conflict with the peasantry, the direct corollary of its close alliance with industrial employers was confrontation with labour. Numerically, the industrial labour force remained relatively small. At the turn of the century, out of a total active population of some 45 million, less than a quarter were nonagricultural employees and only some 2 million were employed in factories and mines. But working-class discontent was fierce and the ability of the industrial proletariat to paralyse large plants and even whole areas by strike action gave them an immediate power of disruption which the peasantry lacked. The grounds for working-class discontent struck even the least sympathetic observer. As in the West, the early stages of industrialization were accompanied by atrocious conditions. Labour's weak bargaining position, combined with the speed with which new industrial centres such as the Donets basin of the Ukraine were developed and older cities such as St Petersburg expanded, ensured that little attention was given to the needs of the work-force. Wages were seldom sufficient to support a family. Workers lived in insanitary and overcrowded rented rooms and cellars where family life was impossible, or in the most spartan and soulless dormitory blocks thrown up by employers. Discipline at work was harsh: use of the birch only faded out in the 1890s, there was no job security, and management imposed fines for the slightest transgression. From the employers' point of view this treatment was made necessary by the nature of the work-force. Throughout the period a high percentage of workers, especially in the newly developed areas and the many enterprises set up in rural areas, were born into peasant families. Even those whose fathers spent some years in industry tended to be brought up in the village. Not only did they lack skills but they did not adapt readily from the rhythm of agricultural life, with its long

5.2 'Corner' lodgers in a workers' flat in St Petersburg in the 1890s. Overcrowded conditions meant that families could rent no more than a 'corner' of shared accommodation. The effect was to fuel discontent and facilitate the spread of radical ideas.

periods of inactivity and frequent holidays, to the demands of modern industry. No matter how deep their urban roots, workers found difficulty in coming to terms with the long hours, unhealthy environment, and frequent accidents at work.

Yet deprivation alone does not explain the militancy and relatively strong political consciousness of the factory proletariat. The specific structure of Russian industry played an important part. The major industrial developments were heavily concentrated in a few key areas of the Empire. By the turn of the century, the central industrial area around Moscow, the north-western area around St Petersburg, the major cities of Poland and the Ukraine employed over 60 per cent of all workers. Moreover, within these areas workers were concentrated in large enterprises to a far greater extent than in the West. In both metallurgical and textile industries almost half the factory workers were employed in plants of over 1,000 workers. This reflected the rapid introduction of the most modern machinery modelled on the West; the need for enterprises in new areas to be self-sufficient in a variety of secondary products; and the repeated, if brief, depressions which hit Russian industry, eliminating competitors and encouraging mergers. This combination of giant enterprises and regional concentration fostered working-class militancy. Sheer size made relations between employers and workers impersonal, facilitated the circulation of radical ideas, and generated a sense of solidarity among workers. It made it easier for workers to appreciate the potential power of strike action: statistics confirm that in general the larger the plant the greater was the propensity to strike. Moreover, where labour disputes in small enterprises might cause little stir, stoppages in major plants proved highly contagious. By the same token, protest in these larger enterprises brought immediate intervention by police or even troops: the workers could not fail to associate the political authorities with the hated employer.

From the mid-1880s there was a marked increase in the incidence of strikes. In 1896 and again in 1897 almost the entire textile industry of St Petersburg was briefly paralysed. The depression which spread from 1899 only temporarily weakened the strike movement and aggravated unemployment and urban discontent. Towards the end of 1902 and during 1903 several important cities in the south, including Rostov-on-Don, Baku, and Odessa, were hit by mass strikes. Government reaction only exacerbated the problem. Such legislation as was passed – on female and child labour, on the length of the working day, and on labour contracts – was feebly enforced. The Ministry of Finance was sympathetic to employers' insistence that their authority should not be undermined. The Ministry of the Interior, too anxious about the security implications of labour unrest to leave matters alone, experimented from 1901–03 with police-run labour organizations which it was hoped would divert working-class energy from political towards economic and cultural aims. These 'Zubatov unions', so-called in honour of the police chief who sponsored them, tended to escape the control of their sponsors and indeed contributed to the explosion of protest which was to shake the regime during 1905.

Mounting social tension was accompanied by the swift development of national consciousness among the Empire's ethnic minorities. According to the census of 1897, only 43 per cent of the population were Great Russians, and the regime's overt identification with them and with the Orthodox Church alienated the minority nationalities. The last two Tsars pursued a heavy-handed if uneven policy of Russification, motivated sometimes by concern to create a uniform legal order and administrative system, but accompanied by measures promoting Russian culture and Orthodoxy and discriminating against minority languages and religions. This tended to push even relatively mild cultural movements, such as that in the Ukraine, in the direction of political protest. The dynamics of the process varied widely. In some cases the government's attempts to tighten its control and impose uniformity created nationalist opposition where virtually none had existed: this was most evident in the Baltic provinces, dominated by a German aristocracy, and in the semi-autonomous Duchy of Finland. Particularly harsh was the treatment of the Jews. By the turn of the century the Empire contained about 5.5 million Jews – almost half the Jewish population of the world. Ever since their incorporation into the Empire under Catherine II and Alexander I, they had been restricted to Poland and the 'Pale of Settlement' to the east of Poland. Not only were they excluded from most professions, but efforts were made to prevent them acquiring land and to limit their access to secondary and higher education. Moreover at moments of crisis – notably in 1881, 1903, and October 1905 – the authorities connived at vicious pogroms against them. The result was evident not only in a growing emigration movement but also in the disproportionately high number of Jews in the most radical parties. National parties of various complexions were set up to represent many of the minorities – from Letts in the north to Armenians and Georgians in the south, and above all the Poles. The long history of Polish resistance played an important part in heightening the regime's suspicions of signs of cultural autonomy anywhere in the Empire, and in fuelling the aggressive nationalist tone adopted by both Alexander III and Nicholas II. Under both tsars the Russification programme in operation in Poland since the 1860s was intensified, but hostility to Russia showed no signs of abating and a large garrison had to be stationed there. Nationalist unrest among the minorities in general, and the Poles in particular, constituted an important ingredient in the upheaval of 1905.

The transformation overtaking Russia's social structure produced major changes in the radical subculture of the revolutionary intelligentsia. They reacted, in particular, to the upsurge in proletarian and, from the turn of the century, peasant unrest. Although as yet their role was peripheral, from the point of view of Russia's subsequent history the new ideology and forms of organization which they adopted in this period merit close attention.

The reaction which followed the assassination of Alexander II had crushed the 'People's Will'. This did not end recruitment to the radical subculture which continued unabated – fed by student unrest and frustration over government regimentation, interference with the syllabus, and efforts to suppress independent student organizations, as well as over the hardship of the growing proportion who were drawn from humble or impoverished noble families. Yet the increasingly effective secret police successfully headed off renewed plots on the life of the Tsar, and a growing number of young radicals began to question not only the tactics of the 'People's Will' but the whole strategy of populism. The sheer failure of efforts to ignite the peasantry, the visible growth of industry and spread of capitalism, the readier response among urban workers to socialist propaganda – all cast doubt on populist assumptions. It was in these conditions that Marxist ideas began to gain currency. Marx's works had already begun to penetrate Russia earlier, but until now they had been used to buttress populist attacks on capitalism rather than to develop a Marxist approach to revolution in

Russia. Many of the groups which formed and dissolved in the 1880s combined elements of populism and Marxism rather than viewing them as two irreconcilable ideologies. But clearer lines of demarcation were emerging. Early in the decade, five *émigré* revolutionaries, three of whom had belonged to the stillborn populist organization 'Black Repartition', founded the 'Emancipation of Labour' group, dedicated to spreading Marxism in Russia. Their leader, George Plekhanov (1856–1918), wrote the founding texts of Russian Marxism, spelling out with crystal clarity the implications for Russia's future that could be drawn from Marx's socioeconomic analysis.

The heart of Plekhanov's message was that Russia was bound to undergo capitalism. The commune was doomed by the spread of market relations: the peasantry would be divided between capitalists and propertyless labourers. Moreover, the development of capitalism, both industrial and agricultural, and the polarization of social classes, was heartily to be welcomed. Only by massive development of her technology and human skill, her 'productive forces', could the economic base for socialism in Russia be laid; only by the formation of an organized proletariat could socialist revolution be carried out. The notion of bypassing capitalism, of direct transition from a primitive peasant society to socialism, was idle Utopianism. The tsar, the old landowning nobility, and all the remnants of her 'Asiatic' order must first be swept away in a bourgeois revolution which would inaugurate the full flowering of capitalism. Only then would follow the final reckoning between capital and labour, the abolition of private property, and the construction of socialism. Russia's revolutionaries must shed their populist illusions, realize that Marx's analysis was fully applicable to Russia, and take their place alongside the proletariat.

From the early 1890s Marxism caught on among young radicals with remarkable speed. For decades the revolutionaries had rejected outright capitalism, the bourgeoisie, and the Western path in general; they had seen the creation of a propertyless proletariat as a disaster to be avoided at almost any cost and had sought to move directly to socialism based on the commune. Now, suddenly, those who clung to these notions were thrown on to the defensive and soon outnumbered. Marxism was all the rage. Several factors contributed to the appeal of the new ideology. It provided answers to every conceivable question with an assurance and a seemingly impregnable logic which the romantics of the 1840s, the nihilists of the 1860s, and the populists of the 1870s had sought but never found. It guaranteed the ultimate victory of the revolution. After decades of failure and the deep self-doubt of the 1880s, its offer of scientific proof that socialism was inevitable exercised a powerful attraction. Whereas the populists had been haunted by the race against time, against the break-up of the commune and the growth of the bourgeoisie, history was on the side of the proletariat. And the vision held out was of a Russia transformed from grinding poverty, ignorance, and rural backwardness into a society that would not only be just and free but modern, dynamic, industrial. Above all, Marx's analysis seemed to be borne out by reality, by developments both in the West, with the rapid rise of the German Social Democratic Party (SPD), and in Russia itself. However inadequate his predictions proved in the twentieth century, Marx did have an unsurpassed grasp of nineteenth-century capitalism and his appeal remains incomprehensible unless this is recognized. His analysis made sense of the social changes overcoming the Empire. A factory proletariat was being formed and, as populist agitators had already discovered, the proletariat bore all the characteristics Marx had depicted – it was brutally exploited, profoundly alienated, and capable of striking heavy blows against employers and government alike.

The Marxist groups of the early 1890s devoted themselves to self-education, fierce polemics against the populists, and propaganda among circles of selected workers. During the mid-1890s, however, they began to turn to mass agitation at factory level and found the workers highly responsive. In 1895 the 'League of Struggle for the Emancipation of the Working Class' was set up in St Petersburg and its members made an important contribution to the major strikes of 1896 and 1897. As local groups multiplied, pressure grew for the formation of a united party. In 1898 the Russian Social Democratic Labour Party was founded, only to be shattered by police arrests. But the effort was renewed and in 1900 Plekhanov's group, augmented by younger recruits, set up *Iskra* (*The Spark*), an *émigré* journal designed as a rallying-point for like-minded Social Democrats. In 1903 a second congress, held in Brussels and London, and dominated by delegates loyal to *Iskra*, re-established the party.

This second founding congress, however, was marred by an immediate schism. The split reflected a portentous difference of approach within the Party. The initial bone of contention was the question of the terms on which sympathizers should be admitted to the Party. One faction (the Bolsheviks – 'partisans of the majority') favoured a narrow definition which would admit only dedicated and disciplined activists, while another (the Mensheviks – 'partisans of the minority') envisaged a much broader party enveloping wide sections of the proletariat. What on the surface appeared a relatively minor issue in fact went to the heart of a fundamental question facing the Social Democrats: that of the relationship between the Party and the rank and file of the proletariat, the class for whom it was designed.

The hard-line approach was articulated by V. I. Lenin (1870–1924). Lenin was the son of an education official in Simbirsk province and trained to be a lawyer. His older brother was a populist executed in 1887 for plotting to assassinate the Tsar, and as a teenager Lenin was drawn into the revolutionary movement. He was a short, energetic man, modest in his tastes and enjoyed a happy though childless marriage to Nadezhda Krupskaia, a fellow revolutionary. He combined outstanding intellectual

5.3 Members of the St Petersburg League of Struggle for the Emancipation of the Working Class, 1897. Lenin is seated in the centre. On his left is I. Martov, Lenin's closest ally until the bitter controversies which split the Marxists in 1903.

ability with a vigorous, highly disciplined, and formidable personality. The remarkable role he played in Russia's development can only be understood in terms of his total immersion – intellectual, emotional, moral – in Marxism. Three fundamental points must be made about his ideological make-up. In the first place, he believed that Marx had bequeathed a method of analysing the social process which was scientific, which went to the very roots of reality. Secondly, he believed an essential condition of the triumph of the proletariat was that it be guided by Marxism. Finally, he was convinced, he knew with every fibre of his being, that he himself had mastered this science of society. It was this absolute conviction which turned a gifted politician into one of history's most significant leaders.

For Lenin, the role of the Party was precisely to provide the guidance, the 'revolutionary theory' which Marxist analysis yielded. The Party must be the institutional embodiment of Marxism. The overriding priority, therefore, was to ensure that the structure of the Party should guarantee its ideological purity. That purity was all too easily sullied. The class enemy, the bourgeoisie and its allies, wielded a vast array of ideological weapons designed to mislead the proletariat. In England they had managed to restrict the horizons of the working class to piecemeal economic goals, to mere trade unionism. He saw similar 'economist' tendencies among Russian activists who considered themselves revolutionaries but in fact were prime carriers of bourgeois distortions. Petty-bourgeois and peasant elements were constantly being drawn into the proletariat, bringing with them innumerable illusions. It was in the very nature of the constantly growing working class that full socialist consciousness, full understanding of the revolutionary destiny of the proletariat, could not be achieved simultaneously by all sections. Initially, in fact, only genuinely revolutionary members of the intelligentsia and the most advanced cadres of the proletariat would be abreast of revolutionary theory. The purpose of the Party was to knit together this vanguard, to build a structure so homogeneous, so ideologically uniform that it would be impervious to infiltration by bourgeois revisionists – or police agents.

Accordingly, Lenin insisted upon an exclusive definition of party membership, speaking in his major tract on party structure – *What Is To Be Done?* (1902) – of a party of 'professional revolutionaries'. Likewise, it was his image of a party united by a scientifically based theory which enabled him to insist upon a steeply hierarchical structure. The 'correct' line on any issue was established not by a survey of opinion within the Party but by rigorous scientific analysis. Once this had yielded a conclusion, there was no room for further debate. To permit dissent within the Party would be to reopen the door to bourgeois deviations. Lenin's approach made the relationship between the Party and the rank and file of the proletariat seem simple. The Party was by definition the vanguard of the proletariat. The social origin of its members, the initial preponderance of intelligentsia over workers, was utterly irrelevant. Contact with less advanced elements might well fluctuate, subject as it was to constant police intervention. But an ideologically sound party had little to fear from this: it could never come adrift from the true interests of the class. And as soon as conditions permitted, the class would come to realize it.

The vigour with which Lenin pressed his own view of the Party played a major role in crystallizing the latent divisions among the Social Democrats. It was in large measure in reaction to Lenin's position that the Mensheviks clarified their ideas. There were major differences within their ranks, a fact which provided a serious handicap in subsequent years, but they all found Lenin's concept of the Party unacceptable. Not that they were unmindful of the dangers of a diluted and 'revised' version of Marxism which so preoccupied Lenin. They too had supported *Iskra* and the creation of a united party, and had condemned 'economism' within Russia and 'revisionism' in the German SPD. Little objection had been raised to the forthright tone of *What Is To Be Done?* when it first appeared. But once the

Party had been firmly re-established, their primary attention switched to the disconcerting evidence of a gulf separating party activists and rank-and-file workers. The problem was real enough. Even at the height of the strike movement of the 1890s there had been a certain amount of friction between workers and intelligentsia. Following the economic downturn of 1899 there had been a brief decline in strike action and contact had become more difficult to sustain. And by the time the workers' movement revived in 1902, the energy of activists was caught up both in party organization and in the challenge posed by the burgeoning liberal and neo-populist movements. For the Mensheviks it was crucial that the Party should not risk isolation from the class it sought to represent.

This was why they adamantly opposed Lenin's vision of the Party. Instead of rapidly expanding the ranks of the Party, it threatened, in their view, to reduce them; instead of bridging the gap between a party dominated by members of the intelligentsia and the working masses, it threatened to institutionalize that gap. To the Mensheviks Lenin's vision smacked of elitism. It was Leon Trotsky (1879–1940), a brilliant young recruit to the party, who expressed most succinctly the interwoven ideological and personal antagonism which Lenin provoked. The effect of Lenin's strategy, he warned, would be that the party substitutes itself for the class, 'the party organization substitutes itself for the party, the Central Committee substitutes itself for the organization and, finally, a "dictator" substitutes himself for the Central Committee'.[2]

Lenin's heavy emphasis on discipline and centralized control within the Party was particularly unattractive to activists drawn from the minority nationalities. Whereas the proportion of Great Russians among Bolsheviks in this early period was about 80 per cent, among the Mensheviks they made up only about one third. In both factions Jews were prominent, but only the Mensheviks attracted a significant proportion of minority nationals, especially Georgians and Ukrainians. When most of the leading Social Democrats, including I. Martov (1873–1923) and, following the congress, Plekhanov, threw their weight against Lenin, the Bolshevik faction failed to gain control of the Party's leading organs.

Some of the implications of the schism became apparent during the upheaval of 1905. The Mensheviks threw themselves into the working-class trade unions and other organizations which sprang up, seeking the fusion of the Party and the rank-and-file proletariat. The Bolsheviks, on the other hand, reacted with much more caution to these institutions and tended to emphasize the need to establish party control over them. A related difference concerned the revolutionary timetable. Both factions of the Party interpreted the upheaval as a 'bourgeois democratic' revolution. For the Mensheviks this implied that state power must pass to bourgeois parties,

---

[2] N. Trotsky, *Nashi politicheskie zadachi* (Geneva 1904), p. 23.

and although the proletariat must play a major, even leading role in over-turning autocracy, it would be madness for the Social Democrats to take part in government. Socialism could not yet be built and they would inevitably disappoint proletarian expectations. Lenin, on the other hand, could see a role for the Party in government. He had much less faith in the revolutionary determination of Russia's bourgeoisie than the Mensheviks, and he emphasized the revolutionary potential of the peasantry. This opened up the prospect of democracy being installed not by a bourgeois government but by 'a revolutionary democratic dictatorship of the prolet-ariat and peasantry'.[3] Such a government, he conceded, was unlikely to sur-vive long. Once noble land had been appropriated, the wealthier peasants would move over to the side of the bourgeoisie, and bourgeois rule would follow. But meanwhile democracy would have been taken much further than the Mensheviks envisaged – and there was even the possibility that, if revolution broke out in the West, the 'dictatorship' might be sustained by aid from socialist regimes abroad. In the event, the outcome of 1905 disap-pointed both factions. But difficult as the schism was for many workers and, indeed, activists to understand or justify, its far-reaching ramifications had already begun to emerge.

By no means all the revolutionaries were converted to social demo-cracy. For a significant minority, Marxism remained a callous and abstract scheme. Were they to applaud while capitalism ruined hardworking peas-ants, imposed the indescribable misery of proletarianization, and yielded fat profits for ruthless exploiters in agriculture and industry? During the 1880s and 1890s populist economists insisted that Russian capitalism was an arti-ficial product of state policy, and that it was doomed by the weakness of the domestic market and its inability to compete abroad. By the late 1890s this argument had become much harder to sustain. Leading neo-populist theorists, of whom Viktor Chernov (1876–1952) was the most influential, emphasized instead the distinction between development in industry and in agriculture. Industrial capitalism was indeed expanding productive power and creating a sharp division between employers and employees. But agri-cultural capitalism was wholly unprogressive, merely exploiting the poor without advancing production in any way. Moreover, the vast majority of the peasantry were already semi-socialist: they were not yet persuaded of the need for collective farming, but they did reject private landownership and depended upon the labour of their own hands. Events in the cities would unfold much as Marx had envisaged, with a phase of bourgeois rule culmi-nating in proletarian revolution, but there was no need for the peasantry to pass through capitalism. Peasant revolution could achieve the immediate 'socialization' of the land and abolition of private ownership in preparation for the ultimate transition to socialist production. Chernov placed less

---

[3] V. I. Lenin, *Collected Works* (London & Moscow 1960–78), IX, p. 82.

emphasis on the peculiar virtues of the peasant commune than had his populist predecessors, and sought to integrate the development of urban capitalism and Marx's insights into his neo-populist programme.

In 1901, encouraged by the resurgence of peasant unrest, several local groups combined to form the Socialist Revolutionary (SR) Party, and were joined the following year by the *émigré* Agrarian Socialist League. Although in theory a homogeneous body directed by a unified Central Committee, in fact the new Party proved decidedly more amorphous than its Social-Democratic rival. Party policy and the implications of party membership were less than clear. It was not until the very end of 1905 that the first Party Congress was summoned and an official programme adopted, and the immediate sequel was the defection of splinter groups to left and right. There were important divisions over tactics – the older guard tended to disapprove of the wave of terrorist attacks mounted by younger members between 1901 and 1907. Moreover, although the Party probably enrolled rather more members among workers, intelligentsia, and artisans than either the Mensheviks or the Bolsheviks in this period, the prime constituency towards which it turned – the peasantry – remained very difficult to organize. The number of peasant members was derisory. Nevertheless, some contact was made with the villages, primarily through teachers and medical assistants, and the SRs were able to exert their influence over the All-Russian Peasants Union, the most important peasant body to emerge during 1905. Despite its organizational drawbacks, and a very sharp decline after 1907, the Party had gained substantial urban support and had seen its faith in mass peasant rebellion vindicated.

The catalyst which transformed this complex pattern of social and political agitation into a direct assault upon the autocracy in 1905 was a disastrous war with Japan. Although Russia's eastern expansion was much less extensive than in earlier periods, she increased her influence over northern Persia and joined in the international scramble for influence in China. But in the Japanese Empire she at last came up against an eastern power developing at a rate comparable to her own, and one capable of offering effective resistance. The conflict arose over rival ambitions in Manchuria and Korea. The Russian approach to negotiations was complacent in the extreme. The issue was of far greater importance to Japan than to Russia, yet the Tsar and most of his ministers expected the Japanese to be easily intimidated. They were not. Emboldened by an alliance with Britain made in 1902, Japan attacked Russian forces in January 1904 and proceeded to inflict a series of devastating defeats upon her by land and sea. In Russia the war aroused no more than a brief flicker of patriotic enthusiasm: years of nationalist propaganda under the last two tsars failed to bear fruit. The war was widely regarded, not without justice, as the product of intrigue at court and among a handful of entrepreneurs. Mobilization was unpopular: there was serious disaffection within the armed forces, dramatically highlighted by the mutiny on the battleship *Potemkin* in June 1905. Repeated doses of bad news from the front generated mounting criticism of government incompetence in all sections of the press; ministerial confidence was visibly shaken; and discontent which had been smouldering for years burst into flame.

Government handling of the crisis was anything but skilful. Alternating attempts at forthright assertion of authority and tentative gestures of conciliation exacerbated the situation. Signs of doubt and division among the authorities played a key part in unleashing disturbances among peasants and soldiers. The use of force against workers, political activists, and minority nationalists simply intensified the incipient revolution and pushed all groups further to the left. By the summer of 1905 the government looked so vulnerable that even irreproachable traditionalists such as the Marshals of the Nobility concluded that political reform was inescapable.

Following the assassination in July 1904 of V. K. Plehve, the notoriously unpopular Minister of the Interior, his successor, D. I. Sviatopolk-Mirsky, tried to soften the government's image. Henceforth peasants were no longer to be subjected to corporal punishment and all their outstanding debts on redemption dues and direct taxes were cancelled. At the same time, censorship and control of public associations was slackened. The result was a tremendous upsurge of liberal and revolutionary propaganda, a campaign of banquets and public meetings to demand reform, a zemstvo congress to draw up specific proposals for change, and the formation of a series of politically oriented white-collar unions. Although leaders of the emergent liberal movement failed – indeed hardly tried – to recruit activists among either students or workers, their open and vigorous campaign impressed and emboldened those lower down the social scale. A final experiment by the police at labour organization backfired disastrously. The St Petersburg Assembly of Factory Workers, set up with official approval in February 1904, broke loose from its sponsors and under the leadership of Father Gapon, a maverick but inspired orator, helped foster a virtual general strike in the capital. On 9 January 1905 the Assembly organized a monster demonstration to present to the Winter Palace a petition which was at once humble and radical. In launching troops against the unarmed, hymn-singing crowds of men and women, the Romanov regime committed one of its greatest political blunders. The effect of 'Bloody Sunday' on political consciousness among workers and peasants alike was by all accounts traumatic. In February an attempt was made to placate working-class anger. The Shidlovsky Commission summoned representatives to be elected by the major factories of the capital. The Commission was never able even to begin its discussions, so radical were the workers' demands, but the elections generated great excitement among the proletariat and provided valuable political experience. In May the efforts of V. N. Kokovtsov, the Minister of Finance, to persuade representatives of the industrialists to agree to improve

5.4 Bloody Sunday, January 1905. Troops open fire on the peaceful demonstration outside the Winter Palace, in which traditional deference was combined with demands for far-reaching social and political reform. The official estimate of the number who died in the violence that followed was 130; unofficial estimates varied from over 200 to more than 1,000. (From a painting by Ivan Vladimirov.)

the conditions of labour collapsed ignominiously. The employers, with new-found spirit, informed the Minister that labour unrest was the result of political rather than econo mic conditions, and withdrew from the discussions. The Tsar's invitation in February for peasant communes to petition their 'little father', far from providing the safety-valve the authorities intended, stimulated peasant activity and heightened their expectations. Encouraged by members of the 'third element', especially village teachers, peasants all over the country drew up demands – first and foremost for land, but also for an end to arbitrary and insulting treatment by officials, for full representation in the zemstvos, for legal equality and free education. By the summer a rudimentary All-Russian Peasants Union had been formed and at its first congress in July it proceeded to demand the abolition of private property in land and the convening of a Constituent Assembly. In August the concession of autonomy to the universities simply turned them into centres for the most frenzied political activity and public debate.

The clearest index of the pressure upon the government was given by the constitutional concessions which the Tsar, despite his profound religious attachment to autocracy, was gradually forced to make. In the autumn of 1904 he was still rejecting the mild suggestion from Sviatopolk-Mirsky, very much along the lines of Loris-Melikov's proposals of 1881, that representatives of public institutions should be co-opted on to the State Council. By February he felt compelled, not least by the need to improve the confidence of Western creditors in Russia's stability, to commit himself to summoning a Consultative Assembly. In August the new Minister of the Interior, A. G.

Bulygin, published details of the (restricted) suffrage for the Assembly. The same month the storm of strikes at last abated, peace was made with Japan, and it seemed possible that the government would recover its balance. But the worst was still to come.

A further outbreak of strikes at the end of September, initiated by printers in Moscow, spread like wildfire, paralysing not only Moscow and St Petersburg but many provincial cities as well. The demands of the workers were more than ever focused upon political change. The Union of Railwaymen brought the railways to a halt, the liberal Union of Unions (formed in May) and leading liberal figures proclaimed full support for the strikes, and many employers showed sympathy by lenient treatment of striking workers. The disparate movements of protest were for a moment united in massive resistance. The regime shuddered. In desperation the Tsar appointed Witte to handle the crisis, committed himself to creating a unified cabinet under Witte's premiership, and on 17 October, reluctant and resentful to the last, issued a historic Manifesto. The autocracy undertook to guarantee full civil liberty, to give major legislative powers to the promised Assembly (the State Duma), and to broaden greatly the franchise on which it was to be based.

The Tsar's 400-word Manifesto immediately divided the forces arrayed against him. The propertied classes rallied to the government and called for a halt to all disturbances. The Union of 17 October (Octobrists), a loose political alliance led by landed nobility and a few prominent industrialists, was formed to work with the Tsar on the basis of the Manifesto. Employers brought maximum pressure to bear on workers in order to restore order: recalcitrant strikers faced lockouts. The liberal centre considered the Manifesto less than satisfactory but sufficient grounds for a return to normality. They formed the Constitutional Democratic (Kadet) Party, dedicated to using the concessions of 17 October as a stepping-stone towards full parliamentary democracy. Moderate unions, including the Union of Railwaymen, called for an immediate return to work.

But widespread resistance and protest demonstrations continued. Although a number of concessions helped to pacify some minority nationalists, the most militant remained unreconciled. Substantial military force had to be used in the Baltic and in Poland where martial law was instituted. The period from October to December saw a rash of serious, though localized, mutinies among soldiers and sailors from the naval base of Kronstadt near St Petersburg to the Far Eastern Army. They were firmly crushed by loyal units, but the implications of unrest within this ultimate bastion of the regime severely frightened the authorities. Most alarming was the failure of the Manifesto to appease peasants and workers. Peasant disturbances – labour and rent strikes, land seizures, and direct assaults on noble manors – peaked precisely during the weeks which followed the Tsar's concessions. The second congress of the All-Russian Peasants Union, meeting in

November, dismissed the Manifesto out of hand, and the announcement that redemption dues were to be phased out altogether made little impact. Troops had to be used on a wide scale in the countryside and peasant disturbances continued through 1906 and into 1907. The proletariat was hardly more impressed by the Manifesto. With moderate unions leading a return to work, there was a brief respite in the strike movement, but in the weeks that followed, the government faced an unprecedented challenge to its authority, centred on St Petersburg and Moscow.

On the very day of the Manifesto a central strike committee in the capital proclaimed itself the St Petersburg Soviet (Council) of Workers' Deputies. With remarkable speed this novel organization gained the confidence of the capital's work-force. Its formation may have owed something to the traditional structure of the peasant commune; its unity and authority were enhanced by the absence of firmly entrenched separate trade unions; and its electoral procedure was drawn directly from the experience of the Shidlovsky Commission. An Executive Committee was formed and individual members of the socialist parties – especially the Mensheviks – played prominent roles: Trotsky briefly held the post of chairman. But the deputies – whose number reached 562 – were elected directly at factory level and were subject to immediate recall. The system of direct democracy made the Soviet immediately responsive to the mood of rank-and-file workers.

Similar soviets had emerged in other cities earlier in the year, but that of St Petersburg took on unique importance. It helped to inspire the creation of soviets elsewhere – among peasants and soldiers as well as workers – and it attempted to liaise between them. Moreover, the functions it took on within the capital – including the setting up of an armed militia, the publication of an uncensored newspaper, the imposition via the printers' union of its own form of censorship, and above all the coordination of strike action – gave it the appearance of rivalling the authority of the government itself. At the end of October, egged on by rank-and-file demands for an eight-hour day, the Soviet endorsed renewed strike action. Early in November it called a second general strike to protest against the repressive measures being taken at the naval base of Kronstadt, in Poland, and elsewhere. This time, however, the attitude of most white-collar workers was decidedly ambivalent, and employers were fiercely hostile, combining lockouts and blacklists to rebuff the attempt by blue-collar workers to impose their right to an eight-hour day. On 3 December, when the Soviet had survived fifty days, the government felt strong enough to arrest the Executive Committee and over 200 deputies and to destroy the organization.

The immediate sequel was an armed uprising in several cities, headed by Moscow. The Bolsheviks played a leading role both in the Moscow Soviet and in the December rising. For over a week government forces were unable to crush guerrilla-style resistance, but the bulk of the army remained loyal and by the second half of December the workers' movement was clearly on the retreat. During the first weeks of the new year ruthless reprisals helped restore order to urban Russia.

The drama of 1905 left a profound imprint upon Russian public life. Both leaders and rank and file at all levels of society – nobility, middle class, workers, and even some peasants – had taken part in open political struggle. They had established new institutions, new parties, soviets, and unions. Radicals and conservatives alike had become politically mobilized. The process had been crowned by the Tsar's undertaking to set up a State Duma, a permanent forum for public participation in the affairs of government. Yet the moment this promise was made, the polarized structure of society was fully exposed. Deep social divisions, briefly overshadowed by the chorus of demands for constitutional reform, came to the fore. On the Left, the effect in political terms was fragmentation. Among the more militant workers, the sense of defeat at the end of the year gave rise to bitter disillusionment with what was seen as betrayal by liberal leaders and professional groups. Fresh credence was given to the class analyses of socialist activists and their warnings that workers must keep 'the bourgeoisie' at arm's length. Among the peasantry, hopes remained high that the forthcoming Duma would effect radical change in the countryside. But the vehemence of their demands, the assertiveness of the Peasants' Union, and their ready resort to direct action made it clear that they would not meekly defer to the relatively cautious counsel of liberal leaders. And that caution was growing. By the end of the year most Kadet leaders, though deeply committed to major social reform and full constitutional democracy, were fiercely critical of continued revolutionary activity. To the Right, the effect was to swing conservative opinion behind Nicholas's regime. The more direct and threatening the pressure from below, the more vocally the propertied classes supported repressive measures. The Octobrists, while regretting official infringement of recently guaranteed civil liberties, heartily endorsed vigorous measures to restore the authority of the government. On the extreme Right, the threat to order and property found expression in the formation of the Union of the Russian People. It was composed of disparate reactionary groups, violently nationalist and anti-Semitic in outlook, whose only regret was that the Tsar had issued any manifesto at all. Before 1905 was out the spectre of social upheaval thus enabled the Tsar's government to regain the initiative.

The end of the Russian Empire (1906–1916)

During the months which followed the Moscow uprising strength was gradually restored to the Tsarist regime. The Far Eastern Army was brought home and a massive French loan floated by Witte helped cover the huge costs of the war and the drop in direct tax receipts from the peasantry. Yet disturbances continued. During 1906 there were frequent strikes and workers energetically set about testing the authorities' ability to uphold the restrictions on trade-union organization. The illegal socialist parties enrolled tens of thousands of new working-class and peasant members, there were repeated student demonstrations, and the number of terrorist attacks on government officials rose. Serious peasant disorders were reported through-out the year, and there were further significant mutinies within the armed forces. These conditions ruled out an abrupt disavowal of the October Manifesto. Repressive measures, it is true, were gradually intensified. Between October 1905 and April 1906, some 34,000 rioters were shot, of whom an estimated 14,000 died. And from summer 1906 the trade unions came under sustained attack as the police moved in to arrest leaders, forbid meetings and close down a growing number outright. But the regime's authority was fragile. Even reactionary ministers were acutely anxious not to risk a repetition of the extreme isolation of 1905. Thus initially the government moved with caution.

An uneasy balance between reform and reaction was reflected in the Duma Statute and the Fundamental Laws issued in February and April 1906. As promised, a Legislative Assembly, the State Duma, was to be established, elected on the broad franchise conceded during December. The Duma's consent was required before any change could be made to the Fundamental Laws; it was to control a portion of the budget; and its members were given immunity against prosecution. On the other hand, the State Council was to be preserved, and was to form an upper chamber designed to counterbalance any radical tendencies in the Duma. Half the councillors were to be appointed by the Tsar, and the other half were to be elected from such reliable institutions as the Holy Synod, the provincial assemblies of the nobility, the zemstvos, and the city dumas, as well as the academic and business communities. This guaranteed an overwhelmingly conservative body: even among elected members, three-quarters were certain to be noblemen. Moreover, even when both houses approved a piece of legislation, the Tsar retained an absolute right of veto, and should an emergency arise while the Duma was not in session, Article 87 enabled him to legislate by decree. The Tsar's control over foreign and military affairs was unqualified. Above all, the government was responsible to him alone: no amount of criticism from the Duma could dislodge his chosen ministers. These arrangements reflected anxiety to conciliate public opinion without losing control of the executive. The same anxiety led to several unsuccessful attempts by Witte and, later in 1906, by one of his successors, P. A. Stolypin, to persuade prominent Kadets and Octobrists to join the Cabinet. On the one hand, leading ministers genuinely wanted to broaden the government's base, but on the other, the Tsar himself was decidedly unenthusiastic and the Kadet leader, P. N. Miliukov, and the other public figures approached gained the clear impression that they would be mere hostages in an administration run in the old spirit.

The First Duma met in April amidst widespread expectations – discounted only by the Social Democrats and SRs who boycotted the elections – of radical change. To the horror of the authorities, who had retained remarkable confidence in the supposed conservatism of the peasantry, right-wing deputies were in a small minority. The largest blocs in the Duma were the Kadets, who benefited both from the socialist boycott and from their skilful use of the indirect electoral system which enabled them to win a disproportionate number of seats, and the peasant deputies loosely bound together in the Trudovik (Labour) Group. They joined forces in demanding a series of profound reforms, including the appointment of a government responsible to the Duma and the redistribution of private land. The Prime Minister, I. L. Goremykin, who had replaced Witte just before the assembly convened, was an old-fashioned bureaucrat and treated the Duma with disdain, dismissing these radical proposals out of hand. The government suggested instead that the nation's representatives discuss proposals for a new laundry and greenhouse at Dorpat University. After two months the Duma was dissolved. The Kadets led other radical deputies across the border to Vyborg in Finland where they issued a manifesto carefully crafted to channel any popular protest away from the revolutionary activity they now frowned upon into the safer waters of passive resistance. The response among peasants and workers was minimal, and the sharp shift to the right among the propertied classes was reflected in a complete lack of support from the zemstvos, where Kadet sympathizers were rapidly displaced by more conservative noble representatives. Nevertheless, the Duma's dismissal

121

6.1   The first State Duma meets in the Taurida Palace, St Petersburg, 1906. The seats are arranged in a semi-circle according to modern constitutional practice. The Chamber is dominated by a huge portrait of the Tsar. It quickly became clear that there would be no constructive dialogue between the government and the deputies, and after two months the Duma was dissolved.

did not signal a return to the pre-October system. Goremykin was replaced by a vigorous new Prime Minister, Peter Stolypin, who was convinced of the need to combine firm assertion of government authority with measures to assuage popular discontent.

A Second Duma was not to be summoned until February 1907, and in the interval Stolypin used Article 87 to implement a series of reforms addressing the problem he saw as fundamental, that of the peasantry. His short-term measures included an increase in resources for the Peasant Bank to facilitate peasant land purchase, and the encouragement of resettlement on vacant land in Siberia. But even before 1905, while Governor of the western province of Grodno, he had become convinced that the only long-term solution was to replace communal with private landownership. This he hoped would foster individual initiative, open the way to improved agricultural methods, and above all create a class of satisfied peasant farmers with a solid interest in the status quo. Russia would develop her own version of the conservative peasantry which formed the backbone of the French Third Republic. His conclusion that the commune had ceased to be a guarantee of order and become a dangerous barrier to economic improvement and social change was now widely shared by the landowning nobility. To dismantle the commune seemed an adequate, and much more attractive, way of assuaging peasant land-hunger than the concession of noble land, which had been gloomily contemplated during the worst moments of 1905. The groundwork for Stolypin's attempt to dismantle the commune had already been laid during investigations of peasant conditions prompted by the risings of 1902. He now legislated to encourage individual peasants to register their communal holdings as private property with a view to exchanging their scattered strips for consolidated farms.

The success enjoyed by Stolypin's 'wager on the strong' has been the subject of controversy ever since. By 1916 a quarter of communal households had registered their land in individual ownership, and up to half of these had received consolidated holdings. Another 2 million in non-repartitional communes were declared private owners, so that together with the areas where the commune did not exist at all, about half the peasant households in the Empire had private ownership. The fairly flexible implementation of the legislation enabled many villages to undertake partial consolidation and reorganization of landholding. The general decline in rural disturbances after 1907 suggested to some observers that Stolypin had successfully diverted the peasantry from their quest for noble land. Yet the view that the reform was jeopardized only by the outbreak of war in 1914 no longer seems tenable. Applications to leave the commune declined long before the war began. Few peasants had the means to set up viable independent farms, and many of those who did contract out of the commune did so only to sell their land. Wealthier households often stood to lose by disrupting existing relationships within the commune. Above all, it was only in the more commercially developed areas, in the west, the south and the south-east, where the commune was already under strong pressure, that the rate of consolidation was high. In the more overpopulated areas, where land-hunger and peasant unrest were most acute, the response was minimal. Among the peasants of Great Russia very few indeed went so far as to move their households out of the village, and there was a steady counterflow back towards communal tenure.

As a result, neither the social nor the political consequences which Stolypin – in common with both liberal and Marxist economists – had expected were forthcoming. The substantial class of independent rural capitalists employing the labour of their landless neighbours failed to emerge. Even among those who left the commune, the tradition of partitioning richer households between the family's sons when they married, and merging unviable households, tended to continue. Together with the vulnerability of even the most flourishing peasant households to the pressure of the State and vagaries of the weather, this greatly reduced the market's tendency to widen the gap between rich and poor. In the central provinces, the economy of a peasant household tended to follow a biological pattern, expanding as the family expanded, contracting as the adults grew old and the children left home. As a result, hired labour in the rural economy remained minimal. Landownership was not becoming more concentrated. Indeed, in the pre-war years 'middle peasant' households were increasing their proportion of the land, output and inventory of central Russia. Clearer still was the political failure of the reform. Peasants who did establish independent farms certainly attracted the hostility of those remaining within the commune. But this intra-peasant division was completely overshadowed by their almost universal belief that the solution to their problems lay in the transfer of noble land into their hands. Through their deputies in the Duma and the zemstvos, peasants continued to express an unequivocal demand for the abolition of noble landownership. The ferocious measures of repression did end the mass protests of 1905–07, but the number of disturbances appears to have risen abruptly in the last years before the war. Moreover, the relative tranquillity of the countryside in the years after 1907 owed little to social change in the village. It is to be explained more in terms of a rapid increase in the amount of land sown, the recovery of grain prices, and a series of excellent harvests.

Stolypin's land reforms did not impress the Second Duma when it met in February 1907. Government attempts to influence the elections had failed to secure a cooperative assembly. The number of right-wing deputies rose slightly, but more striking was the ground lost by the Kadets to the extreme Left. The Kadets were affected by police measures against them, including the debarring of those who had taken part in the Vyborg protest. But the loss of half their seats reflected above all the fact that, while their urban vote held up well, they won little support from more politically-conscious peas-

6.2 A meeting of a pre-revolutionary village commune. Although there are several women present (perhaps drawn more by the camera than the proceedings), the session is dominated by the male heads of the village households.

ants and failed dismally to attract working-class support, which went overwhelmingly to the Social Democrats and SRs who this time decided to contest the elections. The government therefore met bitter criticism, particularly for its emergency measures against revolutionary and terrorist activity, which included the use of courts martial to despatch suspects with minimal formality. Unable to establish any common ground between his proposals and the radical demands of the Left, Stolypin dissolved the Duma on 3 June and, in violation of the Fundamental Laws, drastically altered the franchise on which its successor was to be elected. The representation of the urban population (especially the working class), the peasantry, and the national minorities was cut to a fraction. The Third Duma (1907–12), in which the Octobrists formed the largest group, represented above all the landowning nobility of Great Russia. More than half the deputies were themselves landed noblemen, most of the clerical deputies were clearly identified with them, and they exercised a major influence over the selection of the peasants returned.

125

The stage seemed set for harmonious cooperation between the two houses of the legislature, the Cabinet, and the Tsar. The common ground they shared was extensive. The inviolability of private property was to be staunchly upheld. Peasant land-hunger was to be met by dismantling the commune. Vigorous measures were to be taken to crush any further peasant unrest and to uproot revolutionary and terrorist organizations. There was to be no slackening in the full-scale purge, launched in 1906, of the 'third element' in general and of village school teachers in particular. Cautious moves might be made to improve working-class conditions, but the promised freedom to form trade unions was to be narrowly restricted. The indivisibility of the Empire was to be put beyond question and further steps taken to Russify Poland, curtail the autonomy of Finland, and bring the other restive national minorities into line. Finally, the executive was to remain directly answerable to the Tsar alone. In the event, however, this apparent recipe for unified and effective government proved a disastrous failure.

Stolypin's approach was to present the Third Duma with a long programme of mild reforms. He believed that his agrarian measures must be supplemented by a series of legal and administrative changes designed to reduce social tension and consolidate the government's refound authority. The measures he proposed included greater religious toleration, more lenient treatment of the Jews, reforms of the zemstvos and local government to reduce the division between peasants and the rest of society, extension of primary education, and a genuine effort to discipline local officials and strengthen respect for the law among rulers as well as ruled. Moreover, he believed that the authority of the government would be enhanced by successful cooperation with the Duma in passing the appropriate legislation.

In the eyes of many provincial noblemen and senior bureaucrats, as well as the Orthodox hierarchy, on the other hand, the decline of the revolutionary movement pointed in a different direction. Further reforms of the kind the Premier was proposing seemed to them both unnecessary and dangerous: unnecessary since the masses were now relatively quiescent, dangerous because 1905 had demonstrated that the regime could not afford in any way to weaken its powers of coercion. Stolypin's programme, in their view, would undermine the prestige of the Orthodox Church, encourage the inherently unpatriotic and seditious Jews, and tie the hands of provincial governors and police officials with legal red tape. To reduce the power of the land captain and to give peasants a greater say in their own administration was to invite trouble. And at a time when the government was beginning to pour very substantial sums of money into the zemstvos, provincial noblemen were particularly anxious to maintain ascendancy there in order to channel a decent share of the funds towards their own needs. Finally, this body of opinion, unlike Stolypin, feared that the Duma, far from being a desirable new support for the regime, was a potential bridgehead which liberals and radicals might yet use to capture the all-important executive.

The period of the Third Duma therefore saw Stolypin wage a sustained and increasingly bitter struggle with the forces of the extreme Right. At the outset conservative opposition to the Premier within the Duma was limited to a minority of somewhat maverick deputies, whereas Stolypin had the support of the large Octobrist faction and, on occasion, the Kadets. But outside the Duma he encountered much more formidable opposition. He was exasperated to find that the State Council rejected most of the reforms passed in the lower house. The upper house was dominated by men who, by virtue of both birth and merit, had reached the summit of the civil service or army. They were closely bound by ties of kinship and friendship to upper-class society outside officialdom, many being drawn from ancient families of the nobility and educated at a handful of privileged schools, and many were immensely wealthy landowners. Although their views on the regime's predicament were by no means unanimous, they were predominantly on the conservative end of the political spectrum and inclined to resist Stolypin. A leading part in this was taken by Witte and two other retired ministers, P. N. Durnovo and V. F. Trepov, who were motivated in part by personal jealousy of Stolypin. A major role was also played by the leading landowners who in 1906 had set up an elite pressure group, the United Nobility, to coordinate the defence of their interests. Skilfully exploiting their ready access to senior bureaucrats, the State Council, and the Tsar himself they successfully stymied all reforms of which they disapproved.

The struggle between Stolypin and the far Right was highlighted by two major clashes. During 1908 the colourful Octobrist leader, A. I. Guchkov, raised the hackles of those who abhorred the Duma's pretensions by mounting a scathing attack upon the inefficient administration of the armed forces, symbolized by the high offices of manifestly incompetent grand dukes. Leading conservatives urged the Tsar to beware of any encroachment upon his absolute authority over military affairs, and severely criticized a Duma bill, approved by Stolypin, for implying the Duma's right to make recommendations on naval administration. The bill scraped through the State Council, but in the spring of 1909 the Tsar vetoed it and Stolypin was brought to the point of resignation. He stayed on only at Nicholas's express command and on condition that, in future, he should be consulted on appointments to the State Council. But he was compelled to admonish the Duma's presumption, his alliance with the Octobrists was severely damaged, and he had to look towards the Nationalists, sitting to the right of the Octobrists, for future support in the Duma.

It was over the central objective of the Nationalist Party (formed in 1909) that the second major clash occurred. This was a bill to establish zemstvos in the western provinces where none had been set up in the 1860s for fear they would be dominated by disloyal Polish magnates. Since then the number of Russian landlords in the area had risen substantially and it was they who now demanded the creation of zemstvos to consolidate their influence over the provinces. The bill was framed to ensure that they, rather than the Poles, controlled the zemstvos by creating national *curiae* and cautiously lowering the property qualifications. Stolypin's enemies in the State Council raised the objection to the first provision that it would incite national conflict, and to the second that it would provide a dangerous precedent and encourage pressure for the democratization of other zemstvos. They secured the Tsar's permission to vote 'according to conscience' and in March 1911 proceeded to defeat the bill. Stolypin was enraged. He consented to continue in office only on condition the Tsar suspended both houses, disciplined Trepov and Durnovo by temporary banishment from the capital, and promulgated the western zemstvo bill under Article 87.

The sequel was, to Stolypin, bitterly ironic. The anger of the Tsar at his own humiliation and the bitterness of the majority of the State Council were to be expected, but the Premier's erstwhile allies in the Duma, too, reacted furiously against his high-handed use of Article 87. Instead of hailing the defeat he had dealt the upper house, that graveyard of Duma reforms, the Octobrists savaged the Premier, Guchkov resigned the presidency of the Duma, and the Party was even represented in a deputation which went to see Durnovo off at the railway station. Stolypin's position was becoming untenable, and his fall was widely predicted before he was assassinated, with apparent police complicity, in September 1911.

The same forces which frustrated Stolypin also destroyed the Octobrist Party. The Party's leadership had broadly shared Stolypin's hope that cooperation between Duma and government would strengthen the State's authority while reducing social tension. They had been restrained in their criticism of government infringements of the civil liberties promised in the October Manifesto, and had steered a middle path between right-wing insistence that Russia was still an autocracy and the Kadet view that she now had a constitutional monarchy. Yet the premise on which the Party had been formed proved false. The forces of the Right would not permit the mild reform which it favoured. The Octobrists' landowning constituents were rapidly moving to the right of them, while the Party's support for Stolypin found little favour from an increasingly critical urban public opinion. Such limited local organization as the Party had established wasted away. The Duma faction fell apart. The leadership under Guchkov had always been more committed to the path of constitutional evolution than the rank and file, many of whom had only migrated to the Octobrist flag once they reached the Duma. As Stolypin's star waned, they too tended to drift to the right. The constitutionalist core of the Party, reduced to a mere rump, moved closer to the attitude of moderate opposition adopted by the Kadets and their allies. In the Fourth Duma (1912–17) Guchkov, who lost his own seat, urged the Party to be much more forthright in its attacks upon the high-handed and seemingly aimless administration of Stolypin's successors.

Thus the constitutional development which the October Manifesto had appeared to promise was not forthcoming. The landed nobility recognized the abyss that would open up beneath them should the State become more responsive to urban, or worse still peasant, interests. They therefore frustrated Stolypin and the Octobrists and moved to consolidate their grip on the machinery of state. But in doing so they severely damaged that machinery. There were no more than about 20,000 noble landowners fully enfranchised to vote in the landowners' *curiae* of the Third Duma and the zemstvos, as well as in the provincial assemblies of the nobility. The peasant disorders of 1905–07 had led to panic land sales which only gradually slackened as the nobility regained confidence and successfully diverted considerable resources from the State to their own support. As a result they had severe difficulty in providing candidates for the array of posts – as land captains, marshals of the nobility, and zemstvo deputies – which they had studiously reserved for themselves. With some refusing office, and the most ambitious migrating to lucrative posts in the capital, the result was multiple office-holding by candidates of doubtful ability. The provincial command structure of the Tsarist State was becoming perilously brittle.

More immediately apparent was the impact of their victory upon the coherence of central government. In the first place, relations between government and Duma deteriorated further after Stolypin's death. Although the shift to the right of the bulk of Octobrists provided the government with a potentially well-disposed majority in the Fourth Duma, ministers took no pains to win support and became increasingly intolerant of the slightest criticism. They treated the Duma with contempt and presented it with no substantial legislation. Urged on by N. A. Maklakov, Minister of the Interior from 1912 to 1915, and other reactionaries within and outside the Cabinet, the Tsar went so far as to consider stripping the Duma of its legislative functions. Moreover, even within the executive, power was dangerously dispersed. Nicholas had taken to heart the warnings of Stolypin's enemies that a unified Cabinet under a powerful premier threatened the independent authority of the Crown. He encouraged the breakdown of collective Cabinet responsibility, undermined the authority of Kokovtsov, Stolypin's successor as Prime Minister, and in January 1914 replaced him altogether with the aged Goremykin. The Prime Minister became a mere figurehead in charge of no major department, and individual ministers reverted to reporting independently and in haphazard manner to the Tsar. The result was lack of coordination between different departments. The last pre-war years saw counterproductive oscillations over such questions as the legal rights to be granted trade unions, continuing clashes between the Ministry of Finance and that of the Interior, sharp conflict between civilian and military leaders, massive ill-judged increases in naval expenditure at the expense of the army, and the disruption of an ever more complex administrative structure.

Nor did the myth of an all-seeing autocrat who would himself provide the necessary coordination bear any relation to reality. Not only was Nicholas without the vigour and breadth of outlook this would imply, but his lack of self-confidence and sense of inadequacy deprived him of the air of personal authority necessary for such a role. Moreover, after 1905 the Imperial couple became increasingly cut off from the world around them. Less than charismatic at the best of times, they had never been popular at court. When their anxiety to protect and shield their haemophiliac son led them to withdraw into a very narrow family circle, they incurred the displeasure of even the most conservative members of high society. The most arresting symptom of their isolation was their reckless devotion to Rasputin. This bizarre product of the sectarian movement seemed to the royal couple – and especially to Alexandra – a gift from above. Not only did he appear to have the power to stem the Tsarevich's bleeding attacks, but he was inspired by passionate, if incoherent, religious fervour and seemed to provide living proof of peasant devotion to the Tsar. Yet even the most loyal ministers, even the foremost grand dukes and prelates, regarded him as a charlatan whose doctrine of 'redemption through sin' was but a thin veil for crude depravity. His political influence, before the war at least, was wildly exaggerated, but the sinister light he cast over the royal household severely damaged the image of the Tsar. No amount of censorship could quell public curiosity and disapproval, especially when leading Duma representatives, such as Guchkov, used parliamentary immunity to draw attention to his presence at court. The Tsar's rejection of requests from all sides to investigate the charges levelled against Rasputin and to banish him symbolized and deepened the isolation of the royal couple.

Yet even the most inspiring, politically sensitive, and astute of tsars would have been hard pressed to consolidate the post-Stolypin regime, based as it was on the premise that there should be no unified Cabinet, no cooperation with a Duma of any description, and unqualified support for the landed nobility. For on these premises no government could learn the lessons of 1905. Moreover, there were ominous signs about the continuing effectiveness of the coercive forces which had enabled the Tsar to survive that upheaval – the police, the Cossacks and the army itself. Their ability and willingness to crush unrest were being eroded. The regular police force was small, corrupt and ill-trained. Cossack loyalty was being strained by financial grievances and inadequate land grants. Significant changes were overcoming the army. The officer corps was becoming more professionalized, and as it did so both the War Ministry and a growing number of officers objected to the use of the army for internal 'policing' duties when it should be preparing to face potential foreign enemies. Furthermore, since the military reforms of the 1870s, the period for which conscripts served had been gradually reduced, falling to only three years by the eve of World War I. The effect, as the major mutinies during 1905–06 had already demonstrated, was to make it much more difficult to cut soldiers off from civilian life, accustom them to harsh military discipline and unquestioning obedience, and train them when called upon to repress the peasants and workers from whom they were drawn. And yet the regime remained dependent on just such a call since the pre-war years provided little evidence that popular discontent was abating.

The disruption of war and revolution had brought on a recession, most pronounced in heavy industry, which lasted into 1908. But thereafter recovery began: between 1909 and 1913 industrial growth averaged 8 per cent per annum and the rate was accelerating. The structure of this new phase of industrialization, and its social repercussions, followed broadly the same pattern as before 1905. Improved harvests and higher grain prices created a stronger consumer market and both rural handicraft and factory production in light industry benefited accordingly. At the same time, the government continued to provide the major impetus to heavy industry. The very high level of the national debt ensured that Kokovtsov was a considerably more cautious finance minister than Witte had been, but there was a sharp rise in defence expenditure which went far towards taking over the dynamic role played earlier by railway construction. The banking structure became more sophisticated, and directed increasing sums of domestic capital into industry, while foreign capital continued to flow into Russia. Heavy industry remained restricted to a few areas of the Empire, was further concentrated in large enterprises, and continued to be dominated by a small number of companies organized in a growing network of trusts, cartels, and syndicates.

This development increased the economic power of the commercial and industrial classes. Not only did the numbers of wealthy native industrialists, merchants, bankers and insurance dealers swell, but so too did the ranks of humble businessmen, small-scale manufacturers, self-employed artisans, petty traders and shopkeepers. Yet they made very slow headway in overcoming the political inhibitions which had affected them before 1905. The major banks and enterprises of the capital were in large measure foreign-owned, while their continuing dependence on state contracts and subsidies kept them very close to officialdom. The relationship was lubricated by the free flow of bribes and directorships to senior civil and military officials. The Association of Industry and Trade, set up in St Petersburg in 1906, was a more forthright mouthpiece of business interests than its predecessors, but criticism of government interference was blended with pressure for the State to expand its role in developing the infrastructure of the economy. Moreover, the Association failed dismally in its aspiration to speak for businessmen outside the capital. St Petersburg industrialists remained separated by regional and ethnic differences from the more dynamic entrepreneurs of the south, while their dependence on bureaucratic support and foreign capital was regarded with disdain by the Moscow business community. The narrowly restricted franchise of the urban dumas militated against the development of vigorous municipal politics, and the bulk of small-scale merchants remained culturally inward-looking and politically passive.

Nevertheless, frustration with the political status quo was growing among the business community. The mass of anachronistic Tsarist legislation governing business practice, the tangle of red tape inhibiting the formation of new companies, the haughty attitude of officials, the impossibility of relying upon the law, the domination of the zemstvos by landowners, and the siphoning off of urban taxes to rural needs – all became ever more irksome as business opportunities expanded and businessmen gained in self-confidence. In those few cities (Moscow is the most striking case) where the business and social elites entertained ambitious plans for social reform, expansion of municipal services and widening of the local government franchise, they found their efforts resisted by the Tsarist State. Their frustration led a group of Moscow industrialists, among whom A. I. Konovalov and the Ryabushinsky brothers were prominent, to work for the creation of a party in the Duma which would add the weight of the business community to pressure for reform. In 1912 they formed the Progressive Party, building upon the small groups which sat between the Octobrists and the Kadets. Their aim was not to compete with the other moderate opposition parties: in terms of policies, including franchise reform and the appointment of a government responsible to the Duma, there was little to choose between the Progressive Party and the Kadets. Rather, given the relatively low priority attached to commercial and industrial issues by the Kadets, half of whose Central Committee were or had been university professors, they sought to bridge the entrenched cultural division between the business and professional classes.

The latter continued to expand rapidly in the period. Not only were the numbers of lawyers, doctors, journalists and teachers growing fast, but so too were the ranks of white-collar workers more generally – clerks, administrators and technical specialists in commerce, industry and the service sectors. These groups generally expressed keener resentment than did industrialists and entrepreneurs at the lack of guaranteed civil rights – underlined by repeated interference with university autonomy, the inconveniences of residual censorship, the manifestly inequitable franchise for the zemstvos and urban dumas alike. The 'third element' were frustrated by the restrictions on zemstvo initiatives imposed both by the government and by gentry deputies. Moreover, in the aftermath of 1905, organizations, associations and congresses representing different professions developed markedly in range, size and assertiveness.

In political terms, these groups were generally loyal to the Kadet Party. In each of the four elections to the Duma, the Party won the bulk of the non-working-class urban vote. Yet the growing civic self-confidence of Russia's professional classes was not matched by the mood among Kadet politicians. Party membership, estimated at 100,000 in 1906, dwindled drastically thereafter, few of those who remained paid their dues, and outside a handful of major cities, local branches of the Party virtually ceased functioning except in the immediate run-up to Duma elections. The government's refusal to broaden the franchise for municipal councils – in most cities less than one per cent of the population had the vote – meant that local elections offered little opportunity to stimulate political activity. Above all, the Party's predicament in the Duma undermined Kadet morale.

Throughout the Third Duma, under Miliukov's leadership, they attempted to combine unflinching commitment to British-style constitutional democracy with responsible, constructive opposition to the Tsarist government. It proved a difficult course. The authorities refused even to recognize the legal existence of the Party, viewing it as virtually revolutionary, while the Right and most Octobrists saw the Kadets as irresponsible idealists. To the Left, on the other hand, their opposition appeared spineless. Moderate socialists such as the flamboyant leader of the Trudovik Group, A. F. Kerensky, were able to strike a much more convincing note of outright condemnation of the government, while the Bolsheviks dismissed the Kadets as apologists for the regime. The urge to appease critics of both the Right and the Left produced serious dissension within the Kadet Party. While one wing saw no future without a *rapprochement* with moderate Octobrists, others insisted that the Party must concentrate on its appeal to radical opinion. In the Fourth Duma, despite the misgivings of some, the Kadets did become more outspoken in attacking the government's failure to honour the October Manifesto, but their mood remained deeply pessimistic.

The problem that confronted Russia's liberal parties was that, in the absence of massive pressure from the peasantry and the proletariat, the government showed no signs whatsoever of giving ground. Yet neither Progressives nor Kadets could welcome a revolutionary upheaval over which they would have no control. Indeed, a major factor fuelling their anxiety for reform was the resurgence of the working-class movement after 1911. The government's intransigence seemed a positive incitement to proletarian militancy. The mild labour legislation passed in 1912 to create sickness benefit funds and accident insurance for workers appeared wholly inadequate, and the government continued to place endless obstacles in the way of substantial trade-union organization. There were of course employers – notably in the capital – who opposed even the limited concessions that were made. But the Progressives as well as the Kadets believed that without swift action to improve labour conditions and to channel industrial disputes into orderly trade unions operating within a coherent legal framework, it would be impossible to prevent recurrent threats to the entire social and economic fabric. By 1914, as the strike movement reached alarming proportions, elements in both parties urged the need for liberals to seize the leadership of an incipient revolutionary challenge to the regime. The leading Progressive, Konovalov, opened negotiations with the socialist parties in the hope of creating a united bloc on the left, and went as far as to offer a subvention to the Bolsheviks. Yet only a small minority of liberals shared the view that working-class radicalism might be so easily brought under control. For most, the rigidity of the regime and the extremism of the working class created a sense of helplessness which threatened to fragment both liberal parties on the eve of the war.

In retrospect, liberal pessimism seems thoroughly justified. True, a fragile bridge between middle and working-class aspirations was formed by the commercial press which dwarfed the newspapers founded by the Kadets and Octobrists. At the cheaper end of the market the 'kopeck' press, addressed to workers and the urban lower classes, enjoyed particularly rapid growth in the period. By 1911 there were 29 such dailies and they tended to preach individual self-help and to be broadly liberal in tone. Like the rest of the commercial press, they repudiated socialists' attempts to dub them 'bourgeois' and discouraged notions of class conflict. Their appeal, however, may have owed more to a *pot-pourri* of local and national news, scandal and sensation, serial thrillers and columns written specifically for lower-class women, than to their political orientation. Most of the evidence suggests that the breach between liberals and workers which had opened after the October Manifesto of 1905 remained unbridgeable and that Russia's proletariat was becoming more rather than less radical. With strikes banned, trade unions shackled by a host of regulations, and the road to political reform seemingly blocked by the regime, there was minimal incentive for Russian workers to accept a gradualist, reformist approach towards improving their conditions.

After 1906 labour protest had been temporarily dampened by the government's energetic measures to root out activists and to halt the brief flowering of trade-union organization, and by the effects of the economic recession. But this quiescence proved short-lived. As industrial growth resumed the number of workers in mining and large-scale industry rose swiftly, reaching over 3 million by 1914, and so too did the level of strike action. Moreover, in the last two years before the war there was a dramatic and ominous increase in the proportion of strikes which were regarded by the factory inspectorate as political rather than economic in origin. This trend was sharply accentuated in the spring of 1912 by the furious reaction to news that government troops had opened fire upon a large crowd of striking workers in the Lena goldfields in eastern Siberia, killing some 270. Over half a million workers across the Empire went on strike in protest. Thereafter, the movement gathered momentum, culminating in a massive strike in the summer of 1914.

Working-class conditions improved little, if at all, in the period.

6.3   The Lena goldfields massacre. In 1912 workers in the goldfields in eastern Siberia took strike action against intolerable conditions. Government troops opened fire on mass demonstrations, killing some 270 workers and sparking protest strikes across the Empire.

Although average wages gradually recovered from the sharp drop they had suffered during the war and upheaval of 1905, by 1914 they were, in real terms, still below the pitiful levels of 1903. There were isolated instances of better housing and less oppressive management, but the sheer speed of industrial growth ruled out whatever slim chance there was that oligarchic municipal governments or the employers themselves would adequately cater for the work-force. Moreover, the composition of the work-force did nothing to reduce its militancy. In 1914, two-thirds of industrial workers still had significant ties to the village and these semi-proletarians proved no more amenable to the urban environment than their predecessors. Their deeply rooted grievances as peasants increased their propensity to rebel against treatment which seemed to them unjust. At the same time the number of workers who had cut their ties with the countryside, whose future depended entirely upon the city, was rising steadily. Whether they were older workers with a decade or more of experience in mine or factory, or younger men born and brought up in the city, they tended to be more literate, more skilled, and more politically conscious than new recruits to the city. It was through them that a working-class tradition, nourished by the hope and bitterness of 1905, was transmitted. Hostile though the environment was to the creation of any kind of proletarian culture or organization, a small number of them gradually acquired organizational experience through the trade unions, *ad hoc* strike committees, sickness benefit funds, cooperatives, and underground socialist parties. The combination of a growing tradition of urban protest and class consciousness with a rapid influx of embittered peasants proved highly combustible.

The degree of militancy varied significantly between different plants and cities. Factories which managed to employ a large contingent of women (whose labour cost little more than half that of men) proved relatively untroubled, whereas young male workers, uninhibited by family responsibility, were particularly restive. Large plants with a more highly skilled work-force, notably metal-working factories, remained the most strike-prone. In Moscow, where there was a significant proportion of urban artisans and a diversified industrial structure, polarization between employers and workers was less extreme, and the level of strikes lower than in St Petersburg. Conditions in and around the capital conspired to make it the centre of protest, accounting for almost half the number of strikers recorded for the country as a whole in 1914. Here there was a concentration of massive metal-working plants, an unusually high proportion of urbanized, educated, male workers, particularly rigid management, and the greatest number of socialist activists. It was here that the movement reached a crescendo with a general strike in the summer of 1914, finally broken only days before war was declared.

The repression which followed 1905 hit the revolutionary parties of the Left hard, sweeping many activists into prison or exile. Moreover, not only did defeat discourage potential new recruits from the factories, but the climate was distinctly less favourable to recruitment from the intelligentsia. The number of students in higher education rose steeply, reaching 117,000 in 1913, and as early as 1908 student protest resumed against renewed government restrictions – on the curriculum, on women auditors, and on student organizations. Particularly large-scale demonstrations marked the occasion of Tolstoy's death in 1910. But the proportion of student activists who now became seriously involved in underground politics fell away. Career opportunities in the liberal professions were expanding fast, absorbing most of the radically inclined students. Moreover, despite continued restrictions on civil liberty, the outlets for social and cultural activity increased very rapidly. Russia's educated youth enjoyed unprecedented freedom of expression, reflected in the high point of the 'silver age' with the flowering of avant-garde experiment in art, music, theatre, and literature, epitomized by the symbolists, whose most famous product was Alexander Blok (1880–1921). The theme of social criticism remained prominent in much of this cultural profusion, and a few major literary figures, notably

Maxim Gorky (1868–1936), identified their work with the cause of revolution. But more striking was the new, apolitical emphasis on aesthetics, the greater concern for individual ethics and, indeed, religion. The trend was symbolized by the appearance in 1909 of *Landmarks*, a collection of essays by prominent intellectuals, including several contrite Marxists. They repudiated what they regarded as the sterile tradition of the radical intelligentsia, its utilitarian view of art and its naive faith in positivism, science, materialism, and revolution.

The SRs and Social Democrats alike, therefore, passed through a period of demoralization. Financial contributions from wealthy sympathizers dried up, and the Okhrana devised ever more sophisticated means of planting spies in the revolutionary milieu. The SRs, who until 1908 had devoted much of their energy to terrorist activity, were particularly severely affected when the leader of their 'fighting organization', E. F. Azef, was exposed as a double agent. In the absence of large-scale rural disturbances it was difficult to cultivate contact with sympathizers among the peasantry, especially after the government's mass dismissal of radical village teachers. The Stolypin land-reform seemed at the time a dire threat to the egalitarian peasant ethos upon which the SRs counted, although they did take some comfort from the growing cooperative movement in the countryside. The franchise reform of 1907 virtually ruled out the possibility of exploiting Duma elections for propaganda purposes among the peasantry: having taken part in the Second Duma the Party boycotted the Third and Fourth. No congress was held between 1907 and 1917, and contact between the Central Committee and scattered local committees was tenuous. Nevertheless, the Party's name continued to be identified, both among the peasantry and among workers whose links with the countryside remained close, with the most direct and radical protest against the status quo.

Among the Social Democrats, the number of local committees fell precipitately, and membership, estimated at 150,000 in 1907 had, according to Trotsky, dropped to 10,000 by 1910. The divisions within the Party, briefly overshadowed by the euphoria of 1905–06, were reopened and deepened by the lessons of defeat and by the new, if limited, opportunities for legal activity among workers. Opinion ranged from a small group who favoured virtually winding up the underground organization and concentrating upon legal work, through a variety of Menshevik factions, to the most intransigent Bolsheviks, led by the philosopher A. A. Bogdanov (1873–1928), who favoured exclusive concentration on preparation for a new armed uprising. Lenin combined tactical flexibility with consistent commitment to the idea of a centralized and homogeneous revolutionary party, and to his belief that the peasantry, not the bourgeoisie, would be the workers' ally in the forthcoming revolution. It was a combination which led him to the nadir of his career. During most of 1908 and 1909 because of his willingness to use legal outlets, in the Duma as well as in trade unions and education clubs, he was in danger of being outflanked to the left by Bogdanov. In 1910 he was compelled by Bolshevik activists to accept a form of reconciliation with the amorphous Menshevik 'opportunists' he despised. He was fiercely criticized, not least by leaders of the Second International, for sanctioning so-called 'expropriations' – robberies of public banks and state institutions carried out by party activists. Yet his self-confidence remained unshaken, and his political skill and energy undiminished. In 1909 he successfully engineered the expulsion of Bogdanov from the Bolshevik faction, simultaneously launching an attack on what he regarded as the suspect efforts of Bogdanov, A. V. Lunacharsky (1875–1933), and other Bolshevik intellectuals to refine Marxist philosophy. In January 1912 he organized a small conference of like-minded social democrats in Prague: a new Central Committee was elected and the Bolshevik faction became a fully-fledged independent party. Although Trotsky managed to convene a rival meeting in Vienna seven months later, it proved impossible to forge unity among the non-Bolshevik social democrats, a majority of whose delegations represented non-Russian social democratic organizations within the Empire.

Lenin's 'Party of a new kind' remained a distant approximation of the streamlined, disciplined, centralized body he had in mind: his own authority was far from unquestioned, communication between the leadership in exile and local activists was haphazard, and police arrests repeatedly disrupted the organization. Nevertheless, the combination of a relatively clear Party line and a markedly more radical stance than that of their rivals stood the Bolsheviks in good stead. Where Lenin saw peasant upheaval against private landowners as the source of support for proletarian revolt in the cities, the Mensheviks were inhibited by their concern for a tactical alliance with the Kadets. Bolshevik slogans – an eight-hour day, a democratic republic, confiscation of all noble land – had far more appeal than the wordy, convoluted Menshevik formulae. As working-class protest resumed from 1912, Bolshevik publications achieved much wider circulation than their rivals. It was the Bolsheviks who had greater success both in attracting mass support and in enrolling young activists, increasingly recruited from workers rather than from the intelligentsia. In the Duma elections of 1912 the Bolsheviks won six of the nine labour *curiae*, and by 1914 they dominated the trade unions and sickness benefit funds in the Moscow and St Petersburg regions.

Downhearted Mensheviks suggested that this success reflected the influx into the ranks of the working class of raw youth and, more particularly, undisciplined, primitive peasants. Given time, they would recognize the greater realism of Menshevik moderation: the need to build a sophisticated mass movement along the lines of the German SPD and to harmonize proletarian protest with that of the middle classes in the forthcoming bourgeois revolution. To the Bolsheviks, on the other hand, their success reflected the increasing maturity of the Russian proletariat. In their view, what was exceptional about Russia's social democratic movement, what set it apart from that of the German SPD, was not lack of sophistication but the genuinely revolutionary leadership provided by the Bolshevik Party. Both Mensheviks and Bolsheviks would consider their own interpretation confirmed by developments within the working class during the maelstrom of the First World War.

The background to Russia's involvement in the war lay in the Balkans. As the Ottoman Empire in Europe disintegrated, leaving a number of small successor states, tension mounted between Russia and Austria-Hungary over their rival claims to influence in the area. Russia's anxiety was that no hostile Great Power should gain control of the Straits, which were of enormous strategic and commercial importance to her. The danger that the Central Powers would do so was increased by Germany's vigorous efforts to establish her influence over Constantinople. Austro-Hungarian anxiety, on the other hand, focused upon the threat to her integrity which the new Balkan states posed. In particular the assertive and ambitious kingdom of Serbia exercised a powerful attraction to discontented Serbs and other South Slavs within the Habsburg Empire. In 1908 Austria-Hungary formally annexed the provinces of Bosnia and Hercegovina, which she had occupied since 1878, thereby pre-empting Serbia's hopes of acquiring them. In 1913 Vienna deprived the Serbs of some of the fruits of their successive victories over Turkey and Bulgaria. On each occasion, Serbia turned to Russia for aid, and on each occasion, after advertising her sympathy, Russia backed down and Serbia had to accept a *fait accompli*. The diplomatic atmosphere was further soured by the increasingly aggressive support which Germany lent her Austrian ally. Yet these diplomatic successes did little to calm the nerves of Vienna, already stretched to the point of snapping by nationalist friction among the Habsburgs' Magyar, German, and Czech subjects. When the Austrian heir apparent was assassinated by Serbian nationalists in Sarajevo in June 1914, the Habsburg government resolved to crush the Serbian menace once and for all. Without reference to Russia, Vienna issued Serbia an ultimatum which she could not fulfil, and declared war.

Whether Russia could have avoided a confrontation over the Balkans remains debatable. Certainly the Tsarist regime appeared to have good reason to do so. Both Stolypin and his enemies on the far Right had repeatedly warned of the disastrous consequences that could be expected from involvement in a major conflict. The Japanese War had shown clearly enough, as Durnovo carefully explained to the Tsar, the probability that, whether victorious or not, the regime would be subjected to an intolerable strain which would issue in social revolution. Moreover, in military and diplomatic terms, time appeared to be on the side of Russia. Germany's threatening posture had consolidated the French alliance and encouraged Britain to reach agreement with Russia over their respective spheres of influence in Asia. Italy's own ambitions in the Balkans were drawing her away from the Central Powers, and the Habsburg Empire was in steep and visible

Map 7   Europe in 1914

decline. At the same time Russia's swift industrial growth was financing a major defence programme. The rebuilding of the navy was under way, the army was being rapidly expanded, and in 1913–14 plans were drawn up for a large-scale development of the railway network in the west of the Empire. By 1917, German strategists feared, their so-called Schlieffen plan, which envisaged delivering a knock-out blow to France before Russia could mobilize, would no longer be viable: Russia would be able to mobilize as fast as the other powers and for Germany a two-front war would become suicidal.

Yet the conduct of Russian foreign policy suffered from the structural defects of the regime which Stolypin had tried to rectify. Despite his wholly inadequate grasp of what was a complex diplomatic and military web, Nicholas jealously guarded his personal prerogative in foreign affairs. This ruled out the possibility of well-informed policy formation, let alone the kind of sophisticated weighing of domestic considerations against foreign goals implied by Durnovo's warning. The Cabinet was discouraged from even discussing foreign affairs, and was quite unable to control the Foreign Minister, while the Foreign Minister's control of his own ambassadors was extremely tenuous. Uncoordinated initiatives were taken at different levels of the diplomatic hierarchy and contradictory signals went out to foreign powers.

The effect was to guarantee that at no stage did Russia gain the initiative. She was forced to respond to decisions made in Vienna, Belgrade, Berlin, and Paris. And the series of diplomatic reversals inflicted upon her from 1908 onwards built up a headstream of frustration which by 1914 proved all but irresistible. The moderate opposition parties seized upon the government's humiliation in the Balkans as a powerful weapon with which to berate it. Nationalist indignation in the Duma was intense and the liberal press – with the notable exception of Miliukov's *Rech* – furiously attacked the government's failure to stand up to the Central Powers. Guchkov struck a responsive chord well beyond the ranks of the Octobrists when he denounced the incompetent, anachronistic manner in which the Empire's vital interests were handled. In the eyes of even the most loyal Duma deputies, foreign policy seemed to be in the hands of 'irresponsible' forces, maverick right-wing newspaper editors, and unseen, sinister figures at court. Whether because of his own code of honour, or because he was more sensitive to pressure from below than he cared to admit, Nicholas felt by the time of the July crisis that his options had virtually disappeared: to bow to Austro-German pressure was impossible. Yet even his decision on how exactly to react to the Austrian ultimatum was marked by confusion. Both the Tsar and his Foreign Minister, S. D. Sazonov, were under the impression that it would be possible to mobilize the army against Austria alone in the hope of keeping Germany out of the conflict. It was only after he had ordered this partial mobilization that the Tsar discovered from the High Command that this was not feasible: Russia must mobilize against both

Austria and Germany or not at all. Unable to see any way out, Nicholas gave the order, Germany immediately followed suit, and war ensued.

In Russia, as elsewhere, it was assumed that the war would last no more than a few weeks, and that victory would depend upon the arms and men available for immediate battle. Instead it developed into a seemingly interminable war of attrition. The swift knock-out blow which Prussia had used to such good effect in the 1860s proved impossible to deliver. Modern technology and communications enabled the Great Powers to mobilize and supply millions of men for years on end. Railways enabled the defending power to rush reinforcements forward, while against modern artillery, machine-guns, and rifles horses were too vulnerable, and motorized vehicles too slow and scarce to follow through a breach in the enemy lines. The Russian front was much less static than the western front, since the lines were more thinly stretched and the railway system less developed. But here too the staggering cost of mass attack in terms of men and munitions made for prolonged periods of trench warfare and virtual stalemate. Victory therefore depended upon the sustained mobilization of men and resources. The war put to the test not only the effectiveness of the military machine, but the economic strength, the administrative efficiency, and ultimately the social cohesion and political stability of the combatant powers. It was a test which Tsarism failed to survive.

In direct military engagements the Russian Army was by no means humiliated. Turkey, cajoled into joining the Central Powers, was contained with little difficulty, although it proved impossible to break her blockade of the Straits. Against the ill-equipped Habsburg forces, Russia scored major victories in 1914, and although she was forced into mass retreat in 1915, the brilliant tactics of General Brusilov helped her reassert superiority in the summer of 1916. But against Germany it was a different story. The initial invasion of East Prussia, while relieving German pressure on the French, led to disastrous defeats at Tannenberg and the Masurian Lakes, and during 1915 the Russians were forced to evacuate a vast stretch of territory reaching beyond Poland into the western provinces. In 1916 a renewed offensive which followed Brusilov's success failed to save Russia's newly acquired ally, Romania, and brought further heavy defeats. By 1917, although Germany's attention turned to the west, the breakdown of the old social order in Russia ruled out further effective military action.

This failure reflected more than defeat at the hands of an inherently stronger enemy. Indeed, the *Entente* powers as a whole commanded greater resources than Germany and her allies, and on the face of it Russia's man-power reserves, industrial capacity, and agricultural output gave her every chance of holding her own on the eastern front. It is true that she suffered severely from the blockade of her major trade routes via the Baltic and Straits, but the explanation for her failure lies deeper: it lies in the very nature of her social and political structure. The post-Stolypin regime was too narrowly based and too incompetent to harness the Empire's resources effectively, and the attempt to do so brought social tension to breaking-point.

This dual political and social weakness was clearly visible within the military establishment itself. Nicholas's natural preference for well-born generals on whose loyalty he could rely filled the High Command with aged, reactionary, and unimaginative men. It was typical that before the war the old guard had insisted upon the absolute priority of the antiquated fortress system – thereby condemning a vast quantity of military hardware to redundancy and easy capture once hostilities began. During the first year of the war the Supreme Command proved quite unable to coordinate the northern and southern armies or to provide rational adjudication of their bitter competition for men and supplies. Equally serious was the chasm separating the peasant rank and file from the officers of the Imperial Army, a chasm deepened by the particularly humiliating treatment meted out to the men. The social polarization of rural Russia was imported wholesale into the army. There was no equivalent of the lower-middle-class NCO who did so much in the armies of the West to bridge the gap between upper-class officers and lower-class soldiers. The proportion of middle-ranking officers drawn from educated but non-noble backgrounds had increased significantly since the turn of the century, reaching a majority by 1914, and was to rise steeply during the war – a fact which was to play a significant part in conditioning the army's response to the Revolution of 1917. But the unyielding social prejudice of most senior officers made them very reluctant to promote able men out of the ranks, even after the first battles of the war had wiped out the bulk of the old officer corps. Moreover, instead of dissolving in the face of a common enemy, social antagonism within the army – and the navy, where a much higher proportion of working-class recruits did nothing to improve matters – became worse as the war progressed. The conscription of reluctant reservists from the older age-groups intensified resentment in the ranks. As defeat followed defeat, as the number of casualties, deaths, and prisoners taken climbed, and as the army was driven into retreat, the soldiers' sense of alienation from their officers deepened. Desertion became a serious concern, Russian POWs showed distressingly little anxiety to escape, and an atmosphere of sullen hostility bordering on insubordination became widespread. Accounts of the grim conditions at home reaching soldiers from their wives and mothers did nothing to improve morale. By the winter of 1916–17 the High Command considered large parts of the front unreliable, while in the navy, where frustration was increased by the virtual absence of action throughout the war, the tension between officers and men was even greater.

A similar pattern of government incompetence and mounting social strain unfolded in the organization of the war economy. Like its counterparts abroad, the War Ministry had grossly underrated the quantity of

6.4 Russian troops during the First World War. Inadequately fed, poorly led, and demoralized by repeated losses, large parts of the army both at the front and in garrisons at the rear became disaffected.

shells and firearms that would be required, and during 1914 and 1915 the army suffered a desperate shortage. Yet even after war broke out no Ministry of Supply was set up: the government displayed inordinate faith in a continuing flow of military imports from Britain, France, and the USA, and refused to believe that native industry could produce arms of adequate quality at a reasonable price. It was only after pressure from the military, the Duma, and industry itself that the government was persuaded to place large orders at home. The major companies responded quickly and during 1916 shell-shortage ceased to be a serious problem – but by then the army had become severely demoralized.

Moreover, quite apart from the inept and belated manner in which the munitions programme was launched, the effect of the war effort was to intensify the social instability evident before hostilities began. On the one hand, it involved massive deficit spending: neither normal revenue, which was actually reduced by a quixotic wartime ban on the sale of liquor, nor the floating of public loans could begin to finance the government's vastly increased expenditure. The result was ever-accelerating inflation: prices had quadrupled by the end of 1916. This was the perfect recipe for soaring profits by the large banks and industrial complexes to whom the government directed its military orders, and for profiteering in scarce commodities on a spectacular scale. At the same time, economic mobilization involved a hectic expansion of the urban population, already swollen by refugees from the western provinces. The industrial proletariat rose by a third during the war. What is more, growth was concentrated in large factories, particularly the strike-prone metal-working plants, and both working and living conditions deteriorated below the miserable pre-war level. Wages in most sectors came nowhere near to keeping pace with inflation, queues lengthened as shortages grew, and working-class frustration welled to the surface. A brief period of industrial peace which had followed the defeat of the eve-of-war strike and the initial distraction of war was broken in the summer of 1915. During 1916 the incidence of strikes rose sharply, especially in the capital (renamed Petrograd in tune with patriotic sentiment) where the most frantic wartime industrial expansion took place. The proportion of strikes called in support of explicitly political demands soared, especially in factories where the number of workers who had taken part in pre-war protest remained high. By the winter of 1916–17 urban Russia was on the point of explosion.

What struck most savagely at the soldiers' morale and drove the proletariat beyond the point of endurance was the shortage of food. A variety of factors contributed to the breakdown of supplies. Distribution was affected by an ill-coordinated scramble for supplies by different army sectors, by wartime strain on storage facilities, and by the major reorientation required of the railways, while shortage of agricultural machinery, fertilizer, and labour reduced output on private land. Yet the harvest on peasant land, from where the vast bulk of marketed grain came, was affected much less. Since exports virtually ceased, the Empire should have been able to feed itself adequately. It failed to do so. The fundamental problem was the withdrawal of peasant producers from the grain market. The very success of heavy industry had the effect of starving light industry, including peasant cottage industry, of raw materials. The production of manufactures for sale to the peasantry plummeted and prices spiralled upwards. This deprived the peasantry of any incentive to sell their grain – especially when middlemen ensured that the peasant producer saw a mere fraction of the retail price which grain could fetch. Rather than exchange their grain for depreciating roubles, therefore, the peasantry tended to retain their surplus product – they stored more, ate more, and expanded their livestock holdings. The result was an acute shortage in the army and the cities, as well as in traditionally grain-deficit areas of the countryside, and even where peasants had enough to eat their living standards fell. The government could do nothing. It was in no position to contemplate direct requisitioning, and its very commitment to war production precluded releasing resources again to light industry. Ministers watched helplessly as grain reserves dwindled to dangerously low levels. The announcement of imminent rationing in the capital on 19 February 1917 triggered panic buying, massive queues – and revolution.

Political developments during the war directly reflected mounting social tension. The Tsar remained as steadfastly opposed to reform as ever. This was not the mere caprice of a stupid man. It corresponded closely to the ethos of the High Command, it suited the major industrialists perfectly, and it was energetically encouraged by the United Nobility: they urged the Tsar to resist making any concessions, be it to the Duma or the democratic 'third element' of the zemstvos which might allow central or local government to pass into hostile hands. Some of Nicholas's most notorious blunders were, of course, very much his personal responsibility. In the summer of 1915, following the disastrous retreat of that year, he decided to take personal command at the front. He was motivated by his private sense of honour, by anxiety to overcome the debilitating conflict of authority between the civilian government and the High Command, and by suspicion of the ambitions of his uncle, the Grand Duke Nicholas, whom he replaced. The effect was to identify him personally with subsequent defeats and, more seriously, to increase his wife's influence over ministerial appointments and coordination. Alexandra's anxiety was by now reaching the point of hysteria, and her faith in Rasputin's spiritual and medical gifts was extended to his political judgement. 'Our friend's' support became a crucial, if expensive asset in the bewildering 'ministerial leapfrog' which overtook all the major ministries. It was at the hands of the extreme Right, in the palace of the Tsar's nephew, Prince Yusupov, that Rasputin met his end in the gruesome assassination of December 1916. When at last the combined effect of the breakdown of morale in the army and the ominous growth of the strike movement persuaded Tsarism's most loyal acolytes that Nicholas must go, his identification with Rasputin made the sacrifice easier to contemplate.

So far as liberal opinion was concerned, government incompetence soon silenced the protestations of loyalty which had greeted the outbreak of war. True, commitment to victory was not questioned, and the commercial press remained fiercely patriotic and extremely selective in its reporting of military reversals or even the munitions shortage of 1915. But exasperation grew steadily. The efforts of the professional and business classes to organize assistance for the war effort led to serious friction between them and officialdom. The newly-formed Union of Zemstvos and Union of Towns were quick to offer help in such fields as medical care for the wounded, but found ministers deeply suspicious of even semi-official organizations. Since the conservative leaders of these local government bodies tended to muffle the fierce criticisms made by the 'third element', vociferous demands began to be heard for the democratization of the zemstvos and municipalities. Similarly, Muscovite and provincial industrialists found the War Industry Committees which they set up in 1915 restricted to a very small role in organizing arms production. Even when the government did begin to place large military orders with native industry, the chief beneficiaries were the major companies with good contacts in Petrograd.

Yet the obstacles to translating widespread middle-class frustration into effective political pressure remained formidable. In mid-August 1915, it is true, a broad spectrum of opinion in the Duma was brought together in the Progressive Bloc under Miliukov's leadership. But its demands did not go beyond the call for a 'government of confidence'. Although the small Progressive Party consistently pressed for bolder opposition, Miliukov and the leadership took the view that if they were to go beyond the limits of the law, or even to insist on the old Kadet principle of a Cabinet responsible to the Duma, the effect would be to split the Bloc. Moreover, once the new armaments programme had consolidated the support of Petrograd indus-trialists for the regime and quieted unease in the High Command, the Progressive Bloc proved unable to impose its will on the Tsar. He would go no further than the removal of four particularly unpopular ministers and on 3 September 1915 simply prorogued the Duma. Instead of securing a 'minis-try of confidence' the liberals watched with horror as Rasputin's nominees began to take office in quick succession. For the next year the liberals seemed helpless.

What fatally inhibited liberal opposition was the alarming growth of working-class militancy. As before the war, figures like Guchkov and Konovalov saw the need to respond to working-class frustration before it was too late. They urged that workers be involved in the War Industry Committees, that trade-union legislation be liberalized, and that working conditions be improved, while rank-and-file Kadet sympathizers anxiously tried to establish links with the working class. But many employers, notably the major ones in the capital, were wholly unsympathetic and the rapid rise in inflation made significant increases in real wages highly improbable. This convinced the liberal leadership that there was no alternative but to support a government they despised. Miliukov was warning as early as 1915 that to risk confrontation would be to invite social upheaval, 'to play with fire'.

Towards the end of 1916, as the regime's ability to maintain order – let alone win the war – became increasingly uncertain, liberal attacks on the government regathered momentum. On 1 November Miliukov delivered a sensational speech in the Duma, punctuating a list of the government's shortcomings with the rhetorical question: 'Is this stupidity or treason?' There was talk of engineering a coup and even the grand dukes made sym-pathetic if non-committal noises. Yet until mass strikes, demonstrations, and mutiny forced their hands in February 1917, the leaders of Russia's middle classes remained paralysed by fear of explosion from below.

Throughout the war the government did its best to stamp out political expression of working-class unrest. Further restrictions were placed on labour organizations, legal socialist publications were suppressed, activists were drafted into the army, and the Bolshevik deputies in the Duma were arrested. Yet underground activity continued, and although membership of the socialist parties remained limited there was a steady flow of new recruits. Moreover, as the war dragged on, the most militant stand attracted growing support. A clear measure of the rising tide of radicalism was the fate of the workers' group on the Central War Industries Committee, which liberals hoped would provide moderate labour leadership. When elections to the group were held in the autumn of 1915, Menshevik and right-wing SR delegates who were willing to cooperate won a narrow majority, but the substantial minority of Bolsheviks and left SRs boycotted the Committee altogether. Moreover, the group's policy of coordinating working-class protest with bourgeois opposition to the regime proved unworkable. Unable to consolidate its influence by effective defence of working-class interests, the group soon found its moderate tone out of tune with mounting frustration in the capital. The group only restored its prestige when, in the winter of 1916–17, it moved sharply to the left, joined in calls for what became major strikes on 9 January, the anniversary of Bloody Sunday, and 14 February, the day on which the Duma was to reassemble, and was promptly arrested.

The growing pressure for direct confrontation with the regime was to the benefit of the Bolsheviks. They projected the clearest-cut image of revolutionary commitment. Of crucial importance was their outright opposition to the war. They were by no means alone in denouncing the war. The great majority of socialists saw it as a struggle between rival national groups of capitalists from which the proletariat and peasantry had nothing to gain, and called for peace without annexations or indemnities. Yet the question of how far to carry opposition to the war created major divisions among both the Mensheviks and the SRs, and even leading 'international-ists' such as Martov and Chernov would not take it to the point of welcoming Russia's defeat. Rank-and-file Bolsheviks, on the other hand, admitted no qualifications whatsoever to their revolutionary struggle. If defeat would hasten revolution, so be it. And their view was shared by Lenin. Interpreting the war as the product of desperate competition for markets, of a growing crisis for capitalism in its 'highest stage' – imperialism – he called for the war between nations to be turned into a civil war. He vilified the 'chauvin-ism' which had caused the leaders of the Second International to support their own governments, took a lead in urging radical socialists across the Continent to form a genuinely revolutionary and internationalist Third International, and argued quite explicitly that Russian revolutionaries should welcome Tsarism's defeat. From exile in Switzerland he could not impose his views on those leading Bolsheviks who were unable to approve outright defeatism. But the correspondence between his intransigence and that of the rank and file foreshadowed the distinctive position the Party would adopt once the Romanov regime had at last been overthrown.

Chapter 7 ....

1917

In February 1917 the pent-up frustration of workers and soldiers in Petrograd overflowed and swept away the Tsarist regime. The revolution triggered an explosion of political activity across the Empire. Representative institutions sprang up in bewildering profusion as the masses seized their political manhood. The social struggle which ensued paralysed the army and drastically reduced the level of economic activity. For eight months a Provisional Government formed by liberal and moderate socialist leaders struggled to bridle and direct the energy that had been unleashed. They failed. The aspirations of the masses could not be contained within the formulae advanced by the Mensheviks and SRs, let alone by those of the Kadets. In the countryside the peasantry took matters into their own hands. In the army and the cities mass radicalism was expressed in an upsurge of support for the Bolsheviks. By late October the Provisional Government was helpless in the face of a Bolshevik-organized uprising and the new institutions which the revolution had thrown up installed a Bolshevik government.

From the turn of the year the shortage of food and raw materials in the capital, and the swift rise in prices, had provoked wave upon wave of strikes and demonstrations. Lockouts intensified social antagonism and news of impending bread rationing created panic buying. The long queues in unusually bitter February weather generated mounting anger. On Thursday 23 February, International Women's Day, female textile workers set rolling the snowball which within a week was to overwhelm the government. Their strike quickly attracted the support of metal workers concentrated in the Vyborg District, Petrograd's most militant district. There was no central organization, but numerous socialist cells helped spread the protest and by the weekend the capital was in the grip of a general strike. White-collar workers, teachers, and students joined mass demonstrations and although Sunday 26 February saw troops open fire, the situation rapidly ran out of control.

The police force of 3,500 was hopelessly inadequate. Its roof-top snipers contributed substantially to the 2,000 casualties of the revolution, but failed to intimidate the demonstrators. From the first day the Cossacks proved unwilling even to try to quell the disturbances. Mutiny among the 160,000 soldiers garrisoned in the capital – predominantly raw recruits determined to avoid the front – sealed the fate of the regime. On Monday and Tuesday the government's forces disintegrated as soldiers ignored orders and streamed from the barracks to fraternize with delighted civilian demonstrators. The Tsar's ministers, after making the futile gesture of proroguing the Duma on Sunday, lost their nerve the following day, resigned, and called upon Nicholas to appoint a military dictatorship. The Military Governor, General Khabalov, who had at first refused to confess his helplessness to army headquarters (*Stavka*), now sent desperate messages. Reliable troops under General Ivanov were despatched towards the capital, but before they could reach it they were overtaken by political developments.

The collapse of the old authorities and the swelling tide of insurrection forced the hand of the Progressive Bloc in the Duma. Those on the left of the Bloc eagerly urged that the Duma disregard the decree of prorogation and place itself at the head of the revolution. Moderate liberals, headed by Miliukov, and members to their right were intensely reluctant to overstep the bounds of legality. But as the danger grew of a bloody confrontation between the army and the insurgents – or worse still a collapse of all social order – even M. V. Rodzianko, the Octobrist President of the Duma, was persuaded that it was imperative to create a 'respectable' focus of authority. On Monday a Provisional Committee was formed to restore order and set up a new government.

Rodzianko made desperate attempts to preserve a legal bond between the emergent Provisional Government and the monarchy. On Sunday he had urged the Tsar to appoint a ministry of confidence; by Tuesday he was recommending a ministry responsible to the Duma; two days later, on Thursday, he recognized that no government identified in any way with Nicholas could survive the anti-monarchist fever in the capital. By then the High Command headed by General Alekseev, appalled by news of the revolution spreading to Kronstadt, the Baltic Fleet, and Moscow, had arrived at the same conclusion. On Wednesday they ordered Ivanov's expedition to halt and placed their hopes in Rodzianko and the Duma Committee. The following day, Thursday 2 March, while the Tsar was laboriously making his way back from the front towards the capital, the High Command served notice that he must go. Nicholas gave way and abdicated on behalf both of himself and his son in favour of Grand Duke Michael. Despite every effort at persuasion by Miliukov, who now succeeded Rodzianko as the central figure of the embryonic Provisional Government, Michael judged anti-monarchist feeling in the capital to be running too high for him to accept the Crown. The monarchy disappeared.

What had goaded even the most reluctant Duma rebels into action was the news that a Soviet of Workers' Deputies was being established in the capital – in the Taurida Palace alongside the Duma itself. The initiative for this step was taken by predominantly Menshevik members of the socialist intelligentsia, together with the workers' group on the Central War Industries Committee on their release from prison. On Monday 27 February they formed a Provisional Executive Committee and summoned each factory and company to elect delegates for a plenary session to be held that night. The Executive Committee (EC) elected at this session was composed entirely of members of the intelligentsia, and was dominated by Menshevik and non-party socialists. But overnight the Soviet established itself as a focus for the aspirations of the workers and soldiers of the capital.

The immediate concern of the Soviet leaders was to bring order to the insurrection. A Food Supply Commission was set up to collect and, if necessary, confiscate provisions to feed the needy – and above all the soldiers. A Military Commission was charged with creating military units for use against an expected counter-revolutionary attack, and to prevent the soldiers who had taken to the streets from spreading chaos. Commissars were appointed to oversee the formation of a workers' militia which would keep order in their own districts.

With intervention from the front expected at any minute, the EC felt that speed was of the essence: and the swiftest way to brace the capital and consolidate the revolution was to cooperate with the middle classes. The Food Commission found itself drawing upon the manpower and expertise of the existing bureaucracy, while the Military Commission turned to middle-ranking officers to create the nucleus of organized units. In non-working-class areas of the city the municipal duma, meanwhile, was organizing students and professional men into their own militia, and the Soviet leadership envisaged merging the workers' militia with them. By Tuesday, therefore, the EC was already feeling its way towards an accommodation with social groups whose allegiance was to the liberal deputies of the Duma.

To the rank and file whom the EC aspired to represent, however, matters appeared in a very different light. The workers saw their militia as the most direct expression of their new-found liberty. Already they were overturning the tsarist factory order, electing factory committees to represent them, putting an end to assaults upon their dignity, manhandling and forcibly expelling those foremen and managers they most detested. To surrender their arms and subordinate themselves to the authority of the city militia would be to jeopardize the most tangible gains of the insurrection, to lose the surest guarantee against the return of harsh factory discipline and the hated Tsarist police. The EC was unable to persuade them to accept more than a nominal fusion with the middle-class units, while in practice they remained fiercely independent.

Even more vigorous was the reaction of the Petrograd soldiers to the growing influence of officers in the Military Commission. Like the workers, they saw a direct threat to their most cherished gains. Not only would the brutal discipline of the old army be restored, but they would again be liable to be sent to the front and quite possibly punished for their participation in the insurrection. There was an explosion of anger. On Wednesday 1 March some of the most politically conscious soldiers burst in upon the Soviet and in a dramatic session extracted from it the famous Order No. 1. The authority of both army officers and the Military Commission was to be severely circumscribed. Military units were to elect committees which would retain control of weapons and ensure that there was no return to the degrading conditions of the past. The election of soldiers' representatives to the Soviet was confirmed and in future all orders of the Military Commission were to be subject to the approval of the Soviet. Even the election of officers, already being implemented in some units, was not ruled out.

The enthusiasm with which workers and soldiers rallied to the Soviet suggested to some radical socialists that it was open to the Soviet leadership to establish a revolutionary government in defiance of the Duma Committee. Yet the EC refused to countenance any such idea. Many historians have interpreted this as an act of self-denial. They have pointed to the lack of confidence of the second-rank leaders thrust to the fore while the best-known leaders were still abroad or in Siberia; to the revolutionary intelligentsia's deeply ingrained distaste for state power; to the party divisions within the EC. The most popular explanation has been that the socialists were blinkered by a doctrinaire belief that, in accordance with Marx's theories, the revolution destined to overthrow Tsarism would be a bourgeois affair.

In fact, they did not need to delve into *Das Kapital* to discover that only a revolutionary government which could attract the support of the middle classes had any chance of survival. Not only would it make the revolution more readily acceptable to the provinces, but it would bring over to the side of the insurgents many army officers and bureaucrats, including those in charge of the railway and telegraph networks. In the tumultuous February days, this seemed essential. The workers and soldiers of the capital, for all their enthusiasm, were in no position to organize effective resistance to counter-revolutionary action by regular units from the front. And the EC's fear of such action was soundly based. Ivanov's expedition was halted only because the High Command was persuaded that responsible Duma politicians, firmly committed to the war effort, were gaining control of the situation. A socialist government hostile to military discipline would have been wholly unacceptable to the generals. Neither side could be sure, of course, how the rank and file at the front would react to a trial of strength in the capital. But the proclamation of a Soviet government would at the very least have plunged the country into civil war.

The dominant group on the EC, therefore, was anxious to see the immediate establishment of a liberal government drawn from the Duma. Any delay increased the risk that isolated calls for a Soviet-based socialist government would gather momentum, and that the High Command would try to crush the insurrection. Agreement was hurriedly sought with Miliukov and his colleagues. The EC urged the Duma Committee to form a provisional government which would rule on the basis of civil liberty and the early convening of a democratically elected Constituent Assembly. In their anxiety to gain the commitment of the liberals to the revolution, the Soviet leaders laid down no conditions concerning either industrial law or land reform for their support, and backed down on the immediate proclamation of a republic. So far as foreign policy was concerned, they merely warned that if the new government trumpeted commitment to outright military victory it would fan the flames of anti-war feeling. The soldiers of the capital did insist that the Provisional Government should be recognized only if it confirmed their civil liberties and undertook neither to remove their arms nor send them out of the capital. But the new Prime Minister Prince Lvov, Chairman of the Union of Zemstvos, and the Kadet-dominated Duma Committee could not fail to be relieved at how cheaply the support of the EC had been bought.

When the EC brought the agreement before the full body of the Soviet for approval, however, it was forced to change its tone. To parry left-wing criticism, the EC dwelt not on the common ground but on the distance between Soviet and Duma, and emphasized their resolution that socialist leaders would not enter the government. In the excitement of the moment Kerensky managed to blur this picture by persuading the Soviet that although he had been elected a vice-chairman of the Soviet, he should accept a post in the new Cabinet. But the dominant mood was distinctly guarded: the Soviet would act as a watch-dog over the new liberal government, ensuring that it did not deviate from the democratic programme laid down. It was this arrangement that came to be known as 'dual power'.

The veto claimed by the Petrograd Soviet was merely one facet of the new Provisional Government's unusual status. It inherited a State whose coercive powers had been sharply curtailed. As news of Petrograd's insurrection spread the provincial police force disappeared. In the cities some loyal *ad hoc* militia units were formed, but they were balanced by a workers' militia that was far more responsive to pressure from below than orders from above. Meanwhile at the front, in the garrisons at the rear and, most violently, in the fleet, unpopular officers were ousted. Those who remained found themselves engulfed by a plethora of soldiers' committees insisting upon entirely new relations between officers and men, upon humane treatment, polite forms of address, and full civil rights when off duty. Helpless to stamp out this desecration of military norms, Alekseev and the High Command had recognized by mid-March that the committees

7.1 The first session of the Soviet of Workers' and Soldiers' Deputies in the Taurida Palace, Petrograd, 1917. The sea of deputies to the Petrograd Soviet contrasts strikingly with the formality which had prevailed at meetings of the Imperial Duma in the Palace (see Illustration 6.1).

provided the best chance of maintaining at least some form of order. Yet troops could no longer be relied upon to enforce the law in the interior. Traditional authority was swiftly undermined. The bureaucracy did continue to function but the government's control over it at local level was tenuous. Within days of assuming office, Lvov hastened to replace Tsarist provincial governors, symbols of the old regime who were already being driven from office by local pressure. But the 'commissars' appointed in their place, predominantly zemstvo chairmen, commanded little popular respect and both their jurisdiction and that of the zemstvos and urban dumas – which the government hoped to see as the medium for orderly, legal change and democratization – were challenged from all sides. In most towns, a few of the more 'progressive' members of the local duma, together with liberal and socialist groups, formed 'Committees of Public Organizations' to take charge. They rapidly expanded to include representatives from left-of-centre parties and societies, as well as from the burgeoning array of garrison committees, soviets, trade unions and, in some areas, peasant organizations. Too short of money and recruits to consolidate a regular militia, even these

Committees established no more than conditional authority. Workers looked primarily to a myriad of suburban, city and regional soviets, to newly-formed trade unions, and most directly to their factory committees. These organizations were reluctant to defer to the local Committee of Public Organizations, let alone to the Provisional Government. Likewise, when news of the insurrection spread to the countryside, peasant communal assemblies and committees quickly began to voice their demands, defy the land captains and expel the police. Taxes were left unpaid and by the end of April serious rural disturbances were being reported. At every level deference gave way to rebellion – whether by parishioners against their clergy or students against their professors. Obedience to the law and government depended upon the balance of forces in each locality. However, that balance was slipping with almost unbelievable speed out of the hands of the traditional authorities and larger property owners into those of increasingly radical workers, peasants, and soldiers.

For a few weeks the implications of this dispersal of power were unclear. The overthrow of the Romanovs was very widely welcomed, there were emotional public celebrations all over the country, and expressions of enthusiastic support for the new government poured into the capital. At first most employers showed readiness to come to terms with the new order, the eight-hour day, the establishment of factory committees and the creation of conciliation chambers to adjudicate industrial disputes, and during March and April there was a sharp drop in the number of strikes. Moreover, the initial reforms announced by the Provisional Government were eminently compatible with the surge of political and organizational activity from below. All the classical liberal demands were rapidly decreed: a political amnesty and full freedom of the press, speech, association, and religion; an end to all discrimination based on class, nation, or religion; the abolition of the death penalty and the creation of a fully independent judiciary. Church and State were to be separated, local government democratized, and a Constituent Assembly, elected by universal, direct, equal, and secret franchise, summoned to resolve the country's future Constitution. Russia had become, in Lenin's words, the freest of the belligerent countries.

But the 'honeymoon' period of the revolution could not last. The government was committed to liberal principles, to the right of private ownership in land and industry, to the authority of factory management, to the hierarchical organization of the army. It faced a mounting challenge to the existing social order from workers, soldiers, and the countryside. Lvov and his colleagues hoped to avert confrontation by postponing the resolution of all contentious issues until the meeting of the Constituent Assembly, and ensuring that preparations for the Assembly were none too hasty. It was a vain hope.

The issue which precipitated an open clash was the war. It rapidly became clear after February that the manner in which the war was pursued would condition the entire development of the revolution. Among workers in the capital anti-war sentiment was intense during the insurrection. Attitudes at the front were more complex, and until the last week of March liberal-inclined officers and soldiers' delegates were able to direct fierce criticism at workers for their failure to support the war effort. But by the end of the month anti-war feeling was crystallizing at the front. Instances of fraternization with enemy troops, deliberately encouraged by German officers, multiplied. The rank and file increasingly identified calls for greater effort and more rigorous discipline with the reimposition of the arbitrary authority of officers – just as workers identified it with the authority of factory officials. The demand for rapid steps to a just peace gathered momentum, liberals were rapidly ousted by socialists on the soldiers' committees, and the front demonstratively expressed its greater faith in the Soviet than in the Provisional Government.

Within the government, meanwhile, the interdependence between the war and the social struggle had been immediately recognized. The Foreign Minister, Miliukov, took a particularly firm line. As early as 6 March he was pointing out to his colleagues that without the war 'things would fly apart'. Orderly demobilization of 7 million peasants would be an impossibility in current conditions. Hordes of peasants would pour back from the front, swamp the cities – already beset by the influx of refugees from the western provinces, by food shortage and unemployment – and immeasurably increase the threat to private land. Russia would become ungovernable. As if this were not enough to ensure the government's commitment to the war, the Allies hurried to add their own economic and moral pressure. And in any case the liberal press did its best to convince all sides that the February insurrection had been a protest not against war but against its incompetent conduct. The goals eagerly embraced in 1914, including the annexation of Constantinople, were reasserted. Miliukov lost no time in reassuring the Allies that Russia would uphold the treaties signed by the Tsar.

Miliukov's open adherence to Tsarist goals ran directly counter to popular feeling expressed in the Petrograd Soviet. On 14 March the Soviet issued a famous appeal to the world to move rapidly to a democratic peace based on renunciation by all sides of annexations and indemnities. Street demonstrations, together with direct representations from the EC, soon persuaded Miliukov's Cabinet colleagues that he would have to change the tone of his diplomacy. But he proved difficult to move, and when at last he was prevailed upon to send a statement to Allied governments broadly in line with the Soviet's appeal, he appended a covering note which went a long way to negating the statement. Uproar followed. Demonstrations marking International Labour Day (18 April) rapidly became directed at Miliukov, while middle-class and war veteran counter-demonstrations brought the capital to the brink of civil war. Peace was restored by a firm appeal from the EC. But the government had been shaken to its foundations. The Minister of War, Guchkov, resigned in despair, Miliukov withdrew, and the whole Cabinet threatened to follow suit unless the socialist leaders would throw the weight of the Soviet's popularity behind it by forming a coalition government.

The reaction of the EC to this appeal was of critical importance to the political development of the revolution. During the February insurrection the Soviet leaders, convinced internationalists though they were, had deliberately skirted the issue of foreign policy in their anxiety to see a liberal Provisional Government take office. In mid-March, they had worded the Soviet appeal for peace to satisfy both anti-war feeling and soldiers' demands for effective defence. Faced by an aggressive liberal campaign against their peace policy, Menshevik and SR supporters had then taken the issue to the rank and file at the front, winning overwhelming support for the Soviet position by the end of the month. And now, as tension mounted over Miliukov's intransigence, the EC teetered on the brink of mounting a mass peace campaign. Bolsheviks, left SRs, and non-party socialists on the EC urged that the power of the bourgeoisie should be broken, the way cleared for a Soviet-based government, and the class struggle carried across the frontier to the other belligerent powers.

It was at this point that the fragile unity of the EC was decisively split. The majority, rallied by I. G. Tsereteli, a dynamic and charismatic leading Menshevik just back from exile in Siberia, rejected an unrestrained campaign for peace. The Soviet, in their view, was no longer at liberty to ignore the needs of defence. Its very success in undermining the authority of the liberal Provisional Government and winning the allegiance of workers and soldiers had saddled it with immediate responsibility for the front. This left it with only two realistic courses of action. The first was to sign a separate peace with Germany. This no party was willing to contemplate. It would mean surrendering vast tracts of Russian soil to the Kaiser, greatly enhancing the prospect of continental hegemony for the reactionary German regime, and cutting the ground from under the feet of the Left in Germany. It also seemed a recipe for a civil war in which counter-revolution would be able to make full use of patriotic demagogy. The alternative was to accept that Russia must be defended while pressure was exerted on all the belligerent powers for a general democratic peace.

Once they had adopted this policy of 'revolutionary defencism', the Soviet leaders found it impossible to refuse the Provisional Government's request for coalition. To drive the liberals from office would be to place in jeopardy the cooperation not only of officers, industrialists, and bureaucrats, of zemstvo and municipal duma officials, but quite possibly of the Allies as well. The front would collapse and a separate peace become unavoidable. On these grounds, on 5 May, six socialists, led by Tsereteli and Chernov, entered a coalition Cabinet.

Tsereteli and his colleagues took the step with misgivings but also with hope. They were well aware that they would now be identified with the performance of a government led by liberals. They knew that those who opposed coalition, led by Bolsheviks and radical Mensheviks and SRs, would be at liberty to articulate – and indeed stimulate – impatience for peace and social transformation. The influence over mass opinion which the moderate socialists had hitherto enjoyed was now at risk. But they were buoyed up by the relative industrial harmony of the first weeks after February; by support for their decision from the great majority in the EC, the Soviet plenum, and the first All-Russian Congress of Soviets which met at the beginning of June; by their own apparently overwhelming popularity among workers, peasants and soldiers; and by confidence that they would be able to give a much more radical hue to government handling of labour relations, economic regulation, land reform and the search for peace.

The new coalition pursued two lines in its search for peace. Working through the Soviet, the Mensheviks and SRs tried to organize an international socialist conference in Stockholm, designed to rally anti-war feeling in all countries. They gained some encouragement from parallel efforts by Dutch and Scandinavian socialists, and socialist leaders in Britain and France expressed broad support. But no major Western party was willing to accept that the conference's decisions should be binding on all participants; the French were adamant that German war guilt be recognized; and the Western socialists ruled out participation by the German Majority Socialists. Moreover, the French, Italian, and US governments refused passports to their delegations, and though Soviet efforts continued, by June the prospects of success looked bleak.

Meanwhile, M. I. Tereshchenko, the non-party liberal who had succeeded Miliukov as Foreign Minister, proposed to the Allies that they revise their war aims to bring them closer to the principles enunciated by the Soviet. Although at first the Western governments were anxious not to provoke Russian resentment, the proposal held little attraction for them. They too were conscious of growing war-weariness, but to renounce the glittering prizes of victory seemed a poor method of raising morale. Moreover, the USA's entry into the war in April increased Western confidence in ultimate victory. By early June, therefore, Tereshchenko's efforts had been reduced to an informal invitation to an inter-Allied conference at an indeterminate date with no fixed agenda. It did not help that Tereshchenko himself remained obdurately optimistic about Russia's military recovery; that his own commitment to a compromise peace was at best lukewarm; that he never explicitly renounced Russia's territorial claims; and that Foreign Ministry officials, both at home and abroad, subtly distanced the Provisional Government from the more earnest efforts of the Soviet. But the essence of the matter was that Russia's diplomatic leverage was simply inadequate for the task.

As this fact was borne in upon them, the moderate socialist leaders found it impossible to resist liberal and conservative calls for a new military offensive. They were aware of right-wing hopes that the reimposition of officers' authority would transform the political balance, and that they themselves would be ever more closely identified in the popular mind with the grim implications of a renewed war effort. But there seemed no way out. They could not afford a breach with their coalition partners over the issue. And they were persuaded that only by restoring Russia's military prestige could her diplomatic leverage be increased.

During May and June a propaganda drive was mounted to mobilize mass support for an attack on German positions. It was spearheaded by the inspiring oratory of Kerensky, now Minister of War, and the greatest enthusiasm came from the Right and the commercial press, but the Mensheviks and SRs were fully committed. The peasantry were enjoined to await with patience the convening of a Constituent Assembly – repeatedly postponed and ultimately convened in January 1918 – which would undertake land-reform. Workers were implored to restrain their wage demands, obey management, and increase production to support the front. In the army defencists on the soldiers' committees did all they could to raise morale, restore discipline, and brace the troops for renewed hostilities. The moderate socialists, in short, invested their influence and prestige in the effort to tame mass radicalism.

For many lifelong socialists, of course, it went against the grain to condemn peasant land-seizures, reject the wage claims of workers employed in the state sector, and, in July, tolerate the reintroduction of the death penalty for military insubordination. The coalition was repeatedly disrupted by tension between its partners and when it broke down altogether in July and again at the end of August, only with the greatest of difficulty was a new Cabinet formed. Following each rupture the moderate socialists were subjected to ever greater pressure to repudiate the coalition and take power for themselves. Each time they refused. And instead of deflecting the masses from their goals, the effect was to alienate support from the Mensheviks and SRs and to drive soldiers, workers, and peasants to seek alternative paths to the same goals.

In the case of the armed forces the very effort to restore discipline and launch the offensive was enough to provoke vigorous resistance in the most radical north-western sections of the front – and in the Baltic fleet. Elsewhere, the ignominious collapse of the offensive in the first week of July – itself in large part the consequence of low morale – led in the same direction. Right across the front the influence of moderate socialists went into steep decline. The men began to look for representatives more in tune with their own hatred for traditional authority and their heartfelt war-weariness. During September the army began to disintegrate altogether as officers saw the last shreds of their authority disappear. Bolshevik agitators found a

7.2   The Russian army, 1917: soldiers at the front demonstrate against the war and for radical social change.

dramatic upsurge in support for their demand for a government which would bring peace.

Among workers, too, moderate socialists saw their commitment to the coalition rapidly erode their position. For the workers the central goal was to raise living standards, guarantee employment, and improve working conditions – above all by reducing the working day to eight hours. The revolution seemed to make all this possible. Through factory committees, trade unions, workers' militia and newly legalized strike action direct pressure now could be and was brought to bear upon employers.

Yet the upsurge in working-class activity and aspirations coincided with a catastrophic downward spiral of the economy. The incipient trade breakdown which had helped to spark the Petrograd insurrection greatly accelerated after February. The railways, already severely dislocated by the needs of the army, began to give way altogether amidst the disruption of 1917, and the number of locomotives in working order dropped precipitately. This exacerbated the growing shortage of fuel and raw materials, thereby compelling manufacturers to cut output, lay off labour, and even shut down altogether. The scarcity and high cost of manufactures further reduced the incentive for peasants to market their produce: there was too little to buy with the roubles it fetched. Food shortage in the grain-short areas in general and the cities in particular became progressively more acute and, with the harvest in 1917 well below standard, the situation steadily deteriorated.

Nor was there much that the government could do to improve matters. In administrative terms it was poorly equipped to adopt the far-reaching programme of state-regulation urged by Menshevik economists. In any case, liberal ministers were susceptible to fierce, if ill-coordinated, pressure from industrialists against such intervention, and specifically against controls on the price of manufactures. This, in turn, vitiated repeated efforts to fix the price of grain and eventually drove the government to make forlorn attempts at forced requisitioning from the countryside. As long as the war continued it was committed to channelling resources not towards meeting the aspirations of workers but to supply the army. Moreover, the administrative disruption of the revolution, together with the economic decline, had drastically reduced tax receipts. Lobbying by industrialists helped frustrate proposals for a steep increase in direct taxation, and attempts to float 'liberty loans' fell flat. The only course open was massive deficit spending. Between February and October the money supply doubled, fuelling steep price rises.

In these conditions confrontation between employers and employees became ever more inflamed. Even with the best will in the world, the management of many smaller enterprises would have found it impossible to maintain the level of production and the size of the work-force, or to carry the additional expense of the eight-hour day. All too often, in fact, the will was lacking. From early summer, many larger Petrograd employers made blatant use of the lockout to bring workers to heel and through the press loudly broadcast their resentment against working-class presumption. On the workers' side, after the relative harmony and low level of strike action in the spring, straightforward economic goals gradually merged with more radical challenges to the authority of management. Initially strikes were concentrated among the skilled, relatively highly paid workers who were best placed to wring concessions from employers. As shortages and frustration grew, the strike movement embraced factories where workers had much less bargaining power. When the inflationary spiral made it futile to chase money-wages which lost their value as soon as they had been obtained, and factory closures began to swell the ranks of the unemployed, workers turned to more extreme measures. Factory committees asserted the right to verify employers' claims that raw materials could not be procured, that production must be run down, that workers must be laid off, and encroached further and further onto the sphere of management. The initial emphasis on issues concerning workers' dignity and wage rates was caught up in defensive action to keep the plant open and ultimately led in some

161

cases to factory committees replacing management altogether. The common ordeal, suffered during months of feverish political agitation and organization, greatly intensified class consciousness, not only among traditionally militant sections of the working class but also among the less skilled and uneducated sections. Demand for the 'kopeck' dailies collapsed and workers turned instead to the class analyses offered by the soviet and socialist press. Increasingly, they directed their demands to the government itself – to halt speculation, arrest profiteers, punish hoarding, control prices, ban lockouts, and support factory committees and trade unions against employers' sanctions. Mensheviks and SRs – activists and leaders alike – found their appeals in the name of the country's economy and defence falling on deaf ears. As summer wore on, the workers, like the soldiers, demanded with growing impatience a government responsive to their immediate needs.

An analogous process was taking place in the countryside. As it became clear that the local authorities could no longer rely upon troops to intervene, peasants began to satisfy their age-old land-hunger. As early as May, unrest in areas where there was significant private landholding had reached serious proportions. Apart from a brief decline during harvest, peasant disturbances became ever more widespread and, from September, increasingly violent. Besides seizing land, groups of peasants helped themselves to the timber, the livestock, the machinery, and the crops of private estates.

There could be no common language between this sort of radicalism and the leisurely approach to the land question adopted by the first Provisional Government. Lvov and his colleagues were more willing to envisage drastic land-reform than liberals anywhere else in Europe, but they were determined that it should be orderly, that private landowners should be duly compensated, and that action should be delayed until the Constituent Assembly met. A hasty solution would further disrupt agriculture at a time of critical food shortage. Worse still, it would greatly stimulate political agitation at the front and distract the attention of the peasant army from its military task. They would go no further, therefore, than setting up a hierarchy of Land Committees to gather information for eventual use by the Constituent Assembly and to place the zemstvos on a fully democratic basis. Meanwhile, they sanctioned the use of force to quell agrarian disturbances.

On the face of it, the coalition formed in May and embracing the SR Party had a much better chance of finding common ground with the peasantry. It was with the SRs that politically conscious peasants identified, and SR activists had already taken the lead in forming peasant soviets at provincial, district, and sometimes village level. Yet a serious breach soon became evident between the priorities of peasants and those of the revolutionary institutions claiming to represent them. Not least because of widespread peasant illiteracy, soviets above village level tended to be dominated by members of the provincial intelligentsia. Even when they were deeply sympathetic to the immediate claims of villagers, their attitude was coloured by concerns which the peasantry did not share. In early May an All-Russian Congress of Peasant Soviets faithfully endorsed the peasant demand for the abolition of private landownership without compensation, but at the same time it insisted that this be brought about by legal means and condemned arbitrary seizures. The SRs might support a much more radical final solution of the land problem than their liberal allies, but they too urged that the problem be resolved by the Constituent Assembly.

The predicament into which this led the Party was epitomized by the ordeal of Chernov, their immensely popular leader, who was Minister of Agriculture from May to August. The outstanding theorist of 'peasant socialism', he was anxious that his elevation should mark a tangible step in that direction. He earnestly wished to radicalize government policy. Moreover, he saw a direct connection between peasant impatience with the status quo and the failure of the government's local food committees to persuade the peasantry to yield up their surplus grain. If the government would respond to peasant demands, he believed, the peasantry would be more likely to cooperate over grain supply. Local land committees, which in places were merging with village assemblies and peasant committees, must be legally empowered to supervise the use of private land. Efforts by private landowners to forestall confiscation by selling or dividing their land must be halted. Yet when he issued instructions to this effect he met obstruction from senior officials in the Ministry, and the Cabinet refused to back him.

Chernov's failure owed something to his own indecisiveness and lack of aptitude for administrative detail. But having accepted the premise of coalition, the need to continue the war and maintain the alliance with the liberals, he had little room for manoeuvre. Kadet insistence that landowners be compensated and that the issue be referred to the Constituent Assembly became more rather than less intense as their alarm at mass radicalism grew: they reaffirmed the principle at four successive party congresses during 1917. Chernov's efforts, therefore, were denounced as wholly irresponsible by Lvov and underlay the decision of the Kadet ministers to resign from the first coalition on 2 July. Yet he had not done nearly enough to keep government policy in line with the growing impatience of the village. During the late summer the distance between the SR leadership and the rural masses steadily widened. This did not open the way to a rapid spread of Bolshevik support among the peasants. Unlike soldiers and workers, they were not driven to replace the coalition but simply to emasculate its power in rural areas. Their aspirations could be served as well by an absence of government as by an alternative regime. But local SR activists found that their prestige evaporated if they tried to restrain the peasantry.

The moderate socialists' optimism about cooperation between privileged society and the masses, in short, proved misplaced. They exaggerated

the significance of compromise between political leaders in a situation of acute socioeconomic strife and social polarization in which state power was at a minimum. They underrated employers' resentment against labour's demands, the intensity of officers' frustration with the breakdown of traditional military discipline, and the depth of hostility, both within and outside the Cabinet, to Chernov's efforts at land-reform. Even more significantly, they underestimated the impatience of the peasantry, the determination of soldiers not to go on the offensive again, and the pressures radicalizing workers. Their understanding of the mass mood tended to be based on the upper echelons of the various popular representative hierarchies. They looked to the All-Russian Congress rather than to local soviets, to the Petrograd Soviet rather than to district soviets in the capital, to the trade unions rather than the factory committees, to the provincial land committees rather than village assemblies, to conferences of soldiers' committees rather than to those closest to the rank and file. In each case, the higher-level bodies tended to be less sensitive to popular opinion than lower ones. Elections to them were less frequent, and more of their membership tended to be drawn from the intelligentsia – be it radical journalists, village teachers, or junior officers – at one remove from the mass constituency. The supreme expression of this tendency was the gulf that opened out between the moderate-socialist dominated Central Executive Committee of the All-Russian Congress of Soviets elected in June and popular opinion in factories, trenches and villages.

Social polarization was accompanied by an upsurge in nationalist agitation. The collapse of traditional authority, together with severe economic disruption and competition for grain, inflamed relations between Great Russians and the minorities, and between one minority group and another. It stimulated demands for varying degrees of autonomy all around the periphery, from the Baltic to the Caucasus. In both Finland and Poland most parties were quick to call for outright independence, and organizations claiming cultural and some political autonomy soon sprang up in the Muslim regions as well. Most disruptive was the intransigence of the Ukrainian *Rada*, established in March: initially espousing the cultural interests of Ukrainians, it rapidly aspired to self-government. The proximity of the Ukraine to the front, and its immense economic value, made the issue particularly sensitive. It was concessions made to the *Rada* by Kerensky, Tereshchenko and Tsereteli that finally triggered the Kadet resignations from the first coalition. The interaction of demands for autonomy and independence with the party and social struggles was highly complex. It created the strangest political alliances. At different moments Left and Right, socialists as well as conservatives and liberals, appealed to minority nationalist

---

7.3 Kerensky, Minister of War at the time of the June offensive, was Prime Minister from July 1917, when this photograph was taken.

Map 8   The Eastern front and minority nationalism

sentiment. The far Left found in it a powerful weapon with which to berate the Provisional Government. Right-wing nationalists saw in it a rallying cry with which to check social upheaval and distance their national enclave from the revolutionary vortex of Petrograd. The nationality problem bemused politicians in the capital and defies summary treatment. It is a mistake to argue, as has sometimes been done, that the Russian Revolution owed as much to national as to class conflict. But its impact was important. It accelerated the collapse of Petrograd's authority, it fragmented the middle-class constituency of the Kadets, and it provided further ammunition for radical criticism of the moderate socialist parties.

It is in this context of social polarization that the blossoming of the Bolshevik Party is to be understood. The Party established itself as the major vehicle for opposition against the policies of the coalition partners. Its competitors on the far Left were severely handicapped: the anarchists lacked even a rudimentary national network, and it was with difficulty that radical Mensheviks and left SRs distanced themselves from the main body of their respective parties. The Bolsheviks themselves, despite their independent record in the period since 1905, took time to project a distinctive image. Until April even the Petersburg Committee and the editors of *Pravda* in the capital adopted a position of conditional support for the Provisional Government which differed little from that of the other socialist parties; not until June could workers in Moscow clearly differentiate between Bolsheviks and Mensheviks; even by October they had not done so in the countryside or in many provincial cities. But from the first days of the revolution Bolshevik voices had been loudest among those on the extreme Left. The Party's committee in the militant Vyborg District had been vociferous in calling for a Soviet-based government the moment the Tsar's regime collapsed. Bolshevik activists and middle-ranking officials were already pushing the Party towards outright opposition before Lenin's dramatic return from exile on 3 April.

Lenin lost no time in confounding party moderates by denouncing 'revolutionary defencism' as tantamount to support for a 'predatory imperialist war'.[1] He called for a revolutionary government based on the soviets and empowered to control the banks, production, and distribution. He demanded the confiscation of all private estates, the nationalization of the land, and its management by local peasant soviets. Opposed by the Central Committee of the Party, he appealed over their heads to rank-and-file militants and took by storm the Party Conference at the end of April. His 'April Theses' became official party policy, and to underline the total breach with the Mensheviks he recommended that the Party cease to be called 'Social-Democratic' and adopt the title of 'Communist' (as it did after October).

Lenin's programme was attacked by moderate socialists as irresponsible demagogy. In rejecting revolutionary defencism while refusing to admit that the only alternative was a separate peace, he was shirking the issue. In pronouncing the bourgeois stage of the revolution over, he was recklessly urging the proletariat along a path which ignored their limited numbers and

---

[1] V. I. Lenin, *Collected Works* (London & Moscow 1960–78), XXIV, pp. 21–5.

the backwardness of the economy. He was flouting the fundamental tenets of Marxism – as a scandalized Menshevik exclaimed, he was claiming a throne left vacant for thirty years: the anarchist throne of Bakunin. His programme would guarantee the triumph of counter-revolution. Kerensky, on hearing of what he took to be Lenin's ravings, longed to explain the situation to this poor exile who had obviously lost touch with reality.

Yet Lenin's self-confidence was boundless. Class analysis, he believed, rather than fine phrases and noble intentions, revealed the alternatives facing Russia. No matter how sincere Tsereteli, Chernov, and the other socialist coalition ministers might be, they had become enmeshed in the net of Russian capitalism. The workers of other belligerent countries rightly saw their 'defencism' as a mere veil for the imperialist ambitions of their bourgeois masters. Western workers would only trust and respond to appeals for peace made by a revolutionary government which was engaged in smashing capitalism at home. Moreover, Menshevik fears that a proletarian-led government would be swept away failed to take into account the role of the peasantry: peasant land-hunger guaranteed their revolutionary commitment. And though Lenin admitted that the economy was too backward to make the introduction of socialism an immediate task, the revolution brewing in Germany and France promised massive aid from a socialist Europe.

Lenin's rationale might be beyond most workers and soldiers but his programme was not. It was disseminated in crisp, clear, and hard-hitting propaganda. With the help of energetic agitation, highly effective mass oratory, and a burgeoning party press, Bolshevism occupied the ground towards which growing numbers of workers, soldiers, and peasants were being drawn by the frustrations – and the liberation – of 1917. This, rather than the funds apparently channelled to the Bolsheviks by the German government to destabilize Russia, or any unique brand of party organization, accounts for its success. Indeed, the Party had never conformed less closely to the highly centralized, tightly-knit model envisaged by Lenin in *What Is To Be Done?* For all his prestige, Lenin himself was in no position to impose policy upon the Party. Each major turning-point in the Party's orientation and strategy was fiercely debated by members at every level. A crucial condition for his success in pushing more cautious colleagues on the Central Committee to the left was that the Party's democratic processes, internal elections and numerous local, regional and national conferences mounted during the year gave voice to rank-and-file pressure moving in the same direction. Moreover, although a complex hierarchy of committees quickly took shape, formal policy directives from the centre were followed only in so far as they corresponded to local Bolshevik opinion; the very speed with which membership soared and cells sprang up ruled out close central supervision; and amidst the disruption of the railways and postal services communication between different areas was haphazard. What gave the Party its mass following and developed its strong *esprit de corps* was not its structure but its credibility as the medium for swift and profound socio-political transformation.

The bulk of the Party's new membership was drawn from the industrial proletariat. Progress was most dramatic where confrontation with employers was direct. It was symptomatic that Bolsheviks dominated factory committees long before they ousted the moderate socialist leadership from the trade unions and that they captured local district soviets in the capital long before they gained a majority in the Petrograd Soviet itself. Accurate membership figures are unavailable, but according to the most plausible recent estimate the total rose from about 10,000 in February to some 250,000 or even 300,000 by October. The rate of growth was most impressive in the Petrograd area, where the Party benefited from the feverish atmosphere in the capital, the concentration of seasoned activists, and the large number of Mensheviks converted during the year. The adhesion of Trotsky and the radical 'inter-district' faction in July was an additional bonus. The less polarized social structure of Moscow sustained moderate socialist influence rather longer. But by the summer the Bolsheviks were making rapid inroads in major cities and industrial complexes across the country. And as Menshevik and SR influence declined in both army and navy, Bolshevik cells mushroomed there too and the Party developed a whole network of Military Organizations. Much less impact was made upon the peasantry, whose goals could be achieved by direct action at village level, regardless of the party struggle and the policy of the government. The same was not true for workers and soldiers. The ill-defined relations between the variety of newly created working-class institutions placed a premium on the coordinating role of the Party. Above all, the struggle against employers and for food and raw materials could only be resolved in their favour with the aid of government action, and the State alone could end the war. The Bolshevik Party and programme offered a solution.

It was against this background of rapid, though uneven, radicalization of the masses that the struggle for political power unfolded. As early as June Lenin felt sufficiently confident to tell the first All-Russian Congress of Soviets that his party was willing to take state power alone. Tsereteli and his colleagues, whose control of the Petrograd Soviet and the newly expanded Central Executive Committee of the Congress was in the process of being confirmed, scorned the boast. Yet within days their laughter turned to alarm. The Bolsheviks summoned a demonstration against the coalition for 10 June and only backed down at the last minute when the Soviet majority imposed a three-day ban on all demonstrations. The efforts of the moderate socialists to mount a counter-demonstration a week later were disastrous. Instead of protesting their loyalty to the Provisional Government, the Petrograd workers and soldiers who chose to come out chanted Bolshevik slogans – 'Down with the ten capitalist ministers' and 'All power to the Soviets'. The commencement of the June offensive raised temperatures further: sailors at Kronstadt suspected imminent reimposition of traditional discipline; the Petrograd garrison foresaw their own despatch to the front; and workers struggling for pay rises could see nothing but endless appeals for patriotic patience. The Kadets chose 2 July on which to resign from the coalition, and the following two days witnessed massive armed demonstrations outside the Soviets' Taurida Palace demanding a government based solely on the Soviets.

The July rising was actively encouraged by middle-ranking Bolsheviks, especially from the Party's Military Organizations, as well as by anarchist agitators. But the Bolshevik Central Committee hesitated to commit itself to an outright attempt to overthrow the government. Lenin adopted a 'wait and see' attitude: he neither dissociated himself from the demonstrations nor offered a concrete plan for the seizure of power. This left the demonstrators leaderless. Their intense frustration is captured in a famous scene on the afternoon of 4 July, recorded in the memoirs of Miliukov and those of N. N. Sukhanov, a leading non-party radical in the Soviet. The Soviet leaders sent Chernov out to calm the hostile crowd surrounding the Taurida Palace. But his attempts to explain the attitude of the moderate socialists was met by angry heckling and the furious cry: 'Take power, you son-of-a-bitch, it is being handed to you on a plate.' And when Trotsky, who had publicly endorsed the demand for Soviet power, came to the rescue, he too barely escaped lynching. Yet, without a definite strategy, the demonstration began to lose momentum. By nightfall the crowd was drifting away. At this point the appeals for help from the moderate socialists were at last answered.

In a matter of hours the balance swung against the insurgents. Regiments which until then had remained neutral marched to relieve the Taurida Palace. They were swayed by news that the Soviet leadership had summoned loyal troops from the front, and by growing evidence that the political struggle was degenerating into random street violence. Most serious from the Bolshevik point of view was the sudden credence given to the rumour, which had begun to circulate long before, that Lenin was in the pay of the Germans. The Bolshevik leader, it was pointed out, had travelled from Switzerland to Petrograd by leave of the German High Command; his Party had chosen to undermine revolutionary unity at a critical moment for the Russian offensive; and now word had it that the Ministry of Justice had discovered hard evidence of Lenin's treason. The following day loyalist forces were in control of the situation and the Bolsheviks hastily called off further demonstrations for the time being.

At the time the July rising appeared a major disaster for the Bolsheviks. They seemed to have overreached themselves. The failure of attempted risings in Moscow and elsewhere, and the arrival of loyal troops from the front, vindicated Menshevik and SR insistence that the mood of Petrograd was out of line with the rest of the country. The Soviet newspaper

7.4   The July uprising, Petrograd, 1917. Demonstrators scatter as they come under fire on Nevsky Prospekt, the city's main street.

Izvestiia denounced the irresponsible behaviour of the Bolsheviks and the liberal press blazed against their deliberate treachery. *Pravda* was closed, a number of arrests made – including that of Trotsky – and Lenin was driven into hiding. The Party's influence in the Petrograd garrison plummeted and for a time even the most radical sections of the capital's working class were seriously demoralized.

At the other end of the political spectrum, the débâcle gave a major fillip to liberals and anti-socialists. They took delight in a massive funeral procession in honour of the victims of the July Days – a procession from which workers were notably absent. It was symptomatic of a new stridency that the commercial press now reversed its longstanding refusal to accept the label 'bourgeois' and adopted it with pride. The leading dailies resolutely insisted that the war could be won and that it must take absolute priority over all other issues. Leading industrialists in Petrograd and Moscow became markedly more belligerent in their demands for a restoration of labour discipline. The Orthodox hierarchy, busily organizing a church council to undertake reforms and re-establish the Patriarchate, became more outspoken in its attacks upon the Left. The High Command insisted on measures to restore order in the army, including the reintroduction of the death penalty at the front. Even the dormant Provisional Committee of the Duma showed renewed signs of life. Miliukov foresaw an all-liberal government in the not-too-distant future, and groups to his right began to coordinate support for a military dictatorship.

These developments paralysed the moderate socialists. They clung to the hope that the explosion in the capital was untypical, the product of Bolshevik demagoguery. They persuaded themselves that if they could still find common ground with liberal politicians, then cooperation between responsible workers, soldiers and peasants and 'progressive sections of the bourgeoisie' was still possible. And they remained convinced that for the government to lurch either to the left or to the right would precipitate immediate civil war and the triumph of counter-revolution. While denouncing the Bolsheviks, therefore, they refused to sanction full-scale repression of the Party. And they reaffirmed their commitment to the policies of revolutionary defence and coalition – policies which were now doomed. By the second week in July the objective of revolutionary defence – an early general peace – had disappeared beyond the realm of possibility. The offensive had collapsed and the army was in retreat. Russia was deprived of all diplomatic leverage, the Allies treated her overtures with open contempt, and the Stockholm initiative was hopelessly stalled. At the same time the social struggle continued to intensify, rendering cooperation at government level less and less meaningful.

The moderate socialists did succeed in piecing together a new coalition Cabinet, headed by Kerensky, though only by tacitly conceding that it would resist further pressure from below. Chernov remained at the Ministry of Agriculture, but he was an isolated and helpless figure. Left-wing Mensheviks under Martov denounced this compromise, while the left SRs drew further and further away from the official leadership of their party. By the beginning of August both parties were reporting a serious decline in their popularity and renewed Bolshevik advances. Nor did the participation of the Kadets in the Cabinet do anything to restrain the pressure for drastic action by right-wing elements outside the government.

On 12 August Kerensky staged a 'State Conference' at the Bolshoi Theatre in Moscow to rally support for the government. It was a fiasco. The Bolsheviks, despite opposition from moderate socialists still in control of the Moscow Soviet, organized a successful protest strike, and the Party boycotted the proceedings altogether. It was middle-class organizations and parties which dominated the Conference, and their enthusiasm was reserved not for Kerensky's hysterical appeals for loyalty but for the new Supreme Commander, General Kornilov. Encouraged by business and officer organizations, Kornilov was by now insisting that the government take firm steps to restore discipline in the army, and quell disorder at home. Kerensky, despite his distaste for force, felt himself impelled in the same direction. On 21 August the port of Riga fell to German troops: the net seemed to be closing in on the capital itself. Economic decline continued unchecked. The only hope seemed to lie in a government which had not only nominal emergency powers but effective means of coercion. Since every step designed to create such means – notably the reintroduction of the death penalty in the army – provoked furious protest, the Premier and the General edged ever closer towards taking military action to suppress working-class institutions and impose martial law on the capital.

The upshot was the abortive Kornilov coup at the end of August. At the last moment Kerensky tried to dissociate himself from the coup, realizing that he would be eminently dispensable once the Right was in control. He denounced Kornilov, gained a free hand from his ministerial colleagues to reconstruct the Cabinet, and called upon the Soviet to help defend the capital against counter-revolution. The response was immediate. Garrison troops, sailors from Kronstadt, and armed workers, organized as much under Bolshevik Party auspices as those of the official Soviet leadership, moved quickly to head off the force despatched by Kornilov. Railway workers halted the troop trains and when the men discovered the purpose for which they were being sent into action, they abandoned their officers. Kornilov was arrested and the long-awaited counter-revolution collapsed in ignominy.

Kerensky's equivocal role in the prelude to the Kornilov affair irreparably damaged his popular image. Workers and soldiers were now all but unanimous in calling for 'All power to the Soviets'. Yet still the moderate socialists would go no further than rejecting cooperation with the Kadets, and Tsereteli considered even that an unnecessarily indiscriminate prohibition. Eventually, on 27 September, when a Democratic Conference summoned to resolve the membership of the new government failed to reach agreement, Kerensky was allowed to form a Cabinet in which Kadets were included. The Menshevik and SR leadership, severely disorientated by the precipitate decline in their support, and painfully conscious that to turn to the left now would mean surrendering the initiative to the Bolsheviks, could not agree upon any major reappraisal of their policies. For their part the Kadets, unable to see any hope of containing social upheaval without military victory, and egged on by a commercial press adamant that Germany could not hold out much longer, refused to come to terms with the fact that the army was disintegrating. The government drifted to its ruin.

For the Bolsheviks, on the other hand, the Kornilov *putsch* had provided a major boost. The Party's prestige soared, the disgrace of July was forgotten, Trotsky and the other party members arrested after the July Days were released. The Petrograd Soviet immediately endorsed the call by their spokesman, L. B. Kamenev, for an exclusively socialist government. By 9 September they were able to carry a vote to alter the method by which the Presidium was elected. On 25 September Trotsky became president and the Bolsheviks were in control. They gained a majority in the Moscow Soviet too, and soviet and local elections throughout urban Russia reflected a strong tide flowing in their favour. The moderate socialist leaders were driven back into their stronghold on the Central Executive Committee which had been elected by the Congress of Soviets convened in June. To dislodge them the Bolsheviks successfully insisted on the summoning of a second congress. There could be no doubt that when it met, on 25 October, it would endorse the creation of a purely socialist government committed to a radical solution of the problems of peace, land, and the urban economy.

Bolshevik strategy crystallized in the aftermath of the Kornilov affair. Lenin, watching events unfold from Finland, had decided by mid-September that the time had come to make a direct armed bid for power. The collapse of the army, the surge of peasant violence, and the dramatic advance in Bolshevik popularity convinced him that to delay, to wait even for the new Soviet Congress, was unnecessary, indeed dangerous. Now the Right was demoralized, the government helpless. Should Petrograd fall to the Germans or a separate peace be signed, the situation could suddenly alter. From 14 September, therefore, he bombarded the Central Committee with demands for an immediate seizure of power, even proffering his resignation to force the issue. Two of his leading lieutenants, Kamenev and G. E. Zinoviev, vigorously opposed him, arguing that a rising would place the Party in a perilously exposed and isolated position, and urging that instead recent gains should be consolidated in preparation for the forthcoming Constituent Assembly elections. The Central Committee majority, however, not least because of pressure from middle-ranking party bodies, were gradually won round to Lenin's view. The commitment to an armed rising was carried on 10 October and reaffirmed on 16 October.

To take the strategic decision in favour of an armed uprising was one thing, to decide how it was to be implemented another. As we have seen, the Party was no streamlined, military-style machine, and, for all its popular support, the force at its command should not be exaggerated. True, the call to arms at the time of the Kornilov affair had greatly strengthened the workers' militia and detachments of 'Red Guards', and the Bolshevik role in defeating Kornilov had enhanced the Party's influence among them and helped to restore the prestige of the Party's Military Organization in the garrison. Yet the armed workers' bands remained fiercely jealous of their independence, Bolshevik members were still in the minority, and the energetic efforts which the Party's central organs had recently initiated to coordinate and assert control over them had made limited progress. Equally, the Party's network of cells in the army was patchy and fragmented, and, despite their strong links with militant regiments in the capital and with the sailors in the Baltic Fleet, the leaders of the Party's Military Organization warned Lenin that they could not assemble sufficient force before the Soviet Congress was due to meet. More generally, soundings among workers and garrison soldiers suggested that support for a rising in the name of the Bolshevik Party as such would be distinctly limited and lukewarm. A massive response could confidently be expected, on the other hand, if the Provisional Government were either to move against the Petrograd Soviet or to attempt to prevent the Second Congress of Soviets from meeting. Lenin was persuaded to accept the majority view, most clearly articulated by Trotsky, that the Party's tactics must be adapted accordingly. First, the rising was to be made to appear defensive, a response to government threats to the Left. Second, instead of seeking to overthrow Kerensky through the agencies of the Party, they were to work through those of the Petrograd Soviet. Third, since a premature move might enable the Central Executive Committee to summon help from the front, and even the Petrograd garrison would be confused by a conflict between Soviet and Party, action was to be timed to coincide with the convening of the Soviet Congress.

In the event, the strategies of Lenin and Trotsky dovetailed. Efforts by the government to send the most radical units out of Petrograd aroused acute suspicion among the garrison troops, as did rumours that Kerensky intended to abandon the capital to the Germans. On 9 October, therefore, the Petrograd Soviet voted to set up a Military Revolutionary Committee (MRC) to coordinate measures to prevent a second right-wing *putsch*. The MRC had a substantial left SR membership but was dominated by Bolsheviks. The Party's Central Committee, situated like the MRC in the Smolny Institute, home of the Petrograd Soviet since August, was in direct contact with it. Thus the MRC fused the determination of the Soviet as a whole to defend the Left against any move by the government with the determination of its major Bolshevik figures, headed by Trotsky, to undermine the Provisional Government. It was in view of the government's efforts to transfer garrison troops to the front that on 21–22 October the MRC asserted its own authority over the troops in defiance of the regular military command. It was when Kerensky attempted the closure of the Bolshevik press, the institution of legal proceedings against the MRC, and the raising of the bridges linking working-class districts to the centre that on 24 October workers and soldiers supporting the Soviet directly challenged and overcame government orders. That night, responding to enthusiastic urging by Lenin, who had just arrived incognito at Party headquarters, the MRC went onto the offensive. Subversion of the Provisional Government gave way to the outright seizure of power. The denouement was almost an anticlimax. Key positions in the capital were rapidly seized and Kerensky fled to the front in a vain search for loyal troops. The Cabinet, huddled together in the Winter Palace, could mobilize no substantial force to resist, and even before they surrendered Lenin had drafted the announcement for nationwide distribution that the Provisional Government had fallen.

When the Soviet Congress met later that day it was widely assumed, even among the large bloc of Bolshevik delegates, that a new government would bring together all the major socialist parties. The moderate socialists, however, finding themselves reduced to a small minority in the Congress and enraged by the pre-emptive action of the MRC, denounced the

7.5 The downfall of the Provisional Government, October 1917: the deserted Winter Palace after the arrest of the government ministers.

Bolsheviks and stormed from the hall. After failing to effect a reconciliation, Martov and the left-wing Mensheviks followed suit, consigning themselves, in Trotsky's ruthless epitaph, to the rubbish-bin of history. The Left SRs, who now constituted a separate party and had the second largest bloc of delegates, remained behind and would eventually, in mid-November, form a short-lived coalition with the Bolsheviks. But the way was clear for the Congress to appoint a Bolshevik government, headed by Lenin, which took the name of the Council of People's Commissars.

Confirmed by the Congress, the new government quickly attracted the support of soviets in most of urban Russia. Moderate socialists offered little more than token resistance. Even where they were still in the majority they gave way to pressure from the more radical workers and soldiers, and withdrew from local soviets. In Moscow there was fierce fighting for a week, but the 'committees of public safety' set up in Petrograd and many provincial cities to oppose the new regime were either unwilling or unable to muster armed support and rapidly fell apart. Anti-Bolshevik hopes rested upon the forthcoming Constituent Assembly elections, to which Lenin was pledged, and confidently expected the early collapse of the new government.

The government's position was indeed precarious. It narrowly survived an immediate effort by moderate leaders of the railway and postal workers to force the formation of an all-socialist coalition. In the Ukrainian capital, Kiev, the *Rada* declared full independence before being overwhelmed by soldiers brought from the north under Left-SR command. During the winter there were armed clashes in the Cossack regions, the most serious resistance coming from the Don Cossacks. And even in the parts of the country where the new government's authority had been recognized its coercive power was extremely limited. Neither local organs of the Party nor local revolutionary institutions could be relied upon to accept instructions from above. The preponderance of Bolsheviks in soviets, factory committees, and trade unions was no guarantee that the priorities of the centre would be upheld against those of local activists. In the countryside, moreover, the Bolshevik presence was derisory.

The government's first steps, therefore, its Decrees on Peace and Land, its declarations on national self-determination, and, later, on workers' control of industry, reflected not Bolshevik dogma but mass aspirations which, by the autumn, no power in Russia could withstand. There was no option but to end the war, even when it became clear that this involved signing a separate peace, which was anathema to the Bolshevik leaders. The peasants were authorized to parcel out private land as they saw fit, despite Bolshevik preference for the nationalization of land and immediate steps towards collective farming. Even in the factories, where Bolshevik influence was most deeply rooted, the widespread assertion of direct control by workers went far beyond anything the Party leadership considered compatible with economic recovery. And despite Bolshevik conviction that for the minority nations to break away from Russia now that she was in truly revolutionary hands would be a backward step, the government had to proclaim their right to do so. The People's Commissars were in no position to resist or direct the tide that had swept away Kerensky. No Russian government had ever been more responsive to pressure from below or less able to impose its own will upon society.

But the relationship between state and society was to be swiftly transformed. During 1918 the Right, the Mensheviks, the SRs, Cossacks, various minority national groups, and foreign powers sought to reverse different aspects of the revolution. In the savage civil war which ensued the new government became the rallying point for the defence of the revolution. And in coordinating that defence it forged a new State, possessed of fearsome and highly centralized coercive power.

Chapter 8 ....

Civil War and the consolidation of Bolshevik power (1918–1928)

The Bolshevik leaders came to power expecting the October Revolution to have an electrifying impact upon the rest of Europe. They were convinced by the speed with which the war had radicalized the masses in Russia that a comparable process was under way in the West. The spectacle of a workers' government overthrowing capitalism in Russia would evoke a tremendous response. A forthright peace offer from such a government, coupled with the publication and repudiation of all Russia's secret treaties, would inspire the Western masses to insist upon an immediate end to the war. Trotsky, the first People's Commissar for Foreign Affairs, remarked with character-istic panache that his function would be to 'issue a few revolutionary pro-clamations to the peoples of the world and then shut up shop'.[1] Revolution would spread across the Continent and all Europe would cooperate in the construction of socialism.

Their confidence proved wildly misplaced. Instead of receiving assis-tance from the West, the Socialist Republic found itself confronted by a ring of fiercely hostile neighbours. The first blow was the 'delay' in the response of Western workers to the Soviet Decree on Peace. Allied governments ignored it with impunity and the Germans confidently awaited concrete peace proposals. Lenin quickly decided that, however punitive the German terms, the war must end. The alternative was certain death for the new Soviet government. Idealistic 'Left' Bolsheviks – and the Left SRs – might call for a 'revolutionary' war designed to carry the revolution westward, but the evidence was overwhelming that the army's will to fight had gone beyond recall. After hastily concluding an armistice, the Bolsheviks did all they could to spin out detailed peace negotiations in the hope of upheaval in central Europe. In February Trotsky momentarily dumbfounded the

---

[1] L. Trotsky, *My Life* (New York 1930), p. 341.

178

German delegation by announcing that although Russia was withdrawing from the war, she would not sign a peace treaty. The German High Command, however, soon called his bluff and resumed the military advance. The sequel was the Treaty of Brest-Litovsk, signed on 3 March (New Style).[2] Russia forfeited a massive swathe of western territory, along with much of the former Empire's industrial capacity. Most significant was the loss of the Ukraine, whose nominal independence under German tutelage Russia was compelled to recognize.

By this time, moreover, the Allies had established their first foothold on Russian soil with the avowed purpose of reopening an eastern front against Germany. With consummate diplomatic skill Lenin and G. V. Chicherin, Trotsky's more down-to-earth successor at the Foreign Affairs Commissariat, manoeuvred between the two power blocs. They played upon German recognition that, since no other Russian government would acquiesce in the Carthaginian terms of Brest-Litovsk, it was in Germany's interest that the Bolshevik regime should survive. By offering massive economic concessions, they persuaded Germany to restrain her military pressure in the west and south, enabling Bolshevik forces to check Allied incursions in the north and east. But from June 1918 the international struggle became interwoven with and overlaid by full-scale civil war. The catalyst which sparked off hostilities was a Czechoslovak Legion composed of POWs willing to enlist against the Central Powers. The Czechs were anxious to reach Vladivostok for shipment to the western front, but while strung out along the Trans-Siberian railway line they received orders from the Allies, endorsed by the Bolshevik government, to reroute for Archangel in the north. Suspecting treachery, the Czechs refused to obey and clashed with local soviets over control of the railway. Trotsky – now Commissar for War – furiously ordered their disarming, and in the ensuing confusion anti-Bolshevik forces began to mobilize. The relatively small-scale and scattered shows of resistance in the immediate aftermath of October gave way to the organization of what became substantial White armies as the victims of political and social upheaval attempted to reverse the verdict of 1917.

For two horrendous years Russia was torn by civil war. Coming on top of the exertions and destruction of the First World War, it was a pitiless struggle fought in conditions of economic desolation and extreme hardship. Agricultural disruption culminated in famine and the industrial collapse was without precedent in modern history. The civil war cost between 7 and 10 million lives, if the catastrophic civilian losses due to hunger and epidemic are added to some 800,000 military deaths (over half of them as the result of disease) and upwards of 200,000 victims of internal repression. The

---

[2] The Julian Calendar was replaced by the Gregorian or Western Calendar on 31 January 1918 when the following day was decreed to be not 1 February but 14 February.

Map 9 Bolshevik-held territory during the Civil War

massacre of the Tsar, the Tsarina, and their children by the Reds shortly before fleeing Ekaterinburg was the most notorious of the many atrocities committed on both sides. The Bolsheviks were driven back into the heartland of old Muscovy as White armies attacked from the east, the north-west and the south. A force of 100,000 based in Siberia under Admiral Kolchak approached the Volga in spring 1919. A much smaller army under General Yudenich operating from Estonia briefly threatened Petrograd in the autumn of 1919. The most powerful White army, under General Denikin, was raised in the north Caucasus and Cossack regions of south Russia. In the summer of 1919 it advanced on all fronts – eastwards, westwards into the Ukraine, and above all northwards towards Moscow itself. Moreover, despite the collapse of Germany and the armistice of November 1918, the Allies initially refused to withdraw. Appalled by the challenge to Western capitalism which the Bolsheviks had thrown down, and outraged by the new regime's repudiation of all foreign debts, they maintained their presence for another year, imposed a blockade, and lent considerable financial aid to the anti-Bolshevik forces. But the Whites were fatally handicapped by divisions among themselves. There was almost no coordination between their separate armies scattered around the periphery. Their commitment to the unity of the old Empire and their overt (and virulently anti-semitic) Russian nationalism alienated the national minorities. And as soon as the military leaders asserted control over White-held territory they overruled SR attempts to establish moderate socialist regimes. A White victory, it became increasingly clear, implied a thoroughgoing counter-revolution. There was to be no attempt to win positive support from the peasantry, still less from workers. Most Right SRs, despite their role in resisting the Bolsheviks in the early stages of the Civil War, found this unacceptable, and the Mensheviks condemned the Whites outright.

Nevertheless, the Bolsheviks came close to disaster. Deprived of the major grain-surplus areas and blockaded from the outside world, they suffered from desperate shortages of everything – food, footwear, guns. Hopes of Western revolution continued to run high, and in March 1919 Lenin founded the Communist International (Comintern) to rally far-Left socialists abroad; but bourgeois Europe withstood post-war unrest. The low point was reached in October 1919 when both Petrograd and Moscow – where Lenin's government had moved immediately after Brest-Litovsk – seemed on the brink of falling. Yet they survived. Although Poland, Finland, the Baltic states, and Bessarabia were lost, most of the old Imperial territory was gradually brought under Soviet control. By the summer of 1920 the Reds were in a position to drive an ill-timed invasion by newly independent Poland all the way back to the gates of Warsaw, before being repelled. In November the remnants of the White army in the south, now under General Wrangel, were driven from the Crimean peninsula. The victory of the Reds is explicable partly in terms of the military advantage afforded by control of the Russian heartland. This gave them unbroken and relatively short lines of communication, an asset brilliantly exploited by the Red Army officers gathered under Trotsky. But more fundamental was the fierce loyalty they attracted from many workers, and the preference among most peasants for Reds over Whites. This ensured that the forces under Bolshevik command vastly outnumbered their enemies as the lower classes fought to uphold the post-revolutionary settlement.

The immediate sequel to the October Revolution had been the consummation of the social upheaval of 1917. Russia's social structure was transformed. In the countryside the dispossession of private landowners by the peasantry was already far advanced by October. Now, with government approval, the process was completed. The age-old peasant goal was achieved, rural society was restructured, and the nobility disappeared from the scene. In the cities and major industrial complexes the conflict between workers and employers reached a climax. On coming to power Lenin envisaged taking over only the major industries and the banks. For the time being the bulk of industry would be left in private hands under regulation from above by the Supreme Council of National Economy (VSNKh), and from below by workers. During the first months after October, however, the government was carried forward on a wave of working-class radicalism. This was fuelled not only by euphoria over the establishment of a Soviet government, but also by economic dislocation on a scale which dwarfed the problems of the Provisional Government. The new regime's commitment to end the war led to immediate industrial 'demobilization': an industrial economy already ravaged by shortages of fuel and raw materials was hit by catastrophic contraction of demand for military goods. Faced with the threat of redundancy, and convinced of sabotage on the part of employers – and on occasion technical and clerical staff as well – rank-and-file workers demanded that their enterprises be taken over by the new proletarian State. The government's reservations were fully overcome by the German warning that they would insist on compensation for any German-owned property nationalized after 1 July, and on 28 June 1918 all the major branches of industry were nationalized. The economic base of the bourgeoisie was broken and private enterprise relegated to a peripheral role in the industrial economy.

This massive upheaval in property relations was complemented by drastic institutional change. The ephemeral national representative bodies established by the Provisional Government were swept away. The long-awaited Constituent Assembly, in which Right SRs had a majority, met for just one day, on 5 January 1918, before being forcibly dissolved by the government. At the local level the zemstvos, long resented by the peasantry, were abolished by decree and the city dumas met the same fate. The organizations – and the titles – of nobility and merchants were abolished. The Church was separated from the State, forfeited its property, lost all control over education, was subjected to constant harassment, and saw some of its most venerated places of worship turned into museums of atheism. The old army was disbanded and the established legal and judicial system largely replaced by revolutionary courts. The whole superstructure of the traditional establishment was dismantled. The Tsar's twin-headed eagle, merely uncrowned by the Provisional Government, was torn down and replaced by the hammer and sickle, the twin symbol of worker and peasant power.

On the face of it, the new state structure, enshrined in the Constitution of July 1918, was designed to place power directly in the hands of the masses. Force would, of course, have to be used to overcome the resistance of the old ruling classes and their allies. Strong measures would be necessary to break the resistance of the many bureaucrats and white-collar workers who reacted to the Bolshevik seizure of power by staging a strike. The Kadet Party and those to the right were promptly suppressed, press censorship instituted, and a special security agency, the 'All-Russian Extraordinary Commission for Combating Counter-Revolution and Sabotage' (Cheka), established to root out counter-revolutionary activity. But such measures were regarded as strictly temporary: the vision of the State with which the Bolshevik leadership came to power was little less Utopian than their expectations of foreign revolution. As soon as the exploiters had been finally defeated, as Lenin briefly believed was the case in March 1918, the State could and would cease to be coercive. Lenin himself had provided the most elaborate expression of this vision in *State and Revolution*, written during 1916 and 1917 and published in January 1918, where he speculated on the structure of a classless society. Once exploitation of man by man had ended, the State as a distinctive entity – the coercive machinery of army, bureaucracy, and police – would fade away. The role of central government would be to provide leadership and coordination of the voluntary efforts of a liberated people.

It was in this spirit that, for example, Lunacharsky, People's Commissar for Enlightenment, envisaged his role in overseeing the cultural sphere. While bastions of bourgeois resistance such as the universities and private presses would be brought under 'proletarian' control, he would give wide latitude to intellectuals who sided with the revolution, to the profusion of revolutionary and utopian programmes and experiments which the social and political upheaval unleashed among radical theorists, educationalists, feminists and artists. He would welcome the efforts of those who hailed the new era as one which would sweep away bourgeois art, bourgeois norms of education, bourgeois attitudes to women, marriage, divorce and, of course, religion. He would give his support to Proletkult (the Russian Proletarian Cultural-Educational Association), led by Lenin's pre-war rival Bogdanov, which sought to coordinate cultural and educational activities among workers and foster a distinctive proletarian culture; and the educational reformers and enthusiasts in the Communist Youth Organization

(Komsomol) who battled over rival visions of fusing general and technical education. He would encourage the feminists, championed by the one woman briefly included in the Council of People's Commissars, Alexandra Kollontai, who persuaded the Party to create a Women's Section (Zhenotdel) to promote female emancipation through women's literacy, the establishment of kindergartens and creches, and a propaganda drive against male authority and the patriarchal family. He would also encourage the Futurists and other avant-garde artists and poets, among whom V. V. Mayakovsky (1893–1930) was preeminent, who gave free rein to their sense of a new heaven and a new earth. Likewise, Lunacharsky would provide advice and guidance for the general spread of literacy and education, but implementation would be left to the spontaneous enthusiasm of local soviets. It was this spirit, too, which informed the new Constitution.

Local affairs were henceforth to be run by town and village soviets, directly elected by the working masses. Day-to-day administration would be in the hands of an executive committee appointed by each soviet and directly responsible to it. Above the local level would rise a pyramid of district, county, provincial and regional soviet congresses, each composed of delegates sent by the lower body, capped by the All-Russian Congress of Soviets. This Congress would elect a Central Executive Committee, which, in turn, would appoint the Council of People's Commissars, the government of the Soviet Republic. The system would combine guidance from above with democratic control from below. The State would represent nothing more than the administration of the people by the people.

The Soviet framework had taken shape under the shadow of the Provisional Government, and it was duly extended wherever Bolshevik rule was established. Yet the democratic ideal it represented was flagrantly contradicted by the relationship which actually developed between State and society, between officialdom and ordinary citizens, between the ruling Party and rank-and-file workers and peasants. The State became progressively more coercive and centralized and increasingly removed from mass control. Authoritarian relationships were re-established over the peasantry, in industry, in the new Red Army, in the ever tighter control asserted not only over potentially conservative institutions such as the universities but also over thoroughly radical semi-autonomous institutions such as Proletkult. The bulk of the old bureaucracy was retained and its heavy-handed traditions were carried over into the sprawling new soviet state apparatus that took shape. Although many of the new officials were recruited from the working class and educated peasants, often ex-soldiers, they quickly identified with the apparatus that lent them status and privileges rather than with the classes from which they had been drawn. Lenin's dream that all public officials should be elected and paid a normal worker's wage receded to the horizon. The Cheka, headed until his death in 1926 by F. E. Dzerzhinsky and directly responsible to the party leadership, became firmly entrenched as a nationwide political police force – numbering 40,000 by the end of 1918 and as many as 250,000 in 1921 – and escaped democratic control altogether. Popular participation in decision-making was reduced to a mere charade as the soviets proved quite incapable of asserting themselves over the government and its officials.

For liberal historians, this 'degeneration' was implicit in pre-revolutionary Bolshevik ideology. The Bolsheviks had never shown the slightest interest in such 'bourgeois' constitutional devices as the separation of powers, designed to prevent the erosion of democratic processes. The very concept of the 'vanguard' Party revealing to the less advanced sections of the masses their true interests was inherently elitist. Clearly, these preconceptions did play a part in shaping the post-revolutionary regime and conditioning the leadership's responses to the challenges they faced. But the Party had undergone too profound a transformation during 1917 for this to be an adequate explanation. What guaranteed that it was the authoritarian rather than the democratic currents in the Party which prevailed was the impact of economic chaos and civil war upon the urban masses, and the series of *ad hoc* measures which the regime took to survive.

The most unashamed Bolshevik volte-face was in their approach to military organization. Throughout 1917 they had pressed for democratization within the army, the election of officers, and the abolition of the death penalty. But when faced by the armies of capitalist powers and White generals, the new regime felt compelled to construct its own Red Army on thoroughly traditional lines. Instead of relying on local militia units of armed workers and peasants, a centralized, hierarchical, and harsh military structure was created. The election of officers was discontinued and, despite opposition within the Party, many of those appointed were ex-officers of the Tsar's army. The loyalty of these socially and ideologically alien officers was ensured not by control from below but by attaching to them political commissars – and in some cases by holding their families hostage. The core of the Red Army consisted of the most committed workers, while the bulk, which reached 5 million at the height of the civil war, was made up of peasant conscripts unwillingly forced to choose between Reds and Whites. With the rate of desertion very high, especially when these conscripts were ordered to fight outside their own locality, rigid discipline seemed essential and the death penalty was freely used. In military terms, the results were gratifying. Despite inferior equipment, the Red Army proved a match for the enemy. Trotsky, who masterminded its creation, made full use of centralized control to throw crack troops into the breach wherever they were most urgently needed. But the coercive structure of the Red Army, seemingly demanded by the requirements of modern warfare, did not prove to be an exceptional blemish on the face of a new democratic state. It proved typical of the State's relations with both the peasantry and the working class.

Where relations with the peasantry were concerned, the critical issue

185

8.1 Trotsky haranguing Red Army soldiers in Moscow during the Civil War. Responsibility for the Bolshevik defence brought out both the most dynamic and the most ruthless traits in Trotsky's character.

was grain. The breakdown of the trade nexus between town and country-side, already far advanced before October, gathered pace in the following months. With the loss of the Ukraine the problem of supplying the cities with grain became desperate. The rouble was rapidly losing all value as a medium of exchange, and manufactured goods were in such short supply that direct bartering for grain proved totally inadequate. Force seemed the only answer. *Ad hoc* detachments of workers, soldiers, and officials went into the countryside to requisition supplies. But since the Party's active support in the villages was minimal, their task was extremely difficult. In June 1918, therefore, the government decided to strengthen its hand by mobiliz-ing the poorer peasants against the richer villagers (pejoratively dubbed 'kulaks' – exploiters) who were assumed to be hoarding grain. Committees of Poor Peasants were to be set up to requisition grain, both for themselves and for the cities. Peasants with virtually no property of their own would join hands with the urban proletariat in overcoming the selfishness of the kulaks, and would be encouraged to take the first steps towards collective farming. The socialist revolution would be extended to the countryside.

The experiment was a disaster. The assumption that social differentia-tion in the village had reached the point where it could be fanned into open class warfare proved unfounded. Although farming implements and live-stock were still not evenly divided among the peasantry, the seizure of private land during the revolution had had a levelling effect. Contrary to Bolshevik belief, the numbers of both rich and very poor households had fallen, and the vast majority remained 'middle' peasants, relying almost entirely upon working their own plots of land. This is not to deny elements of tension within the village – not least between generations as self-confident, assertive sons returned from the war and, often egged on by young wives, demanded partition of the household's land and the break-up of the extended family. Equally, there was severe conflict between different rural regions, between 'grain surplus' and 'grain deficit' areas, and between neighbouring villages. But confronted by the demands of alien townsmen, each village tended to close ranks behind the traditional communal structure. Even in the areas where the Poor Peasant Committees did show some vitality, a large proportion of their members – destitute craftsmen and former workers, soldiers and domestic servants – had either never farmed as peasants or had ceased to do so. Their concern was to secure grain for themselves, rather than for the requisitioning detachments, and they showed little interest in collective farming.

In the winter of 1918–19 the Party began to disband the committees and by March 1919 Lenin was openly regretting the way in which the middle peasants had been attacked and alienated. But there was no let-up. With the civil war raging, and grain required for the Red Army as well as the cities, forced requisitioning was intensified. An urban-based hierarchy imposed quotas drawn up on the haziest information about peasant stocks and with minimal concern for peasant needs or the damage inflicted on peasant agriculture. And, in mimicry of the age-old strategy of the Tsarist State, villagers were made collectively rather than individually responsible for meeting quotas. To the wealthiest minority of peasants, notably in Siberia, and to the Cossacks of the North Caucasus, even the Whites seemed preferable to the depredations of the Reds. In the Ukraine, where the Bolsheviks continued to use Poor Peasant Committees, hatred of both sides in the Civil War generated a remarkable independent peasant army. Under the anarchist leader Nestor Makhno, it survived until the White collapse left it face-to-face with the Red Army. Elsewhere, although the spectre of a White victory was generally enough to keep peasant resistance passive, villagers did all they could – by reducing sowings, concealing stocks, trading grain for the products of cottage industry, and selling it on the black market – to evade the voracious regime.

In these conditions, rural democracy was doomed. The district soviets, which in the course of the Civil War became responsible for rural administration, were unable to win popular support. Attendance at their assemblies fell away as control passed to their executive committees. These were dominated by party members recruited largely from among younger, more literate and often ex-army peasants, whose links with the village became increasingly tenuous. The soviets established at village level failed to displace the traditional peasant communes, whose members viewed the emergent new state structures with mounting hostility. Bolshevik Party membership among peasant farmers remained negligible and the Bolsheviks became increasingly suspicious of any political expression of peasant discontent. Not only the Right SRs but also the Left SRs, the Bolsheviks' early coalition partners, were subject to growing constraints. It was in March 1918, in protest against the Treaty of Brest-Litovsk, that the Left SRs had resigned from the government. In July the Party engineered the assassination of the German Ambassador in Moscow, hoping to jeopardize the peace and force the government into a revolutionary war. At this stage Lenin was careful to leave the door open to reconciliation with all but the most intransigent Left SR critics of his regime. But relations between the two parties were permanently soured by the policy of forced requisitioning. For the Left SRs this was a criminal betrayal of the worker-peasant alliance. Relations were further embittered when, in late August, an SR terrorist shot and wounded Lenin. Although it was not until after the Civil War that all rival socialist parties were finally suppressed, non-Bolshevik political activity in the countryside was tightly circumscribed. With the Food Commissariat, backed by armed 'food brigades', the Cheka and the Red Army confronting the village head-on, democratic consultation with the peasantry was out of the question.

The deterioration in relations between the new State and the working class was a more complex process. Of critical importance was the issue of power within individual nationalized factories and mines. Nationalization in itself had not resolved the question of the proper relationship between management and workers. Should management be taken over by the elected representatives of the workers within each enterprise? Or should authority be vested in the hands of a government appointee? Later generations of socialists have seen this issue as the very heart of socialist revolution: relations at the point of production govern the distribution of power throughout society. Unless workers are in control here, they will not retain control of the State, however magnificent the letter of the Constitution or sincere the socialist convictions of the political leadership.

Individual labour leaders said as much at the time, and the movement for workers' self-management gathered real momentum, especially in Petrograd. For a few weeks rank-and-file euphoria over the prospect of workers proving themselves capable of running industry affected wide sections of the Party. Lenin himself redrafted the November Decree on Workers' Control to strengthen the role of workers in management. As the economic crisis plumbed new depths, however, the preoccupation of government leaders swung dramatically to the need to maintain production. By the spring of 1918 Lenin was urging the need for strict industrial discipline and wage differentials to ensure the cooperation of bourgeois specialists. This could not be achieved, he believed, if management reflected the whims of the work-force. Firm one-man management was essential.

The tide quickly began to turn. Workers' attempts to retain managerial authority in their own hands were not helped by the chronic rivalry between grass-roots factory committees and the more hierarchical trade-union organizations. When this struggle was resolved in favour of the latter, and factory committees were absorbed into the trade-union structure, the ties between labour leaders and the rank and file were weakened. More fundamental, however, was the impact of economic collapse upon the working class. With the wheels of industry grinding to a halt, bread rations falling below subsistence level, and money losing all value, workers streamed from the cities in search of bread – Petrograd lost 1 million inhabitants in the first six months of 1918. Those who remained spent much of their time in search of food and became increasingly demoralized and unreliable. This led labour leaders themselves to accept the need for harsher discipline. And though they might continue to regard themselves as workers' representatives, their attempts to forbid strikes and impose discipline by introducing workbooks, bonus incentives, and even piece rates and the threat of dismissal widened the gulf separating them from the rank and file. Rather than being representatives of the workers, they became agents of the State, almost indistinguishable from officials of VSNKh and the Commissariat of Labour. Deprived of its leadership and increasingly disorientated, the movement for workers' management began to lose ground. From June 1918 a collegial form of management, including only one-third elected workers, was laid down as the norm for nationalized enterprises. Control began to pass out of the hands of the work-force and into those of managers appointed by the State.

This process was greatly accelerated by the Civil War. On the one hand, the government, desperate to maintain essential military production, became more and more committed to one-man management. Managerial authority was steadily strengthened, to the point where work camps were instituted for recalcitrant workers. On the other, urban depopulation reached catastrophic proportions. Supplies from the countryside slowed to a trickle, industrial production fell to a mere fraction of the 1917 level, and as malnutrition and disease took hold, the drift to the countryside from the major cities became an exodus. Between the revolution and 1921 Moscow's population fell by more than half and Petrograd's by over two-thirds. The proportionate fall among factory workers was much greater. What made matters worse was that those who remained at the factory bench tended to be least fitted for leadership. This reflected the manpower needs of the new regime. It was the politically committed who provided the best material for the repeated recruitment drives launched by the Red Army. It was the literate who could most readily be drawn into the swelling Soviet bureaucracy. Among those left at the factory bench, the proportion of women, relatively less assertive and less well educated, rose steeply and within each factory the rank and file found themselves more and more helpless to retain any managerial role. The proletariat of 1917 was transformed out of all recognition. By 1920 one-man management was the rule.

In the eyes of the Bolshevik leaders, this development was unavoidable. They scorned Menshevik and Western Marxist cries that it was a betrayal of socialism. Large-scale modern industry by its nature required specialized and forceful management. Central control was essential if production by different enterprises was to be coordinated. The savage reduction in the size and strength of the working class caused by the Civil War made the enhanced role of the State critical. In any case, since discipline was enforced by the appointees of a proletarian government, it constituted a form of proletarian 'self-discipline' orchestrated by the vanguard of the class. But the effect on working-class democracy was fatal: the breach between management and workers at the factory bench was mirrored in a growing estrangement between the Party and the working class. Discontent over conditions in the factories, miserable pay and rations, the relatively privileged treatment of bourgeois specialists, managers, and officials alike, as well as mass unemployment, rubbed off on the Bolsheviks. Working-class hostility was to some extent mitigated, it is true, by fear and hatred of the Whites, by deep resentment of the supposed hoarding and selfishness of the peasantry, and by the Party's vigorous, colourful and sustained propaganda drive to justify its actions. There was general recognition of the need for rationing and the Party gained credit for the abolition of charges for available municipal services and public transport as well as for efforts to support workers' schools, libraries and theatres. As we have seen, many workers responded to repeated recruitment drives for the Red Army and some workers willingly supported the *subbotniki*, days on which the party appealed for voluntary labour to shore up the decaying urban fabric. Moreover, amidst the desperate struggle to secure a high-priority ration card, to beg, barter and steal food and fuel, workers resorted more to individual survival strategies than to collective action and political protest. Yet the Party's hold on working-class allegiance was seriously eroded. The Bolshevik response was to take full advantage of the force at their disposal. The Cheka and the Red Army were neither stable nor streamlined instruments of coercion. But the Bolsheviks enjoyed a monopoly of organized force of any kind in Red-held territory, and in any case for their rivals to take to the streets would be tantamount to aiding the counter-revolution. Democratic processes in the urban soviets were deliberately undermined. On the one hand, as in the countryside, opposition socialist parties which began to revive and give expression to workers' discontent, were attacked. Menshevik, urban SR, and anarchist activists were hounded by the Cheka and their press severely circumscribed. They were driven from effective representation in the soviets, and sporadic attempts to found new parties were swiftly crushed. On the other, the soviets were rapidly 'bureaucratized'. Elections became less and less frequent and meaningful.

Soviet executive committees, dominated by Bolsheviks, ceased to be responsive to pressure from below. The process ran right through the Soviet pyramid. At the apex the Supreme Congress and indeed its Central Executive Committee lost control over the Council of People's Commissars. Severely weakened by the devastating impact of economic dislocation and civil war, rank-and-file workers lost control over the Soviet State.

The corollary of the decline in mass democracy and the establishment of the Bolsheviks' political monopoly was the transformation in the nature of the Party. In the first place, from being a mass organization of workers, it became a body of officials. Members were removed from the factory bench to take leading roles in institutions of all kinds – not only factory committees, trade unions, the various organs of the soviets, and the full-time party apparatus, but the Cheka, the Red Army, and the state bureaucracy. By 1922 over two-thirds of party members were administrators of one kind or another. In the second place, it became the source of decision-making power at every level. The chairman of the local soviet took his instructions from the local party committee. It was the Central Committee of the Party which guided the Council of People's Commissars. And through the development of what became known as the *nomenklatura* system, by which party committees drew up a list of sensitive posts and eligible candidates under their purview, the Party exercised control over significant public appointments of every description at both national and local level.

Equally important was the drastic impact of the Party's new role upon inner-party democracy. In the early months after October, party organization had been loose and local organs remained as responsive to the views of local members as to pressure from above. The major issues of the day were openly and vigorously debated, the row between Lenin and the 'Left Communists' over the separate peace with Germany being the most dramatic instance. But when civil war flared up and the regime's survival seemed to hang by a thread, the Party underwent a rapid process of centralization. In part this was the result of a sustained drive from above to streamline the central organs of the Party and to tighten party discipline. At the beginning of 1919 the authority of the Central Committee was partially delegated to two smaller bodies. A five-man Politburo was to handle urgent political decisions while a five-man Orgburo was entrusted with organizational matters and party appointments – both being served by a formalized Secretariat of the Central Committee. Confronted by civil war, Lenin and his colleagues became ever more impatient with democratic nicety. The Party must provide the rigorous command structure necessary to mobilize men, material, and food from an increasingly impoverished society. But the closing of ranks was also encouraged by ordinary members; policy disputes were restrained and local cells themselves urged greater control from the centre in order to maximize the use of limited personnel and resources against the counter-revolution. Moreover, the sheer growth in the administrative burdens placed upon party members left less and less time or energy for democratic political consultation. The rapid turnover of membership during the Civil War further weakened grass-roots influence. The proportion of 'veterans' shrank as they fell victim to the Civil War, political disillusionment and the purge of inactive and unreliable elements. A vigorous recruitment drive in the autumn of 1919 rapidly replenished numbers, which approached 600,000 by the following spring. But the careerist motives of many of the new recruits – ambitious workers, young peasants returning from the army and seeking a life outside the routine of the village, and white-collar workers and officials anxious to secure their jobs and gain promotion – inhibited them from challenging their seniors. Party cells met less often and were ever more dominated by the local committee. The local committee, in turn, was increasingly bound by instructions from above, and the same process set in all the way up the committee ladder. The chain of command through which authority was exercised was that of the committee secretary. At each level the secretary gained clear ascendancy over his own committee. And these key posts were more and more often filled by appointment from above rather than election from below. Thus, as the Party's priorities shifted from political and ideological struggle to administrative and military activity, it became an increasingly pliant instrument at the command of the leadership.

The destruction of democracy during the Civil War generated among the party leadership an illusion that almost proved fatal. Far from recognizing that socially and economically Russia was now far more backward than in 1917 and light years removed from the conditions which Marx had envisaged as the point of departure for socialism, they were mesmerized by the seemingly limitless scope for state direction. The policies adopted to cope with the military emergency, which in retrospect became known as 'War Communism', could be retained to organize civilian reconstruction. During 1920 Trotsky, the leading 'Left Communist' N. I. Bukharin, and for a few months Lenin himself shared the euphoric dream that these policies provided a blueprint for direct transition to socialism. With inflation rendering the rouble virtually valueless, money would permanently disappear and the market mechanism of capitalism would be replaced by planned production and distribution. Grain requisitioning was therefore continued and measures against the ubiquitous black market were intensified. In the autumn of 1920, since the peasantry had retaliated by cutting back their crops, an attempt was even made to set up 'sowing committees' to impose production targets upon them. In industry petty enterprises employing as few as five workers were nationalized. Lenin was particularly enthusiastic about the establishment of a commission (GOELRO) to plan the electrification of the whole country, while Trotsky became the champion of a comprehensive programme of industrial reconstruction based upon dictatorial control of the economy. The command structure and bureaucracy of the Red Army were to provide the basis for the direction of labour resources into the most critical areas. Highest priority was to be given to engineering, fuel, and, above all, the railway system which epitomized the reality of 'War Communism', reduced as it was to chaos by the destruction of lines, unrepaired rolling-stock, conflicts of authority and a rate of absenteeism that made a nonsense of timetabling. Labour conscription was to be made universal, the trade unions turned into obedient instruments of the State, and discipline imposed with military rigour.

It rapidly became clear that on this occasion the State had overreached itself. With the 1920 harvest falling to some 60 per cent of the pre-war level, discontent mounted in both city and countryside. Towards the end of 1920 peasant disturbances became widespread, there was a major revolt in the province of Tambov, and requisitioning had to be suspended in thirteen provinces. During the winter industry was hit by repeated strikes, party spokesmen were howled down at workers' meetings, there were protest demonstrations, hostile resolutions were passed, and non-party Soviet delegates became outspoken in criticism. The climax came with a revolt by sailors and workers at Kronstadt in March 1921. An anti-Bolshevik Provisional Revolutionary Committee demanded political freedom for all socialist parties, free elections to the soviets, and the replacement of requisitioning by free trade in grain. Though the Bolsheviks denounced the revolt as a White-inspired plot, and the Red Army stormed across the ice to crush it, the writing was on the wall.

An economic U-turn proposed by Lenin was hastily approved by the Tenth Party Congress, meeting at the time of the Kronstadt rebellion. The Bolsheviks came to terms with a mixed economy and 'War Communism' gave way to the New Economic Policy (NEP). Grain requisitioning was to be replaced by a fixed tax, set at a considerably lower level than the requisition quotas, and, from 1924, collected in cash rather than kind. The tax was to be levied on individual households, rather than on the principle of joint responsibility of a whole village, the peasantry were permitted to trade the remainder of their produce, and restrictions on other forms of private retail trade were lifted. At the same time, the Party backed down from the militarization of labour and Lenin and Zinoviev rallied a majority to defeat Trotsky's line on turning the trade unions into disciplinarian organs of the state apparatus. In the following months industry, too, was reorientated to market principles. Although the major enterprises remained in public ownership, they were instructed to operate upon strictly commercial lines, relying upon the market to determine production, price, and wage levels. A few were even leased to private entrepreneurs and smaller enterprises were denationalized.

The introduction of NEP successfully defused the explosive situation of 1921. Drought that summer, coming on top of widespread crop failure the previous year, devastated a peasant economy whose basic food and even

193

seed stores had been eroded by the years of grain requisitioning. The result was horrific famine and mass cholera and typhus epidemics in the winter of 1921–22 – the epilogue to eight years of man-made carnage. So desperate was the situation that substantial famine relief was accepted from the capitalist West. But thereafter, relieved from requisitioning, the peasantry regained the incentive to raise production and from 1922 agriculture began to pick up quickly. By 1926 the grain crop had reached pre-war levels, there was a sharp increase in non-grain production, and by 1928 peasant living standards, measured in terms of livestock and food consumption, had reached a new high. Industry took longer to recover from the nadir of 1920 when production was only one-fifth of the pre-war level. Artisan manufacturers soon re-established the trade nexus with the peasantry, but larger-scale factory production, and especially heavy industry, remained depressed until 1924. At first peasant demand was so weak that industrial prices collapsed. Then in 1923 the nationalized industries combined to force prices up and the terms of trade moved so heavily against the peasantry that demand fell away. By the end of the year, however, industrial prices had fallen back, a new currency restored peasant confidence, and trade revived. By the end of 1925 industry was approaching the level of output achieved before the war.

Neither the failure of 'War Communism' in 1920 nor the retreat into NEP, however, signified the restoration of Soviet democracy. The notion of a return to a democratic, militia-style army was finally laid to rest at the Tenth Party Congress. The bulk of the Red Army was demobilized but the brutalizing experience of civil war had severely weakened democratic currents within the Party. The tens of thousands of party members returning to civilian life injected a crude, swaggering and militaristic strain into Bolshevik style, rhetoric and mentality. Moreover, the effect of Kronstadt, the naked exposure of the Party's extreme unpopularity, was to rule out any political concessions to rival parties. While positive support for the Bolsheviks within the factories stood at its lowest ebb, and peasant hostility was manifest, the regime could not afford to slacken its political grip. Moreover, during the 1920s, the very success of NEP made political pluralism seem suicidal: it would merely invite 'counter-revolutionary' organization, give voice to hostile 'bourgeois' elements, to 'Nepmen' and kulaks. Drastic measures, therefore, were taken against the remnants of the Menshevik and SR parties and their leaders were imprisoned or exiled. The Soviet Union became a one-party state.

The Party's political monopoly seemed indispensable, too, in establishing control over areas regained from the Whites, particularly where national separatist feeling was pronounced. One-party rule was the fundamental premise underlying the Constitution of the Union of Soviet Socialist Republics (USSR), ratified in 1924, which created a quasi-federal union between the Republics of the Ukraine, Belorussia, and Transcaucasia and

8.2   The Smolensk street market in Moscow, September 1921, shortly after the introduction of NEP. The busy scene reflects the quick re-establishment of small-scale trade.

the giant Russian Socialist Federative Soviet Republic (RSFSR). The Constitution not only recognized separate governments for each Union Republic, each with its own flag and symbols of sovereignty, but boldly proclaimed their right of secession from the Union. Yet this did not reflect the slightest willingness to countenance independent policy-formation by the minority republics, still less any future break-up of the Union. Nor was the party leadership under any misapprehension about the existence of strong separatist currents: national resistance to incorporation in a centralized Soviet state had been fierce, particularly in the Ukraine and Georgia. But Lenin, unlike his much more abrasive Commissar of Nationalities, J. V. Stalin (1879–1953), whom he accused of 'Great-Russian chauvinism', was anxious that minority sensibilities should not be unnecessarily offended. Indeed, during the 1920s the Party actively promoted in education and public life the language and culture not only of the major minority nationalities but even of those which hitherto had had little in the way of a literary culture.

Likewise, during the 1920s there was a sustained drive to increase the proportion of non-Russians recruited to the Party and appointed to posts within the local party and state apparatus. But the premise of concessions to the minorities on the constitutional structure and scope of cultural autonomy was the Party's monopolization of political life throughout the USSR.

Nor was the end of the Civil War accompanied by any slackening of internal party discipline. During 1920, when Lenin and Trotsky were committed to intensifying 'War Communism', a minority of Bolsheviks had openly criticized the leadership. To tighten central control within the Party and to increase coercion over workers just when the White threat was receding, they argued, was unjustifiable. A so-called 'Democratic-Centralist' opposition objected to the leadership's reliance upon appointment and discipline rather than consultation with party members. 'A fish begins to stink from the head,' warned V. N. Maksimovsky, one of their leaders. 'The Party at its highest levels is beginning to succumb to the influence of bureaucratic centralism.'[3] A more widespread 'Workers' Opposition' demanded that the trade unions should take the central role in economic management, rather than being used as mere instruments of discipline in the hands of the party leadership. In part this opposition reflected no more than rivalry between the trade-union and VSNKh elites and Trotsky's military hierarchy – as well as personal hostility to the Commissar of War himself. But it reflected, too, genuine misgivings that the regime should rely so exclusively upon force in its relations with its supposed social base, the proletariat. The alarming winter of 1920–21, however, culminating in the Kronstadt rising, swept the ground from beneath the opposition's feet. Even to those who sympathized with their criticisms, dissent seemed a luxury the Party could not afford. The same Party Congress which approved NEP also imposed a fateful ban on the organization of 'factions' within the Party and threatened offenders with expulsion. Although nominally temporary, the ban was to become permanent. The expression of dissent within the Party became ever more difficult.

At different moments during the 1920s all the leading Bolsheviks lamented the repercussions of this trend. They criticized the widening gulf separating the Party from rank-and-file workers, the lack of genuine consultation with the lower echelons over policy, and the impact on party life of appointments from above. Moreover, they began to perceive the enormous power which the system of appointment was concentrating in the hands of the Central Secretariat. It was the Secretariat which controlled the appointment of individual party members to key posts throughout the country. The careers of party officials were thus becoming increasingly dependent upon their loyalty to the Secretariat. The result was to give to the central administrative organs enormous influence over the make-up of Party

---

[3] *Deviatyi s'ezd RKP (b). Mart–Aprel 1920 goda* (Moscow 1960), p. 49.

Congresses and thus of elections to the Central Committee and the Politburo itself. A process was set in train by which power at the centre gradually moved from the Politburo to the Secretariat. While Lenin was in command this process remained somewhat masked, since his authority over his colleagues owed nothing to personal control over the Secretariat. But before he became incapacitated in 1923 and died in 1924, Lenin himself expressed alarm at these developments. In part his alarm arose from his growing distaste for the man whom he had himself helped to acquire a unique and pivotal position at the apex of the Party – simultaneously a member of the Politburo, the Orgburo and, from April 1922, General Secretary – Joseph Stalin. In the memoranda he dictated from his sick-bed in the winter of 1922–23, his so-called 'last testament', Lenin specifically warned of the dangers of leaving such power in the hands of anyone so rude, intolerant and capricious.

Successive Party Congresses resolved upon a variety of counter-measures against the 'bureaucratization' of the Party. A 'Central Control Commission' was set up to root out careerist elements. There were repeated purges of 'unworthy' members. From 1924 a major recruitment drive was launched, specifically aimed at raising working-class membership. The Central Committee was steadily expanded. The Secretariat was instructed to 'recommend' rather than appoint candidates for key posts. All to no avail. It is true the proportion of members drawn from the working class and still engaged in manual labour rose as membership climbed from under half a million in 1924 to over a million in 1928. But the vast majority of new recruits had no more than primary-level education and exercised little influence over senior officials. Moreover, every attempted remedy depended for implementation upon the existing secretarial hierarchy. Yet it was precisely this hierarchy whose power was at issue. Far from checking centralization, the effect of each palliative was further to increase the power of the Secretariat.

It was against this background that a dramatic struggle over power and policy took place within the Politburo during the mid-1920s. That Stalin gained the ascendancy over Lenin's other heirs is to be explained first and foremost by his position at the centre of the party apparatus. Through his confidential personal secretariat and the close links he forged with the leadership of the secret police, he acquired access to privileged information, not least concerning the other leaders. Through the Orgburo and the party Secretariat he had unequalled influence over the Politburo agenda, over the implementation of Politburo resolutions, and above all over the appointment of Party officials. The ever-growing number of middle and higher-ranking Party members promoted by and indebted to the General Secretary gave him a clear advantage over his rivals. But this was not the sole source of his success. It is a mistake to assume that in the 1920s his allies and appointees were all mere placemen willing to endorse whatever course he cared to choose. Stalin also proved highly sensitive to the hopes and anxieties, the pride and the prejudices of the upper echelons of the Party. The twists and turns in his own attitude to the dilemmas of the 1920s closely mirrored majority opinion among them. And the more often he emerged as spokesman for the majority, the easier it became for him to portray his critics as out of step, disloyal, and reckless of the interests of the beloved Party.

The central question at issue was the tempo and means of industrializing Russia. For the Bolsheviks, the restoration of pre-war industrial production could be no more than a beginning. Until revolution spread to the West, military security and ideological independence seemed to require that the Soviet Union build an industrial base comparable or superior to that of the other Great Powers. In domestic terms, too, large-scale industrialization seemed essential. It was through industrialization that a social structure dominated by petty-bourgeois peasants would give way to one founded on a mass working class committed to common ownership. Moreover, Russian Marxists had always viewed the productive power of modern factory industry as the prerequisite for socialism. It alone would provide the economic base for the wealth, the leisure, the mass education, and cultural richness which they associated with full-blown socialism. Their international predicament, their sense of social isolation, the entire ideological framework within which the leadership operated demanded that peasant Russia be transformed by large-scale industrialization.

The aim was clear. The means were not. The basic problem, as they saw it, was one of capital. To move beyond the restoration of existing machinery required investment. The construction of new factories, mines, dams, railways, and roads involved massive expenditure before any return could be expected. Where were the funds to come from? Witte, confronted by the same problem in the 1890s, had relied overwhelmingly upon foreign loans financed by 'savings' extracted from Russian peasants and workers. At first the Bolsheviks too hoped that the West, even before succumbing to revolution, would provide a source of capital. When the foreign trade blockade was lifted in 1920, and the following year a trade treaty was negotiated with Britain, they sought direct loans and offered concessions to foreign entrepreneurs for the development of specified areas of the economy. At first only Germany – herself desperately short of capital – proved willing to be drawn into closer relations with the Soviet pariah. But Bolshevik hopes remained high. The West would surely find it profitable to overcome ideological distaste and, in exchange for token compensation for the debts repudiated in 1917, would invest in Russia. In 1924 the British Labour government led the way in granting *de jure* recognition to the regime and opened trade negotiations involving considerable investment. Before the draft treaty was ratified, however, the Labour government fell and in November the new Conservative administration rejected the package.

For most Bolsheviks, the British decision was crucial since both France and the USA were markedly more hostile. With post-war Europe regaining stability, Western revolution was becoming an increasingly remote prospect. The Soviet Union stood alone. But to conclude that the revolution was doomed, that October had been based on a gross misjudgement of Western prospects, was unthinkable. It was a month later, in December 1924, that Stalin first spoke of the prospect of building socialism in one country. His claim that Lenin himself had believed this possible was dubious, but he was articulating the conclusion towards which foreign and domestic isolation was driving the regime. In doing so he took a major step towards identifying his own leadership with faith in the future.

Of itself, the act of faith that Russia could build socialism on her own still failed to explain where the funds for investment would come from. In the mid-1920s, the official party line, endorsed by Stalin, remained firmly wedded to NEP. Its most enthusiastic spokesman was Bukharin, editor of *Pravda* since 1917 and a full member of the Politburo from 1924. He believed that the market mechanism of NEP provided a method of accumulating the capital necessary for industrialization. As peasant agriculture developed, their demand for industrial goods would expand. Consumer industries would be able to make economies of scale and raise efficiency so that industry itself would furnish some of the necessary surplus. At the same time, a judicious combination of tax and price policies would 'pump over' part of peasant income into the industrial sector. Even the kulaks, by their efficiency, would unwittingly hasten industrialization. At the same time, he argued that in social terms NEP represented a realistic road to socialism. The middle and poor peasants would gradually be won round to common ownership and production. Starting with the small credit and trading co-operatives which were being created in their thousands by peasant communes, and on which Lenin had come to set great store, the State would lead them step by step to realize the advantages of merging their strips of land as well. They would move away from their petty-bourgeois aspirations and voluntarily set up collective farms. For Bukharin it was axiomatic that the State must uphold the alliance, the *smychka*, with the peasants, and avoid any return to the confrontation of 1921. By maintaining a balance between agriculture, consumer industry, and heavy industry, the regime would gradually guide the Soviet Union towards industrial development and 'come riding into socialism on a peasant nag'.

From the start, however, NEP had aroused grave misgivings within the Party. As a brief tactical move it might have been unavoidable in 1921. But to his critics Bukharin's scenario seemed to imply a protracted retreat from the heady promise of October. It seemed to pander to the 'capitalist' as against the 'socialist' sector of the economy, to give priority to agriculture rather than industry. Convinced as the 'Left' oppositionists were that the peasants were now at last rapidly dividing between rich and poor, they saw

199

Bukharin's strategy as a victory for the kulaks who, they believed, controlled the bulk of the grain supply. In their eyes, moreover, he appeared to dodge the crucial issue of capital accumulation. E. A. Preobrazhensky, their most trenchant economist, argued frankly that the major source of capital for industrial development must come from the peasantry. To pretend that this could be done in sweet harmony was unrealistic. Kulaks as well as Nepmen, the tens of thousands of petty traders and small-scale private manufacturers flourishing as capitalism re-emerged, must be heavily taxed to serve the needs of industry. Passive estimates of future trends must be replaced by an active investment programme designed to speed up industrialization.

The potential support for a more 'heroic' approach to the building of socialism extended far beyond the ranks of a few prominent 'Left' economists and politicians. NEP frustrated the idealism of party members old and new, especially among the rapidly growing Komsomol. It exasperated Red Army warriors returning triumphant to civilian life, eager to reap the rewards of victory and accustomed to overcoming obstacles with swift and drastic action. The painfully slow improvement in working-class wages and working conditions, the dilapidated and overcrowded housing, the rudimentary medical provision, and above all the high rate of urban unemployment seemed to fly in the face of the Party's *raison d'être*. There was deep resentment that 'bourgeois' managers and specialists should be running factories, staffing state planning agencies and continuing to enjoy the privileges and favourable differentials which the leadership had used to win them over during the Civil War. Moreover, the economic volte-face of 1921 seemed to be complemented by a similar retreat in other fields where radicals had championed the immediate introduction of 'proletarian' culture and social norms. Lenin had, in fact, always regarded many of the more extreme programmes with scepticism and insisted that Russia's cultural heritage be preserved. In practice, economic chaos and civil war had ensured that, even at their height, most of these experiments made very limited impact upon urban life and none at all upon the peasantry. In the case of the attack upon the traditional family, radicals were thrown onto the defensive by the hostile reaction of working-class as well as peasant women and the problems posed by the millions of children orphaned by the Civil War. Where religion was concerned, the party leadership preferred to concentrate upon atheist propaganda rather than forcible suppression of religious institutions which ran the risk of alienating believers, especially among the peasantry, and creating sympathy for priests. Having briefly supported a reformist challenge to patriarchal authority among Orthodox priests, the Party reached a *modus vivendi* with Church leaders and in 1923 released Patriarch Tikhon from a year's imprisonment. But there remained a strong millenarian current, fed by and feeding the utopian dreams of avant-garde artists and intellectuals, which ran against the grain of the compromises associated with NEP.

The nature of these compromises should not be misconstrued. In the cultural sphere, as in every other except that of the rural economy, the tolerance granted by the Party was narrowly subscribed. Yet the Commissariat of Enlightenment, under Lunacharsky, did not throw its full weight behind the challenges which Marxist scholars presented to an older generation, or respond to the demands from militants in some fields that a single radical orthodoxy be imposed. Instead, it reached a conditional rapprochement with the old cultural elites. Despite party censorship, and although they were heavily dependent on state-run institutes and publishing outlets, non-Marxist specialists and intellectuals – historians, social scientists, psychologists, natural scientists – were given considerable scope for research and publication, and they remained an overwhelming majority among the members of the Academy of Sciences. The agrarian sociologist, A. V. Chaianov and his colleagues, for example, were able to pursue their debate with agrarian Marxists over the issue of whether or not market relations were breaking up the traditional peasant family farm and generating social differentiation in the village. Likewise, non-Marxist artists and writers, the so-called 'fellow-travellers', enjoyed a measure of independence. As a result, despite the decimation of the pre-war cultural elite – many of whom had been among the estimated 2 million Russians who emigrated after the revolution – the 1920s were a period of great creativity and innovation, reflecting the euphoria, the tragedy, the drama through which Russia had passed. Several major novelists established themselves, including B. Pilnyak (1894–1937), I. E. Babel (1894–1941), and M. A. Bulgakov (1891–1940), while Boris Pasternak (1890–1960) consolidated the reputation he had made with his collection of poems on 1917, *My Sister Life*, and O. E. Mandelshtam (1891–1938) wrote his most famous poems. But the relatively privileged status of these non-workers and non-Communists contradicted the whole ethos of the Party.

Moreover, during NEP the Party's political monopoly was fully exploited to propagate this ethos, to establish the new Bolshevik orthodoxy. The revolution had opened a new era in human history. It had brought the proletariat to power. In cooperation with the peasantry, the workers of the Soviet Union were building the first socialist society, an egalitarian society in which the masses would at last be free of exploitation. This was the meaning of Bolshevik rule: the Party was the vanguard of the proletariat. It had forged the mighty alliance of workers and peasants which had overthrown the brutal oppression of bourgeoisie and landowners and exposed the cynical phrasemongering of the Church. It had routed the savage White attempt at counter-revolution. It had repelled the rapacious invading armies of the capitalist powers and continued to uphold the revolutionary settlement against the vicious hostility of Western governments. On Lenin's death, this process of legitimizing the Party's rule was increasingly focused upon his image. From 1924 the cult of the departed prophet was developed by all the

8.3 Lenin lying in state, January 1924. Tomsky, Zinoviev and Kamenev look on. Lenin's body was subsequently embalmed and preserved. His mausoleum on Red Square, with its constant queue of reverent visitors, became the focal point of a cult that was almost religious in tone.

Bolshevik leaders. Lenin's 'last testament', which had been critical of all his major lieutenants, was quietly suppressed as they vied with each other to sing his praises – none with more fervour than Stalin. It was Lenin who had formed the Bolshevik Party, preserved it against the ruthless attacks of the Okhrana, led it to glorious victory in October, and laid the foundations of the Soviet Union. The personification of Marxist science, he was credited with the mind of a genius. On posters, statues, coins, and stamps his far-seeing gaze was projected across the country, the old capital was renamed to honour him, and his body was preserved in a massive mausoleum on Red Square. Identification with him became the touchstone of loyalty to the revolution, the Party, the State. And however earnestly Bukharin might insist that Lenin had come to see NEP as more than a stopgap, his legacy was of greater inspiration to those impatient for change.

What is more, despite official commitment to Bukharin's gradualism, the economic policy pursued during the mid-1920s was laying the groundwork for more active state intervention. From the moment NEP was adopted, the regime took great care to limit the scale of free enterprise. The state monopoly of foreign trade was retained, and wholesale trade was dominated by state and cooperative institutions. Moreover, as the economy recovered, state control was gradually extended. From as early as 1924 private retail trade and small-scale industry, always dependent on the state sector for the supply of manufactures and raw materials, were cut back by the use of tax and administrative measures. Where labour was concerned, the Party took a variety of steps to consolidate its influence. It retained firm control of the trade unions and ensured a rapid recovery in membership, both by making the unions responsible for an expanding system of social insurance as well as cultural and educational opportunities, and by allowing them some latitude to represent workers against management and in wage bargaining. By enrolling over half a million new working-class party members, as well as rapidly expanding Komsomol, the recruitment drives of the mid-twenties sharply raised the Party's presence on the shop-floor. Besides the sustained propaganda drive celebrating the proletarian commitment of the Party, the incentives for joining and identifying with it were heightened by providing loyal workers with opportunities for promotion into administrative positions and improved access to higher education. Moreover, energetic efforts were made to draw workers into discussion with managers and specialists through production meetings and conferences. None of this guaranteed general compliance with party wishes. Working-class discontent was real. The efforts to cut costs, raise productivity and intensify labour met with passive resistance and in 1925 provoked a significant outbreak of strikes. But hostility was directed as much against managers (and Nepmen) as against the Party: indeed party members often took a lead in criticizing management. Moreover, the effect of the high levels of unemployment and intense competition for jobs was to create sharp divisions amongst workers themselves, notably between those who were thoroughly urbanized and those who were newly-arrived migrants from the countryside, and to limit the scope for the working class to exert pressure independently of or against the Party.

State control made least headway in agriculture. As late as 1925 concessions were made to reduce the restrictions which the Land Decree of October 1917 had imposed on peasants leasing land and hiring labour. There was minimal progress in forming state and collective farms: in the mid-1920s they were responsible for little more than 2 per cent of gross farm production. Over 90 per cent of peasant households continued to farm scattered strips of land regulated only by the traditional peasant commune. The rural soviets established little authority over the commune or legitimacy in peasant eyes. And although the number of rural party members rose to 300,000 by 1927, less than half of these were peasant farmers. The Party remained thinly represented in the village and its rural organization was poorly coordinated and unreliable. But, nevertheless, there was growing confidence that as the State tightened its grip on trade, it could take a more active role in regulating the market to ensure a steady flow of grain at acceptable prices.

This extension of control was made possible by the gradual strengthening of the whole machinery of State. The Red Army, rapidly run down

203

after 1920, was reformed and gradually built up after 1923. Great care was taken to make a military career attractive by granting a variety of privileges to officers and welfare and other benefits to soldiers and their families, and the proportion admitted to the Party rose significantly. The secret police, renamed the OGPU and attached to the Commissariat of the Interior, established an extensive network to root out at source the slightest hint of 'counter-revolution'. The bureaucracy, after contracting sharply with the abandonment of 'War Communism', expanded steadily, especially in the provinces, and a sustained policy of raising the wages of lower-paid officials markedly improved morale. The low educational level of many new officials made for duplication and inefficiency, and 'bureaucracy' remained a dirty word in the Party, but by the late 1920s the Bolsheviks had a more reliable and elaborate administrative apparatus than the Tsar had ever commanded.

Nevertheless, a thoroughgoing reassessment of NEP was firmly rejected by the Politburo majority, the Central Committee, and successive Party congresses. This was in part because of genuine doubt over the viability of any alternative, and fear that a more adventurous policy would involve renewed confrontation with the peasantry. But it was also because the economic debate became intertwined with the power struggle which developed as Lenin gradually faded from the scene during 1923. It was Trotsky who was most forthright in criticizing current policy. The 'Left' course became inseparably bound up with his name. Trotsky's outstanding role in October and the Civil War, his prowess as an orator and theorist, the respect accorded him by Lenin himself suggested that he might inherit Lenin's mantle. To the other leading members of the Politburo – Zinoviev, Kamenev, and Stalin – the prospect of serving this high-handed, haughty ex-Menshevik was intolerable. His championing of the 'Left' course was enough to damn it in the eyes of the 'triumvirate'. They denounced his criticisms and successfully destroyed what they perceived as his bid for power. With Stalin in control of the Secretariat, Kamenev heading the Moscow Soviet, and Zinoviev that in Leningrad as well as being chairman of Comintern, they were well placed to minimize representation of the opposition in the upper reaches of the Party and to weed out Trotsky's supporters in the army. Although Trotsky bitterly attacked the use of administrative power to settle a political debate, his dictatorial record under 'War Communism' made him an incongruous champion of party democracy. In any case, his disdain for the minutiae of political manoeuvre, his meek acceptance of the principle 'my party right or wrong', and his recurrent bouts of illness, made him an unexpectedly feeble opponent.

With Trotsky's defeat and resignation as Commissar of War in January 1925, the 'triumvirate' broke up. Zinoviev and Kamenev became alarmed at Stalin's growing power and his skilful identification of himself as Lenin's closest and most loyal disciple. They themselves now took up many of the themes of the Left Opposition. The excessive concern of Bukharin –

and by implication Stalin – for the peasantry, they claimed, was permitting the kulaks to hold the regime to ransom. The current version of NEP made it impossible to extract the necessary grain surplus for exports and investment and would lead to degeneration. Their criticisms gave expression to genuine frustration within the Party. But they, too, came up against the impassable barrier of the Secretariat's control. Early in 1926 Kamenev was ousted from the leadership of the Moscow Soviet, while Zinoviev was removed from his base in Leningrad and, at the end of the year, was replaced as chairman of Comintern by Bukharin.

Their effort to recover lost ground by joining forces with Trotsky in the so-called 'United Opposition' in 1926 was doomed from the start. Its formation coincided with a highly successful year for NEP, seemingly justifying the optimism of Bukharin and Stalin. There was a record harvest and grain procurement went much more smoothly than in 1924 or 1925, rising by 25 per cent, while the price paid by the State fell by 20 per cent. The opposition stood condemned for believing that socialism in Russia was impossible without revolution abroad. In fact by this time Trotsky's concern, unlike Preobrazhensky and many on the Left, was to warn against autarky and to stress the role in Russia's industrialization that Western trade and investment must play even before revolution spread across the Continent. But since long before 1917 his name had been identified with the view that a lone socialist regime in Russia could not survive. With the opposition steadily losing all access to the press, his complaint that it was illogical to denounce him both for being a 'super-industrializer', urging unrealistic targets, and for his lack of faith in Russia went unheard. The dual charge stuck.

The denouement followed when in 1927 the international climate suddenly worsened. In April the leadership was badly shaken when the policy of cooperation with the Chinese Nationalists was destroyed by Chiang Kai-Shek's massacre of Chinese Communists. In May Britain broke off diplomatic relations with the Soviet Union. This was followed by a sharp deterioration in relations with France. In the atmosphere of xenophobia that developed, the opposition's insistence that in one form or another Soviet prospects depended upon closer integration with the West became politically suicidal. With Bukharin and Stalin more or less disingenuously cultivating a war scare, something approaching panic set in. The opposition was castigated not only for lacking faith in the Soviet Union and pandering to the capitalist enemy, but for treason. The OGPU, whose new leader, V. R. Menzhinsky, worked closely with Stalin, gathered 'evidence' of their supposed preparations for a *coup*. Their desperate attempts to appeal to the public outside the Party were promptly crushed by the OGPU. The leading figures were drummed out of the Party and banished from Moscow. Trotsky was exiled to Central Asia and in 1929 expelled from the Soviet Union.

At the very time the Party leadership under Stalin and Bukharin were

8.4 Stalin (front right) waves his party card during a vote at the 15th Party Congress, December 1927. The Congress confirmed the expulsion from the party of the 'Trotskyists and Zinovievists'. Also in the picture (front left) is A. A. Rykov, Lenin's successor as Chairman of the Council of People's Commissars, himself short-ly to be denounced as a leader of the so-called 'Right Opposition'.

denouncing the 'super-industrialists' and reaffirming NEP, they were also adopting ever more ambitious plans for investment in heavy industry. Where Stalin is concerned, the paradox reflects in part sheer cynicism: from at least as early as 1926 he had, in fact, come to share their vision of a dramatic industrial breakthrough. But his stance – upholding NEP while distancing himself from Bukharin's most forthright defence of the com-promises inherent in it, denouncing the adventurism of the Left while hold-ing out the promise of rapid industrial advance – closely matched the mix-ture of apprehension and frustration widespread within the Party. Moreover, the mid-1920s saw a remarkable growth in optimism throughout the Party – fully shared by Bukharin – that industrialization could be greatly accelerated without jeopardizing NEP and the *smychka*. This optimism was first expressed during 1925 by economists, most of them non-Party men, working in Gosplan, the State Planning Commission set up in 1921. The collection of basic economic statistics and the construction of a coherent model of the economy by Gosplan was itself a major source of confidence. They began to urge on the leadership a tantalizing vision of the future in which massive investment in heavy industry would be combined with a rise in the living standards of both workers and the majority of peasants. The bumper harvest and economic successes of 1926 added grist to the mill. By the spring of 1927 Gosplan had drafted a comprehensive Five-Year Plan – the period of five years being chosen to allow for the vagaries of the harvest. Experts and managers within VSNKh, citing demands from spokesmen for major industrial branches and regions for massive investment in their own particular bailiwick, criticized Gosplan's targets as too conservative and the two bodies vied with each other to produce ever more enticing visions of the future. Once Trotsky and the 'super-industrializers' had been defeated, the Politburo itself began to press the experts to raise the projected targets. In an atmosphere of mounting euphoria the optimists of 1927 were left behind, and those who expressed doubt over the feasibility of the new targets found themselves rapidly losing influence. The plan was constantly revised upwards and when in March 1929 the Politburo was presented with a final draft containing 'basic' and 'optimum' variants, they enthusiastically endorsed the latter.

The targets set for investment, which was to be concentrated in heavy industry, far exceeded anything the Left Opposition had envisaged. But even more striking was the wildly unrealistic assumption that this could be achieved without depressing living standards. In industry, labour productivity was to rise by 110 per cent, allowing for a dramatic increase both in investment and in consumption. In agriculture, not only would private peasant yields rise, but some 15 per cent of households would be drawn into efficient collective farms as mass-produced tractors and other farm machinery became available. Total agricultural output would rise by 55 per cent. The plan envisaged a simultaneous expansion in the volume of grain retained in the village, marketed in the city, and exported.

The true implications of the new tempo of industrial investment began to emerge well before the final plan was approved. By the winter of 1927–28 it was already imposing a heavy burden on worker and peasant alike. Wages began to fall and pressure to increase discipline and effort by workers intensified. Every means was used to maximize the elements of genuine enthusiasm among workers: honorary titles and privileges were awarded to outstanding workers and massive publicity used to encourage others to emulate their achievements. At the same time, managers acquired new powers to punish and dismiss disorderly, drunken, and unreliable workers and the trade unions placed ever more emphasis on raising productivity and less and less on immediate improvements in conditions.

Even more dramatic was the impact upon the peasantry. To help finance investment the State held down the price paid for grain. At the same time resources were diverted away from consumer industries serving peasant needs. Moreover, industrial prices were cut, with the result that such goods as were available were rapidly bought up in urban areas and seldom found their way to the countryside. The shortage of manufactures was made even worse by the steady squeeze placed upon private traders and by the war-scare of 1927 which triggered panic buying and hoarding in towns and cities. The village, therefore, suffered from an acute 'goods famine'. The market mechanism of NEP, delicate from the start, was seriously disrupted. Throughout the 1920s, with the disappearance of private estates, the sharp decline of enclosed private peasant holdings, and the reduction in the average land area available to peasant households, a much smaller proportion of agricultural output had been marketed than before the war. Although land use had been rationalized to some extent, investment in improved techniques had been minimal. As repeated hiccups in grain procurement in the mid–20s had shown, few peasants produced a surplus so great that they could be relied upon to sell it at artificially depressed prices. From 1927, in so far as it made sense at all for peasants to trade for cash amidst a goods famine, the price policies of the State placed a premium not upon grain but upon industrial crops, livestock and dairy produce. Accordingly, peasants expanded their output of these products and preferred to sell them rather than their surplus grain. The upshot was that in the autumn of 1927, with peasants in most regions finding little incentive to market their grain, the State purchasing agencies could not nearly meet their requirements. Determined that peasant recalcitrance should not jeopardize industrial growth, Stalin instituted 'extraordinary measures', forcibly requisitioning grain in Siberia and the Urals. Peasant confidence, on which NEP rested, was shaken to the core.

A minority in the Party, the so-called 'Right Opposition' headed by Bukharin, A. I. Rykov, Chairman of the Council of People's Commissars, and the trade-union leader M. P. Tomsky, now protested. Although they had shared the optimism of 1927, they now urged that, even if investment targets had temporarily to be lowered, 'extraordinary measures' must end, grain be imported, and the prices offered to peasants raised. But it was too late. While officially 'extraordinary measures' were renounced, the bulk of the leadership, headed by Stalin, refused to raise the grain price significantly, to slacken the pace, or to lower the targets. They were prepared to take the gamble that the State was now strong enough to overcome all obstacles to an industrial breakthrough, including passive resistance by the peasantry. The following winter a new version of 'extraordinary measures' was introduced, private outlets for grain were rapidly closed down, and rationing began to be introduced in the cities.

The commitment to forced industrialization had gathered irresistible momentum. It had unleashed the pent-up frustration that NEP had generated within the Party and among worker activists enthused by the socialist vision held out to them. It promised a return to the heroic tradition of October and the Civil War, to an attack on all the bourgeois deformities of NEP in culture, law, and social life. Every field was infected by this militant, millenarian atmosphere. In place of the 'united front' policy, which had failed so dismally in China and elsewhere, Comintern moved abruptly towards a policy of extreme polarization, denouncing foreign socialists as the supreme evil. The new mood was skilfully encouraged by Stalin. The proletarian offensive, he proclaimed, would provoke intensified resistance by hostile elements. In the summer of 1928, amidst massive publicity, a group of 'bourgeois' specialists from the Shakhty region of the Donbass were publicly tried for foreign-inspired sabotage. Similarly, the grain shortage was blamed on deliberate kulak defiance: to oppose rapid industrialization, to criticize forced requisitioning was tantamount to supporting the class enemy. To do so at a time of supposed foreign danger was treason. The Right Opposition was isolated and denounced, and its leading figures removed from office. The Soviet State embarked upon a programme of social engineering without precedent in human history.

Chapter 9 ....

Stalin's revolution from above (1928–1941)

Between 1928 and the German invasion of 1941 the Soviet Union underwent a spectacular transformation. The industrialization achieved during the period of the First, Second, and (truncated) Third Five-Year Plans (1928–32, 1933–37, 1938–41) was truly revolutionary in scope. The emphasis throughout was upon heavy industry, upon engineering and metallurgical works, together with the fuel and transport connections on which they depended. In established industrial centres such as the Moscow and Leningrad regions, old factories were modernized and expanded and entirely new industries brought into being. In the south and east whole industrial complexes, towns, and major cities were thrown up. Most striking was the combine centred on Magnitogorsk in the southern Urals and Stalinsk in the Kuznets basin. Massive new coal-mines and steelworks were opened, quadrupling total output in these key sectors during the period. Electricity generation increased ten times with the help of a number of gigantic dams, including the huge construction on the Dnieper. The existing railway network was broadened and extensive new lines laid down, while several vast canals, notably that linking the Volga and the White Sea, were dug. The infrastructure for the exploitation of Russia's resources was expanded out of all recognition.

The overall rate of industrial growth achieved is hotly disputed. Different methods of measurement yield sharply divergent results; light industry languished far behind heavy industry; and the quality of output in some sectors was too poor to make international comparisons meaningful. Whereas Soviet indices grossly inflated the growth rate, some post-Soviet Russian estimates are lower even than those made by sceptical Western commentators. Nevertheless, it seems probable that overall industrial output in 1940 was 2.5 times the volume of output in 1928. This expansion was by no means evenly spread over the period. The First Five-Year Plan, which was proclaimed fulfilled nine months early, saw the largest number of

9.1 Kuznetsk, 1932. A blast furnace in the Kuznetsk combine, one of the massive industrial developments undertaken during the First Five-Year Plan.

construction projects initiated, but many were completed only in the mid- or late 1930s, and it was not until then that they began to contribute to output. Moreover, there were severe setbacks. The winter of 1932–33 saw a drop in output and in the rate of investment, and from 1937 onwards most production indices climbed much more slowly as defence expenditure soared and the Red Army was expanded in response to the threat from Nazi Germany. Nevertheless, by 1941 the Soviet Union had established a mighty, if crude, industrial base.

There were three key ingredients in this achievement. The first was an extremely high rate of investment. The labour and the materials necessary for construction projects which took years to give any return had somehow to be paid for. The millions of workers digging, carrying, building, and assembling machinery had to be fed, housed, and clothed. The burden was increased by the low level of both labour and management skills. During the period of the First Five-Year Plan labour productivity actually fell and resources had to be poured into education and training schemes for workers, and for hundreds of thousands of technicians, industrial managers, and administrators. In addition, the machinery being installed in factories and mines had to be paid for. During the early years the great bulk of it had to be imported from the West. The availability of Western technology and a significant number of Western technicians was, of course, a precondition for the whole industrialization drive. But these imports had to be financed at a time when the onset of the Great Depression had reduced to rock-bottom world prices for Russia's traditional primary produce exports. Total investment during the period approached 25 per cent of gross national product (GNP), reaching 30 per cent in 1932. What made this historically high level particularly remarkable was that, unlike Witte's investment drive in the 1890s, it was achieved with minimal foreign credit. Soviet investment could be financed only by domestic accumulation, by restraining internal consumption, by forced saving. The deprivation, especially during the most difficult early years, was horrendous. A society in which most people already lived all too close to the breadline experienced a drop in living standards without precedent in peacetime.

The second key ingredient was the massive mobilization of underutilized labour. In little over a decade the urban population leaped by 30 million. The industrial labour force rose from one eighth to one third of the working population. Although the pool of urban unemployed bequeathed by NEP, together with wives of workers already living in the city, accounted for part of this increase, the great bulk was drawn from the peasantry. The countryside, of course, was heavily overpopulated and much of the adult peasant population was in effect underemployed, but the speed at which the shift was achieved was phenomenal. Equally remarkable was the fact that the major urban migration took place in 1930 and 1931 when working-class living standards were under greatest pressure. Millions of peasants were 'attracted' to industrial employment despite chaotic overcrowding in the cities, minimal food rations, and the complete absence of basic amenities.

The third ingredient was the vast expansion in the scope of state power. Private enterprise, already severely restricted before 1928, was virtually eliminated. Independent manufacture and commerce were taken into public hands and, with the collectivization of agriculture, almost all the means of production were brought into the hands of the State. This made it possible to concentrate effort on priority areas and for the central planning agencies to direct the different sectors of the economy accordingly. Broad goals identified by the party leadership were translated by Gosplan into a detailed plan which, in theory at least, covered all major fields of the economy. The rapidly proliferating and increasingly specialized economic commissariats were then given the task of subdividing the production targets for their particular sector between republics, regions, cities and individual plants.

The means by which investment and labour were mobilized and the entire economy brought under state control involved the use of force – force on a scale which beggars the imagination: whole social groups were brutally coerced and individual security undermined. The apparatus of coercion established during the 1920s was vastly expanded. At its centre stood the state security police, the NKVD (as the OGPU became in 1934), assisted by a network of ubiquitous informers. The NKVD was involved in each facet of the industrialization drive – the collectivization of the peasantry, the enforcement of labour discipline, the supervision of industrial management, welfare provision, education and the cultural field in general. It oversaw a sprawling penal system. The size of the detained population is the subject of fierce controversy. But even if the grimmest estimates – 16 million in 1938 – are wide of the mark, the memoirs on which they are based bear witness to the monstrous image of the NKVD and the fear it inspired. And even if newly-available archival material suggests much lower figures for those detained at any one time, the overall number to pass through the NKVD's hands remains astronomical since there was a constant flow in and out of detention. The number held in prison repeatedly approached half a million. The number of exiles in 'special resettlement areas' – predominantly peas-ants in the early and mid-thirties, supplemented at the end of the period by deportees from newly-annexed Baltic, Polish and Ukrainian territories – was at least twice that figure and possibly many times larger. Most notorious were the corrective labour colonies and above all the viciously harsh labour camps of the GULAG, where life expectancy was pitifully short. Even according to the lowest, most scrupulously documented estimates, their numbers approached 2 million by the end of the decade. Moreover, the forced labour of detainees provided the NKVD with an economic base of its own. This underpinned its freedom not only from public control, but even from supervision by the Party. While the party hierarchy shadowed that of the State and economy, the NKVD monitored the conduct and loyalty of party members themselves. Only at the highest level were the roles reversed: the leadership of the NKVD was appointed by and responsible to the Politburo. But in the course of the 1930s, as Stalin's ascendancy over his colleagues grew, he established personal control over the police hierarchy. In 1936 he forced through the appointment of his protégé N. I. Yezhov, a zealous advocate of drastic measures against corruption and misconduct among party officials, to head the NKVD. The sequel was the 'Great Terror' of 1936–38, which, of all the stains on Stalin's record, has been least satis-factorily explained. The proud claimant to Lenin's mantle unleashed the NKVD against tens of thousands of leading party figures – industrial man-agers, officials, intellectuals, officers, and members of the Politburo itself.

Until the 1960s the label generally used in the West to describe the social order under Stalin was 'totalitarian', and in the post-Soviet period it has been eagerly taken up by Russian historians. The term highlights some of the cardinal features of the 1930s. Not only was personal security totally destroyed, but with every working citizen effectively an employee of the e, the scope of state power did in a sense become total. Thus, besides direct legal and punitive sanctions, the State commanded the sanctions available to it as employer and as the source of welfare benefits in housing, education and health care. Virtually all social relationships were mediated through the State, and the very distinction between the political-legal power of the State, on the one hand, and the more or less autonomous economic, social, and cultural activity of the citizen, on the other, was effaced. Moreover, the democratic and federal facade of this Leviathan was a charade. The 'Stalin' Constitution of 1936 recognized eleven Union Republics (the three Slav republics of Russia, Ukraine, and Belorussia; the three republics of the former Transcaucasian Federation: Georgia, Armenia and Azerbaizhan; and five Central Asian Republics: Kazakhstan, Kirgizia, Uzbekistan, Turkmenistan and Tadzhikistan), as well as lower tiers of 'autonomous' republics, regions and areas to accommodate some of the smaller nationalities within the Union Republics. In theory, all power belonged to the working people, who expressed their will through the election of a pyramid of soviets and republican governments, which voluntarily delegated authority to the federal, or Union, government in Moscow. In practice, control over the policies pursued by the 'totalitarian' State was monopolized by one party bound by allegiance to an all-embracing official ideology and structured to concentrate decision-making power at the apex. But the image the label conjures up of a one-man dictatorship acting through streamlined state machinery to remould a passive society at will needs substantial qualification.

As far as the leadership is concerned, the pall of secrecy hanging over the decision-making process at the top was so thick that despite the opening of the archives, historians can still catch no more than the occasional glimpse. By the end of the period, certainly, Stalin's personal power had reached prodigious proportions. The cult surrounding his personality approached deification. On public occasions of all kinds tribute was paid to the great 'father', to his all-seeing genius, to this source of almost miraculous inspiration. His immediate colleagues stood in terror of him. He recklessly imposed his own views even in fields where his knowledge was negligible. His personality – a singularly repulsive concoction of power-lust, megalomania, cynicism, and suspicion, further envenomed by his wife's pathetic suicide in 1932 – affected the fate of millions. But evidence is mounting that during the crucial early stages of the industrialization drive, at least until 1936, Stalin by no means went unchallenged. The most forthright denunciation not only of Stalin himself but of forced collectivization, frantic industrialization and the whole thrust of official policy, was a bulky 200-page document by M. Riutin which circulated among Central Committee members in 1932. Riutin had been expelled from the Party two years earlier, but it seems that when Stalin now demanded that the death penalty be applied, a Politburo majority defeated him. The supposed threat posed by S. M. Kirov, the Leningrad Party Secretary, the reported invitation to him by several delegates at the Party Congress in 1934 to take over as General Secretary, and the rumour that he secured far more support than did Stalin when the Congress elected the new Central Committee, are unproven. But by the mid-30s there does appear to have been growing friction among the leadership over the problems that confronted them. Rather than reflecting the single will of the General Secretary, the regime's policy was the outcome of genuine, though unpublicized, struggle and debate within the upper reaches of the Party.

The machinery of State, extending from the centre of power to far-flung cities and villages, was anything but streamlined. The police, administrative and party bureaucracies alike were in a state of hectic growth and ceaseless flux, bedevilled by poor communications across a vast country embracing a hundred different nationalities, marred by gross waste and inefficiency, racked by regional and sectoral rivalries, and open at every level to corruption and abuse. For all the appearance of a rigid hierarchy, of officials bound to obey orders at peril not only of their jobs but of their liberty and even their lives, the leadership was constantly frustrated by its own servants. Not surprisingly, Moscow's plans proved again and again to be out of touch with reality. In 1929, to take one example, it had been estimated that the industrial labour force would rise by some 50 per cent by 1932. In fact, it doubled. Few of the extremely high production targets of 1929 – which were raised even further during 1929 and 1930 – were achieved. Indeed the economic development of the period bore only the most general relationship to the Five-Year Plans, or even to the more detailed One-Year Plans, drawn up in Moscow. The 'planned economy' hardly deserves the name. Based on extravagant optimism about such key variables as weather conditions and foreign demand for Soviet exports, it lurched from crisis to crisis. It was beset by bottlenecks and imbalances, began massive programmes only to halt them half-finished, entailed waste on a colossal scale, and virtually abandoned vast and vital areas of the economy, such as housing and health provision, as residues left to fend for themselves. Neither the statistical information nor the instruments of control available to the centre approached the level of sophistication suggested by the 'totalitarian' model. The power of the centre was enormous, but it was power of the most crude, clumsy, and often counterproductive kind.

The major defect of the totalitarian model, however, lies elsewhere. This is in the impression it conveys that Soviet society was a cowering mass responding only to orders from above. Such a view distorts the dynamics of Soviet industrialization. On the one hand, the panoply of devices used to motivate and discipline the labour of workers and peasants proved dismally unsuccessful. Peasant apathy, neglect and petty insubordination on the newly-created collective farms amounted to a form of passive resistance which all the seemingly unlimited power of the State could not overcome.

Likewise, no matter how furiously the State hurled down decrees against the high turnover of labour, or against absenteeism, slipshod work, defiance of management and damage to machinery, it proved unable even to approximate to the degree of control over the individual worker to which it aspired. As on the collective farm, what happened on the factory floor was in large measure beyond its control. No less important a qualification of the totalitarian image is the fact that, in addition to coercion, the State drew not only upon the fierce enthusiasm of a highly motivated minority but also upon the active support of many more who were won over by the untold opportunities which industrialization opened up for individual advancement. Moreover, the backdrop of international tension against which it was carried out provided powerful justification, even in the eyes of those who gained nothing. From the war scare of 1927 until the Nazi invasion of 1941 there was almost chronic fear of an impending attack upon the Soviet Union. This created an atmosphere in which national security seemed to depend upon cooperation with party policy, and anything short of fulsome commitment easily came to be seen as treason. The Stalinist industrial breakthrough was marked by a blend of ruthless coercion, deliberate and unwitting insubordination, and genuine consent. Only by grasping the nature of this blend is it possible to understand the most astonishing decade in Russian history.

The supreme victims of coercion were the peasantry. The confrontation over the procurement of grain in 1928 became progressively more acute. The quantities collected during the second half of 1928 and the early months of 1929 were disappointingly low: this was in part because adverse weather had severely hit the crop in southern Ukraine and the North Caucasus, but it reflected above all the State's refusal to raise the official price for grain. In desperation, Moscow looked to western Siberia, where there was an excellent harvest and the proportion of peasants with a significant surplus was relatively high. Taking a lead from Stalin, who had urged that somehow middle and poor peasants must be mobilized against kulaks, party officials in Siberia devised a method of bribing and browbeating some of the poorer peasants within a given village to give a show of support, however lukewarm, for confiscatory measures against their richer neighbours. Stalin hailed the 'Ural-Siberian Method' as a popular and ideologically sound development of class warfare. Its success emboldened him and increased eagerness within the Party finally to break the back of what was seen as deliberate kulak sabotage of the construction of socialism.

The solution adopted was to collectivize agriculture. This had always been the long-term goal of the Bolsheviks. The irrational waste of small-scale production would be replaced by the enormous productive power of large-scale mechanized farms. The narrow, petty-bourgeois horizons of the peasantry would give way to socialist consciousness and the division between workers and peasant, industry and agriculture would be gradually erased. Hitherto, however, it had always been stressed – by Lenin, by oppositions both Left and Right – that the essential preconditions for successful collective agriculture were the willing cooperation of the great majority of peasants, and the availability of modern agricultural machinery. As a result, during the 1920s the few state and collective farms that existed had been neglected and virtually no thought had been given to testing different models or developing precise plans for setting up new farms. But in the feverish atmosphere of 1929 these considerations were ignored. The decision to collectivize was fired by immediate anxiety to secure guaranteed supplies of grain for urban consumption and export. The objection that there was minimal support in the villages, and only a pitiful stock of agricultural machinery available, was overridden. Stalin and his allies professed to see a dramatic upsurge in voluntary collectivization and local enthusiasts stressed that vast collective farms would greatly increase output even before tractors began to pour off the production line. Regional party organs were urged to accelerate collectivization in selected areas, and in the autumn of 1929 the Central Committee decided upon a full-scale collectivization drive.

As in the days of the Poor Peasant Committees, the Party hoped to draw positive support from 'poor' peasants, deemed the immediate beneficiaries of collectivized agriculture, and to persuade the middle peasants by a sustained publicity campaign. Once again Bolshevik expectations were disappointed: coming on top of increasingly indiscriminate grain requisitioning, the campaign met with minimal peasant support. On the contrary, the vast majority of peasants were bitterly hostile. There was widespread and in some areas violent resistance.

The advantage, however, lay with the city rather than the countryside. In part this was simply because the peasants were generally unarmed and lacked any means to coordinate efforts made in thousands of isolated villages. The network of rural soviets was dominated by the Party, while the village commune, although it had enjoyed unprecedented autonomy under NEP, remained narrowly parochial. But the peasantry was also weakened by the Party's success in isolating and destroying the villagers most likely to provide leadership. The campaign was carried out in terms of a decisive class struggle against the richer peasant, the kulak. Stalin threw his full weight against any attempt to draw these 'cunning enemies' into the collective farms. Those identified as kulaks were to forfeit their property and be driven from the village. Nor was brutal treatment reserved for the tiny percentage of peasants who could seriously be considered 'rural capitalists', exploiting the labour of other peasants: to resist collectivization was enough to be denounced as a 'kulak hireling' and dealt with accordingly. The campaign could hardly have been less orderly or methodic. In many areas local party and state officials, accompanied by police and military units, resorted to indiscriminate violence which exceeded the letter if not the spirit of Moscow's orders. To lend assistance – and strengthen the resolution of local officials who proved reluctant – tens of thousands of workers were recruited to take part. Most celebrated were the so-called 25,000ers, an elite group of volunteers hastily trained in the winter of 1929–30 and despatched to the countryside to assist in cajoling the peasantry into collective farms, and in establishing the farms once they had been created on paper. By March 1930, almost 60 per cent of the browbeaten and bewildered peasants had been driven to enrol.

Nevertheless, peasant hostility was enough to check the campaign. Even if active resistance could be crushed, passive protest threatened to have disastrous economic consequences. Rather than see their livestock taken over by alien institutions, the peasantry resorted to slaughter on a wide scale, selling or consuming the meat. Moreover, the disruption of the early months of 1930 seemed likely to jeopardize the spring sowing. Alarmed, the leadership drew back. On 2 March, with characteristic political acumen, Stalin took personal credit for calling a halt in a famous *Pravda* article headed 'Dizzy with Success'. Blame for excesses was placed on the over-enthusiasm of local officials, and the peasants were offered the option of withdrawing from the collectives. Over half those enrolled promptly did so. This retreat, however, did not signal a return to voluntary collectivization. Encouraged by a very good harvest in 1930 – a year of exceptionally favourable weather – the Party resumed the forced collectivization drive. The size of each collective farm was greatly reduced, generally being based on one or two village settlements, thereby making the new structure margin-ally less bewildering for the villagers. And the peasantry did extract one per-manent concession from the Party: each household was permitted to retain a plot of somewhat less than an acre for its own use, together with a small amount of livestock. But there was to be no going back on the basic prin-ciple: those who resisted collectivization were subject to swingeing penalties and the mass exile of kulaks was stepped up. By the end of the decade the number of independent peasant farmers had fallen from over 90 per cent in the 1920s to 2.6 per cent of the rural population.

Soviet agriculture was collectivized at the cost of untold human misery. Living standards in the village fell catastrophically as rural handi-craft and private trade collapsed and, above all, the peasantry lost control over the crop. For some the consequences were fatal. Serious harvest failures in 1931 and 1932, brought on by the dislocation of collectivization and exacerbated by severely adverse weather conditions, caused horrendous famine in 1933. Some 5 million people, predominantly in the Ukraine, died of disease and starvation. Even for those who survived, the shock of collec-tivization was traumatic. Tens of millions of peasant men, women, and chil-dren had the most basic rhythms of their lives brutally broken. Not only was the dignity they derived from a sense of independence harshly under-mined, but the transfer of property was accompanied by an assault upon their entire culture. There was a massive campaign against religion, most village churches were shut down and the great majority of the clergy uprooted. Without destroying peasant faith, this deepened their sense of alienation and oppression. For the victims of 'dekulakization' the ordeal was even worse. Stalin's commitment to destroy the kulaks 'as a class' signalled the wholesale deportation of up to 5 million peasants. Exiled to remote regions of the east and north, the older men, women, and children eked out a meagre existence in forced settlements, while many of the able-bodied men were herded into rapidly expanding labour camps.

In economic terms, too, collectivization dealt a staggering blow to the countryside. The slaughter of livestock triggered by the initial campaign made an immediate impact upon draught power, fertilizer, and animal produce. Moreover, the damage took years to repair because of the chronic shortage of food and fodder in the village. 'Dekulakization' removed many of the ablest farmers just when the complex shift to collective methods placed a premium upon skill and initiative. In any case, minimal effort was made to draw upon peasant expertise. The old peasant commune was abolished and although in theory each farm was the property of its members, in practice management was taken out of peasant hands. The farm's 'elected' chairman was effectively a party appointee, and in the early years these posts were often taken by the workers sent out to help impose collectivization. Moreover, because peasant labour proved so apathetic, and results so disappointing, the authorities replaced chairmen with dizzying frequency and intervened more and more often in the detailed running of the farms. This interference not only alienated the peasantry further, but was often so arbitrary and based on such flimsy knowledge of agriculture in general and local conditions in particular that it exacerbated the disruption. The most serious defect of the system was the lack of incentive provided for the peasantry. This ensured that their initial hostility became deeply entrenched. Their level of pay, in cash and kind, depended upon the surplus left after state requirements and running costs had been met. With the State's appetite seemingly insatiable, this was a derisory sum. Moreover, since a good crop merely led to higher compulsory deliveries to the State, collective farm labour seemed sheer drudgery. Contrary to the whole ethos of collective farming, the peasantry devoted as little effort as possible to tilling, tending and harvesting the land. Far from expanding, therefore, agricultural production as a whole dropped steeply during the early 1930s, with the grain harvest substantially below pre-collectivization levels. And when slow recovery did set in – after a disastrous harvest in 1936 – a wholly disproportionate contribution was made by the peasants' cherished household plots into which they poured their time and energy.

So damaging was the impact of collectivization that some historians have even denied that the agricultural sector of the economy made any overall contribution to the industrialization drive. It is true, of course, that considerable resources from industry had to be devoted to providing tractors

9.2 Collective farm workers are marched off to the fields. Farm managers found it impossible to overcome the hostility and apathy peasants showed towards collective-farm work.

simply to restore total draught power to the pre-collectivization level. And the peasantry gained some compensation for the ludicrously low grain procurement prices by selling fruit, vegetables, wool, meat, and dairy products from their private plots on the special collective farm markets. But the over-all effect of collectivization was completely to subordinate the peasantry to the city, the needs of agriculture to those of industry.

The State secured an unshakeable grip upon the grain harvest. Instead of having to buy grain at a price acceptable to the peasantry, the State collected its requirements at nominal prices, freely defaulting on promised supplies of industrial goods. When the crop was particularly poor, the peasantry naturally tried to withhold the 'quotas' set, but with management responsible to the Party, it became impossible to conceal stocks and in 1932 the death penalty was imposed for stealing collective farm livestock or crops. Officials who failed to extract the required quantities of grain – whether through compassion or inefficiency – were ruthlessly dealt with. Where necessary, shock brigades invaded the farm and stripped stocks bare. Moreover, even tighter and more regular control was established by concentrating tractors and other scarce machinery in separate state-run machine-tractor stations (MTS): the grain was collected the moment it had been harvested and threshed. In 1930 and 1931 grain exports soared to pay for vital capital goods imports, and, regardless of peasant needs, the swelling urban population was fed. With the exception of 1932–33, the 1930s saw state procurements steadily rise – and this at a time when the harvest was at best inadequate. The peasantry were the major victim of forced saving.

Besides squeezing grain from the peasantry, collectivization also played a vital role in bringing about the massive shift of labour which underlay Soviet industrialization. The most notorious aspect of this shift was the use made of forced labour. Millions of kulak deportees, supplemented for years ahead by peasants arrested for stealing state and kolkhoz property or failing to meet minimum work norms, were put to work in the most inhospitable regions of the north and east. There can be no doubt that their slave labour in construction, mining, and lumbering – in regions so severe that free labour would have required exorbitant incentives – made a significant contribution to industrialization. In addition to those incarcerated in the camps of the GULAG, many more were used outside the camps in the construction of roads and canals and even played a part in building such cities as Magnitogorsk. The brutal treatment of these prime victims of collectivization established a precedent for the exploitation of the political and national groups repressed in the later 1930s and 1940s. The early Bolshevik notion that sanctions should rehabilitate rather than punish offenders was abandoned. The arbitrary and violent exercise of authority spread throughout the body politic.

Collectivization also played a wider role in driving millions of peasants into industrial labour. By 1930 the pool of urban unemployed had dried up. With urban living standards falling sharply and rationing extended to all major goods, migration to the city, running at 1 million during the later 1920s, might have been expected to dwindle away. Instead, for the next three years it soared to the staggering figure of 3 million a year. This was the direct result of collectivization. So dreadful were conditions in the village – especially for those who ran the risk of being denounced as 'kulak hirelings' – that even the abysmal conditions in the city seemed preferable. By the end of 1932 the rural exodus was so great that a system of internal passports was introduced to try to prevent peasants leaving their collective farms without police permission.

Although the workers' experience of the industrial breakthrough bore no comparison to the peasant ordeal, it was grim. The forcible depression of working-class consumption played a critical role in making possible the high rate of investment. Much the worst period was from 1929 to 1933. While urban population growth exploded, housing space rose by less than half the planned area and overcrowding reached sordid and degrading proportions. Family life became virtually impossible and individual privacy was out of the question. Wherever bottlenecks developed in the economy the expansion of light industry was sacrificed to the needs of heavy industry. Given the virtual elimination of artisan production – and private shops – the result was acute shortage, a vigorous black market, and all the frustration and humiliation of endless queues and contemptuous service. Rationing of both food and consumer goods was extremely tight and average real wages fell precipitately.

The nadir was reached in 1933. During the Second Five-Year Plan period conditions began to improve. Whereas the initial version of this plan, drawn up in 1932, had maintained overwhelming emphasis upon investment in heavy industry, during the gruelling year of 1933 the balance was substantially revised. The final version, adopted at the Party Congress of February 1934, increased significantly the resources devoted to light industry and consumer goods. During the 'three good years' which followed, rationing was gradually phased out, health and social security provision improved, and real wages began to recover. Life, nevertheless, remained hard, and towards the end of the decade, as the proportion of the budget spent on defence soared from 11 per cent in 1935 to over 32 per cent in 1940, consumption was again cut back.

Besides suffering wretched conditions, the working class were also subjected to a panoply of measures designed to enforce rigorous labour discipline. For the central planners, labour productivity and efficiency represented an absolutely critical variable on which much else depended. Yet the bulk of the new labour force was entirely lacking in industrial skill and experience. Moreover, they reacted to harsh and unfamiliar working conditions by small-scale, more or less deliberate insubordination and carelessness, by indulging in drunkenness and absenteeism, and by changing their jobs with a frequency that bedevilled management. Contrary to expectations, productivity during the First Five-Year Plan fell drastically. The regime was presented with a formidable challenge: the raw recruits had somehow to be welded into a disciplined and stable labour force. The piece-rate system of wage payment was extended to most industries, and the authority of both management and technical and engineering specialists was steadily increased. A decree of November 1932 empowered managers to dismiss unsatisfactory workers, to withdraw their ration cards, to evict them from factory housing, and to deprive them of social benefits. Later in the decade even more stringent measures were introduced: in addition to an internal passport every employee had to carry a labour book recording details of his or her labour performance. The most draconian decrees were issued in 1940, on the eve of war. Holidays were cut and the working day extended without additional pay. Absenteeism – which was defined so as to include arriving twenty minutes late for work – made a worker liable to criminal law penalties and even a term in prison. Above all, special permission was required to leave one job for another and here too the punishment for violation was imprisonment.

Taken at face value, these decrees suggest a working class helpless before the State's determination to harness them to the industrialization drive. But in reality the ever harsher tone of labour legislation reflected the failure of earlier measures, the failure of successive steps to bend workers to the will of the authorities. What undermined the regime's efforts was the fact that workers retained a rudimentary amount of autonomy and bargaining power. This was guaranteed by the enormous demand for labour entailed in the ambitious targets of successive Five-Year Plans. The effect was to compel managers to compete with each other in order to secure and retain labour, thereby limiting their ability to discipline their workers. Their treatment of individual workers might be arbitrary, but if the management of one factory was too heavy-handed, workers could move on and sign up in another where the demands made upon them were less exacting, wages were higher or conditions better. Moreover, there was little incentive for managers to extract maximum effort from their workers or to confess slovenly work practices, defective production and spare capacity to their superiors. To do so would only lead to the imposition of higher targets and thereby increase friction between them and their workers. Even the fiercest decrees, therefore, were blunted by managers' inhibitions about implementing them.

Workers' resistance to the will of the State, however, was inchoate and inarticulate. Its economic consequences were incalculable, comparable only to the apathy and lethargy of peasants on the collective farms. But it was the effort of millions of workers pursuing individual strategies to better their lot rather than coordinated collective action. It did not present a direct threat to the regime's political stability. Despite the vast expansion of its ranks, the Soviet working class, heir to the most effective tradition of revolutionary protest in Europe, failed to mount any concerted attack upon the Stalinist State. This was primarily a reflection of the tight grip that the Party had established over all public organizations and media. With the defeat of the Right Opposition the Party itself no longer offered a medium for the expression of criticism. Any attempt at organized opposition, whether within or outside the Party, faced immediate intervention by the growing NKVD. Strikes were out of the question and from 1929 the purged trade unions became straightforward adjuncts of management, concentrating upon discipline and productivity, with minimal concern for improving welfare and wages. The political quiescence of Soviet workers is to be explained, too, by the profound divisions among them. One facet of this was the tension between native workers within the minority republics and the large number of migrant Russian workers. More generally, the massive influx of raw recruits from the countryside quickly reduced the hereditary proletariat to a minority and greatly widened differences in terms of skill, education, culture and experience. It rendered the 'working class' highly heterogeneous, intensified mutual friction, and militated strongly against the development of solidarity among them. With its better-educated and more experienced members being rapidly promoted off the factory floor, as we shall see, the Soviet working class was in no position to mount organized pressure for change.

Yet there was more to the acquiescence of workers than friction among them and sheer repression. For one thing, even during the harsh early years, they were by no means uniformly hostile to the new order. Sparse though the workers' diet might be, factory canteens guaranteed basic rations, and their needs were given clear preference over low-grade white-collar workers. For those previously unemployed, forced industrialization was a decided blessing. For many families the impact of the sharp fall in real wages was to some degree cushioned by the rapid increase in the number of women employed. Moreover, the campaign to raise productivity provided workers with new opportunities. Millions benefited from the mass adult literacy campaign of the 1930s. Every effort was made to encourage workers to acquire new skills through a wide range of training schemes. After the first tumultuous years of the 'great turn', during which there was a resurgence of radical egalitarianism, measures were taken to provide wage incentives for skilled workers. As early as 1931, Stalin began to deride 'petty-bourgeois egalitarianism': skilled workers should be rewarded by suit-able differentials. Both large wage increases and honorary awards were heaped upon shock brigades and outstanding workers: the most famous symbol of this was Aleksei Stakhanov, a coal-miner who produced fourteen times the norm – inspired of course by thoughts of Stalin. He received mas-sive publicity and 'Stakhanovs' appeared in other industries. These 'Heroes of Labour' played an important part in raising labour norms in line with improving machinery and skills, and widening the differentials between skilled and less skilled workers. With between 10 and 15 per cent receiving wages significantly above average, the effect upon working-class attitudes was by no means negligible, even if the less skilled were resentful.

In addition to the incentives used to attract positive commitment from at least a skilled minority, there was a powerful and sustained propaganda campaign to mobilize the hearts and minds of ordinary workers, to exhort them to greater effort, and to identify the industrialization drive specifically with the cause of the proletariat. This campaign was at its most dramatic during the early years of the First Five-Year Plan, from 1928 to 1931. Through press, posters, and factory meetings the Party sought to explain matters in terms of the interests of the working class. The inferior status of manual labour in the mixed economy of NEP was denounced in favour of an egalitarian society in which the masses, the rank-and-file workers, would at last receive their due. The policy of offering the status of party member to workers was vigorously pursued: some 2 million were admitted during the First Five-Year Plan, and by 1932 workers by current occupation consti-tuted almost 50 per cent of total membership. Initially, there was a surge of real enthusiasm among a minority of activist workers. While some, as we have seen, volunteered to assist with the 'battle for grain' and the implementation of collectivization, others vied with one another to increase productivity, and urged fellow workers in workshops and whole factories to engage in 'socialist competition', to speed production and to exceed planned targets. Groups of a dozen or so young workers, initially often with little encouragement from management, trade unions or the Party, formed 'shock brigades' to act as models of responsibility and self-discipline. Despite hostility from new recruits from the countryside as well as from older, skilled workers, they sought to raise output and efficiency by experimenting with new methods and by rationalizing production. Soon, however, both the 'shock worker' movement and the movement for socialist competition were taken up by the Party and the planning agencies, and turned into a national campaign. From 1930 the enthusiasm of the early shock brigades was rapidly diluted as millions enrolled as shock workers for form's sake and for the rewards membership would bring, rather than out of genuine commitment, and in later years the cult of manual labour became more muted. Nevertheless, the vision of 'building socialism' continued to be publicized through every possible medium. Bedazzling statistics of industrial achievement, improved health services, and social security provision were paraded, and to generate working-class pride and enthusiasm, the press published countless heartwarming reports of heroic efforts by individual men and women. The plan held out the promise of a rapid rise in real wage levels. And even if life was hard for their generation, the educational opportunities open to their children were expanding very swiftly, and the promise of a head-start in life encouraged a rapidly rising proportion to join the Party's youth organizations, the Pioneers and Komsomol.

Though workers might experience harassment and high-handed treatment from the authorities, the press and radio projected an ideal image of the normal condition of Soviet life. It is in this context that repeated calls by the Central Committee for less arbitrary rule should be seen. During the mid-1930s there was a substantial press campaign encouraging individual workers to criticize officials who exceeded legal bounds and obstructed the supposedly benign intentions of the great leader. In February 1935 a commission was established to revise the Constitution, and during 1936 there was wide-scale public consultation about the proposed text. In December Stalin proudly introduced 'the only thoroughly democratic Constitution in the world', resplendent with universal, direct, secret, and equal suffrage, and the full panoply of guaranteed civil liberties. The immediate sequel of the Great Terror made a mockery of the Constitution, but there can be little doubt that official propaganda succeeded at least to some extent in colouring the perceptions of rank-and-file workers. At the very least, the regime's monopoly of public discussion helped to pre-empt the development of a coherent anti-Party critique among workers.

What is certain is that propaganda of a much more negative kind struck a highly responsive chord among many workers. This was the denunciation of relatively privileged 'traitors'. The precedent was the Shakhty trial of 1928. The revelation of 'sabotage' and 'wrecking' by bourgeois specialists in touch with foreign enemies stirred powerful emotions. For the next three years, 'specialist-baiting' was widespread. It was fostered by repeated calls by the Party and press for vigilance, for the unmasking of 'Shakhtyites', and by the 'discovery' of a series of diabolical anti-Soviet organizations – in 1930 the 'Toiling Peasant Party' and the 'Industrial Party', in 1931 the Menshevik 'Union Bureau'. Economists, agrarian and industrial specialists, former SRs and Mensheviks were declared to have an extensive network of spies and wreckers permeating the organs of government. They were accused of deliberately sabotaging planned production – setting the targets too high, or too low, disrupting the supply of everything from coal to fish, and plotting the armed overthrow of Soviet power. The Great Terror of 1936–38, as we shall see, followed a similar pattern. Major public figures, including previous 'opposition' leaders such as Zinoviev, Kamenev, and Bukharin, were publicly tried for a variety of heinous crimes and plots against the Soviet Union, masterminded from abroad by the arch criminal Trotsky. A vicious combination of physical and psychological torture induced many of the accused to confess, and they were duly convicted and executed. The charges were false and in retrospect seem too absurd to be even plausible. But in the highly charged atmosphere of the industrialization drive, with the Party controlling all public comment, selective reporting of carefully stage-managed trials carried conviction. They played upon genuine fears of the traitor within, upon memories of foreign intervention, upon deep resentment at the privileges enjoyed by these *intelligenty*. Just as Stalin had predicted, class warfare was intensifying: foreign and domestic enemies alike were trying to undermine the mighty effort of the Soviet people. The witch-hunt served as a powerful conductor of the bitterness and disappointments of the 1930s. Here at last was the explanation for the discrepancy between the splendid official production figures and the squalor of daily life, here at last was an outlet for the frustration built up at work, in the apartment shared with half a dozen other families, in the endless queues.

The major beneficiaries of the economic *tour de force* were the white-collar workers. Industrialization everywhere generates a vast expansion of non-manual labour. In the Soviet case the centralized management of all aspects of the economy involved particularly explosive growth of the state bureaucracy, while the burgeoning party and police hierarchies added a further dimension. By the end of the 1930s the total number of white-collar workers approached eleven million, or some 16 per cent of the employed population. Of course, many of these had menial clerical and auxiliary tasks and were markedly less privileged than skilled workers. But hundreds of thousands of new industrial managers, technical specialists, and senior administrators were appointed. The number of graduate engineers alone rose from 47,000 in 1928 to 289,000 in 1941; the total number of employed graduates reached 750,000 while the number occupying posts of graduate status but without themselves having formal higher education was several times greater.

The experience of the white-collar elite, who came to be known collectively by the old label 'intelligentsia', was no bed of roses. At the outset of the industrialization drive a large proportion of specialists in most fields were non-party men. During the first tumultuous phase of the 'great turn' they came under fierce attack. Particularly hard-hit were specialists working in production and in the state bureaucracy. They were the prime victims of the campaign associated with the Shakhty affair of 1928, deliberately launched by Stalin to pulverize latent support for the moderation of the Right Opposition. The campaign of denunciation, enthusiastically taken up by rank-and-file workers and militant members of the Party and Komsomol, affected 'bourgeois specialists' in almost every field. A non-proletarian background was sufficient grounds for suspicion of indifference or even hostility to the 'building of socialism'. Significant numbers were arrested or at least driven from their posts.

In the middle of 1931, however, this campaign was abruptly halted. The change was signalled by Stalin in a major speech in which he suddenly proclaimed that most specialists had seen the light and could now be trusted. There were two main reasons for this volte-face. In the first place, by 1931 the number of 'red' specialists in industry was soaring. The trained personnel bequeathed by NEP could not begin to meet the economy's needs, so that the great majority of the new elite had to be educated and trained in the course of the industrialization drive. In the First Five-Year Plan period enrolments in higher education almost trebled, approaching half a million, and there was an abrupt shift to technical and production-related subjects. Moreover, from the outset Stalin and the leadership had stressed the need to train 'our own' specialists. Colleges were ordered to take high quotas of working-class students. Tens of thousands of selected workers, most of them party members, were provided with crash courses. In 1931, as a result of the campaign to promote adult Communists and workers from the factory floor, two-thirds of students in higher education were aged 23 or over. Many more were promoted without formal qualifications: indeed, the scale of upward mobility so exacerbated the shortage of skilled labour that in October 1930 a temporary halt was called to such promotions. But already suspect '- bourgeois' specialists were rapidly being outnumbered by new specialists drawn from socially and ideologically sound proletarian backgrounds. Equally important in triggering the change of course was the disruption caused by 'specialist-baiting'. Managers began to complain that they could not afford to lose experienced personnel. Moreover, specialists were directly involved in monitoring labour performance and implementing measures designed to raise labour productivity. To subject them to harassment ran counter to increasing official emphasis upon the need to tighten labour discipline, respect technical expertise, and buttress authority within each enterprise.

From 1931, therefore, the status and privileges of the white-collar elites began rapidly to improve. Managers and technical specialists alike were positively encouraged to impress workers with their superior status, and steps were taken to raise both their prestige and their morale. The new trend affected all sections of the Soviet intelligentsia. The old Bolshevik principle that party officials should be paid no more than skilled workers was openly abandoned. Indeed, the tendency evident under NEP for the higher ranks in the Party, the state apparatus, the police, the army, the cultural field, and the economy alike to acquire a wide range of privileges, including special access to rare consumer goods and housing, rapidly accelerated. This was extended to the field of education where discrimination in favour of the children of workers by current occupation was dropped and at the end of the decade school fees were introduced for the upper-secondary and tertiary level. In December 1935 the Central Committee adopted as party policy the notion that the ultimate ideal was for all Soviet citizens to be raised to the level of the technical intelligentsia. The Party's recruitment policy reflected the same trend. At the end of 1932 all recruitment was suspended and in the next two years a large proportion of the recent worker – and smaller peasant – influx was purged. When large-scale recruitment was resumed in 1939, discrimination in favour of worker applicants was abandoned and the great majority of new members were drawn from white-collar occupations. The proportion of Party members currently engaged in manual labour fell rapidly. As yet only a fifth of those with specialized or higher education (the intelligentsia) were party members, but the correlation between social privilege and party membership was becoming ever closer.

This growing elite was the major source of support for the new order. Its members, the great majority drawn from peasant or proletarian backgrounds, had good reason to identify with the Soviet system. But while their material rewards were increasing, they too were subject to coercion. Once the 'specialist-baiting' of 1928–31 subsided, pressure was most intense upon those responsible for the economy, the party officials charged with overseeing different regions and branches of the economy, the state officials of the proliferating industrial commissariats, and the directors of individual enterprises. It was not merely that they had no security of tenure in their posts and were moved at will from one post to another, or from one region to another. More fundamental was the endemic conflict between these officials and the authorities at the centre. There was permanent tension between, on the one hand, the desire of industrial and agricultural managers and officials to secure low, or at least feasible targets, which they could claim to have met successfully and, on the other, suspicion at the centre that they were underrating capacity when production quotas were being set and exaggerating production when results were reported. As we have seen, they hoarded labour, exceeded wage norms, and covered up their workers' desultory and slipshod work patterns. Moreover, officials bent the rules, struck illicit deals with suppliers of fuel and raw materials, and, above all, tolerated monstrous waste and the production of faulty or even useless goods as they ignored guidelines on quality and devoted all their energy to achieving the overriding gross output targets. This, in turn, gave rise to informal 'family circles' linking officials within and among different hierarchies. In seeking to ensure that 'their' Republic, commissariat, region, city, or enterprise secured scarce labour and raw materials, officials in the Party, the state bureaucracy, enterprise management, and, indeed, the procuracy and the police colluded in unofficial networks designed to conceal failures, circumvent unwelcome directives, and evade scrutiny from Moscow. Often enough, moreover, these networks were lubricated by patronage, nepotism, bribery and embezzlement.

To local officials and managers these practices seemed unavoidable and, indeed, evidence of skilful and effective management. The targets imposed upon them were so high, the directives on wage levels, quality control and output so incompatible, the difficulties of securing adequate labour and materials so acute, and the penalties for failure so grave that corners had to be cut. Likewise, many came to regard the occasional favour to a friend or illegal supplement to their own income as the necessary and justifiable rights of office. But in Moscow's eyes, such practices appeared not only as corruption and contravention of socialist legality but above all as potentially disastrous to the industrialization drive. Here, it seemed, was the real source of the successive economic setbacks and crises which marked the 1930s. The State's own officials were distorting the plan, defying orders, obstructing and misleading the centre, and throwing the economy into confusion. With mounting frustration the Politburo sought means to impose its will.

One method was to appoint plenipotentiaries to break through what appeared from Moscow to be deliberate obstruction. A variation on this theme was the practice of placing a number of ethnic Russians in key positions within each non-Russian republic on the premise that they would resist the embrace of local cliques. Another was to threaten the heaviest legal penalties for falsifying figures and abuse of office. A third strategy was to invite pressure from below, to encourage workers to denounce instances of abuse of power, nepotism, corruption, inefficiency and mismanagement by officials and industrial managers. One important motive behind the official support for the Stakhanovite movement in the mid-1930s was to compel management to adopt new production methods, by combining pressure from above with demands by model workers from below. Likewise, positive encouragement was intermittently given to ordinary citizens to write to the press to expose instances of dishonesty, incompetence and injustice. Yet another strategy, adopted in different forms in 1933, 1935 and 1936 and designed to tighten control over officials who belonged to the Party, consisted of repeated attempts to 'cleanse' the Party, to verify the credentials of members, to expel those who from incompetence, inertia or opposition failed to observe instructions and party norms. To the same end, there were repeated calls for 'self-criticism' and for the renewal of party democracy. In each case, however, Moscow came up against the mutual protection afforded by local cliques. And the more senior the offending officials, the better placed they were to evade and deflect intervention from the centre.

None of these strategies, therefore, appeared effective. By the mid-1930s the issue was giving rise to divisions within the leadership itself. As the economic hierarchies became ever more closely intertwined with that of the Party, middle-ranking officials began to find spokesmen in the Politburo. The 'Stalinists' became divided over how best to tackle the malfunctioning of the state and economic apparatus. More cautious members of the Politburo urged that the difficulties facing officials be taken seriously and that targets be somewhat moderated. Prominent among these were G. K. Ordzhonikidze, the Commissar of Heavy Industry, and possibly Kirov, the popular Leningrad Party Secretary, whose convenient assassination in December 1934 may well have been Stalin's own work. Stalin, V. M. Molotov (Chairman of the Council of People's Commissars until Stalin himself took over on the eve of war) and other 'super-industrializers', on the other hand, were adamant that the problem lay not in high targets but in inadequate and disloyal personnel. Rather than give way to what they saw as a threat to the tempo of industrialization, they resorted to the most drastic measures to root out and smash the corrupt networks of officials they held responsible for economic setbacks.

It is in these terms that the most plausible (though by no means fully satisfying) hypotheses to account for the scale of the Great Terror of 1936–38 have been advanced. The Great Terror is among the least adequately explained phenomena of Soviet and indeed of all modern European history. It is not difficult to identify the conditions which made it possible: the feebleness of barriers to the abuse of state power and specifically police power; the brutalized political culture bequeathed by the Civil War and collectivization; the close censorship of the media, information and public debate; the restriction of policy-making to a narrow elite within the Party; the leadership's sectarian arrogance and blood-curdling indifference to taking human life, epitomized by Stalin himself. Nor is it difficult to imagine why Stalin might want to destroy the one-time lieutenants of Lenin who were given the star roles in the great show trials of the period. The pleasure he took in their fear, humiliation and death suggests that he had long harboured vicious resentment against his former rivals. Moreover, although by the mid-1930s they were defeated men willing to heap praise upon the great leader, it is conceivable that he was wary lest one or other of them emerge as a figurehead for manifest dissatisfaction with his rule. He may have genuinely feared high-level conspiracy among those who had reason to hate him and have seen merit in using them as scapegoats for economic failures. Much more perplexing is the toll taken on current leaders of the Party, the arrest and disappearance of men promoted by the General Secretary himself, of thousands upon thousands of loyal Stalinist officials. Although the scale of the devastation inflicted upon the Party remains uncertain, the Terror extended far beyond the lists of 40,000 victims Stalin is reputed to have signed personally. During the period between 200,000 and 240,000 party members were expelled and a high proportion of them were either executed or disappeared into the camps. Some of the details were provided by Khrushchev in 1956. Of the 139 full and candidate members of the Central Committee elected in 1934, 70 per cent were arrested and shot. More than half the delegates to the Party Congress of 1934 were arrested. By 1939 only 7 of 136 regional secretaries of the Moscow region were still in their posts. The party leadership of every Union Republic was devastated for supposed nationalist tendencies, Georgia and the Ukraine being particularly hard hit. Foreign Communist Party leaders did not escape, contact with foreigners was extremely dangerous for Soviet citizens, and from 1934 the punishment for flight abroad was death. Along with the top ranks of the Party went thousands of officials associated with them in local party organizations and the various state agencies, commissariats, and branches of the economy which they headed. The leadership in every field and every organization – education, the trade unions, the judiciary, the Komsomol, the military – was decimated. In some cases the victims were associated with key figures who had at some moment opposed Stalin. In others, as in the almost suicidal devastation of the officer corps, which was accompanied by the abolition of national units within the army and the imposition of Russian as the language of command, it is just conceivable that Stalin feared conspiracy or believed bogus evidence of treason supplied by Nazi Germany. Even members of the NKVD itself fell victim – because they lacked the stomach for their task, because they provided such perfect scapegoats for excesses, or because they knew too much.

It is as the product of the ultimate attempt by Stalin and his allies to impose order on the party-state apparatus that the havoc wreaked upon the Party and the intelligentsia in general may best be understood. Their method was the wholesale dismissal, arrest and, in many cases, execution of suspect officials. Their instrument was the NKVD, headed by Yezhov. Although in some areas the NKVD had itself become enmeshed in 'family circles' of local officials, it appeared much more responsive to orders from above than the party hierarchy. With a permanent presence in every arm of the bureaucracy and every major enterprise, the security police closely monitored both the economic performance and the political sympathies of significant officials. The precedent for dealing with unsatisfactory officials had been set

9.3 A virulent 1937 caricature of Trotsky. Surrounded by the tools of his grisly trade and the symbols of his Nazi allies, the arch-criminal washes his hands in the blood of Soviet Russia.

during the most violent years of confrontation with the peasantry. Thoroughly loyal rural officials had at times felt compelled to report that it was simply impossible for the peasantry in their particular area to meet the grain quotas imposed. They had been ruthlessly punished. Under instructions from Stalin the NKVD now carried through the much more bloody purge of 1936–38.

The purge, however, was not carried out in terms of a campaign against mere economic incompetence or financial corruption, but rather in terms of an assault upon politically motivated sabotage. Stalin and his allies were either unable or unwilling to recognize that the very nature of the command economy, beset with imbalances, bottlenecks, and confusion, led even the most loyal and diligent officials to bend the rules and opened the door wide to abuse. In any case, to have admitted as much would have been to call into question the legitimacy of the 'planned economy', Soviet-style socialism and Communist rule itself. They therefore portrayed every malfunction as the deliberate handiwork of 'wreckers' motivated by political hostility to socialism, of 'traitors' infected with the disease of Trotskyism and obedient to imperialist enemies of the motherland. And all loyal citizens were urged to be ever vigilant, to do their utmost to unmask these agents of evil and expose them to the authorities. Victims could be denounced as 'enemies of the people' for anything from economic failure, through financial irregularity and falsifying data, to high-handed wielding of managerial power – or some connection, however tenuous, with a colleague, friend or relation whose 'guilt' had been established. Equally, they could be denounced on the grounds that at some stage, no matter how long ago, they had been associated with anti-Party activity – with the SRs or the Mensheviks, with the 'Right Opposition' or the 'Left Opposition'. Judged in these terms, there were few officials whose record was blameless. And the best form of defence for current officials with much to hide was not to question the need for vigilance but rather to deflect the attentions of the NKVD by pointing the finger elsewhere – be it at rivals, at subordinates, at those who might otherwise denounce them, or, most easily, at those who did indeed have a past record of political opposition. As a result, the NKVD net was cast extraordinarily wide. The combination of 'guilt by association' and the existence of very real 'family circles', linking officials within and among different hierarchies, led the secret police from one arrest to another. With NKVD officials themselves frantic to demonstrate their own vigilance and unmask their full quota of spies and saboteurs, the Terror gathered a momentum of its own. Stalin and his group had unleashed a monster which, besides devastating the upper- and middle-ranking officials who were its prime target, reached out further and further, beyond the Party and state apparatus into fields unconnected with economic production, at humble office-holders, and, to a much lesser extent, at ordinary workers. The proportion of 'counter-revolutionaries' in the GULAG, though never exceeding 'non-political' criminals, soared and according to figures recently published by the KGB itself (the successor to the NKVD), no less than 681,692 people were shot in 1937 and 1938.

A vital ingredient in the assault on the leading cadres of the Party and the State was the active part played by citizens far removed from the centres of power. There were several reasons for this. Amidst chronically high tension over real and imaginary foreign threats, spy-fever easily took hold. For those about to step into dead men's shoes or with a score to settle, there was a positive, if unattractive, motive for initiating denunciation. Even for those who had nothing to gain and saw through police fabrication it was safest to identify with the witch-hunt for traitors and fascist hirelings. But above all, tacit and sometimes vocal support from below for the purging of officials must be understood in terms of profound popular discontent. Workers eagerly seized the opportunity to vent their anger against arbitrary and abusive managers and privileged party officials. Stalin and those members of the leadership who had encouraged ordinary workers to be outspoken in their criticisms were taken aback by the vehemence of protest from below.

This was one reason why at the end of 1938 the assault on the Party and the generalized Terror abated. Those who had favoured drastic measures were made uneasy by the potential threat posed to the whole regime. To perpetuate internecine strife within the apparatus of the State might eventually trigger mass unrest. Already the confidence and authority of officials and managers had been severely shaken and their ability to discipline workers weakened. Moreover, it became increasingly difficult to believe that the Terror was winnowing out the most corrupt, unreliable and incompetent officials. Far from improving efficiency, it was manifestly damaging the economy. Key hierarchies, including Gosplan itself, had suffered a loss of personnel which threw them into confusion. The decimation of the country's skilled and experienced specialists, administrators and managers was proving a poor remedy for economic failures. With the international situation darkening, Stalin called a halt. At the end of the year Yezhov was dismissed – and subsequently arrested – and replaced by L. P. Beria, a dissolute fellow-Georgian who was to remain at Stalin's side to the end.

If the destruction of incipient opposition within the Party had been a major object of the Terror, the aim had been achieved. Stalin's political domination was beyond question; he no longer faced even the limited resistance offered by such figures as Ordzhonikidze, who had committed suicide; and it seems probable that the ambitious Third Five-Year Plan, formally approved in 1939, reflected the victory of the 'super-industrializers'. But the Terror had done nothing to overcome the inherent malfunctions of the command economy or to turn the party-state apparatus into a streamlined, orderly and obedient instrument at the disposal of the leadership. Nor had it done anything to reverse the trend for the regime to become ever more closely associated with the white-collar elite rather than the working class for which it claimed to act. Indeed, the sequel to the Terror was the most draconian series of decrees aimed at tightening labour discipline, accompanied by further enhancement of the elite's power and privilege. And between 1939 and the outbreak of war in 1941, during which party membership doubled, it was upon that elite that recruitment was overwhelmingly concentrated.

The experience of the cultural intelligentsia during the industrialization drive followed a pattern very similar to that of the intelligentsia as a whole. Between 1928 and 1931 they were caught up in the campaign against 'bourgeois' specialists. Indeed, the Shakhty trial was the trigger for what contemporaries called a 'cultural revolution'. In some fields, such as history and the social sciences, much of the initiative came from the party leadership. Scholarly research into developments in the countryside could not be tolerated once the attack on the peasantry was under way. The link between Lenin and Stalin, between October and the 'second revolution', the revolution 'from above', between Russia's backward economic development and the possibility of building socialism in one country – these were themes too politically sensitive to be left to scholars. But the cultural revolution was not merely a matter of manipulation from above. It, too, gathered a momentum of its own.

In field after field radical groups took up the cry for a decisive class struggle against 'bourgeois' traitors. The accusation of indifference to and alienation from the masses touched an acutely sensitive nerve among members of the old intelligentsia, and in any case resistance was impossible. Non-Marxists were denounced and purged for their class affiliation, and Marxist scholars, teachers, lawyers, architects vied with each other to establish the new orthodoxy in their own field, to demonstrate their *partiinost*, their identification with and commitment to the party line. In every academic field, from philosophy to the sciences and even mathematics and town planning, a new 'front' in the class war was opened and a frantic search made for truly 'proletarian' approaches. In many fields no clearly defined party line existed, and in the apocalyptic atmosphere of 1929 and 1930 Marxist theorists who had been no more than peripheral under NEP came to the fore. Marx's dream was coming true, socialism was taking form, the market was giving way to planned distribution, the end was in sight for all that was bourgeois – from the State to the family. The 'League of the Godless', founded in 1922, seized the opportunity to launch a full-blooded assault upon the Church, together with a furious atheist propaganda campaign. The legal profession was possessed by visions of the imminent withering away of law as private property disappeared and 'comrades' courts' took over criminal cases. Educational theory was dominated by those who saw the beginning of a new age in the stupendous expansion of the student body, the virtual collapse of the universities, the purging of children of 'bourgeois' parents at all levels, and the mass enrolment of adult workers. Schools as separate institutions would merge into the wider community as the barriers between intellectual and manual labour, between learning and production were broken down. In literature, the Association of Proletarian Writers (RAPP) and even more radical groups were able at last to launch the attack on bourgeois individualism they had been urging on the Party throughout the 1920s. Authors were exhorted to address themselves to issues of immediate relevance, to join in the construction of socialism, to commit themselves to their own 'planned' literary output. There was a full-blown cult of the machine while individual heroes – and even individual authorship – were denounced as self-indulgent, elitist, bourgeois.

Initially, this militant upsurge was welcomed by the party leadership. It served a useful propaganda purpose and silenced moderate voices. Esoteric disputes about literary form or legal theory might make little impact on working-class attitudes, but constant eulogizing of the proletariat, of the virtues of the heroic worker, played some part in deepening the sense that the regime was 'ours'. There was popular appeal, too, in the humiliation of the privileged, the highly educated, the aloof. Moreover, daily news of the exposure of bourgeois agents in the cultural field added weight to the accusations against technical specialists. Equally, the cultural revolution helped to pre-empt criticism of official policy. It pulverized any conceivable opposition from the intellectual elite, whether within or outside the Party. In this atmosphere there was no chance that working-class discontent, let alone the anguish suffered by the peasantry, by Nepmen and artisans, and by the 'bourgeois intellectuals' themselves, would be publicly articulated.

But just as the attack on 'bourgeois' technical specialists had triggered the cultural revolution, so the *rapprochement* with them in 1931 signalled its end. In some fields the radicals had already proved so disruptive and their ideas so impractical that a reaction set in without prompting from above. Now the euphoric dreams of 1929 and 1930 came under fire from the Central Committee itself, as the leadership became increasingly concerned to tighten discipline and inculcate basic skills. Stalin set the tone. He firmly asserted that in the immediate future, with the Soviet Union surrounded by hostile capitalist powers, the State, far from disappearing, must become more powerful. The 'legal nihilists' were thrown onto the defensive and both civil and extremely harsh criminal law codes were firmly re-established. In education, too, extravagant visions gave way to a much more traditional approach. The emphasis on technical education remained pronounced, as did the large dose of ideology in the curriculum, but at secondary level the authority of teachers and exams alike was re-established, and the universities were restored. Earlier attacks on the family gave way to emphasis on parental responsibility and authority, and the more extreme anti-religious activities of the Komsomol and the 'League of the Godless' were toned down.

This 'Great Retreat' of the early 1930s brought relief to those purged and hounded during the cultural revolution, and many non-Marxist scholars and writers were rehabilitated. But the upheaval of 1928–31 had brought a fundamental change to the cultural world. There was to be no return to the experiment and *élan* of the early post-revolutionary period or to the relative freedom of NEP. It was not merely that Marxism-Leninism was to be treated as the guide to all knowledge, but the party leadership's views were to be taken as the key to that guide. Centralized party control, to which the militants had enthusiastically appealed at the height of their influence, was now established in every field. Even over issues in which politics seemed no more than tangentially relevant, the tastes of the new guardians of Soviet culture were uniformly imposed – be it in the narrow restrictions placed upon innovation in art and music, or in the heavy, stylized architecture and statues of 'Stalinist baroque' in which the regime chose to celebrate its triumphs. In more obviously sensitive areas, the trend towards centrally imposed uniformity was even stronger, and the measure of cultural autonomy enjoyed by the minority republics was further narrowed. Growing emphasis on the Russian language was one facet of this: at school all children were to learn Russian as their second language, if not their first. Likewise, the 'Great Retreat' saw further, if more measured, anti-religious measures which hit minority religious groups, including Muslims, Buddhists, Baptists and the Armenian and Georgian Churches, as much if not more than the Russian Church. The new orthodoxy was not only stifling but often absurd as specialists took their cue from Central Committee statements or the almost casual remarks of Stalin himself. Enormous damage was done to research in areas as diverse as biology and psychology.

In some respects the new dispensation was an improvement on the cultural revolution. In literature, for example, RAPP was disbanded, while Gorky led a call for greater respect for traditional literary values. But there was no question of defending art for art's sake: the overriding purpose of literature remained its contribution to constructing socialism. All authors were gathered into the Union of Soviet Writers, directly under Central Committee control, and constrained by a new literary orthodoxy: 'Socialist realism'. The Union recommended a short list of novels – including *And Quiet Flows the Don* by M. A. Sholokhov (1905–) written in the late 1920s – whose structure and approach were to be universally adopted. Literature was to be didactic, it was at once to describe contemporary life and to hold up an inspiring model for emulation. The 'positive hero' replaced the machine as the central figure. His struggle to overcome his own inadequacies and reach the level of conscious commitment to socialism was to serve as a microcosm of humanity's progress from spontaneous struggle to the conscious construction of socialism. Above all, whatever the genre or subject-matter, writers were to convey the message of optimism, the inevitable victory of socialism. Works which failed to conform had no chance of being published and many of the most gifted figures of the age, including Pasternak and the great lyric poet Anna Akhmatova (1889–1966), chose 'the genre of silence'.

The impact of the Great Retreat on intellectual life was epitomized in the field of history. The leading figure on the historical 'front', M. N. Pokrovsky, was publicly denounced, and the party leadership took control over the direction – and the conclusions – of historical research. Textbooks directly reflected the Party's political preoccupations and the prejudices of Stalin himself. There was much more emphasis on the progressive role of the Tsarist State and of Russian leaders such as Ivan the Terrible and Peter the Great, and a clearly nationalist celebration of the achievements of Great Russia at the expense of the minority nationalities. A new orthodoxy – narrow, rigid, and lifeless – was laid down from above. The *Short Course* in the history of the Communist Party, written under Stalin's direct supervision, became dogma. For sixteen years, from its publication in 1938, this crude distortion of the past, vilifying not only all the opponents of Bolshevism but also the leading opposition figures within the Party, became the basic text from school to professorial level. It moulded the view of the past impressed upon generations of Soviet students.

For the cultural intelligentsia, conformity with the wisdom of the Central Committee was no guarantee of security. Between 1936 and 1938 both the radicals of the cultural revolution and their opponents were subjected to the ravages of the Terror. In every field – in pure and applied science, in medicine, in history, and in all the creative arts – numerous leading figures were denounced as 'enemies of the people' and arrested. Vulnerable to a strong anti-intellectual current in the NKVD and to cynical denunciation by rivals, the cultural intelligentsia worked in an atmosphere of fear and suspicion. The rewards for those who survived were considerable, but Soviet intellectual life suffered crippling inhibitions against independent thought or criticism of the official line even when offered in the most constructive spirit. The cultural intelligentsia shared to the full both the material privileges and the acute insecurity of the white-collar elite.

The industrialization drive was carried out in an atmosphere of sustained tension over international affairs. Ever since the war-scare of 1927 Soviet leaders had warned of imminent foreign attack. During the early years, there may have been an element of disingenuousness in the alarm expressed by the leadership. The spectre of foreign aggression and intrigue was of immense propaganda value. It provided the pretext for the recurrent witch-hunt against the enemy within. The need to 'catch up' with hostile neighbours had fuelled the increasingly strident nationalist note in the Party's appeal. 'We are fifty or a hundred years behind the advanced countries', warned Stalin in 1931. 'We must make good this distance in ten years. Either we do it or we shall go under.'[1] But hostile Western rhetoric and Soviet diplomatic isolation were real enough. The memory of Allied intervention in the Civil War was fresh, and belief in the impatience of the capitalist powers to destroy the centre of the world revolutionary movement was deeply ingrained.

Soviet efforts to meet the perceived threat consisted of two virtually contradictory approaches. On one level the Foreign Commissariat, where

---

[1] I. V. Stalin, *Sochineniia* (Moscow 1946–51), XIII, p. 39.

Chicherin was replaced in 1930 by M. M. Litvinov, tried to improve relations with all the Western powers. Olive branches held out by the short-lived British Labour government in 1929, by France in 1931, and by Roosevelt's administration in 1933 were eagerly seized upon, and the relatively warm relationship with Germany established in the early 1920s was maintained. On another level, through Comintern, the militant policy adopted in 1928 was vigorously pursued. The hostile intentions of bourgeois governments were to be checked by revolutionary agitation. Scorning compromise, Western Communist parties launched their most bitter attacks upon their social-democratic rivals. Western socialists were denounced as 'social fascists', and accused of betraying the proletarian cause by cooperating with bourgeois parties and, in the late 1920s, actively fostering a *rapprochement* between Germany and the Western powers which from Moscow looked distinctly sinister. The policy chimed in perfectly with Stalin's *démarche* against Bukharin and the Right Opposition, with the apocalyptic atmosphere of 1928–31, and with the predilections of militant sections of the major foreign Communist parties. But it flew in the face of the Foreign Commissar's conciliatory stance. Moreover, it was upheld through a period of six years during which the onset of the Great Depression drove Japan into alarming expansion in the Far East and turned the political and diplomatic scene in Europe upside-down. The policy proved most disastrous in Germany, where the virulently anti-Soviet and anti-Slav Nazi bandwagon was beginning to roll. Ideologically predisposed to write off Nazism as a desperate capitalist appeal to the petty bourgeoisie of no more than passing significance, and inclined to welcome Hitler's hostility to the other Western powers, the Comintern committed a fateful blunder. In January 1933, his way cleared by the bitter divisions between German Communists and social democrats, Hitler became Chancellor.

By 1934, with Germany now recognized as the overriding threat, the two lines of foreign policy appeared to converge. The Foreign Commissariat stepped up its efforts to align the Soviet Union with the Western democracies. In 1934 Russia entered the League of Nations. Litvinov's voice was loudest in insisting on the virtues of collective security against aggression from revisionist powers, and in 1935 a mutual assistance pact was signed with France. At the same time Comintern policy was at last reversed: the final reckoning with capitalism slipped to the bottom of the agenda as the fight against fascism took precedence. Fraternal parties were instructed to close ranks not only with socialists but with liberal democrats as well. In France, Spain, and elsewhere Communists joined in the formation of anti-fascist popular fronts.

Yet the underlying tension between the Soviet Union's courting of the Western democracies and her identification with Communist revolution was not so easily relieved. It led to contortions in Soviet foreign policy that became ever more cynical and counterproductive. Every effort was made to square the circle during the Spanish Civil War, which broke out in 1936. With Hitler and Mussolini actively supporting Franco and the Right, Moscow decided to respond in a limited way to pleas for assistance from the Spanish Republic. Shipments of arms – paid for by Spanish gold – were channelled to the Republic through the Spanish Communist Party. But rather than concentrating their efforts upon rallying popular support for the Republic, the Spanish Communists were instructed to focus their energies upon enticing Britain and France into the war against the Right. The anarchists and other radical Left factions were ruthlessly crushed in the hope of making the Republican cause respectable in London and Paris. The policy was a complete failure. Republican *élan* was sapped while in Britain and France the establishment looked askance at the growing influence of the Spanish Communists. From the end of 1937 Soviet aid was gradually curtailed and the Republic abandoned to its fate.

With Hitler becoming ever more overtly aggressive, and Japan probing Soviet defences in the east, where serious battles were fought in 1938 and 1939, Moscow's anxiety to break out of her diplomatic isolation intensified. But the authoritarian regimes of her immediate neighbours, Romania and Poland, remained fiercely hostile: the Poles spurned offers of mutual assistance, convinced that irreconcilable Nazi-Soviet differences left them free to manoeuvre between their two giant neighbours. The Baltic states fell increasingly under German influence. The Western governments, actively seeking to appease Germany, also refused to respond. To Western distrust of Bolshevism was added contempt for the Red Army. Although Soviet rearmament had begun in earnest in 1937, what impressed foreign opinion was the destruction of the High Command in the Terror. The Soviet Union was conspicuously excluded from the international agreement at Munich in September 1938. Even after Hitler's invasion of Prague in March 1939 had exposed the futility of appeasement, Chamberlain and the rudderless Third Republic pursued military discussions with Moscow in the most desultory fashion. The Western powers could propose no way round Polish and Baltic refusal to countenance cooperation with the Soviet Union, and horror at the thought of Soviet troops crossing their territory to resist Germany. This suggested to Stalin that Britain and France were not sincere and would come to terms with Hitler. Confronted by the frightful prospect of facing alone a German thrust to the east, as well as the possibility of renewed attack by Japan, the Soviet Union was driven to desperate measures. Responding to feelers put out from Berlin, Stalin performed the most abrupt diplomatic volte-face of the century. In May 1939 Litvinov was replaced by Molotov, anti-Nazi propaganda was sharply toned down, and on 23 August 1939 a Ten-Year Non-Aggression Pact was signed with Nazi Germany. Sure of Soviet neutrality, Hitler promptly invaded Poland, thereby precipitating the declaration of war by Britain and France.

The pact had much to offer the Soviet Union. In return for a wide

9.4 Molotov signs the Nazi–Soviet Non-Aggression Pact on 23 August 1939. He is watched by Stalin (left centre) and Hitler's foreign secretary, Ribbentrop (left).

range of raw materials, Germany supplied her with valuable industrial and military imports. Moreover, the way was also opened for the reacquisition of most of the western territory lost at the end of the First World War. Under the terms of a secret protocol of the pact, eastern Europe was divided into two spheres of influence, and while Germany overran northern, central, south-eastern, and western Europe, the Soviet Union, too, took full advantage of the agreement. Eastern Poland – with a population of some 13 million, just over half of them Ukrainians and Belorussians – was occupied; Estonia, Latvia, and Lithuania (the latter transferred to the Soviet sphere in a postscript to the secret protocol) were incorporated under coercion into the USSR as Union Republics; Finland, after putting up stout resistance in the winter war of 1940–41, was forced to make territorial concessions designed to secure Leningrad's defences; and Romania was deprived of Bessarabia, which was given the trappings of nationhood as the Union Republic of Moldavia. With the help of mass arrests and the deportation of some 1.5 million people considered potentially hostile, Soviet rule was extended over 20 million new citizens.

But the USSR paid a heavy price for the pact. The Soviet image as the staunchest foe of fascism, successfully cultivated during the 1930s, was severely tarnished. Foreign Communist parties were placed in the impossible position of justifying Moscow's accord with Hitler. Worse still, the pact left the rest of the Continent helpless before the Nazi onslaught: Stalin was taken aback at the speed with which France collapsed. When Russia's turn came, she would feel the full force of the German Army. And that moment was not long delayed. As early as December 1940, frustrated in the west by the Battle of Britain, Hitler drew up a timetable for 'Operation Barbarossa'. The Nazi invasion was launched the following summer. The political system, the social cohesion, and the industrial might of the new Soviet order were subjected to a devastating ordeal.

World War and Cold War (1941–1953)

The German invasion, launched at dawn on Sunday 22 June 1941, caught the Red Army almost fatally unprepared and the Soviet Union suffered catastrophic defeats. This disastrous start can be traced to Stalin's firm conviction that Hitler would respect the terms of the Nazi-Soviet Pact at least until 1942. In part because of his exaggerated notion of the wealth and power of Britain, for so long the centre of the capitalist world, he could not believe Hitler would dare to move eastwards while the western war was still in the balance. Indeed, during 1940 Stalin and Molotov were so confident that they increased their demands on Germany: the USSR occupied Northern Bukovina in Romania, although this had not been agreed in the secret protocol, and pressed Hitler to accept that the Soviet sphere of influence should be extended to include Bulgaria and that traditional Tsarist dream, the Straits. Nor was this complacency and the strategic risks which it led the Soviet Union to take challenged by military leaders, so cowed were they by the Terror. Far from preparing for in-depth defence, Soviet strategy was based upon the rash assumption that, in the event of war, the Red Army would be in a position to move rapidly onto the offensive. No preparations were made for the evacuation of population or plant from the industrially developed western regions. Moreover, when the Germans attacked, the newly incorporated western territories – where anti-Soviet feeling ran deep – had still to be fully fortified, yet the defences of the 1939 frontier had already been weakened. Even in the last weeks and days before the invasion, despite repeated warnings, Stalin remained adamant that rumours of an impending attack were unfounded: at worst Hitler was manoeuvring to strengthen his hand for peaceful bargaining. Accurate Soviet intelligence reports were dismissed as unreliable, and clear warnings from the US and British governments were treated as deliberate ploys to embroil the Soviet Union in war. The growing alarm of frontline commanders was met by firm orders to avoid reacting to any 'provocation' from the Germans. When at last it was borne in upon Moscow that war had begun, the front was in utter disarray and the order to go on to full-scale offensive merely compounded the confusion. Confidence in the regime was rocked by the lack of warning and there was widespread panic. Stalin himself appears to have been so stunned by his monumental miscalculation that momentarily he expected to be ousted. The battle-hardened German Army smashed through Soviet lines, cut their communications, destroyed the bulk of the Soviet Air Force on the ground, and swept into the interior.

Soviet losses during the first months of the war were enormous. By November, the Germans had occupied a broad swathe of the most heavily populated and industrially advanced Soviet territory. Almost two-thirds of coal and steel production were lost, together with some 40 per cent of the land under grain crops and the same proportion of the railway network, while the population of the occupied areas was over 80 million. Casualties already ran into the millions and between 2 and 3 million soldiers had been taken prisoner. For many the ordeal had only just begun. To the north, Leningrad was surrounded and a siege of epic proportions began. To the south, Kiev fell after desperate resistance and heavy losses. The major German thrust was at Moscow itself. At the end of November, with Soviet production drastically curtailed and the Red Army at its lowest ebb, the German Army reached the suburbs of the capital, which teetered on the brink of chaos as pandemonium spread among officials and ordinary citizens alike.

Yet Russia survived. The bitter winter stalled the German advance, and Japan's decision to strike south rather than join Hitler against the Soviet Union freed invaluable troops from the Far East. Nevertheless, the premature offensives on which Stalin insisted were costly failures and 1942 saw renewed German advances, culminating in the monstrous battle for Stalingrad. Of no more than limited strategic value, the straggling city on the Volga became the supreme test of the two war machines. From August, the Germans began to launch furious attacks on Soviet positions, advancing further and further into the city. Every street, every square, every house became part of the battleground; the railway station changed hands more than a dozen times; the bloody, pitiless struggle epitomized the unique ferocity with which the war on the eastern front was fought. Yet the Germans, mounting simultaneous offensives in the north and the Caucasus, had overreached themselves. By November 1942, with industrial production from the east rapidly picking up, the Soviet Army was poised for a devastating counterattack. Despite the damage the Germans had inflicted, for Hitler the defeat at Stalingrad was disastrous. The knock-out blow had failed. Already news was coming in from the north that the Leningrad blockade had been breached. The initiative was passing to the Russians.

The following summer saw one last major German offensive at Kursk,

Map 10   The Great Patriotic War

10.1 House-to-house fighting in Stalingrad. By the winter of 1942 the furious struggle for Stalingrad had reduced the city to rubble.

where casualties ran even higher than at Stalingrad. But thereafter the battlefront swung inexorably back from east to west. Kiev was liberated in November 1943, Sevastopol in May 1944, Estonia and Latvia in the autumn. By the end of 1944 all Soviet territory had been freed from enemy occupation, German control of the air had been broken and the Red Army was bulldozing its way through six eastern European countries. The governments of Romania, Bulgaria and Hungary were overthrown, and under new governments these countries switched sides and declared war on Germany. The Germans were driven from Poland in the first weeks of 1945. Soviet aid played a subsidiary role in liberating Yugoslavia, where a powerful resistance movement flourished under Tito's leadership, and in Czechoslovakia Prague was occupied on 9 May. By then Berlin itself, 'the lair of the fascist beast', had fallen and the Red Army had linked up with Allied forces on the River Elbe. As agreed with the Western Allies, three months after Germany's surrender the Soviet Union joined the coalition against Japan – a move rendered superfluous in military terms by the annihilation of Hiroshima and Nagasaki.

In accounting for the Soviet victory, the foolhardiness of Hitler's adventure in the east must be recognized. He set out to smash an enemy whose industrial output was already comparable to Germany's own, whose untapped resources were far greater, and whose population was twice the size. He relied upon the *Blitzkrieg*, despite Russia's legendary capacity to absorb initial defeat and retreat into her vast hinterland. And his megalomania, bloated by his astonishing diplomatic and military triumphs of 1936–40, led him again and again to overrate the efficacy of 'racial superiority' and sheer willpower. The invasion force was not equipped for a winter campaign, and when the *Blitzkrieg* failed, Hitler imposed his will on his generals in arbitrary and fanatical fashion, forbidding vital strategic withdrawals and wantonly dividing German forces between conflicting goals. Equally costly was the political price of Nazi racist doctrine. The army was ordered to give no quarter to the subjugated Slavs: far from playing upon minority nationalist and peasant discontent with Soviet rule, the *Untermenschen* were treated with a savage brutality perfectly designed to rally even the most disaffected elements behind Stalin. Nor was Germany free to concentrate solely upon the Russian foe. The invasion was launched before Britain had been dealt with, and Hitler gratuitously joined Japan's war against the USA without securing reciprocal support from the Japanese against Russia. In a protracted war Russia would be assured of western military supplies, primarily from the USA. By 1943 the material delivered under Lend-Lease, food as well as the trucks, jeeps and communications equipment in which Russia was severely deficient, was providing a valuable supplement to Soviet war production and beginning to release resources to shore up the desperate civilian economy. Although it was not until June 1944 that a Second Front was opened in the west, pressure from the Western Allies, both at sea and on the periphery, placed an upper limit on the effort that Germany could devote to the major struggle in the east.

Nevertheless, the Soviet Union was the victim of an assault of truly gigantic proportions. She faced the largest and most proficient invasion force the world had ever seen. The German Army swept into Russia on the crest of a wave. Initially it enjoyed a distinct advantage in the quality of its *matériel* and of its communications system, and it could draw upon the resources of most of Europe. The war effort Russia mounted to drive out the Germans was by any standard prodigious – all the more so in view of the catastrophic scale of her initial losses.

In the course of the war some 25 million men served in the forces, the great bulk of them in the Red Army, which gained steadily in effectiveness. Stalin as Supreme Commander was a decidedly mixed blessing, only learning the value of strategic withdrawals after the men on the ground had sustained horrific losses. But German officers were shaken by the speed with which the army and the Soviet officer corps, headed by Marshal Zhukov, recovered from the ravages of the Great Terror. In part this reflected the draconian sanctions imposed for failure. From July 1942, military police were ordered to shoot soldiers who retreated without orders, while officers whose units collapsed were to be sent to virtually certain death in penal battalions. In part it was the result of positive steps to improve the organization, raise the morale, and change the ethos of the army. Officers found their authority enhanced at the expense of that of political commissars, traditional insignia and privileges of rank were introduced, and the lack of respect for officers and slack discipline of pre-war years were rapidly reversed. Party membership was liberally conferred upon officers and soldiers alike and honours and praise were heaped upon those who enjoyed success. But above all, it reflected common purpose. After the initial disasters, the rank and file showed a dogged courage and determination, an ability to survive on wretched rations, which went a long way towards compensating for the superior education and training of German troops.

To arm and supply this massive force, the whole balance of the economy was violently recast. During the retreat, over 1,500 major enterprises, together with several million civilians, were evacuated from the war zone to the east and hastily converted to war production. New industrial complexes were frantically developed and expanded in regions beyond the reach of the Germans. In 1943 over half the working population were employed in fighting and supplying the war effort and at peak more than half the national income was devoted to armaments. Investment, meanwhile, plummeted and civilian consumption fell to pitiful levels as strict rationing was introduced, not only for food but for clothes and basic household goods. To sustain industrial and agricultural production while so much of the regular workforce was at the front, unprecedented demands were made upon men and women of all ages. For the Soviet Union, this was total war in the truest sense.

To direct and coordinate the war effort, absolute power was vested in a small Council for State Defence whose original members were Beria, Molotov, K. E. Voroshilov, G. M. Malenkov – and Stalin. Its orders were binding on all institutions and all individuals. Operating both through the state, soviet, party and police hierarchies and through *ad hoc* plenipotentiaries it strove frantically to maximize economic and military mobilization. Formally at least, centralized control was brought to its apogee. Moreover, the regime made ruthless use of the full panoply of its legal powers and punitive sanctions. All able-bodied men and women were legally obliged to work. Not only was it illegal to change jobs without permission but holidays were cancelled, the working week was often seven days, the working day was lengthened to eleven hours, and even after hours civilians were called upon to contribute in a thousand ways to shoring up the home front. Workers in enterprises close to the front, and those in transport, were placed under martial law. Those who abandoned their jobs without authorization were to be declared deserters and tried by military tribunal. Summary justice was meted out to those the NKVD found guilty of spreading panic and demoralization and the death penalty was reimposed for theft from state and collective farms. Though the numbers released from the GULAG and labour colonies rose, there was a steady inflow and the annual camp death-rate reached 20 per cent.

Yet this catalogue of central decrees and coercive measures was only half the story. As the pre-war years had shown, force alone could not ensure that orders from above were obeyed. Moreover, amidst the chaos of invasion, with key economic sectors thrown into confusion, communications disrupted, most of the central party and state apparatus evacuated from Moscow and relocated in the east, and the administrative system drained of hundreds of thousands of key personnel called to the front, the centre was fully stretched in trying to mobilize resources for the military. During the first half of the war, the attempt at comprehensive planning was in effect replaced by emergency *ad hoc* measures overwhelmingly focused upon supplying the front. The Council for State Defence could not hope simultaneously to organize by fiat the countless auxiliary services needed to sustain civilian life. Central direction and the ruthless imposition of discipline, therefore, were accompanied by a significant loosening of the reins of party and state control in some fields. There was a dramatic shift in the tone and indeed the language used by Stalin and the party leadership. With the country's very survival at risk, they played down ideological divisions and did all they could to identify the spontaneous upsurge in both Russian nationalism and Soviet patriotism with the 'great banner of Lenin'. They appealed to the tradition of Donskoi and Alexander Nevsky, Suvorov and Kutuzov, and even pursued open *rapprochement* with the Church. Pressure upon believers was sharply curtailed, the 'League of the Godless' disbanded, and permission was given to fill the Patriarchate, vacant since 1925. Censorship remained, private radios were impounded and private telephones disconnected, but official propaganda became much less concerned with the niceties of party doctrine. Non-party writers enjoyed greater intellectual freedom and non-party specialists and scientists were entrusted with highly responsible official and advisory posts. Party and police supervision of activities unconnected with or beneficial to the war effort became markedly more relaxed. Beneath the highly centralized formal structure, local authorities and managers were given wider discretion and autonomy, be it in organizing rationing or securing labour and raw materials. Peasants and urban workers were left unmolested when they took over unused land for their own use.

In short, the war effort depended to a large extent upon popular initiative and voluntary commitment. Indeed, the most positive effect of draconian wartime legislation was in underlining the leadership's resolution, bracing public morale at the moments of gravest peril, and buttressing popular determination that the war could and would be won. It was this determination that was decisive. It explains why millions gave far more to the war effort than coercion could ever have extracted, poured into the voluntary militia, engaged spontaneously in 'socialist competition', and worked to breaking point in industry and agriculture. It explains why industrial productivity held up so well despite wartime disruption, mass malnutrition, barely human living and working conditions, and an industrial work-force drastically recast as skilled and experienced men were called to arms and replaced by untrained ex-peasants, youths and women (almost 60 per cent by 1943). It explains how the country was fed at all, despite the German occupation of the best land, the loss to the army and industry of three-quarters of the able-bodied menfolk working on the collective farms, the requisitioning of most of the horses, and the virtual collapse of mechanization. The 'command economy' enjoyed the popular support whose absence had so profoundly handicapped it in peacetime. The picture was, of course, by no means uniform. Neither crime nor evasion of work ended: theft, abuse of the rationing system, absenteeism and illegal changing of jobs continued. There were some instances of large-scale disaffection, notably in the newly-annexed western areas and the Caucasus, where the Germans did condescend to curry support among local minority nationalities, and some 800,000 POWs, demoralized beyond the point of endurance, consented to serve alongside the Germans under the captured General Vlasov. But the overwhelming majority identified wholeheartedly with the struggle against the hated Nazis. Even to those who suffered greatest deprivation the demands of the authorities made infinitely better sense than had those of the 1930s. Behind the German lines, resistance was fierce and, the longer the war dragged on, the greater the damage inflicted upon German forces by partisans, especially in the Ukraine and Belorussia. The same resolve was shown in cities, towns, and villages across the country. The supreme test of civilian morale and resilience was the 900-day siege of Leningrad. Although engulfed by hunger, cold, lice, and death, the city refused to surrender.

Hitler's invasion, the titanic struggle on Russian soil, and the triumphant but protracted drive to Berlin left a trail of incalculable human and material destruction. Public catastrophe mingled everywhere with private grief. The population was more than decimated: out of some 200 million in 1941, between 27 and 28 million people died – two-thirds of them civilians – and many more were maimed. The victims of Leningrad alone exceeded the combined total of British and American wartime deaths. The economic destruction, too, beggars the imagination. Whole cities were reduced to rubble. Countless villages were laid waste, machinery destroyed, and livestock slaughtered. And on top of German destruction was the heart-rending self-inflicted damage of the Russians' 'scorched earth' retreat: the Dnieper Dam, the pride of the First Five-Year Plan, had been deliberately dynamited. Merely to make good the material damage would, it is estimated, have taken the labour force of 1940 anything from three to seven years.

10.2 A forlorn couple on the streets of besieged Leningrad drag away a corpse for burial. During the 28 months of its ordeal the city was devastated by starvation and disease.

The emotional impact of the 'Great Patriotic War' is difficult to exaggerate. Its depth and intensity can only dimly be grasped by Anglo-Saxons – even by the generation which experienced the war in the west. The pitiless struggle, the contemptuous, bestial Nazi treatment of Soviet civilians and POWs, the searing racial insult, left its mark on every ethnic, every religious, every social group. The ordeal generated a sense of solidarity within the Soviet Union that had been absent before the war. It conferred upon Communist rule and the Soviet system an entirely new legitimacy in the eyes of the generation who lived through it, and transformed Stalin into a genuinely popular national hero. Official celebration of the regime's achievement evoked an incomparably deeper response than appeals to the fading memory of October. The war had placed at the disposal of both Stalin and his successors a pool of emotional capital on which they drew freely for decades. It predisposed the Soviet public to accept the leadership's dire warnings about renewed threats from abroad. At home, bitterness, discontent, and division would resurface soon enough. But the effect of the war upon popular attitudes to foreign affairs would endure. Hitler's adventure had aroused a sense of moral outrage, of national indignation which bears comparison with the impact of the holocaust upon Jewish consciousness. It guaranteed, as censorship alone never could, overwhelming and uncritical popular support for every *démarche* of post-war Soviet foreign policy.

Victory brought a dramatic and complex change in the international position of the Soviet Union. On the one hand, it enhanced her military and diplomatic weight out of all recognition. The destruction of the Third Reich, following as it did upon the humiliation of both France and Italy, left a power vacuum on the Continent. With Britain's imperial commitments placing a definite limit upon the role she could play, Russia emerged from the war incomparably Europe's greatest power. Yet the manner in which she exerted her new-found influence, primarily in eastern Europe but later in Asia too, provoked the hostility of a massive Western alliance headed by the emergent American superpower. The mutual suspicion that developed reached a degree of intensity which was aptly christened 'Cold War'.

Temporarily, of course, Hitler's aggression had driven Russia and the Anglo-Saxon powers into each others' arms. Military strategy was never closely coordinated, but both sides acknowledged the assistance of the other and an element of genuine warmth crept into the relationship. While the Red Army fought alone on the Continent, the Western view of the Soviet Union and of Stalin himself altered significantly. For a time there was a widespread belief that Soviet society had undergone a permanent change for the better, and both Churchill and Roosevelt felt themselves within an ace of establishing a genuine understanding with Stalin. For his part Stalin paid tribute to his Western allies, welcomed the material assistance received through the Lend-Lease arrangement, and was immensely relieved when in June 1944 the Second Front was opened in the west.

10.3   Stalin and Churchill flank the ailing Roosevelt during the conference at Yalta (in the Crimea), February 1945.

As the tide turned against Germany, however, relations between the Soviet Union and her Allies deteriorated. When the 'Big Three' first met, at Teheran in 1943, preoccupation with the common enemy ensured relative harmony. By the time of the Yalta Conference, in February 1945, only a fragile and ambiguous agreement could paper over the growing dissension; and the atmosphere at Potsdam in August 1945 was frankly acrimonious.

In part this was the product of ill-feeling over the conduct of the war. For Stalin the cardinal test of Allied good faith was the issue of the Second Front. From the outset, Russia's overriding plea to the West was to draw off pressure on the Red Army by opening a new front in Europe. The Allies were full of good intentions: Roosevelt rashly promised there would be action in 1942, Soviet hopes were raised again in 1943, yet D-Day was ultimately postponed until 1944, by which time virtually all Soviet territory had been liberated. There was inevitable bitterness that it should have been delayed so long while the Red Army bore the main brunt of the *Wehrmacht*. The postponement fuelled Soviet anxiety – recurrent to the very end of the war, despite the flow of political intelligence from their agents in the West – that underlying hatred of Communism would lead the Allies to come to terms with Germany. Intermittent and unofficial feelers put out to the West from Berlin were viewed with the utmost gravity: Moscow was convinced that Churchill failed to bring Hess to trial because he might prove useful in arranging a peace deal with the Germans. From Moscow it seemed an age before substantial material aid began to arrive; when it did so, the Allies seemed to expect grovelling gratitude for a contribution that cost not one drop of blood; and when peace came, Moscow took offence at how abruptly Lend-Lease was curtailed. The last chapter in the war against Japan was a further source of estrangement. Whereas as late as the meeting at Yalta in February 1945, the Western Allies were urgently pressing for a Soviet declaration of war on Japan as soon as Germany was defeated, by the summer it seemed plain that they wished to exclude the USSR and deprive her of any share in the fruits of victory in the Far East. At the very end of the war, Western atomic power introduced a new dimension to Soviet fear and suspicion. During the war, despite the well-informed intelligence reports reaching Moscow about the 'Manhattan Project', Stalin had underrated its significance. As a result he was aghast at the American display of its devastating power in Japan.

From the Western viewpoint, Soviet anxiety on each score was misplaced and bordered on paranoia. There was never any question of Britain signing a separate peace. If either side was to be suspected of contemplating such a step, the signatory of the Nazi-Soviet Pact was surely the more likely candidate – and there is evidence that, in desperation, Stalin did put out feelers in 1941 and possibly again in 1943. The Second Front was postponed for what seemed thoroughly sound military reasons: Western caution reflected not cynical foot-dragging about aiding the Red Army but the indelible impression made by the carnage on the western front in World War I. As for the abrupt cessation of Lend-Lease, Britain was as much a victim as the Soviet Union. Where the Far East was concerned, the Soviet Union did, after all, secure South Sakhalin and the Kurile islands, the Japanese territories she had long coveted. And however much some American officials might relish the impression Hiroshima would make on Moscow, the wish to minimize Russian involvement in the Far Eastern war and intimidate the Russians was not the primary motive for dropping the bomb.

However, it was not conflict over the conduct of the war which lay at the root of post-war hostility. Nor is the very fact that the European power vacuum was filled so rapidly by the Russians and the Americans sufficient explanation for the Cold War. Diplomatic competition of a traditional kind, of course, was bound to place a strain upon their relationship, as unprecedented and dazzling diplomatic opportunities opened out before both Washington and Moscow: while Soviet troops occupied Poland, Romania, Bulgaria, Hungary, Czechoslovakia, the eastern zones of Germany and Austria, and, for a time, part of Yugoslavia, the USA rapidly gained paramount influence in the areas liberated by the Western Allies. But both sides saw considerable advantage in maintaining the wartime amity even after

Hitler's fate was sealed, and both seemed willing to accept that an accommodation would have to be found.

Soviet perceptions at the end of the war are, of course, extremely difficult to reconstruct. It remains a crippling handicap for historians of the Cold War – as it was for Western diplomats at the time – that so little direct evidence of the process of foreign policy-making in Moscow is available. But two primary Soviet goals seem clear enough. The Great Patriotic War had heightened national preoccupation with security to the point of obsession. Even in the dark days of 1941, with the Germans at the gates of Moscow, Stalin had made it absolutely clear to the British government that the USSR would insist upon retaining all the territorial gains of 1939–41 and that there could be no question of restoring Polish independence under an anti-Soviet government: Poland had too often been the corridor for Western aggression. And as the Reich crumbled the future of Germany itself became of crucial importance in Soviet eyes. Of almost equal concern was compensation for the staggering economic damage Russia had suffered. She was determined to extract maximum reparations, both in current produce and industrial plant, not only from the fallen Reich but from erstwhile German satellites as well. Both goals were served by the care Stalin took, once ultimate victory was beyond doubt, to maximize the territory that fell to the Red Army rather than to Western forces. And both encouraged the Soviet Union to prolong the Red Army's occupation of eastern and central Europe. Soviet security might be permanently assured if a line of buffer states running from Poland right down to the Balkans could be consolidated. Likewise, even when reparations had been collected and the confiscation of supposedly German assets, whether in Berlin, Budapest, or Bucharest, had been completed, military leverage might be used to dictate advantageous trading terms to the liberated countries.

Yet Stalin's approach to the fluid post-war situation appears to have been thoroughly pragmatic. He was not fired by a sense of mission, by any ideological commitment to the spread of socialism and revolution. Certainly there was a deep reservoir of hostility to the capitalist West in Moscow, which some of his lieutenants began to draw upon from as early as 1944. Moreover, the trumpeting of the Red Army's liberation mission did arouse expectations among exiled eastern European Communist leaders in Moscow that they would return home to institute swift sociopolitical transformation. But Stalin's outlook by 1945 was light years removed from that of Lenin and Trotsky in 1920. Already in 1943 he had abolished the Comintern – though without dismantling much of its secretariat – apparently in part to blunt any concerted pressure from these affiliated parties. His cavalier treatment of vigorous Communist revolts in China and Greece clearly showed that his overriding priority remained, as in the 1930s, what he perceived as strictly Soviet interests. And during 1944 and 1945 he was more than willing to deal with non-Communist parties and politicians in eastern Europe.

His diplomacy was characteristically wily. He skilfully played upon every sign of discord between his wartime allies. But he had no master-plan to establish Communist regimes in central and eastern Europe, let alone further afield. He was quite willing to think in terms of spheres of influence. During Churchill's famous visit to Moscow in 1944, Stalin showed himself happy to respect paramount British influence in Greece in exchange for Russian domination of Romania. He repeatedly compared Soviet interest in Poland to British interest in France and settled for Finnish neutrality rather than risk military confrontation with the West. After Hiroshima, it is true, he poured resources into developing Soviet atomic power and meanwhile, to avoid giving any impression of fear or intimidation in the face of the bomb, became more rather than less intransigent over disputed issues. But the speed with which he demobilized the bulk of the Red Army at the end of the war does not suggest a willingness to launch the ruined country on a military crusade. In his first post-war speech, in February 1946, he warned of capitalism's inherent instability and its hostility towards the Communist world, but he was far from convinced by those in Moscow who predicted an imminent 'general crisis of world capitalism'. On at least two occasions in 1945 Moscow raised the question of an American loan and, as late as 1947, Stalin appears to have seriously entertained the hope of securing large-scale credit from Washington.

For their part, the Western powers accepted as inevitable a very considerable increase in Soviet diplomatic weight once Hitler had been defeated. Distasteful though they found it, they recognized the benefits of keeping post-war relations amicable. Reconstruction in western Europe would be arduous enough without a renewed arms race. Moreover, London and Washington acknowledged the legitimacy of Soviet concern both for security and for compensation. At Yalta and at Potsdam they accepted her claim to the lion's share of reparations. And as early as 1942 the British government had come to terms with Soviet paramountcy in much of eastern Europe. Although Roosevelt was less willing to accept the notion of a Europe divided into 'spheres of influence', he too explicitly accepted the Soviet need for 'friendly governments' in the countries of eastern and central Europe, and dreamed of a post-war world in which the Great Powers would cooperate through the nascent United Nations Organization.

These hopes, however, were disappointed. The fundamental issue over which the rift developed was the manner in which Moscow secured her influence over her neighbours. The problem was that the Soviet Union had so little to offer. Economically, far from being in a position to provide commercial or financial aid she was in desperate need of reparations. Territorially, the acquisitions she had made in 1939–41 had been at the direct expense of some of her neighbours, while for all of them the absorption of the Baltic states was an ominous precedent. With the crushing of Germany, even the diplomatic protection Russia could offer had lost its attraction. In most eastern European countries, moreover, there was a deeply rooted tradition of hostility to Russian power which the unruly and sometimes bestial behaviour of the Red Army did nothing to counterbalance. With few exceptions, therefore, non-Communist parties viewed Soviet domination with abhorrence. The only means by which a pro-Soviet orientation could be entrenched was through the medium of local Communist parties.

To make matters worse, only in south-east Europe, in Yugoslavia and Albania, were local Communist parties strong enough to come to power by their own efforts. Elsewhere, they had no hope of doing so. The traditional Right in eastern Europe, it is true, emerged from the war thoroughly demoralized and discredited, having collaborated more or less actively with the Nazis, while parties of the left and centre had gathered momentum in the underground resistance. With the collapse of fascism and Nazism, the political spectrum throughout the Continent shifted to the left. Yet while they recovered from the devastation of the purges of the 1930s, Communist parties still had distinctly limited popular appeal – not least because of their allegiance to the forbidding giant in the east. Soviet influence, therefore, implied not only the elevation of local Communist parties, but their elevation through the crude intervention of the Red Army and the NKVD. This was a recipe guaranteed to poison the wartime alliance.

Nowhere was the problem more acute than in Poland. Poland had the fiercest anti-Russian tradition, a tradition rooted in centuries of conflict and nurtured by the vigorous life of the Catholic Church. She had been the chief victim of Russian expansion in 1939–41. During the war, the London-based government-in-exile – which commanded widespread support in the Polish underground – steadfastly refused to come to terms with this territorial loss. Moreover, wartime developments created an absolutely unbridgeable division between Moscow and the London Poles. In 1943 the Germans announced their discovery of the Katyn massacre, the remains of some 4,000 of 10,000 Polish officers butchered during the Soviet occupation of eastern Poland in 1939. The London Poles promptly denounced the Russians, who denied their responsibility and severed relations. The following summer, when the Red Army entered eastern Poland, a Communist-dominated 'National Liberation Committee' was set up in the city of Lublin. The London Poles saw this as a prelude to the establishment by Moscow of a puppet regime in Warsaw. On 1 August 1944, in an attempt to establish beyond question their claim to be 'the rightful masters' in Poland, the underground Home Army launched a quixotic rising against the Nazis. While the Germans were crushing the rising with untold brutality, Stalin displayed icy indifference. In retrospect it seems probable that the Red Army was not in fact in a position to intervene in time, but Moscow did the minimum to help and made it abundantly clear that the annihilation of the Home Army was by no means unwelcome. Polish bitterness knew no bounds. As Stalin himself admitted in a moment of weakness, there was no chance whatsoever of a democratically elected Polish government accepting Russian suzerainty. Left to her own devices Poland seemed guaranteed to gravitate to an anti-Soviet orbit. When the Nazis were driven out the following winter, therefore, the Lublin Committee was installed in Warsaw. The Western Allies protested, pressing the case for the inclusion of the London Poles in the new government and demanding free elections with international observers. The Russians, with more or less subtlety and frankness, blocked every demand.

On its own the Polish problem might not have wrecked the wartime alliance. But between 1945 and 1948 the pattern was repeated throughout eastern Europe. Reluctant to alienate the West more than necessary, Moscow tried at first to achieve the impossible, retaining democratic forms that would be acceptable to the West while upholding Russian influence. Only in Czechoslovakia, where the respected non-Communist President Beneš had worked throughout the war for just such a pro-Moscow democratic coalition, did the tactic work even temporarily. Elsewhere, it failed dismally. In Romania, as in Poland, the Party was far too weak to make free elections and Russian influence compatible; in Bulgaria the relatively vigorous Party itself took the initiative in carrying out a vicious purge of the opposition parties. In Hungary the elections of 1945 inflicted an alarming reversal on the Communists.

To the West Soviet behaviour was unacceptable. In part it was a matter of moral outrage: the increasingly callous Soviet attitude – epitomized by the Soviet reaction to the Warsaw rising of August 1944 – could not fail to arouse fury. But what fuelled and sustained Western hostility was the spectre of Moscow's hand stretching out much further – right into western Europe, the Middle East and Asia. It was in the West that the war and a vigorous role in the underground resistance had had the most rejuvenating effect on Communist fortunes. In France, Italy, Belgium, and Greece they had gained a genuinely mass following, far from enough to win a democratic election but sufficient to mount formidable challenges and to cause acute concern in London and Washington; and they were outspoken in protestations of loyalty to Moscow. Concern over the Middle East was fuelled by Moscow pressing Turkey for concessions over control of the Straits in the summer of 1945, and proving suspiciously slow about honouring the agreement that all foreign troops in Iran, including Soviet forces in the north, would be withdrawn early in March 1946. With Europe's overseas colonies, especially in Asia, severely destabilized during the war, the scope for Soviet expansionism seemed in Western eyes almost limitless. In the USA, by the time of Roosevelt's death in April 1945, stiff resistance to the Red threat was already becoming a major electoral asset. Under President Truman, American policy in Europe became focused above all upon social and political stabilization and the exclusion of Communists from power. In March 1947 the President committed the USA to the policy of containment. American financial and if necessary military resources would check Communist influence wherever necessary – starting with Turkey, Greece, and Iran, where Soviet pressure seemed most intense.

Overt hostility from the West quickly reawoke the darkest suspicions in Moscow. Although the record of Allied intervention in the Civil War and hostility during the 1920s and 1930s had been played down during the war, it had not been forgotten. Tension rapidly mounted. The decisive break came when the US Secretary of State, Marshall, launched the European Recovery Programme. The Soviet Union and her satellites were invited to take part, despite the fact that Congress would be extremely unlikely to ratify aid to the 'Reds'. In the event it was the Soviet team at the Paris Conference of June-July 1947, led by Molotov, who broke off negotiations. Marshall Aid was denounced as an imperialist ploy to subvert Soviet independence and those eastern European countries which had shown interest in taking part were called to heel. Two months later the Communist Information Bureau (Cominform) was formed to underline the solidarity of the Soviet Union, her allies, and the fraternal parties of France and Italy.

As trust broke down completely, the Soviet Union became less and less concerned with Western sensibilities. In Poland, Romania, Bulgaria, Hungary and Czechoslovakia Stalin imposed with the utmost brutality regimes dominated in each case by the national Communist Party. And as the international situation became increasingly polarized, a series of bilateral political, military, and economic treaties bound these countries ever closer to the Soviet Union. In 1948 a dramatic breach with Tito's regime in Yugoslavia added a further incentive for Moscow to consolidate control over her satellites. As the one Communist regime which did not depend either for its creation or its survival upon Soviet support, the government in Belgrade had from the start shown a marked degree of independence. Tito's approach towards the West was much more aggressive than was Stalin's. Where Moscow prevaricated, Belgrade was outspoken, willingly offering aid to the Communists in the Greek Civil War and enthusiastically encouraging Communist revolt in Asia. In this, Tito was apparently supported by some of Stalin's more militant comrades, notably the faction identified with A. A. Zhdanov. Stalin's attitude may have been coloured by sheer dislike of Tito's independence as well as suspicion over his close ties with Zhdanov and party leaders in Leningrad. Equally important was the Yugoslavs' resentment over the hard bargain driven by the Soviets in economic negotiations, and Stalin's hostility to Tito's plans for a federation of Communist states in the Balkans. Soviet hopes that Stalin's word would be enough to persuade Tito's colleagues to overthrow him were disappointed. In June 1948 the Yugoslav Party was expelled from Cominform, trade was broken off, and the Party was denounced for bourgeois nationalist deviations. Party leaders elsewhere in eastern Europe hastened to protest their loyalty and those who had shown any inclination to resist Moscow's diktat were purged amidst a spate of show trials. The new 'People's Democracies' began to implement social and economic programmes closely modelled upon the Soviet prototype.

It was in this context that the joint occupation of Germany broke down. The defeated Reich, and the capital, Berlin, had been divided into four zones (Soviet, American, British and French). From the start disputes over the process of extracting reparations had fuelled mutual suspicion. To the Russians, the West appeared to be placing artificial obstacles in the way of the Soviet Union gaining due compensation; for their part the Western powers became increasingly irked at the prospect of subsidizing Germany while she was milked by the Russians. As events in eastern Europe under-mined East–West relations, opinion in Washington and London began to move in the direction of rehabilitating and integrating the Western occupa-tion zones into the 'free world'. As early as 1947 the British and American zones were merged, and the French zone joined them the following year. In 1948 a new currency was introduced in the Western zones and the first steps were taken towards restoring German national political institutions. Parallel steps were being taken in the Soviet zone, but Moscow had no desire to see the greater part of Germany re-emerging as part of an anti-Soviet alliance. In an attempt to forestall the permanent absorption of western Germany into the capitalist 'bloc', Moscow imposed a blockade on West Berlin. Coming as it did shortly after the final assertion of Communist power in Prague, this move was viewed in the West as a crude attempt to suck the western sectors of the city into the Communist 'bloc'. An Anglo-American airlift broke the blockade and lingering isolationist sentiment in Washington was irrevocably overcome. In April 1949 the North Atlantic Treaty Organization (NATO) gave formal shape to the Western Alliance. The fol-lowing month saw the foundation of the Federal Republic of West Germany under Chancellor Adenauer's fiercely pro-Western leadership. The Soviet zone gained the trappings of statehood at the end of the year.

Europe was divided into two hostile blocs. Peace movements in the West found themselves patronized and, in the eyes of many, tainted by Moscow. An 'Iron Curtain' was drawn across Europe. And as the demarca-tion line began to set firm, Cold War tension was brought to a new pitch by a chain of momentous events in Asia.

Soviet involvement in Asia took a very different form from that in eastern Europe. Here Moscow was a relatively passive beneficiary of post-war upheaval. The war had fatally weakened the grip of the British, French, and Dutch upon their overseas imperial interests. It had also nurtured increasingly militant independence movements from India to Indonesia. Local Communist parties figured prominently in few of these. But in the bipolar context of the Cold War, even non-Communist nationalist leaders tended to regard Moscow as a natural source of support against the Western powers.

Map 11   The Soviet Union and Eastern Europe after the Second World War

Soviet reaction was cautious. The discomfiture caused to the Western powers was naturally welcome, but Asia figured low in Soviet priorities – as the exclusion even of the Chinese Party from Cominform suggested. Having secured handsome territorial concessions from defeated Japan, and extracted a satisfactory arrangement to enhance Soviet influence in north-eastern China, Stalin tended to react to events in the east rather than to take the initiative. He encouraged the Chinese Communists – whom he once scornfully dubbed 'margarine Communists' – to reach an accommodation with the Nationalist government, and Soviet advice to other Asian Communists on the attitude to be adopted towards 'bourgeois' nationalist liberation movements vacillated with little regard for local conditions. Moscow committed minimal resources to aid the series of extreme left revolts that broke out in Burma, India, Indonesia, Malaya, and the Philippines.

From 1949, however, the Soviet Union was drawn ever more closely into Asian affairs. The Chinese Communists' prolonged struggle against the Nationalists ended in triumph and in October they proclaimed the foundation of the People's Republic of China. Exhilarating though the Communist victory was, Soviet enthusiasm was less than fulsome. The immediate result, after all, was a series of Chinese requests – for economic aid, military guarantees, and territorial concessions – which seemed to offer Russia no short-term benefit. It was only after six weeks' hard bargaining in Moscow that Mao Zedong extracted from Stalin a Treaty of Friendship.

The following year, the unstable post-war settlement in Korea, which bordered upon both Communist giants, exploded into civil war. At the end of the Pacific War, the country had been split between Soviet occupation forces in the north and those of the USA in the south. Both sides had eventually withdrawn, leaving the country divided between two well-armed local regimes locked in bitter political and ideological rivalry. In June 1950, apparently with Stalin's consent rather than on his initiative, the Communist regime of North Korea invaded South Korea. Following so hard upon Mao's triumph in neighbouring China, the invasion stung the USA into action. With the support of the UN – which the Soviet Union happened to be boycotting temporarily in protest against Communist China's exclusion from the world organization – American forces repelled the invasion and drove into the north. The Chinese, alarmed at the proximity of American troops and at the increasingly belligerent tone of American anti-Communism, poured 'volunteer' forces into the north. The American-led UN forces were checked and in June 1951, with the war bogged down near to the pre-war frontier, two years of frustrating armistice negotiations began.

The Soviet Union, though readily selling arms to the Communist belligerents, had declined to become directly involved. But the Korean War had extremely grave implications for her. In the USA the northern invasion was interpreted as part of a world-wide strategy for the spread of Moscow-dominated Communist influence. Washington's reaction was to extend her defence umbrella right across non-Communist Asia. In Indo-China, where France was experiencing growing difficulty in containing the challenge to her imperial authority launched in 1946 by the Vietnamese nationalist movement led by Ho Chi Minh, the USA took on a growing share of the military burden. She hastily reached a final peace settlement with Japan (1951) and expanded the military bases she had established there. In Europe, too, the war served to heighten tension. Repeated Soviet efforts to reopen the question of creating a unified, neutral Germany were ignored, and Washington began to press for the creation of West German forces and their integration into NATO. Above all, the US defence budget soared. The Soviet Union was locked into an open-ended arms race against an American-led alliance commanding vastly superior economic resources.

The combined effect of the Great Patriotic War and the Cold War which followed it was to reinforce many of the harshest economic and political features of Soviet life. The wreckage which the Nazis left in their wake necessitated a vast programme of reconstruction. In the countryside whole areas had been left severely short of livestock and implements. Most able-bodied male peasants had been recruited into the army and industry and many never returned to the land. The devastation was compounded when in 1946–47 European Russia was hit by the worst drought of the century. Urban conditions, too, were abysmal. Some 25 million people had been left homeless and the basic amenities of many cities had been destroyed. Food and manufactures were in desperately short supply. To restore the industrial base of the western provinces – the flooded mines, the bombed factories, the shattered railway network – massive resources were required. Training and education programmes had suffered severely during the war; battle casualties among men of prime military age had left a dire shortage of skilled labour; military service and evacuation had uprooted millions. Given the scale of the economic catastrophe, the reparations and favourable trading agreements exacted from the 'People's Democracies' could provide no more than limited assistance. Much of the effort of the 1930s would have to be undertaken again.

The Cold War only made matters worse. On the one hand, it ensured that, as in the 1930s, the strain of a huge investment programme would not be eased by foreign credit. On the other, it committed the Soviet Union to massive defence expenditure at a time when the civilian economy was in acute need. With national income in 1945 standing below that of 1940, the country was competing with the combined might of much of the Western world. To counter the American atomic monopoly and consolidate control over eastern Europe, the Soviet Army was expanded from 1948 and maintained at a level above 4 million men; the modest wartime navy was expanded, with special emphasis on developing a submarine fleet; and major resources were devoted to building a Soviet atomic bomb (1949) and a hydrogen bomb (1953). It is difficult to establish just how large the military budget was. Official figures may well underrate it, though even they indicate that the percentage of the budget spent on defence in the late 1940s dipped only slightly below 20 per cent and in 1952 was over 25 per cent: it absorbed a much higher proportion of national income than equivalent expenditure in the West. By the late 1940s the first tentative steps were being taken towards placing part of the defence burden upon the eastern European satellites, but this brought the Soviet Union minimal relief until after Stalin's death.

When reconstruction got under way, the regime reverted to a pattern that in most respects duplicated that of the 1930s. From 1943 Gosplan, headed by N. A. Voznesensky, who had been brought onto the Committee for State Defence in 1942, had begun again to prepare comprehensive plans and in 1946 the Fourth Five-Year Plan (1946–50) was launched. Both this and the Fifth Five-Year Plan (1951–55) set ambitious goals for increased production of consumer goods, but in practice overwhelming priority was given to heavy industry. As before the war, light industry and agriculture were starved of resources. The State continued to procure grain at abysmally low prices, and the remuneration for work on collective farms remained derisory. The illegal wartime expansion of private plots was halted and reversed, while the heavy wartime taxes imposed on private produce were retained. Moreover, firm steps were taken to cut peasant demand for consumer goods. During the war some peasants had accumulated very considerable savings from sales of the produce from their private plots. In 1947 a carefully designed currency reform virtually wiped out these savings. Minimal efforts were made to improve retail outlets in the countryside, village amenities remained rudimentary, and rural living conditions were barely above subsistence level.

Such attempts as were made to raise agricultural productivity were quintessentially Stalinist. The 'Stalin Plan to Transform Nature' – including a massive tree-planting programme, the diversion of several major rivers, and the construction of five huge hydroelectric power-stations – was designed to counteract both erosion and drought. Eventually the power-stations did contribute to the country's electrification, but the grandiose vision of raising vast new stretches of forest and of bringing millions of acres under irrigation came to nothing, and the peasants bore the brunt of the whole undertaking. Somewhat less far removed from reality, though of very doubtful value, were the reforms sponsored by N. S. Khrushchev (1894–1971), the ebullient Politburo member who had made his name as Secretary of the Ukrainian Party. In the hope of enhancing economies of scale, specialization and mechanization, many of the smaller collective farms were merged, the total number falling from 250,000 to under 100,000 in three years and continuing to decline thereafter. At the same time, the standard farm labour squad was sharply increased in the belief that smaller groups ('links'), often made up of extended peasant families, perpetuated precollectivization attitudes. Khrushchev also entertained visions of concentrating peasant households in modern 'agrotowns', thereby narrowing the differences between peasants and workers. But in the post-war years there was no chance that the necessary investment would be forthcoming.

Although workers received clear priority over peasants, and opportunities for acquiring technical skills expanded enormously after the war, their conditions too were grim. Rationing was only abolished at the end of 1947; shortages of food, clothes, and consumer goods remained acute; and it was not until 1950 that real wages recovered to pre-war levels. As in the 1930s, workers' representatives were much more concerned with improved discipline and efficiency than with the conditions of labour. The authority and status of managers were firmly upheld and the harsh eve-of-war labour decrees were not revoked. In practice, with millions of soldiers being demobilized and evacuees flooding back to the western provinces, and with housing conditions atrocious, laws against moving from one job to another proved increasingly difficult to enforce. Likewise, the pre-war pattern of tacit collusion between managers and workers to conceal slack work practices reasserted itself. But the material quality of life was wretched for the countless workers coming to terms with the human wreckage of war and invasion, families uprooted, young men maimed, young women widowed and a skewed demographic pattern that deprived many more of the opportunity ever to marry at all.

The renewed industrialization drive saw further differentiation in status and life-style between the upper strata of white-collar workers and the mass of workers and peasants. This was broadly reflected in the Party's admissions policy. A significant proportion of the workers, peasants, and rank-and-file soldiers admitted to the Party during the war lost their membership and the predominance of white-collar members was firmly re-established. By the end of Stalin's rule it is estimated that over 75 per cent of party members occupied white-collar positions. Of course, many white-collar positions conferred neither higher status nor better wages than did skilled manual labour. But the relatively privileged way of life of officials in the upper echelons of every hierarchy – in the bureaucracies of Party, State and economy, as well as the army and police – became increasingly pronounced. Their special access to food, goods, and housing was an invaluable privilege in conditions of shortage and overcrowding. Generally speaking their security, too, began to improve. The incidence of drastic intervention from the centre against local managers and state officials declined. As in the 1930s, Moscow found severe limits to the effective control that could be exercised through either the police or the Party. Once again, recalcitrant local networks re-emerged as officials in each hierarchy responsible for one particular area or sector of the economy were drawn together both by personal links and by their common interest in parading the successful 'plan fulfilment' of their bailiwick. Moreover, the tendency was reinforced by the relative autonomy managers and officials had enjoyed during the war and the new confidence this had enabled them to acquire. The result was to magnify deviations from the general plan laid down in Moscow, as the more powerful regions and ministries asserted their own interests. New constraints on the power of the centre were beginning to emerge, although this tendency would become much more pronounced after Stalin's death.

So far as political conformity was concerned, however, there was no more room for dissent at the top of the social ladder than at the bottom. The instruments of coercion – the secret police, the labour camps, censorship – remained firmly in place. The Party's political monopoly and control over the trade unions and both urban and rural soviets was still absolute. And within the Party, democratic processes remained an empty charade. Although the Politburo, together with the Central Committee, regained formal supremacy after the war, in practice, key decisions were made by *ad hoc* groups chosen or sanctioned by Stalin. The Central Committee failed to meet at all for five years between 1947 and 1952, and it was only in 1952, after an interval of 13 years, that a new Congress was held. Stalin remained General Secretary and Chairman of the Council of Ministers (as the Commissars were renamed in 1946) and retained a virtually free hand in decision-making – when he cared to exercise it. Between 1944 and 1948 he appears to have been unwell and made extremely few public appearances and statements. But his personal domination of the leadership was unchallenged; he could make or break his lieutenants; and in the aftermath of the war, the personality cult reached its most absurd expression. As soon as victory had been won, leading military figures, headed by Zhukov, were withdrawn from the public eye and every laurel heaped upon Stalin himself. The victory was his victory and his genius was recognized as the guiding light in every sphere of human knowledge and activity. Flattery of Stalin was the safest course. On every public occasion, in every connection his praises were sung. Deification reached the point where a committee was established to ensure that he reached the age of 100. His writings took clear precedence over the classic texts of Marxism-Leninism, and official policy moved further and further from the spirit of Marx or indeed Lenin.

It is neither easy nor edifying to penetrate the mind of the 'Generalissimo' in his last years. Any description of his character reads like an endless catalogue of the most obnoxious vices – insufferable pride, savage indifference to human suffering, suspiciousness bordering on paranoia, monumental hypocrisy. The whole atmosphere was darkened by his style,

---

10.4 The Stalin Cult reached bizarre extremes during his last years. This photograph shows a slide portrait being projected on to a cloud over Red Square during celebrations to mark Stalin's 70th birthday, 21 December 1949.

Огонёк

№ 52 ДЕКАБРЬ 1949
ИЗДАТЕЛЬСТВО «ПРАВДА»

his sadistic treatment even of venerable henchmen like Molotov (who saw his own wife arrested), his readiness to use murder to remove political obstacles, his utter contempt for peasants. Many of the most bizarre, even pathological, aspects of official policy bore his stamp.

How far Stalin's defective personality was in itself responsible for the repressive conditions of post-war Russia is more debatable. It was clear to the leadership as a whole that amidst the general hardship of the post-war years, with every Union Republic, every minority nationality, every region, every city and every social group crying out for additional resources, individual grumbling and frustration could all too easily find political expression. The danger seemed greatest where the war had done most to undermine the authority of the Party.

First, there were the areas originally annexed between 1939 and 1941 – eastern Poland, the Baltic states, Bessarabia, and northern Bukovina. The relative indifference or even support with which the German invasion was met here (especially in Estonia, Latvia, and Lithuania) fully exposed just how shallow were the roots put down by Soviet power. When these territories were reabsorbed at the end of the war, therefore, a series of drastic measures was taken to entrench Soviet power and to bring the new citizens into line with the rest of the country. Anti-Soviet political organizations were destroyed, industry was renationalized, and large estates were distributed to the peasantry. The year 1948 saw the beginning of forced collectivization and the mass deportation of kulaks to labour camps. This was accompanied by brutal police measures in both the countryside and the cities strongly reminiscent of the 1930s.

Second, there were the long-established western areas of the Soviet Union which had been cut off from Moscow. In the Ukraine, Nazi occupation had stimulated local nationalism, weakened the collective farm system, and left a number of scattered partisan groups who resisted the reimposition of Moscow's authority. As Soviet power was re-established, the gravest suspicion fell upon any hint of 'bourgeois nationalism', whether among local party officials or intellectuals, and here the turnover among party secretaries was much higher than elsewhere. In some areas entire nationalities were convicted of collaboration with the Germans. In 1941 Stalin had already ordered the mass deportation of the Volga-Germans on the assumption that, left in a vulnerable area, they would throw in their lot with Hitler. During the war local Russian party leaders denounced the Crimean Tatars and several Muslim tribes of the Caucasus for conniving with German occupation forces. In fact, although the Germans had sought, with the help of *émigré* leaders, to rouse them against the Soviet Union, few had betrayed their country and many had served honourably in the Red Army. Yet the moment the Germans had been driven out, some 1.5 million were uprooted *en masse* and sent penniless to Central Asia, the Urals, and Siberia. Even party officials belonging to the 'punished peoples' were despatched – though they did escape the murderous conditions in which the rank and file were forced to travel. The authorities may have suspected that their Muslim faith made these national groups susceptible to influence from Turkey. But the majority of the deportees were women and children and their political weight minimal. Within a decade Khrushchev was to admit that such brutal and indiscriminate punishment of whole nations defied not only the principles of Marxism-Leninism but common sense.

The same might be said of the treatment meted out to POWs returning from German captivity. They suffered from the authorities' assumption that foreign contact, however involuntary, implied unreliability, guilt, and possibly treason. The secret police went through the motions of 'screening' them to identify which of them had betrayed the Soviet Union, but in fact the vast majority were automatically arrested. The labour camps were not only retained but, despite an appallingly high death-rate, the number of inmates reached an all-time peak on the eve of Stalin's death.

The concern to re-establish party authority triggered a fierce drive to reinforce rigid political discipline throughout the country. From as early as 1944 vigorous steps were taken to raise political consciousness within the Party and the criteria for membership were stiffened. Particular care was taken to pre-empt any political aspirations among army leaders and the commissar system was refurbished to ensure party control over the army. During 1945 pressure for strict ideological orthodoxy and loyalty to the party line mounted steadily. In the post-war years this campaign, which was at first particularly identified with Zhdanov, whose responsibilities included the fields of culture and ideology, became increasingly vicious and engulfed ever wider dimensions of Soviet cultural life.

The particular form that the *Zhdanovshchina* took was conditioned by the legacy of the war and the impact of the emergent Cold War. Popular patriotic fervour and anti-Germanism mingled with official suspicion of the corrupting influence of the individualism and relative affluence of the West. As post-war tension mounted, the West was damned as both bourgeois and hostile, both degenerate and anti-Russian. Xenophobia, more or less cynically exploited by the party leadership, reached pathological extremes. There was a furious drive against any taint of Western influence. Cultural exchanges of every kind – even soccer matches – were broken off. It became illegal to marry a foreigner. Intellectuals who implicitly or explicitly showed respect for things Western were mercilessly denounced for 'cosmopolitanism'. In an orgy of nationalist self-congratulation, absurd claims were made for the cultural achievements of Russians – including responsibility for many of the world's greatest scientific discoveries. The *Short Course* was republished and historical research restricted to themes and conclusions that celebrated Soviet – and especially Great Russian – achievements. Censorship over literature, art, cinema, theatre and music was sharply tightened from 1946. Many prominent intellectuals were publicly subjected to crude denunciation. The sparkling satirist M. M. Zoshchenko (1895–1958) was an early victim, and the list of victims, including S. M. Eisenstein (1898–1948), Shostakovich, and Prokofiev, reads like a roll-call of Russia's most gifted creative artists. The tone of official attacks was epitomized by Zhdanov's venomous assault upon the lyric poetry of Akhmatova, whose popularity had been all too clearly demonstrated during the war: 'It would be hard to say if she is a nun or a whore; better perhaps to say that she is a little of both, her lusts and her prayers intertwine.'

The structure and form of 'socialist realism' were rigidly upheld. Tributes to Stalin and the Party, together with an idealized version of Soviet life, were mandatory. For novelists more or less in sympathy with the regime, this was not intolerably restrictive. They were able to express some of the subtle shifts in the tone of public life that had taken place since the 1930s. They showed a new concern with the quality of private life, with material comfort, with the trappings of gentility – and their heroes tended to be relatively refined managers and specialists rather than workers. Their work was as openly didactic as in the heroic days of the first Five-Year Plans, urging dedication and self-discipline, but it also addressed the private concerns of a more settled, more 'bourgeois' white-collar elite. For more independent spirits, Stalin's last years were utterly oppressive. A Pasternak might command too much popularity and moral authority to be cowed. A rare public rendition he gave in 1948, in which he demonstratively distanced himself from officialdom, was given a rapturous reception. And it was under the shadow of the *Zhdanovshchina* that he began work on *Doctor Zhivago*. But many victims of the post-war witch-hunt were driven to despair by the atmosphere of suspicion and fear of denunciation. For them it was, in the words of Pasternak's cousin Olga Freidenburg, professor of classical philology in Leningrad, 'an epoch that tramples poetry in the dust and spits on the human spirit'.[1]

The sciences suffered from an equally outrageous exercise of arbitrary political power. The almost paranoid concern for secrecy, the narrow restrictions on gathering social and economic statistics, as well as the infallibility accorded every word uttered by Stalin, stultified the social sciences. And his authority was freely used to destroy scholarly analysis in a whole range of fields, from physiology to linguistics. Most notorious was the absolute authority conferred upon the biological theories of T. D. Lysenko, who convinced the leadership he had developed a revolutionary approach to agronomy and plant-breeding that was unknown to 'bourgeois' science. For almost two decades the Soviet study of genetics was based upon an amalgam of dubious hypothesis and sheer fantasy. Although the party line in any

---

[1] E. Mossman, ed., *The Correspondence of Boris Pasternak and Olga Freidenburg 1910–1954* (London 1982), p. 325.

given field was almost always couched in Marxist phraseology the study of Marxist theory itself became petrified. When the notion that such an entity as international science existed could be damned as un-Marxist, no more than the shell of Marxist theory survived. Marxism was what Stalin and the leadership said it was.

The various currents that fed the *Zhdanovshchina* – xenophobia, national insecurity, party demagogy and the evil genius of Stalin himself – converged on the oldest of prejudices: anti-Semitism. A major stimulant was the emergence of the State of Israel in 1948. Initially, the Soviet government had supported its foundation, but the enthusiasm with which the Jewish triumph was met by Soviet Jews alarmed the regime. As the bonds between the USA and Israel strengthened, the official Soviet attitude became increasingly hostile. The quintessential Zhdanovite smear, 'rootless cosmopolitan', became a virtual synonym for Jew, and Jewish organizations, journals, and intellectuals became uniquely vulnerable to attack.

The price that intellectuals paid for public denunciation after the war was more likely to be dismissal, disgrace, and expulsion from their union than banishment, imprisonment, or death. But the ultimate penalty was paid by some, and life at the highest political levels, close to Stalin himself, remained decidedly dangerous. The cost of failure in the factional struggles which raged in the leader's shadow was as likely to be death as peaceful obscurity.

Western observers at the time and Western scholars ever since have had grave difficulty in identifying individual members of Stalin's post-war Politburo with consistent policy attitudes. There certainly were divisions over a range of issues – foreign policy, regional policy, agriculture. But the factions that emerged tended to be bound together less by common issues of principle than by personal loyalty based on patronage and a measure of personal sympathy. The most spectacular post-war rivalry was fought out between Stalin's two chief lieutenants in the Secretariat, Zhdanov and Malenkov. Behind each was arrayed a network of officials who owed their advancement to one or other of the two protagonists. Other members of the Politburo were able to remain neutral, although Beria, who continued to head the secret police, appears to have allied with Malenkov. Stalin's attitude was entirely characteristic. He tolerated the struggle, intervening only to ensure that neither side built up too powerful a position. In 1946 and 1947 Zhdanov's faction gained the advantage, but even before Zhdanov's fatal illness in the summer of 1948, Stalin had moved to check his power. The close ties which Zhdanov and his associates in Leningrad had established with the Yugoslav Party appear to have incensed Stalin and proved a major liability following the break with Tito. Malenkov, with the assistance of Beria, moved against Zhdanov's faction. During 1949 leading party figures in Leningrad and elsewhere, including Voznesensky, were dismissed, arrested and shot or disappeared into the Gulag.

The 'Leningrad affair', however, did not signal Malenkov's firm grip on the succession. According to Khrushchev, it was precisely to counter-balance Malenkov that he himself was promoted to the Secretariat by Stalin in 1949. In 1951, Beria's position was shaken when Stalin accused party officials in his home province, Mingrelia in Georgia, of planning to secede from the USSR and compelled him to carry out a drastic purge. And in his last year Stalin appears to have laid the groundwork for a purge which Malenkov, Beria, Molotov, and even Khrushchev feared might engulf them. The Nineteenth Party Congress, held in October 1952, saw the Politburo replaced by a much larger Presidium, and Stalin's old lieutenants were swamped by new men. In January 1953 *Pravda* announced the discovery of a plot among a group of (mostly Jewish) doctors in the Kremlin to assassin-ate leading party figures. Calls for vigilance against the enemy within were ominously reminiscent of the 1930s. But whatever Stalin had in mind, it never came to fruition. The ageing tyrant suffered a stroke on 1 March and died four days later.

Chapter 11 ....

Stabilization under Khrushchev and Brezhnev (1953–mid-1970s)

Much of Stalin's legacy remained in place for a generation. The country's borders did not alter, her superpower status was upheld, and her estrangement from the West remained profound. Political and economic power remained fused in the hands of the State. The Party, backed by the KGB, continued to exercise control over all forms of public organization and mass communication, and Marxism-Leninism remained firmly entrenched as the prescribed ideology. Yet in the course of the first two decades following Stalin's death, within this seemingly rigid framework, there took place a qualitative change in almost every facet of Soviet life.

As soon as Stalin was safely interred alongside Lenin in the mausoleum on Red Square, his heirs moved to curtail political violence and arbitrary arrest. The 'Doctors' Plot' was promptly denounced as a fabrication, and during the succession struggle which followed the only contestant to meet a bloody end was Beria. The chief motive behind his arrest in June 1953 and subsequent execution appears to have been the alarm of his Politburo colleagues at his control over the secret police. But thereafter, political disgrace no longer spelled death. Malenkov, who at first seemed the likely heir to Stalin's leadership, was forced to resign as Prime Minister in 1955, but remained in the Politburo until 1957. Even then, when the emergent new leader, Khrushchev, successfully rallied the Central Committee against a hostile majority on the Politburo, the defeated 'old guard' paid a relatively light, if galling, penalty. Molotov, Stalin's immensely experienced Foreign Minister, for example, was relegated to the embassy in Mongolia. And when in 1964 Khrushchev in turn alienated his colleagues in the leadership, the great showman was forced into retirement and his name became taboo. His successor as party leader, L. I. Brezhnev (1906–82), General Secretary from 1964 to 1982, died in office, and the few Politburo members who fell from grace faced honourable retirement. The days of physical elimination had passed.

Changes in the rules of political struggle at the top were matched by a general reduction in the use of coercion following Stalin's death. There was an immediate, if limited, amnesty, a public call for a return to 'socialist legality', and in private the new leadership began to articulate criticism of the way Stalin had exploited his independent control of the KGB. The secret police were firmly subordinated to party control once more, while uprisings in several labour camps during 1953 and 1954 brought the future of the whole camp system into question. The most dramatic break from the past came at the famous closed session of the Twentieth Party Congress in 1956. Despite the forebodings of some of his colleagues, Khrushchev took it upon himself to spell out to stunned party delegates a selective catalogue of Stalin's crimes. He cast no doubt, of course, on the legitimacy of the Party's claim to rule. The emphasis was firmly on the mass terror launched against loyal members of the Party, many of whom Khrushchev mentioned by name, and upon Stalin's irresponsible and often disastrous interference in otherwise thoroughly sound economic and military planning. He was also at pains to distance Stalin's personality cult and all the crimes to which it gave rise from the achievements of the revolution, of collectivization, and the industrialization drive. He specifically stressed Lenin's distrust of Stalin. But the Terror, the mass arrests, the uprooting of whole nationalities – all were explicitly denounced. Although the speech was not published in Russia, edited versions were circulated at party meetings all over the country and before long its message was widely known.

Party conservatives feared that so fundamental a blow to the perceptions to which a whole generation had become accustomed would destabilize the system. Their fears were heightened when, within months of Khrushchev's speech, disturbances in Poland and a full-scale revolt in Hungary broke out against regimes intimately identified with the discredited leader. For a time open criticism of Stalin was checked. But in 1961 Khrushchev again took the lead and this time publicly and openly aired the crimes associated with the personality cult. The Central Committee resolved that the remains of J. V. Stalin were not worthy of a place alongside Lenin in the great mausoleum and they were removed.

The exposure of Stalin was accompanied by a variety of steps to undo the most oppressive features of his regime. Already the secret police had forfeited control over the economic empire of the labour camps which had underpinned their independence, and following Khrushchev's secret speech in 1956 the camps, where serious unrest had broken out, were almost all dismantled and several million prisoners returned to civilian life. For countless families the sense of relief and even gratitude was immense, and there was a general and palpable relaxation of tension in the atmosphere. A major symbol of the reduction in coercion was the repeal in 1956 of the draconian pre-war legislation imposing criminal penalties for absenteeism and 'unauthorized departure from enterprises and institutions'. Freedom of employment was restored. At the same time officials in the party and state hierarchies, as well as industrial and collective farm managers, were relieved from the threat of arrest for economic failure. Punishments for corruption and crime remained heavy and in some cases were increased, and dissent from the basic tenets of the Soviet system was punished in a variety of ways – from internal exile to incarceration in a psychiatric hospital and deportation. Ordinary citizens remained conscious that the KGB was alert and its methods of surveillance increasingly sophisticated. But police intervention took on less and less arbitrary and unpredictable forms. As time passed, the politically conformist gradually gained a sense of security under the law.

The most perilous moment for a bad regime, in Tocqueville's famous words, is when it seeks to mend its ways. Both Khrushchev and his more cautious colleagues were conscious of the risk that 'destalinization' and the return to 'socialist legality' involved. Unlike Stalin, they would be unable to ignore mass deprivation. Expectations of tangible improvements in Soviet life would gather pace. With the machinery of terror curbed, discontent might find dangerous expression – be it through an unstable and demoralized labour force, an upsurge in nationalist unrest among the minorities, or even disenchantment among the more privileged groups. Trepidation ensured a general consensus, running from Malenkov and Khrushchev to Brezhnev and his colleagues, that the reduction of coercion must be complemented by measures to consolidate and broaden support for the system.

Their success was remarkable. The post-Stalin generation saw Russia become more stable than at any time since the days of Alexander I. The recipe for this stability was based upon two key ingredients. The first was a marked and general improvement in the standard of living. The second was the paradoxical combination of military might and chronic national insecurity which was Stalin's legacy. Both were exploited to the full to rally mass support behind the Soviet system. Despite the slackening of censorship and cultural control which accompanied 'destalinization', the Party did all it could to ensure that, from cradle to grave, every citizen was convinced that both material progress and peace depended upon 'Soviet socialism'.

What made possible the dual commitment to increased consumption and superpower status was the extremely rapid economic development achieved in the period to the mid-1970s. The growth in agricultural production left the stagnation of Stalinist days far behind. Under Khrushchev, the main source of increased output was the 'virgin lands' campaign of 1954–56. Massive tracts of unused land in Kazakhstan, Siberia, and the Urals were ploughed up and brought under cultivation. Much of this land was acutely susceptible to drought and wind erosion, making the harvest highly erratic and the long-term benefits doubtful. But it did give a major short-term boost to output. In addition, Khrushchev initiated a fundamental reversal in the relationship of the agricultural sector to the rest of the economy. From being a major source of funds for industry, it became a major recipient. Procurement prices paid by the State for grain were sharply raised in an attempt to improve incentives, there was a large increase in the wages of workers on state farms, and Khrushchev took the first steps towards providing a comparable fixed wage for collective farmers. At the same time a sustained increase began in investment in mechanization, irrigation and fertilizers. Each of these policies was taken further under Brezhnev. By the early 1970s rural wages were fast approaching those of unskilled urban workers, procurement prices continued to rise despite the massive subsidies required to keep retail prices stable, and the share of total capital investment devoted to productive investment in agriculture exceeded 20 per cent.

The growth in production, it should be stressed, was far from satisfactory and fell far short of the returns expected from the increase in land cultivated and enormous investment outlays. The overall improvement was highly uneven, marked by frequent and sharp setbacks because of harvest failure, and almost invariably failed to meet planned levels. Many of Khrushchev's panaceas proved costly failures, and disappointing results in the early 1960s – culminating in a disastrous harvest in 1963 – helped to bring him down. After initially taking steps to encourage private-plot production, between 1958 and 1963 he placed new restrictions on it in a forlorn attempt to compel peasants to throw their energies into working for collective and state farms. The series of administrative reorganizations in the period fared little better. The decision in 1958 to abolish the MTS and sell the machinery to collective farms imposed a heavy short-term burden on the farms and few of them were equipped to maintain or repair the machinery. The supposed economies of scale to be gained by amalgamating collective farms into larger units and converting many into state farms failed to materialize. While both state and collective farm managers were notionally given more autonomy, in practice ill-considered interference continued both from local party officials and from the centre. The most notorious case was Khrushchev's irrational enthusiasm for maize, which was imposed in manifestly unsuitable regions. Between 1959 and 1964, highly promising local experiments with the so-called 'link' system, designed to increase motivation by giving a team of 9–11 peasants full responsibility for working a piece of land and enabling them to benefit directly from improved output, were frustrated. Most local party officials and farm administrators, anxious lest the autonomy involved render them redundant, denounced the experiments as 'petty-bourgeois' and incipiently capitalist, while the mass of peasants not involved in the experiments resented their success and the way their relative efficiency highlighted how slack were conventional farm labour practices. For all the improvement in procurement prices, no solution was found to the fundamental problem of peasant apathy and lack of incentive. Despite the massive increase in investment, productivity per farm worker rose very slowly. Every year millions of troops, townsfolk, students and, indeed, schoolchildren had to be mobilized to assist with the harvest. UN estimates

11.1 Threshing grain on a state farm in Kazakhstan. Massive investment in the mechanization of Soviet agriculture contributed to a period of sustained increase in output in the first two decades after Stalin's death.

indicating that Soviet agriculture achieved a faster rate of growth both in volume and per capita than any other major region of the world underscore just how dire the situation had been under Stalin. Nevertheless, although by Western standards Soviet agriculture remained extremely inefficient, between 1950 and 1975 gross agricultural output more than doubled.

The growth in industrial production was even more striking. Until well into the 1950s, much of this growth arose from post-war reconstruction and the major projects launched under Stalin. Until the 1970s, the urban work-force expanded at a rate of over 1.5 per cent per year, as the size of the population recovered from the war and renewed its upward trend, and as migration from the countryside continued apace. New mineral resources were discovered and exploited and major new industrial developments were undertaken in Siberia. Heavy investment in new plant and machinery, together with an impressive training programme, helped ensure that labour productivity, while remaining well below Western levels, gradually rose. As in the case of agriculture, the return on investment fell short of expectations. Industry continued to be handicapped by many of the dys-functions that had emerged under Stalin: slipshod work practices; mana-gerial preoccupation with quantitative targets rather than with quality or economy in fuel, raw materials and labour; resistance to technological innovation; and a planning system grossly distorted by falsified economic data and in-fighting between different bureaucratic hierarchies. Repeated administrative reforms made limited impact. In 1957 Khrushchev tried to overcome the refusal of the central ministries to coordinate their efforts and eliminate duplication by transferring their powers to regional economic councils. The new bodies rapidly developed a new but scarcely less wasteful form of 'localism' and the reform had run into severe difficulties even before Khrushchev's successors reversed it. In 1965 a series of changes introduced by A. N. Kosygin, Chairman of the Council of Ministers, sought to increase both the autonomy of managers and their incentive to cut labour and other costs and raise quality. In practice, instructions from the central ministries continued to rain down upon enterprises, and the supposed rewards for technical innovation and increased productivity were insufficient to out-weigh overriding concern to achieve quantitative targets regardless of cost and waste. Nevertheless, according to Soviet statistics, from the beginning of the Fifth to the end of the Ninth Five-Year Plan period (1951–75) national income expanded at an average annual rate of almost 8 per cent. Although Western and recent Russian estimates are lower, and the rate of expansion certainly declined towards the end of the period, the overall eco-nomic growth was substantial. Between 1950 and 1975 the gross national product more than quadrupled, rising from some 33 to 61 per cent of that of the USA. With the population increasing by some 40 per cent – from 178 million in 1950 to 253.3 million in 1975 – the rise in per capita output exceeded 5 per cent a year. Consumption, of course, did not rise nearly as fast. The output of defence and heavy industry continued to grow more rapidly than that of consumer goods. Even when in the Ninth Plan (1971–75), for the first time, a higher rate of growth was set for consumer goods than producer goods, the goal was not fulfilled. Yet this did not pre-vent a rise in living standards without parallel in any previous period of Russian history.

From the start Stalin's successors made quite explicit their belief that an improvement in mass welfare was essential. There was a new note of urgency in the Central Committee's commitment, contained in the announcement of Stalin's death, to the 'maximum satisfaction of the con-stantly growing material and cultural needs of the entire society'.[1] Malenkov's 'new course' was designed to associate his bid for the leadership with a general wage increase and an undertaking to shift resources from defence and heavy industry towards the production of consumer goods.

---

[1] *Pravda*, 6 March 1953, p. 1.

Khrushchev successfully rallied state and party officials in the heavy industry and defence sectors against the 'extremism' of Malenkov's proposals, but at the same time he championed the consumer sector *par excellence*: agriculture. And once he had successfully secured the leadership, he identified the Party's claim to legitimacy ever more closely with the improvement in the quality of life. He positively invited comparison between American and Soviet material achievements, and in 1961 a revised programme of breathtaking optimism was adopted by the Party. Abundance in basic consumer necessities was to be achieved within two decades. By 1980 the material base would be achieved for the transition to begin from socialism to the ultimate Utopia of communism.

Khrushchev's successors eschewed such gratuitous hostages to fortune. They regarded the flamboyant gesture as typical of all that was worst in Khrushchev and relegated the ultimate goal to an uncertain date in the future. But their major criticism of him was precisely that his various economic panaceas – drastic restructuring first of the state bureaucracy and then of the Party, a crash programme of investment in the chemical industry – created disruption without accelerating growth. Though their approach would be more cautious, more incremental, throughout their tenure of power Brezhnev and his colleagues made quite clear their concern to guarantee a steady improvement in the standard of living.

There was of course no question of fulfilling Khrushchev's imaginative goals, but sustained improvement was apparent in every aspect of both urban and rural life. The social services made dramatic advances. In 1956 there was a major expansion of the pension scheme for the aged, disabled, and sick. In 1964 comprehensive coverage was extended to collective farmers, who hitherto had been covered only by their own inadequate mutual aid funds. By stages the minimum and average level of pensions was raised, additional benefits such as those for maternity were increased, and the retirement age was gradually reduced. The education system, which had suffered grievously during the war, was being rapidly expanded even before Stalin's death. At every level the number of places grew enormously: in kindergarten and nurseries from under 2 million before the war to almost 12 million in 1976; in higher education from 0.8 million to 5 million; adults taking courses designed to upgrade skills rose from 9.5 million to over 33 million. At secondary level the school-leaving age was raised in 1958 from 14 to 15. The expansion of the free health service was equally spectacular. By the late 1970s the number of doctors and hospital beds available per head of the population exceeded the comparable figure in Britain and the USA. The improvement in urban housing was less dramatic, and overcrowding remained severe, but average per capita space more than doubled between the early 1950s and the late 1970s. The cities saw continuous improvement in the provision of public leisure facilities – holiday resorts, parks, restaurants, theatres, cinemas, museums, libraries. Conditions in the

11.2   The Troparevo residential estate, Moscow. In the period from the 1950s to the 1970s Moscow and other Soviet cities saw the proliferation of large-scale, uniform apartment blocks in the expanding suburbs.

countryside remained much more primitive, but the general provision of electric light and running water, at least in the form of a village pump, represented marked progress.

In addition to the development of social services and amenities there was a great improvement in the supply of consumer goods. The provision of meat, fruit, and vegetables increased enormously, and average calorie consumption rose very sharply. Food prices remained heavily subsidized: a sharp price rise in 1962 provoked widespread protest, riots and, in the city of Novocherkassk, a virtual general strike which left the authorities extremely wary of repeating the expedient. There was a steady rise in the output of clothes and shoes, and the 1960s saw the mass production of consumer durables – washing machines, refrigerators, vacuum cleaners. By the late 1970s even in rural areas the vast majority of households had a television set. Despite a consistent policy of improving public rather than private transport, during the 1970s even the number of private cars slowly began to climb.

The quality of the services and goods made available under Khrushchev and Brezhnev is, of course, much more difficult to measure than their quantity. In few areas could they compare with those of western Europe. But in terms of the training of doctors and teachers, the variety of food and clothing, the elegance of furniture and fitments the progress was manifest. And on top of everything else, the working week was gradually shortened and the length of paid holidays extended. By any measurement, the standard of living had by the 1970s shown a remarkable improvement since the harsh conditions of Stalin's last years.

In absolute terms every income bracket made substantial gains. In 1956 Khrushchev sharply raised the minimum wage, and in the 1960s the wages of collective farmers ceased to depend on the vagaries of the harvest, were standardized, and step by step brought up towards those of state farm workers. Wage rises for white-collar workers in the service industries, in clerical posts, and primary level teaching, tended to be less generous and more fitful – reflecting in part the fact that the vast majority of these posts were occupied by women, whose wages as often as not were regarded as supplementary to those of the main breadwinner. But skilled workers saw a steep rise in their wages, and, for those higher up the social scale, besides a steadily growing salary there was a myriad of fringe benefits – ranging from privileged access to goods and services to chauffeur-driven cars and even domestic servants. Although expectations rose at least as fast as living standards, every stratum had reason to appreciate the material achievements of the Soviet system.

Rewards were, of course, by no means equally distributed. True, there were recurrent efforts to improve the position of the most disadvantaged – inspired by the need to attract labour into the least sought-after occupations and regions as much as by any ideological commitment. The relative deprivation of the peasantry declined very sharply, in part because of the growing need to restrain the flight from rural areas. The stress on universal free services and various attempts at positive discrimination in education in favour of the children of workers and peasants were designed to benefit the worst off. Successive Five-Year Plans aimed, with some success, to reduce the disparity between developed and undeveloped regions. By the late 1970s, nevertheless, there was still a great gulf between the richest republics of the Baltic and the poorest of Central Asia, between the spartan life-style of remoter villages and the modern facilities of the great cities. The income gap between the richest 10 per cent and the poorest 10 per cent did show a clear decline over the period, falling well below the equivalent gap in West Germany and the USA, but by the end of the 1970s it was still comparable to that in France or Britain.

Yet in a sense this stratification of income levels served further to consolidate support for the Soviet system. For sustained economic development provided very considerable scope for upward mobility within the social hierarchy. There could, of course, be no repetition of the overnight promotion of workers into management that had taken place in the early 1930s. But millions benefited from the opportunities for a gradual rise in social status. As urbanization continued – the urban population increased from 33 per cent of the total in 1940 to over 50 per cent in 1960 and almost two-thirds by 1980 – the collective farmer was likely to see at least some of his children rise into the ranks of the urban working class. As industrial production became increasingly sophisticated, the demand for skilled workers outstripped that for unskilled workers, providing many opportunities for workers to better themselves – and even more for their sons to do so. From the 1960s the regime deliberately increased the number of 'closed' enterprises engaged (in theory at least) in sensitive military production, and offering a variety of privileges to the labour-force, thereby creating particularly advantageous openings for hand-picked workers. Similarly coveted was the *propiska* granting the right of residence in one of the major cities – Moscow, Leningrad, the republican capitals, and other large urban centres – where the standard of living, the amenities, the cultural life, and the job prospects were distinctly superior. Expansion was fastest of all in white-collar posts requiring higher education, which ensured substantial upward mobility for many within the white-collar stratum as well as for the successful children of those lower down the social scale.

Scattered opinion surveys confirm the common-sense assumption that upward mobility – be it through entry to a major city, a 'closed' enterprise, or a higher social bracket – tended to deepen the individual's commitment to the Soviet system. The regime, moreover, did everything to strengthen the association between career success and political conformism. The prime mechanism used was that of party membership. In return for an explicit commitment to the values of the Party, the citizen greatly enhanced his or her prospects of promotion. At the highest levels this had long been the case. Through the *nomenklatura* system, the Central Committee and the regional committees of the Party took responsibility for ensuring that key posts in every hierarchy under their surveillance went to those whose loyalty was beyond doubt. But during the period the range of posts dominated by party members constantly grew, while even for those who did not gain promotion, entry to the Party brought a number of informal benefits. Not surprisingly, an invitation by the local committee to join the Party was eagerly sought and readily accepted. Total party membership soared – from 6.9 million at the time of Stalin's death to almost 16 million by 1977. Party representation gradually rose in every stratum, even among collective farmers where it had long been very low. By the late 1970s more than one-fifth of all men over the age of thirty were party members. The proportion in the white-collar stratum with higher education was even higher, reaching over 50 per cent. For the ambitious and the dynamic in every walk of life the route to conventional success lay through identification with the Soviet system.

Nowhere was this more significant than in binding the intelligentsia – political, economic, scientific, cultural – of each minority nationality to Moscow. The nationality-based federal structure was further elaborated during the period. When the 'Brezhnev' Constitution was introduced in

1977, the USSR consisted of fifteen Union Republics (the three Baltic Republics and Moldavia having been added to the eleven Union Republics of the 'Stalin' Constitution), twenty 'Autonomous Republics', eight 'Autonomous Regions' and ten 'Autonomous Areas'. The hierarchy broadly corresponded to the size of each national minority. Thus of the twenty-two ethnic groups with a population of over one million, fifteen had their own Union Republic, another four had 'Autonomous Republics', leaving only the German and Polish population with no territorial base, and the Jews with a token and largely uninhabitable 'Autonomous Region' situated in the Far East. All but seven of these thirty-eight 'autonomous' units belonged to the giant RSFSR, with a further three in Georgia and two in Azerbaizhan reflecting the patchwork quilt of minority peoples in the Caucasus, and one each in Tadzhikistan and Uzbekistan. The party leadership was well aware of the danger that this structure would not only preserve but, as literacy and urbanization spread, increase national consciousness, and that it would provide a ready-made framework for nationalist self-assertion against the centre. To avoid provoking such self-assertion, considerable leeway was given to the use of the native language and the development of native culture, and the majority of leading posts in public life in almost every one of these territorial units were deliberately reserved for members of the dominant local nationality. But in a sense this only increased the danger of nationalist pressure. To contain such pressure without having to resort to overt force, the leadership relied in part upon constant appeals to Soviet patriotism and the ideal of a steady 'drawing together' of the family of nations; in part upon the inter-ethnic tensions and conflicts of interest which encouraged the units to appeal to, rather than present a united front against, Moscow; in part upon the presence of a substantial Russian minority within most non-Russian territories and their intermarriage with the minorities; and in part upon the appointment of Russians to a number of strategically placed positions within the local party and KGB apparatus. But above all the centre relied upon its hold over the local elites: it was on the party-based patronage dispensed from Moscow that they depended for their posts, their privileges and their security.

The second major source of the system's domestic stability arose from the field of foreign policy. The regime was able to take full advantage of the psychological legacy of Hitler's invasion and the Great Patriotic War. It had the best of both worlds. On the one hand, it could take credit for maintaining peace, for each diplomatic success, and for every sign of Soviet strength and military security. On the other, it could play upon popular fear of war and foreign aggression whenever the international scene darkened. Diplomatic success and diplomatic reversals alike served to consolidate support behind the regime. And every major field of Soviet foreign involvement provided plenty of both.

First, there was her tense relationship with the USA, the one power whose military potential exceeded her own. Shortly after Stalin's death, Russia established herself beyond question as one of the two members of the exclusive club of superpowers. In August 1953 she exploded her first nuclear bomb. In 1957 she successfully launched Sputnik I into orbit and demonstrated her capacity, as the Soviet news agency, Tass, boasted, to target rockets on any region of the globe. Sputnik made an enormous impression on domestic opinion and fostered alarm in the USA that the USSR had opened out a 'missile gap'. Khrushchev, it is true, overplayed his hand. Under President Kennedy, the USA responded to the perceived threat with a rapid expansion in military expenditure; the 'gap' was soon exposed as a myth; and Khrushchev's attempt in 1962 to steal a further march by placing nuclear missiles on Cuba went awry. Nevertheless, by the late 1960s Soviet nuclear capacity began to match that of the USA and by the early 1970s, with the American military budget weighed down by the Vietnam war, she had achieved broad strategic parity. Beneath this nuclear umbrella, the Soviet Union built up formidable conventional forces. Although in his early years Khrushchev had imposed sharp cuts in the size of the army, from 1960, in part because of American military expansion, these were thrown into reverse. Despite no more than limited help from her eastern European partners in the Warsaw Pact (1955), the USSR maintained conventional superiority in Europe; in the late 1960s and early 1970s she rapidly expanded her forces in the Far East; and the development of the navy made her a first-class sea power.

This military power had an ambiguous effect upon Soviet security. On the one hand, it made the spectre of capitalist aggression, which had haunted the country ever since 1917, appear less menacing. Before he died even Stalin had at times cast doubt on the inevitability of renewed war with the capitalist powers. After Stalin's death Malenkov explicitly argued that nuclear power had made the Soviet Union virtually invulnerable. The new mood of relative confidence saw the USSR assist in negotiating an end to the Korean War in 1954, agree to withdraw from its occupation zone in Austria, surrender its bases in Finland, and restore diplomatic relations with Yugoslavia and Israel. In 1956 Khrushchev officially endorsed the concept of 'peaceful coexistence' and the view that nuclear war was too horrendous to contemplate. In Moscow's eyes, Soviet military strength was giving even the 'warmongers' in Washington pause before attempting to 'roll back the tide of communism'. Even in the fiasco of Khrushchev's Cuban adventure, the Soviet role was successfully portrayed at home as that of injured peacemaker. And later in the decade a great triumph was claimed for 'the peace-loving Soviet people' when, supposedly against their every instinct, the Americans were driven to the conference table. In 1969 the two superpowers entered into Strategic Arms Limitation Talks (SALT), and three years later they signed the first SALT Accord.

At the same time, however, the arms race generated acute insecurity and fear of war. The NATO partners collectively continued to outspend those of the Warsaw Pact. There seemed a recurrent danger that despite the Soviet commitment to peace – constantly celebrated through the media – war would break out. Even superpower negotiations to control the arms race were only mildly reassuring. The SALT Accord placed all too generous a ceiling on the nuclear capability of each side, and later in the 1970s, efforts to agree upon further SALT terms broke down altogether. Shadow-boxing with lethal nuclear weapons was perfectly designed to rally popular support behind the regime.

Eastern Europe provided a similar blend of demonstrable Soviet power and constant anxiety. Far from relinquishing the hegemony Stalin had established in the area, his heirs consistently regarded the security of the 'socialist commonwealth' as an extension of Soviet security itself. Through Comecon, the Council of Mutual Economic Assistance set up in 1949, they progressively strengthened the economic bonds linking the eastern satellites to Russia, and under the Warsaw Pact they perpetuated Soviet control of the armed forces of the six People's Democracies. They were able to take pride in their success in ensuring that the West refrained from interference in the area. The 'counter-revolutionary' Hungarian appeal for outside aid against Russian domination in 1956 went unheeded, and there was no question of Western intervention in aid of the Czechoslovak challenge to Russian power in 1968. Indeed, from the mid-1960s western Europe proved eager to improve political and commercial relations. Towards the end of the decade West Germany took the lead in furthering international *détente*. She normalized her relations with East Germany and recognized the Polish borders established in 1945. The seal was set on a series of treaties by the European Conference on Security and Cooperation in Helsinki in 1975. For the Soviet Union, the major significance of the Conference's Final Act, which included sections on economic relations and human rights, was Western recognition of the post-war political and territorial settlement in Europe. The West had come to terms with Russian hegemony in the east.

At the same time, however, recurrent bouts of unrest within eastern Europe could not fail to feed Soviet insecurity. In 1956 Soviet forces were sent into Hungary to crush the uprising. In 1968 it was the turn of the 'Prague Spring' to be suppressed by Warsaw Pact forces. Even less dramatic signs of instability sent shivers of unease through Moscow. The buffer zone, after all, lay immediately before NATO's front line. Khrushchev's dramatic efforts between 1958 and 1961 failed to dislodge the capitalist powers from their galling – and tiresomely prosperous – enclave in West Berlin or to dissuade them from installing nuclear weapons in West Germany. The construction of the Berlin Wall stemmed the flow of refugees to the West but a divided Germany provided a constant source of unease about possible future German 'revanchism'. At home the regime could easily summon up spectres from the past to justify the most ruthless action in ensuring ultimate

Soviet control. But the result was to undermine Moscow's claims to lead the oppressed peoples of the world, weaken the allegiance of Communist parties further afield, and virtually destroy the general sympathy from foreign radicals on which she had been able to count before the war.

In the Third World, too, grounds for self-congratulation were balanced by new threats to Soviet security. Soviet influence reached further and further afield. Besides the military protection she could offer would-be clients, she began to channel limited funds into development aid and, above all, during the 1970s she rapidly increased her arms exports. The Soviet point of view became a considerable factor in every corner of the globe. On the American doorstep, she forged the most intimate links with Cuba in the early 1960s, and admitted her to Comecon in 1972. On the Chinese doorstep, her chief satellites were Mongolia, admitted to Comecon in 1962, and Vietnam, admitted to Comecon in 1978. In South Asia she developed close diplomatic and commercial links with India. In the Middle East, South Yemen moved firmly into the Soviet orbit, Syria and, for a time, Egypt looked to the Soviet Union to counterbalance American support for Israel, and in 1978 a Treaty of Friendship was signed with the new military regime in Afghanistan. In Africa her most dramatic, if indirect, intervention came in the 1970s with the introduction of Cuban troops into the affairs of a number of states, most notably Ethiopia and Angola.

The roll-call of new clients fell well short of the Soviet Union's aspirations. Moscow was as baffled as Washington by the readiness with which humble Third World governments would abruptly repudiate their giant patrons. Indeed, between the late 1950s and the late 1970s the number of Soviet-dominated governments outside eastern Europe declined markedly. Yet after Khrushchev's fall, direct Soviet involvement tended to be cautious and low-key. Rebuffs could be borne fairly easily. Moreover, such successes as the West enjoyed were portrayed as evidence of the expansionist and militarist nature of the 'imperialist' powers, while every reversal they suffered was portrayed as a victory for progress, democracy – and, by implication, the Soviet Union. The list of those reversals was a long one – including the débâcle of Anglo-French intervention over Suez in 1956, the decolonization of Africa, and above all the abject humiliation of the USA in Vietnam.

There was, however, one major source of unease in the Third World. From the late 1950s there emerged a new threat, less easy to fit into the Marxist-Leninist lexicon than that of the imperialist West, but scarcely less emotive: China. The Sino-Soviet dispute arose from a complex tangle of issues. The two countries shared the longest common border in the world and China deeply resented Soviet determination to retain disputed territory secured in the nineteenth century. Peasant China confronted a range of economic problems quite unlike those of industrialized Russia, and in trying to cope with them Mao developed a brand of Marxism-Leninism which conflicted with Moscow's orthodoxy. American hostility to China, her refusal

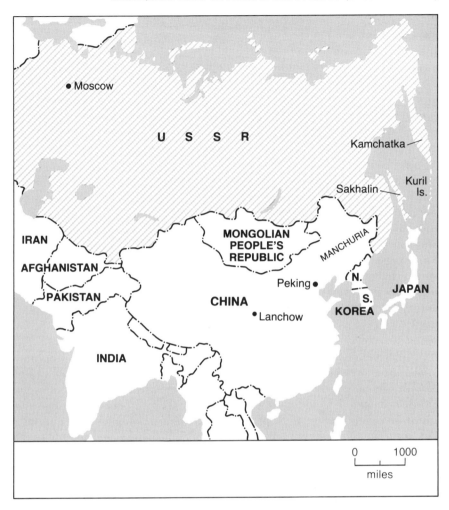

Map 12   The Soviet Union and the Far East

to recognize the Communist regime, and her defence of Taiwan ensured that Peking took a much more aggressive attitude towards the West than did Moscow. Every sign of moderation in Moscow, from a partial reconciliation with Yugoslavia, to the climb-down over Cuba, was criticized in Peking as '- capitulationism'. While Moscow feared Peking would recklessly draw her into a catastrophic war with the USA, the Chinese were furious at lukewarm Russian support. By the end of the 1950s relations had deteriorated enough for Moscow to interrupt her military and industrial aid. By 1960 the breach was public. An open struggle between the two countries began, both for the support of other Communist parties, and for influence in the Third World.

Relations reached their lowest point in the late 1960s when there were significant border clashes. In 1969 the Chinese Party led several others in boycotting the last of a series of periodic international Communist congresses organized by the CPSU. For the USSR, the 'yellow peril' took on an even more ominous image when relations between the USA and China very rapidly began to thaw. Once the USA had withdrawn from Vietnam in the early 1970s, the two governments reached an accommodation which could not fail to alarm Moscow. The spectre arose of an unholy alliance between the bristling arsenal of imperialism and the teeming millions of China.

It remains difficult for the historian – as it was for foreign statesmen at the time – to be sure how the foreign situation was perceived from the Kremlin. Official expressions of alarm may genuinely have reflected the fears of a generation of leaders indelibly scarred by the Great Patriotic War. On the other hand, they may have reflected conscious manipulation of public opinion. What is certain is that the combination of a mighty military build-up and a chronic state of insecurity had a powerful effect upon public attitudes. In the 1950s and 1960s Soviet citizens had extremely limited access to interpretations of international affairs other than those of the Kremlin. In the 1970s, the reception of Western broadcasts became much more common in the major cities, making it more difficult for the Soviet media to remain silent about unwelcome international developments. But even then there was an overwhelming predisposition to accept Moscow's version of events – and to ostracize those who did not. The authorities had no difficulty in smearing the small dissident movement that emerged in the 1960s and 1970s as unpatriotic, disloyal, and even treasonable. The sustained Jewish pressure to emigrate to Israel was viewed in the same light and constantly nourished age-old anti-Semitism. The association between patriotism and the Soviet system appears to have been widely accepted – and nowhere was it more vigorously propagated than in the army, through whose hands more than half the male population passed while doing military service between the ages of 18 and 20.

Throughout the period the material incentives and patriotic pressure to conform politically were maximized by all the propaganda resources at the command of the Party. With 'destalinization', it is true, centralized control over the intellectual world did become considerably more subtle and less coarse. It was inevitable that there should be a cultural 'thaw' corresponding to the reduction of coercion in other spheres. But this thaw must be seen in context: there was no let-up in the authorities' determination to mould Soviet consciousness, to minimize access to information that ran counter to the official line, and to vet the ideas to which Soviet citizens were exposed.

Once the leadership itself began to attack Stalin's method of rule and the absurdities of the personality cult, the ground rules for censorship were shaken. In literature, the change in the atmosphere became apparent almost immediately. The canon of 'socialist realism' was not abandoned, but the constraints it imposed on individual writers declined from the mid-1950s. The Khrushchev period saw an upsurge in both poetry and prose whose tone was light-years removed from the atmosphere of the *Zhdanovshchina*. The new scope for original, exhilarating, even mischievous work was exemplified by a young generation of poets including Andrei Voznesensky (1933–) and Evgenii Yevtushenko (1933–). During the 1960s and 1970s avant-garde writers devoted increasing attention to private life and domestic drama devoid of any political message. Many of them markedly softened the characteristically didactic tone of Soviet literature. The scope for social criticism, too, gradually widened. In the later 1960s and 1970s, the so-called 'village writers' explored the devastating impact of collectivization on peasant life. They played upon themes – rural tradition, religion, national identity – which called into question many of the axioms of orthodoxy.

A similar pattern developed in other intellectual fields. The xeno-phobia of the late 1940s gave way to increasing interchange with foreign scholars. Party supervision became very much less restrictive. Under Khrushchev, Stalin's *Short Course* was denounced and there was a sudden blossoming of original research on a whole range of historical topics which had been taboo in Stalin's day. No work was complete without a genuflec-tion in the direction of Lenin, and under both Khrushchev and Brezhnev the most independently-minded historians were sharply disciplined for exceed-ing the limits of official tolerance. But the contrast with the stultifying con-straints of the Stalin period was marked. Empirical research in the social sciences not only recommended but was treated with growing respect by party leaders and even such prime casualties of Stalin's era as sociology revived. Academic economists were positively encouraged to contribute to policy formation, and with the acceleration of post-war technological change – the so-called 'scientific and technical revolution' – the authorities became increasingly anxious that Soviet scientists and engineers be released from the kind of dogmatic constraints typified by Lysenko's pernicious influence. If access to specialized foreign sources and even carefully super-vised travel to the West was necessary, so be it. Resources were poured into the development of scientific research. Step by step, as in literature, avant-garde scholars pushed back the boundaries of censorship. By the 1970s, the more specialist journals, with a restricted and essentially elite circulation, provided a forum for increasingly explicit discussion of sensitive socioeco-nomic questions, and within closed party conferences treatment of contem-porary problems appears to have become even more candid.

Yet in every field ultimate party control over the printed word and the public statement remained intact. Just as personal security for ordinary cit-izens was assured on condition that they accepted the basic premises of the system, so the intellectual was free within a defined range of inquiry. The precise contours of the permissible constantly changed, and greater tolerance in one field could easily go hand-in-hand with greater repression in another. During his last years in power, for example, Khrushchev pursued an aggressively anti-religious campaign: half the parishes of the Orthodox Church were disbanded in the early 1960s, the number of functioning monasteries shrank further, many churches closed, and responsibility for church buildings and finances was taken away from priests. The Baptists and other Protestant denominations faced new restrictions on evangelism and control over public ritual was tightened. Under Brezhnev, religious persecution eased somewhat but, on the other hand, overt criticism of Stalin was sharply curtailed. Under both leaders, however, the guiding principle remained the same: every form of mass communication must continue to deepen public commitment to the Soviet system, foster optimism, and parry unhealthy influences from the bourgeois West. Permission to travel abroad depended upon evidence of unquestioning loyalty. Works in which the authorities detected criticism of the very bases of the Soviet system – which in the minds of Khrushchev's successors included frank analysis of Stalin's crimes – were systematically suppressed. The most spectacular clashes with the authorities were in the field of literature. Pasternak held out no hope that *Doctor Zhivago* would appear, and when its publication in the West (1958) won him the Nobel Prize, he would not accept it in person for fear of being punished by permanent exile. Alexander Solzhenitsyn's *One Day in the Life of Ivan Denisovich*, a devastating exposé of life in the camps, did appear in 1962, with Khrushchev's personal sanction. But the Soviet Union's best-known writer was able to publish only a mere fragment of his subsequent works and rapidly fell foul of Khrushchev's successors. The limited tolerance of the censorship was displayed in the later 1960s and 1970s by a number of public trials in which several prominent authors were convicted of anti-Soviet propaganda. Solzhenitsyn's deportation to the West in 1974 was only the most famous instance of a substantial emigration – voluntary or otherwise – of talented writers, musicians, and artists as well as scholars working in a whole range of fields from history and sociology to the pure sciences.

For every piece of literature contriving to cast doubt on the basic superiority of the Soviet system there were countless works celebrating its achievements, lauding the heroes of the revolutionary movement, the exploits of the Bolsheviks during 1917 and the Civil War, the self-sacrifice of the period of the first Five-Year Plans, and, above all, the heroism of the Great Patriotic War and the material and cultural progress of the post-war period. Radio, television, the cinema, the press, and the great bulk of printed material were geared to support the party line. The cardinal virtues of Soviet socialism – loyalty to Party and country, hard work and commitment to the common good, adherence to atheism and materialism, faith in the future of socialism and rejection of bourgeois individualism – were constantly reiterated in every discipline and through every arm of the mass media. These values were inculcated from the most tender age. Enrolment in the childhood organizations of the Party – the Octobrists (age 7–9) and the Pioneers (age 10–14) – became almost universal, while about 30 per cent of Soviet youth went on to enter the Komsomol (age 14–28). The education system did all it could to ensure that successive generations of pupils should appreciate their good fortune in belonging to Soviet society. That message permeated the entire school curriculum. With academic success the key to opportunity in later life, deference to authority in school remained deeply embedded in parents and pupils alike. By the late 1970s, when the pre-1917 generation had almost disappeared and those born since the war accounted for nearly half the population, virtually the whole of society had been brought up on an intellectual diet controlled by the Party.

The post-Stalin period, then, saw the Soviet system come to rest upon a much broader base of support. In the process, naked coercion gave way to a more amorphous and complex form of control. There was a marked dispersal of power within the political system.

This is not to imply that formal participation by the masses in the political process took on radically new significance. The grandiose claims made for Soviet democracy still bore little relation to reality. In the new Party Programme of 1961, it is true, Khrushchev went so far as to resuscitate the notion that, as a coercive body manned by appointed, salaried officials, the State was 'withering away' and being replaced by public self-government. The 'dictatorship of the proletariat' was giving way to 'the State of the whole people', the Party of the proletariat to the Party of the whole people. The soviets were reverting to their original role of placing power directly in the hands of the masses. The USSR stood on the threshold of communism in terms of political organization as well as material abundance.

For the most part Khrushchev's vision remained just that. In limited areas, bureaucracy did yield ground to voluntary public action, be it in the form of comrades' courts or people's volunteer guards. Public participation in the work of local soviets did revive; the executive committees found themselves open to considerably more pressure from rank-and-file deputies; and regular elections, though quite unrelated to the selection of candidates, did provide an occasion for the electorate to press local needs and grievances upon deputies. Moreover, although it was conceded that in most fields state officials were still necessary, ordinary citizens were positively encouraged to lodge complaints – provided they did so individually and never as a group – against corruption, inefficiency, and heavy-handedness. Within the Party, too, ordinary members were encouraged to speak out more freely at meetings. A Party-State Control Commission was set up to lend weight to constructive criticism from below.

Yet even this timid movement towards 'public self-government' soon lost momentum. Khrushchev's populist style won him few friends among

officials, and under his successors the demise of the State, like so much of Marx's dream, was postponed to the distant future. Not that there was a return to the Stalinist past. The Constitution of 1977 endorsed – with much less flamboyance – many of the reforms Khrushchev had hailed. The right of individuals to criticize overbearing officials was upheld, and was widely exercised, either through the medium of (carefully filtered) letters to the press, or through the People's Control Commission which had replaced Khrushchev's Party-State Control Commission in 1965. The democratic processes of the soviets, the duty of the executive to respond to deputies, and deputies to consult their electorate, received detailed attention. But posts both within the State and the Party continued to be filled by appointment rather than competitive election from below. The executive organs of the soviets remained incomparably more responsive to instructions from above than to the deputies. The Congress of Soviets remained a mere rubber stamp, invarial·'·· and unanimously endorsing the proposals of the Council of Ministers – which itself remained subordinated to the Politburo.

This is not to deny that the relationship between officialdom and ordinary citizens altered. Although virtually every active citizen was employed by the State and depended upon it for a livelihood, rank-and-file workers were not simply the passive victims of directives from above. Most significant was their freedom to move from one job to another, officially restored in 1956. The labour market, of course, was far from unfettered: 'closed' enterprises and restricted access to major cities placed barriers in the way of free movement; it was only at the very end of the Brezhnev period that collective farmers obtained the right to an internal passport – and even then the right of movement of the 20 per cent of the working population still engaged in agriculture was far from absolute. But given the chronic labour shortage and the guarantee of full employment, the proportion of workers changing jobs every year ran at the high rate of some 20 per cent. Thus the pattern that had emerged in the 1930s, which the drastic pre-war legislation had been designed to overcome, was perpetuated. Despite the absence of independent labour organizations or free collective bargaining, workers exercised a measure of leverage. The leadership itself repeatedly urged that the trade unions should be more active in alerting management to worker dissatisfaction. Moreover, the fact that workers could seek alternative employment created strong competition for labour between different enterprises concerned much more to achieve output targets than to raise productivity. It compelled management to make some response to pressure from below for improved working conditions and ensured that wages regu-

---

11.3   Krushchev addresses the 22nd Congress of the Soviet Communist Party in October 1961, applauded by F. R. Koslov (centre) and M. Suslov (right). The Congress endorsed Khrushchev's visionary, and wholly unrealistic, Party Programme.

larly exceeded the levels fixed by government. It severely reduced the ability of managers to impose their will on the factory-floor, overcome absenteeism, penalize slipshod work practices and improve efficiency. It provided an important mechanism through which the masses could bring pressure to bear for higher living standards and against attempts to intensify labour. Workers might be in no position to challenge the basic structure of the system, but they were able to evade many of the demands it attempted to make upon them.

Far from wilting, however, the bureaucratic State continued to expand. Officialdom of one kind or another continued to mediate and supervise a vast range of social activity, from production and exchange to the running of chess clubs and antiquarian societies. It was within this all-embracing Party-State, among its countless officials and institutions, that the most significant shift in the political system took place. Extreme centralization gave way to an ever more diffuse distribution of power.

At the summit, Stalin's heirs endorsed the principle of 'collective leadership'. In practice, it is true, control of the Party Secretariat continued to confer primacy. It was from this base that Khrushchev defeated Malenkov and that Brezhnev gained ascendancy over Kosygin and his other Politburo colleagues. The First or General Secretary still enjoyed a wide measure of control over appointments within the hierarchy and thus over election to both the Central Committee and the Politburo. In his time Khrushchev succeeded in ousting his declared opponents from the Politburo, and in 1961 he pushed through a major change in the composition of the Central Committee. Moreover, the leader's ultimate control over critical foreign policy decisions remained intact; both Khrushchev (until his last years) and Brezhnev ensured that the armed forces were headed by men on whose personal loyalty they could rely; and the international status they enjoyed, as well as the terrifying nuclear power for which they were ultimately responsible, helped foster a considerable personality cult around both leaders. Yet in fact the post-Stalin decades saw the power in the hands of the party leader tempered by a growing range of constraints.

The very fact that both the Politburo and the Central Committee resumed regular meetings from 1953, thereby establishing regular procedures for decision-making, limited the scope for the *ad hoc* and arbitrary methods favoured by Stalin. Moreover, the composition of both party organs became increasingly stable. Under Brezhnev the stability of the Politburo was almost proverbial: the few new members admitted were coopted by an ageing membership who tended to favour venerable officials cast in very much the same mould as themselves. In part, no doubt, the continuity in both bodies reflected Brezhnev's satisfaction with his colleagues. But Khrushchev's experience had demonstrated that the flow of power was by no means one-way. It was by appealing to the Central Committee that Khrushchev had defeated his enemies on the Politburo in 1957. In 1960, the promotion of F. R. Kozlov, reputed to be highly critical of aspects of both his domestic and foreign policies, as 'Second Secretary' of the Central Committee appears to have represented a warning to the First Secretary. In 1964, it was by the consensus of both Politburo and Central Committee that Khrushchev was removed from office. Lacking the charisma of Lenin and the independent police power of Stalin, subsequent leaders could no longer take their senior colleagues for granted.

There is limited direct evidence of the internal working of these two key bodies. The Central Committee became too large – reaching 287 in 1976 – and met too infrequently to act as a day-to-day decision-making body. But it provided a forum within which its members – leading figures from all the key institutions in the country, including the national and regional party apparatus, the major ministries, the military, the police, and the trade unions – tended increasingly to act as spokesman for their particular bailiwick. Behind the monolithic image of the Soviet system, within the confines of the one-party State and a command economy, there developed a form of political competition between different 'interest groups', different ministries, different republics and regions. There is no discernible pattern according to which individual members of the Politburo voiced sectional interests. But both the party leader and the Politburo found their room for manoeuvre narrowed by pressure from spokesmen for the more powerful regions and ministries.

At the same time, the control which the policy-making elite as a whole exercised over the sprawling network of officials below it suffered significant erosion. For one thing, the pre-war tendency for officials to identify with the interests of their particular organization, whether it was responsible for a particular region or branch of the economy, strongly reasserted itself. The tendency was exacerbated by the increasing complexity of an advanced industrial economy and of the state bureaucracy charged with running it. Moreover, the curbing of the KGB left full-time party officials as the major agency on which the centre depended for supervision of the hierarchy of state bureaucrats and economic managers. But, as in Stalin's time, all too often local party men, even when they commanded the high level of administrative and economic expertise required, lacked the will to act as the eyes and ears of the centre. A party secretary charged with overseeing a given sector or region was anxious that his parish should appear in the best possible light; to a large extent, therefore, he shared the same interests as the officials within his purview. Regardless of the spirit of the Party and the plan, his primary concern was to ensure that his parish was not lumbered with excessive targets, that it secured priority access to the resources it needed, and that in general it gave no grounds for intervention by his superiors in Moscow.

Khrushchev did make several attempts to shake up both the state and party bureaucracies. This was one of his aims when, in 1957, he replaced most of the ministries with regional economic councils; he carried through a major purge of local party secretaries in 1960 and 1961; in 1962 he divided the Party between parallel hierarchies responsible for agriculture and industry and limited to three the number of times that leading officials could be elected to the same office. Each of these moves was bitterly resented by the officials affected, and his successors made plain their rejection of such 'harebrained' schemes. 'Trust the cadres' was the Brezhnev watchword.

It became ever more common for the centre simply to promote local cadres rather than impose men from outside on a given locality. It was generally only in the most brazen cases of corruption and incompetence that Moscow intervened to purge local officials. Party officials, state bureaucrats, and enterprise managers became increasingly secure and correspondingly less sensitive to directives from above. To the exasperation of the centre, they bent the rules in achieving some of the targets set them, ignored others, presented fictitious reports of both production potential and fulfilment, and resorted to private embezzlement on an apparently increasing scale. Passive resistance to unwelcome policy initiatives could be offered with impunity. Khrushchev and Brezhnev found one reform after another running into the sands of vested interests entrenched within the machinery of State. With the leadership unable to assert its authority and increasingly unwilling to disturb the local networks over which Stalin had spilled so much blood, the 'command economy' mutated towards a form of bureaucratic consensus.

Stagnation and decline
(mid-1970s–1985)

Towards the end of the Brezhnev period the 'bureaucratic consensus' of the post-Stalin decades came under increased strain. The rapid rate of economic growth upon which it was based slowed markedly. By the late 1970s, according to Soviet estimates, the annual growth of national income was running at little above 4 per cent, falling to 3.2 per cent in the early 1980s. American and recent Russian estimates suggest that growth was even more modest and that the rate continued to decline to the point of stagnation in the early 1980s. The general deterioration was partially masked by increased output of oil and the huge rise in the world price of oil: this paid for substantial imports from the West to alleviate some of the most serious shortages, whether of grain, or in the areas of technology or managerial science. But the contrast with the 1950s and 1960s was dramatic.

Some elements of the explanation are clear enough. Not only was relatively little new land being brought under cultivation, but the virgin lands in particular suffered from severe erosion. Weather conditions, too, happened to be particularly disadvantageous: the harvest of 1975 was disastrous and those of 1979, 1980, 1981, and 1982 very poor. Vast though her natural resources were, the Soviet Union suffered along with the rest of the world from the growing cost of energy, of extracting minerals and raw materials – and of conservation. By the late 1970s the annual increase in the urban work-force had declined to little over 1 per cent per year, reflecting the gradual deceleration in population growth and urban migration, and the virtual exhaustion of the reserves of female labour still to be drawn upon. Only in Central Asia did population growth remain rapid, but Muslim villagers showed distinct reluctance to migrate to the city – let alone to permit their womenfolk to do so.

Increased production, therefore, was coming to depend very largely upon improved efficiency and labour productivity. On the face of it, the Soviet Union seemed well placed to take full advantage of the accelerating 'scientific and technical revolution' of the computer age. Her impressive record in training and education seemed geared to provide her with a skilled work-force capable of exploiting modern technology. Her rate of capital investment, though gradually declining as current consumption rose, was still running by the end of the 1970s at a level that compared favourably with other developed countries, and successive Five-Year Plans placed enormous emphasis on mechanization of every sector of the economy.

In fact, however, the return on capital investment and the increase in productivity steadily declined. Various explanations have been advanced. As regards the land, attention has focused on the problems of supervision and incentives. To supervise the work-force on one of the Soviet Union's ever larger state or collective farms was incomparably more difficult than to supervise specialized factory workers serving a production line. Agricultural workers were called upon to perform a great variety of tasks in different seasons of the year, to observe irregular hours, and to respond to the unpredictable behaviour of the weather. The need for incentives which induce self-motivation was therefore all the greater. Yet here, too, agriculture – and especially crop farming – posed problems of its own. The individual worker, aware that the success of his efforts during a season depended on a great host of factors outside his control – above all on the effort his fellow workers chose to make – responded lethargically to a system designed to reward or penalize indiscriminately the entire labour force. Yet the nature of most tasks on the farm made an individual piece-rate system of payment impractical. The problem was highlighted by the one area in which the individual peasant required no supervision and could see a direct relationship between the effort he or she expended and the reward: the private plot. The size of the village plots remained firmly restricted; new generations of better-paid, younger farm workers showed declining interest in them; and their share in total food supply gradually fell. Nevertheless, they continued to absorb a disproportionate amount of peasant labour time and to be incomparably more productive than state and collective farm land. While the official view remained that they would disappear as socialized production increased, under Brezhnev the Party frankly acknowledged their positive contribution.

Stalin's heirs, as we have seen, had tried various bureaucratic reforms and efforts to improve supervision and raise motivation. In 1982 yet another major administrative reorganization was undertaken. A new, over-arching hierarchy responsible for all aspects of agriculture was to be created in an attempt to overcome poor coordination between state and collective farms and the industrial sectors serving them. Whereas this tended in the direction of centralization and imposed new constraints on farm managers, the following year saw the Party adopt, in principle at least, a radical move which pointed in the other direction. M. S. Gorbachev, the Politburo member responsible for agriculture, officially endorsed a version of the 'link' system, under which small groups of peasants were to be permitted to contract full responsibility for a given piece of land throughout the year, thereby providing a direct connection between individual effort and ultimate rewards. As in Khrushchev's day, when experiments with a similar system had briefly flowered before being officially condemned, local officials, farm managers and most farm workers showed little enthusiasm. The measure, which in the eyes of traditionalists was a betrayal of principle, a first step towards private enterprise, exploitation and unemployment, reflected the leadership's exasperation at the chronic inefficiency of collectivized agriculture.

In industry, a different set of explanations has been advanced for the declining increase in productivity. Western critics from the Left stressed the damaging effect on morale and commitment of a system in which rank-and-file workers played a minimal role in managing and controlling their own political, social and work environment. Whereas in Khrushchev's day the regime still exuded confidence that it could tap hidden depths of mass enthusiasm and social commitment, the Brezhnev regime tacitly accepted that the key to improved performance lay in incentives. The Soviet citizen was still constantly urged to work harder for the common good, and a full panoply of medals, decorations and publicity continued to be used to encourage labour effort. But dismayed party stalwarts increasingly complained that the old slogans were regarded with cynicism by an ever more apathetic younger generation.

For champions of the free market, Soviet economic problems were the product of a fundamentally flawed structure. Without the discipline of unemployment, or the threat of it, the labour force naturally became slack, idle, and all too inclined to disrupt production by constantly changing jobs. As for management, fettered by central planning and lacking the stimulus of competition and the profit motive, it naturally shunned innovation and tolerated inefficiency. The problems of waste, bottlenecks, and shoddy goods were the inevitable result of an economy based on public ownership and central planning.

The sophistication of Soviet military technology, not to mention her achievements in space, suggests that not all aspects of her economy were as inefficient or incapable of innovation as these strictures imply. Yet defence was the priority sector *par excellence*. It made the first claim upon all resources – material, manpower, and research. And from the outset, the command economy had proved itself extremely effective at achieving selected priority goals. What eluded it was the organization, through one unified plan, of balanced growth. And the problem of doing so without the guidance of the market mechanism became more difficult as the range of civilian goods and services required widened. The more complex the directives handed down from above, the more certain it was that they would be mutually contradictory. It was one thing to ensure that an enterprise

299

produced a given quantity of shirts, wrist-watches, or cans of fish. It was quite another to monitor quality, to match supply and demand, to predict needs, to satisfy a public ever more concerned with the niceties of variety, taste, style, and fashion.

Soviet economists, pointing to the recurrent recessions suffered by the West during the 1970s and early 1980s, argued that nothing could be more wasteful than the mass unemployment, industrial stoppages, and frivolous consumerism of capitalist society. But at the same time they acknowledged many of the shortcomings stressed by Western economists and tacitly implied by the significant concessions made to the market in reforms undertaken in eastern Europe – with some success in the case of Hungary. They rehearsed many of the arguments which had inspired Kosygin's unsuccessful reform in the 1960s. They paid particular attention to the problem of persuading managers to give higher priority to improved productivity and consumer satisfaction. They focused on the tendency for managers to hoard labour and resist technical innovation. Accustomed to permanent labour shortage – itself the product of chronically over-ambitious national plans – managers preferred to retain excess labour rather than risk underfulfilling their production quotas. Equally, they had too little incentive to adopt modern technology. Installing new plant involved a temporary halt to production, and in any case was likely to lead to a higher output target rather than any sustained benefits to the enterprise. Moreover, given the pace of technological change, what was required was not a once-and-for-all innovation but a constant, dynamic replacement of obsolete machinery. Similarly, with their eyes fixed above all on targets set in terms of volume, managers tended to give relatively little attention to quality.

The 1970s and early 1980s, therefore, saw an almost constant stream of reforms, generally minor and often on an experimental basis, to try to overcome these problems. The most notable included efforts to grant greater autonomy to individual enterprises; to speed technical innovation by merging research institutions and production enterprises; to place greater stress on productivity targets; to award bonuses for cuts in the labour force; to devise a system of incentives and penalties which depended upon the quality of the products turned out; to strengthen the hand of the consumer by encouraging feedback and undertaking a limited form of market research. Although these reforms enjoyed temporary, localized success, each ran into vested interests within the system and their impact was limited.

The dispersal of power had ruled out any miracle panacea being forcibly administered from above. In any case, the 'gerontocracy' of the late 1970s and early 1980s showed little inclination to risk drastic change. In his last years Brezhnev became little more than a figurehead and was unkindly pronounced 'brain dead' years before he expired in 1982. His immediate successor, I. V. Andropov (1914–1984), was more alive to the depths of the problems confronting the country and signalled his determination to tighten

12.1   May Day in Red Square, 1984. The Soviet leaders watch from Lenin's mausoleum on the left, while the massive poster dominating the parade proclaims peace. The traditional public holiday was the occasion for officially organized nationwide parades designed to demonstrate the socioeconomic achievement of, and popular support for, the Soviet system.

measures against slack labour and corruption and his willingness to seek radical solutions. It was during his brief rule that the leadership received the so-called 'Novosibirsk Report', a scathing critique which called for fundamental changes to the entire Soviet system, written by Tatiana Zaslavskaia, a leading sociologist at the Novosibirsk Insitute of Economics. But Andropov fell ill within months of coming to power, and the term of his ailing successor, K. U. Chernenko (1911–1985), who took office in February 1984, was from the outset generally regarded as a stop-gap before a new generation of leaders took over. Yet inertia from above was not enough to remove the constrictions on initiative from below. From the late 1970s, evidence accumulated that the economy was failing to keep pace with the constant increase in the demands made upon it.

On the one hand, the economic cost of superpower status rose remorselessly. From the late 1950s, the leadership had recognized that the only way to perpetuate Soviet influence in eastern Europe was to reverse the exploitative relationship established in the aftermath of the war. The terms of trade between the USSR and her Comecon partners were allowed to swing dramatically in favour of the latter. In the early 1970s the abrupt rise in the world price of oil, for supplies of which the eastern European satellites depended on the Soviet Union, very substantially increased the effective subsidy paid by Russia; and as her satellites ran into grave economic problems and amassed large Western debts, they placed a growing burden upon the Soviet economy. In the early 1980s the USSR's anxiety to maintain her hold over the satellites was intensified by the flowering of Solidarity, the free trade union movement which shook Poland in 1980 and 1981. A smaller but significant additional burden was the aid and subsidized exports, primarily in arms, extended to Third World clients. Above all, the military budget, both conventional and nuclear, grew steadily. Although NATO appears to have regularly outspent the Warsaw Pact alliance as a whole, the Soviet Union's burden remained unique. For all its post-war expansion, her economy remained much smaller than that of her superpower rival – and her partners contributed much less than did those of the USA. The most recent estimates suggest that during the 1970s Soviet defence absorbed at least 17 per cent of GNP – a proportionate burden no less than twice that borne by the USA. Moreover, the cost of matching the Americans threatened to soar at the end of the 1970s with the onset of what has been called the 'Second Cold War'.

Relations between the superpowers, having thawed considerably in the *détente* of the early 1970s, deteriorated thereafter. In part this was the result of rapid changes in nuclear technology and the development of qualitatively improved weapons: the anxiety generated was particularly acute where short-range 'theatre' weapons, which had not been covered by the SALT talks, were concerned. Mutual suspicion was both fed by and reflected in the decision of both sides in the late 1970s to introduce a new generation of more sophisticated weapons into the European theatre. It was fed, too, by developments in the Third World. For Washington, a major purpose of *détente* had been to shore up the status quo in the Third World by dissuading the Soviet Union from lending support to revolutionary threats in Latin America, Africa, the Middle East and Asia. Yet between 1974 and 1980 radical governments came to power in no fewer than fourteen Third World states – from Ethiopia, Zimbabwe and the ex-Portuguese colonies in Africa, through Cambodia, Laos and South Vietnam in South-East Asia, to Afghanistan and Iran in the Middle East, and Nicaragua in Latin America. The cause of these upheavals varied widely, as did the complexion of the new regimes installed, and in most cases Soviet support played a distinctly minor role. But from Washington, badly bruised by humiliation in Vietnam and stung by the spectacle of Cuban troops intervening in Africa, Moscow's hand seemed omnipresent. The Carter administration (1977–81) responded by a substantial increase in military expenditure and the establishment of full diplomatic relations with China, accompanied by a number of military agreements. A simultaneous improvement in relations between China and Japan, where Soviet insistence on retaining the four disputed islands annexed in 1945 rankled deeply, did nothing to soothe the Soviet sense of insecurity.

At this point international tension was sharply heightened by the one

12.2 Soviet solders fight off an attack in Afghanistan. The cost of the war, in diplomatic and economic terms as well as in terms of lives lost, proved much higher than the Soviet leadership had foreseen.

occasion on which Moscow resorted to direct armed intervention outside Europe: Afghanistan, 1979. Within a year of bringing the country into her sphere of influence, the USSR found her client regime tottering. Reluctant to leave the country to its own devices, the Soviet Union despatched troops of her own. Already uneasy about Ayatollah Khomeni's revivalist regime in Iran, she may have feared the possible repercussions for her own Central Asian republics of chronic instability in another adjoining Muslim state. The result of the action, however, was uproar in the West, an American grain embargo, a virtual halt to SALT negotiations, a damaging boycott of the Moscow Olympic Games the following year, furious denunciation from Peking, and condemnation throughout most of the Middle East. Not only was the war extremely costly, both economically and in terms of some 14,000 servicemen killed, as the country proved (predictably) difficult to pacify, but it gave credence in the West to those who saw the USSR as inherently aggressive and expansionist. In the USA, Carter was pilloried by the resurgent 'new right' for failing to stand up to what his successor, Ronald Reagan (1981–89), would dub 'the evil empire'. Reagan came to power committed to a massive arms build-up: annual US military expenditure rose by more than 50 per cent between 1980 and 1985. Moreover, in March 1983 Reagan introduced the Strategic Defence Initiative (SDI) which, it was claimed, would render Soviet offensive capability obsolete by providing the

303

USA with a space-based shield for its missiles, or even a total shield for all US territory and the ability to attack Soviet cities with impunity. Ill-defined though SDI was, in Moscow's eyes it injected an alarming new dimension into the nuclear balance and demonstrated American determination to regain strategic ascendancy. Relations hit a new low in September 1983 when the Soviet airforce shot down a South Korean airliner which had accidentally veered off course and was taken for a spy-plane. Disarmament talks were stalled and Moscow faced the spectre of a monstrously expensive new chapter in the arms race.

At the same time, consumer expectations continued to rise. For a generation, living standards had steadily improved and the Party continued to promise ever greater things to come. An increasingly urban, well-informed and sophisticated population aspired to a level of education and job satisfaction, a standard of living, a quality of life which the economy was hard-pressed to provide. Popular appetites were fed by the fabled riches of a privileged few, and for the first time knowledge of the much higher living standards enjoyed abroad became sufficiently widespread to make a significant impact. There was steadily increasing contact with the wealthier satellites of eastern Europe. And although it was only a small elite who experienced Western luxury at first hand, a much wider public gained access to Western broadcasts, Western pop music, books, and even clothes.

The symptoms of unsatisfied demand and frustration were unmistakable. At the most basic level there was the ubiquitous queue. The Soviet citizen had to queue for everything, from bananas to motor cars, from television repair services to a larger apartment. Even when in absolute terms production increased, shortages were chronic. Money wages rose faster than output, and since the price of many basic goods – including food – remained virtually frozen, demand constantly exceeded supply. Cynical commentators pointed to the ample supply of vodka as a deliberate device used by the authorities to absorb some of this excess money: certainly Soviet alcohol consumption in the 1970s was very high by international standards. At the same time, although the interest rate on deposits was derisory, personal savings climbed to what by Western standards were astonishing heights.

Predictably enough, money that could find no other outlet lubricated an ever wider black market along with a network of bribery and corruption. For a fee every queue could be jumped, every shortage overcome. A private citizen who stuck to the letter of the law was placed at a severe disadvantage in all his or her dealings, be it with the department store, the garage mechanic, or indeed the doctor. Likewise, the management of an enterprise had to be ready to pay above the odds – whether for raw materials, transport, or spare parts. Every hierarchy of the State and Party, too, became permeated by bribery. Moreover, chronic shortages sustained a flourishing 'second economy'. Not only was there a large black market for the many goods in short supply, but there was considerable illegal private enterprise in repair services, light industry, and even construction. It is almost impossible to quantify the 'second economy', but impressionistic evidence suggests that it expanded rapidly during the 1970s and, according to some Western and recent Russian estimates, it constituted as much as 15 per cent of GNP.

There was comparable evidence of frustration, unsatisfied demand, and an illegal 'market' in employment and education. As the rate of growth slowed down, so too did structural change in the economy and the scope for upward social mobility. Yet career aspirations continued to rise inexorably. Particularly marked was the impact of better education and wider horizons upon the expectations of women: the high rate of both abortions and divorce suggests that a younger generation of women was increasingly reluctant to subordinate career prospects to family life or male ambitions. The effects of promotion blockage were visible at every social level. In the countryside, those willing to remain in the village at all experienced growing difficulty in gaining access to the more skilled ranks of mechanics, lorry-drivers, and tractor-drivers. At the other end of the social pyramid, more and more graduates were forced into jobs for which they were overqualified – the oversupply of engineers being particularly marked. Greatest friction was evident between these two extremes. Surveys of school-leavers confirmed that the vast majority of those of blue-collar background looked down on manual labour and aspired to white-collar jobs. Yet the prospects of such promotion failed to keep pace with demand. Resentment was particularly bitter over competition for that coveted passport into the ranks of the intelligentsia: a place in higher education. The tendency – which Khrushchev had decried but proved unable to reverse – for the well-educated to use their relative affluence and social advantage to ensure that it was their offspring rather than those of workers and peasants who dominated the universities and colleges became more and more pronounced. The swift upward mobility of earlier decades gave way to a pattern which implied something much more like hereditary status and inevitably generated intense frustration.

Nevertheless, collective and organized protest was minimal. There were occasional demonstrations over food and housing shortages as well as pay, but disturbances were quickly brought under control and none approached the severity of the riots triggered by price rises in 1962. Although it is still unclear how frequent strikes were, the few that were reported appear to have been isolated and short-lived. Attempts made in the late 1970s to form an independent trade union were rapidly crushed. There was greater evidence of the way in which competition over resources and posts exacerbated friction between different ethnic groups and counteracted official efforts to enhance Soviet rather than separate national consciousness. For all the official stress on socialist equality and fraternity, and on the bourgeois nature of nationalism, the majority Great Russians (52.4 per cent of the population in 1979) tended to view the poorer republics as a drain on

12.3 Pollution. The degradation of the environment with attendant health hazards became a major issue in the late Soviet period, inflaming nationalist feeling among the minorities and Russians alike. Here the sky over Nizhnitagil, a centre of heavy industry in Sverdlovsk province subsequently dubbed the most polluted city in the world, is blackened by belching factories.

their own resources. There was tension over access to education, housing and jobs between those Russians (25 million by 1985) living in non-Russian republics and the native majority. The latter, in their turn, tended to regard the Russians and the RSFSR as unjustly privileged. Among minority nation-alities, sporadic protest broke out over a variety of issues, notably language, religion and the environment. The gradual extension of Russification – through the status of Russian as the second official language where it was not already the first, as well as through its use in the army – served as one focus for opposition. A striking instance of mass protest took place in 1978 in the Georgian capital of Tbilisi, when the regime was persuaded to back down from a proposal to demote Georgian as the Republic's official state language. Fear of provoking a nationalist response led the post-Khrushchev leaders to be more selective in their sustained (but far from triumphant) drive against religion: they were particularly cautious where faith was most vigorous – notably among the Georgians, Armenians, Muslims and Lithuanians. There were, however, many minor instances of protest, includ-ing a petition with 148,000 signatures (for the reopening of a cathedral) organized in 1980 by the Catholic Church in Lithuania. A third focus of nationalist protest was over the siting of major industrial projects and Moscow's seeming indifference to the damage inflicted on the local environment. Ecological issues contributed to repeated protests by small groups of nationalists in the Baltic Republics and the Ukraine. Some of the sharpest friction involved protest by one minority against another – notably by Armenians in Nagorno-Karabakh, an 'Autonomous Region' subordinated to Azerbaijan, and by Abkhazians, who resented the subordination of 'their' Autonomous Republic to Georgia. In the case of Russian nationalism, although its symptoms grew – in nostalgic literature, in concern for historical monuments, in protest over environmental damage, in everyday prejudice and discrimination against national minorities – it was of greater political significance as a current within the establishment rather than as a focus for anti-Communist protest. The same may be said of the most notorious expression of inter-ethnic bitterness – anti-Semitism. Jews remained relatively over-represented within the Party, but, as many of the 250,000 Jews who emigrated between 1968 and 1980 testified, resentment and discrimination against them continued unabated both within and outside the Party. Yet anti-Semitism was associated more closely with support for than criticism of the existing order. With the elite of each major national group strongly motivated to uphold the system, expressions of national identity which challenged the status quo failed to gather momentum.

The only sustained and explicit political opposition was that expressed by the dissident movement. When, in 1966, Khrushchev's successors attempted to tighten restrictions on critical literature by having two prominent writers, A. Sinyavsky and Y. Daniel, convicted of anti-Soviet propaganda, a section of the cultural intelligentsia protested vigorously. They succeeded in wrong-footing the regime by focusing on official abuse of the law and the Constitution. During the following decade the dissidents drew attention to a host of offences against civil liberty and human rights – rigid restrictions on emigration, the use of psychiatric prisons to intimidate dissenters, the imprisonment of individuals for their religious faith, the steadfast refusal to restore the Crimean Tatars to the homeland from which they had been uprooted in 1944. During the 1970s, dissident *samizdat* (illegal) publications, headed by the *Chronicle of Current Events*, flourished. The movement included outstanding figures in several fields – Solzhenitsyn, the nuclear scientist A. D. Sakharov, the former army general P. G. Grigorenko, the historian Roy Medvedev – and during the 1970s small dissident groups, championing national as well as human rights, emerged in most of the non-Muslim Union Republics. Abroad, their heroism and integrity attracted enormous publicity. In 1974 the US Congress went so far as to make a major trade agreement dependent upon improvement in the Soviet record on human rights. The moral protest and the cultural vitality of the dissident movement commanded worldwide respect and the rich current of independent criticism they nurtured played a part in eroding respect for the regime at home. Yet the number of committed dissidents at any one time does not appear to have exceeded a few thousand. Cooperation between different national groups was limited, they established minimal contact with rank-and-file workers, and they forged no sustained organizations comparable to those of the pre-revolutionary underground. During the late 1970s the internal reform and refinement of the KGB, overseen by its then head, Andropov, took a heavy toll. Many leading figures were driven into exile, and by the end of the decade the earlier mood of optimism had passed. Given the grounds for popular dissatisfaction, the political impact of the dissident movement appeared remarkably limited.

Overt opposition to the Soviet system, in short, remained decidedly muted. Although social frustration was real enough, and evidently intensifying, the conflict to which it might have been expected to give rise was contained. The Party's political monopoly, consolidated during a period of peace and economic progress without parallel in Russian history and jealously guarded by the KGB, remained unshaken, even as that progress ground to a halt. Paradoxical as it may seem, it was not from below that the initiatives which destabilized and ultimately destroyed the Soviet system were to come, but from above: from the party leadership itself.

Chapter 13 ....

Perestroika and the fall of the Soviet Union (1985–1991)

From the late 1970s, the gravity of the Soviet Union's predicament was increasingly borne in upon the leadership. Even though popular discontent had not begun to threaten the stability of the State, and though, for all her diplomatic problems, the country faced no immediate threat to her security, the myriad symptoms of that predicament were plainly visible from the Kremlin. The abortive economic reforms of Brezhnev's last years, the anti-corruption and discipline drive launched under Andropov in 1982, the desperate efforts in the early eighties to slow the arms race and dissuade the US from its SDI programme – all bore witness to anxiety. Military leaders were painfully aware that an economy in which computers had barely appeared at all could not long compete with the laser beams of the West. The protracted struggle and rising casualty rate in Afghanistan did nothing to shore up their confidence. The planning agencies watched with mounting frustration as economic growth ground to a halt. Repeated harvest failures necessitated massive grain imports and placed a heavy burden on the balance of payments. Ministries responsible for social welfare were conscious of failing dismally to meet the demands made upon them. While the upper echelons of the Party were themselves cushioned from consumer shortages, they were well-placed to appreciate that the gap between the Soviet Union and the West – in terms of technological innovation, productivity and living standards – was rapidly widening. Alongside complacent official propaganda were increasingly gloomy prognostications, albeit coded or published in journals with restricted circulation, from military, economic and social-welfare specialists. While some of these warnings might be dismissed in time-honoured fashion as seditious and anti-Soviet in inspiration, many came from loyal party members with access to senior figures in the Kremlin. Although official statistics and propaganda continued to place the most positive gloss on matters, the triumphalism of the Brezhnev period became increasingly hollow and, under Andropov, was sharply toned down.

While it was one thing for the leaders of the ruling Party to realize that all was not well it was another to risk destabilizing the system from which their power and their privileges flowed. That they did so owed much to the new General Secretary appointed on Chernenko's death in March 1985, Mikhail Gorbachev (1931-). He used his position to promote far-reaching reform. He led his government in reappraising elements of the status quo which, under his predecessors, had seemed immutable, and set his personal imprint on a host of initiatives taken in both domestic and foreign policy. For at least the first four of his seven tumultuous years in office, he displayed a dynamism, panache and willingness to experiment that marked him out as a most unusual politician. Scarcely less remarkable was his reluctance to resort to overt coercion, even when confronted by the abject failure of his efforts and the swift erosion of his own power. With all his strengths and weaknesses, Gorbachev crucially affected the timing and pace of change.

So novel did Gorbachev appear, exuding a vigour and openness of mind his immediate predecessors so manifestly lacked, that commentators marvelled, in the words of former British Foreign Secretary Denis Healey, how the Communist system could have thrown up as leader someone 'so nice and human'. In fact, much that was novel about him – his relative youth, his familiarity with Western culture and the world outside the Soviet Union, even the presence at his side of a high-profile, intellectually assertive and cosmopolitan wife – simply reflected the arrival of a new generation at the summit of the party. At last the Brezhnevite gerontocracy, born before World War I and moulded by Stalin's dictatorship, the Great Patriotic War, and the depths of the Cold War, was giving way to younger men whose formative days in the Party had been spent during the relative domestic and international thaw of Khrushchev's day. True, this did not guarantee the emergence of a radical leader. There were many among the new generation, including Gorbachev's rival for the leadership, G. V. Romanov, whose record in public life suggested that they would have embraced reform much less willingly. But the appointment of a man of his stamp as General Secretary was no bizarre fluke, nor was his commitment to reform a personal whim.

Moreover, the discontinuity between Gorbachev and his predecessors should not be exaggerated. Since joining the Party as a law student at Moscow University in 1952, he had enjoyed conventional, if rapid, promotion up the party ladder. He became first secretary of the committee of his home town, Stavropol, at the age of 35 and took over leadership of the regional party organization in 1970. The following year saw him brought onto the Central Committee; in 1978 he was appointed to the Secretariat; and by 1980 he was a full member of the Politburo. In part, no doubt, he owed his ascent towards the Kremlin to a combination of administrative competence, sobriety and financial integrity. Such fine bureaucratic attributes commanded respect, even if they were not sufficient (and often not necessary) conditions for a successful career in the party apparatus. But what was indispensable for promotion to the inner sanctum in Moscow was the support of powerful figures at the summit of the Party. That he enjoyed such support – notably from M. Suslov, chief guardian of ideological orthodoxy in the 1960s and 1970s, Andropov, KGB chief until he succeeded Brezhnev as General Secretary in 1982, and the long-time Foreign Secretary, A. A. Gromyko, who ultimately nominated him for the leadership itself – reflected more than their recognition of valuable talent. He would never have won their confidence had he not shared in large measure their values and assumptions, had there been the slightest doubt about his commitment to Communist rule. In fact, like them, he believed in the central tenets of Marxism-Leninism, in the progressive role that the Communist Party had played, in the superior social justice delivered by the Soviet system, and in the ultimate victory of socialism over capitalism.

It was his faith that the system over which he presided was fundamentally sound, that it could be reformed without being destabilized, which gave Gorbachev the confidence to take the initiatives he did. While he was conscious that there was much that was wrong with the Party, that corruption and indolence abounded, he was inspired by the romantic halo which Soviet historiography cast over the Party of Lenin's day. He was convinced that, cleansed and revitalized, the Party really could bring together the best and the brightest to offer moral and political leadership of a quality sufficient to win democratic approval. Equally, while he was well aware of social tension, he accepted the orthodox view that such tension was transitory. The common ownership of the means of production had removed fundamental clashes of interest between different social strata. Likewise, economic interdependence, intermarriage between ethnic groups, and a shared Soviet cultural and historical heritage provided a solid bond between the different nationalities. Given the creation of new resources, a resumption in the steady rise in living standards, and more open (if guided) debate and airing of society's problems, public discontent could be contained and assuaged. While he knew that economic growth had slowed almost to a standstill, he was convinced that this arose not from the very nature of the system but from a 'braking mechanism' which had come into play after the early triumphs of socialist construction. This, too, could be solved by adapting rather than abandoning the 'socialist' commitment to social ownership, central planning and full employment. In the international sphere, unlike his predecessors, he had concluded from his Western contacts that Soviet security and international standing would be enhanced rather than imperilled by a drastic reduction in nuclear arms. Certainly Gorbachev was conscious that he and his allies were embarking upon a drastic break with precedent: 'If not us, then who? If not now, when?' was the evocative phrase he used in the summer of 1986.[1] But he was convinced that the stability of the Soviet Union and the maintenance of Communist Party rule were compatible with far-reaching reform.

What buoyed up this confidence was the overwhelmingly positive response to his early reforms. It could hardly be otherwise. Gorbachev's slogans – economic *uskorenie* (acceleration) and *perestroika* (restructuring), greater *glasnost* (openness) in public life, and *demokratizatsiia* (democratization) – were so elastic and the ultimate destination so unclear that all could at least pay lip-service to them. The dictates of party discipline inhibited those officials most committed to the status quo from overtly challenging their own leader, while many middle-ranking officials positively endorsed his analysis and eagerly seized upon the opportunities for promotion opened up by his drive against 'dead wood'. A broad spectrum of white-collar workers both within and outside the Party welcomed the new scope he promised for professional autonomy and initiative; some, including teachers and medical workers, benefited from an early and sharp wage rise. The creative intelligentsia were delighted by increased intellectual and artistic freedom. Among workers, scepticism was greater from the outset, not least over Gorbachev's emphasis on intensifying labour and stretching differentials. But they, too, could hardly oppose the proclaimed goals of the new leadership. Naturally enough, individuals in every stratum of society, every bureaucratic hierarchy, every branch of the economy might prefer that the drive against waste, overmanning, slack work-discipline, illegal earnings and petty corruption should not start too close to home. As citizens and as consumers, however, they could not but welcome in principle an assault upon the restrictions and frustrations of Soviet life.

Yet Gorbachev's faith that this common interest would sustain support for his initiatives could not have been proved more grievously misplaced. The attempt to reform society from above unleashed forces for change which the government proved wholly unable to control. It ignited a cultural and ideological revolution, unhinged the economy and sent it into steep decline, ruptured the State and destroyed the Communist Party. It detonated an explosion which ripped apart the Soviet system, broke up the USSR, recast international politics and sent shock waves across the world which continue to reverberate.

As we have seen, it was in the international sphere that the General Secretary enjoyed greatest room for manoeuvre and the most direct personal control over policy, and it was here that Gorbachev signalled most clearly and consistently the radical departure his appointment marked. Without at first abandoning the notion of a long-term struggle between 'socialism' and capitalism, he quickly went well beyond the rhetoric of co-existence. The 'new thinking' he proclaimed was based on the premise that there were

---

[1] *Time*, 5 January 1987, p. 54.

13.1 Summit in Geneva, November 1985, the first of four such meetings between Gorbachev and Reagan. The atmosphere proved much more harmonious than in earlier US–Soviet summits and pointed towards the transformation that was to overcome superpower relations.

global issues which transcended differences in ideology and class: the degradation of the environment, the exhaustion of the world's natural resources, the impoverishment of much of the Third World. None was more important than the danger of nuclear annihilation. Any miscalculation here would be the end for all: 'There will be no second Noah's Ark'.[2]

In a series of initiatives which bewildered US State Department officials, Gorbachev and his Georgian Foreign Minister, E. A. Shevardnadze, made drastic efforts to break the log-jam on arms limitation talks. They froze the deployment of Soviet short-range nuclear missiles in Europe, announced a unilateral moratorium on nuclear testing, and in the Party's new Programme of 1986, committed themselves to seek the destruction of all nuclear weapons on both sides by the end of the century. At the UN in December 1988 Gorbachev announced that within two years the Soviet armed forces would be cut by 500,000, and promised a reduction and redeployment of tanks to defensive positions in both Europe and Asia. The Americans responded with caution, but the change in the international atmosphere was palpable. Between November 1985 and the summer of

---

[2] M. S. Gorbachev, *Perestroika: New Thinking for Our Country and the World* (rev. edn, London 1988), p. 12.

1988, four summit meetings were held with President Reagan, followed by a further three with President Bush, culminating in a meeting in Moscow in July 1991 which saw the signing of a Strategic Arms Reduction Treaty committing both sides to cut their weapons stock by 30 per cent. Reagan conceded that the USSR had ceased to be an 'evil empire' and in 1987 Gorbachev was named Man of the Year for *Time* magazine; he was lionized in western Europe where his emphasis on mutual concern for 'our common European home' struck a deep chord; and in 1990 he was awarded the Nobel Peace Prize. Moscow made plain its determination to defuse tension in regional conflicts across the globe. Assistance to radical movements in the Third World was slashed; troop cuts in Afghanistan began in 1986, formal withdrawal was agreed in April 1988 and completed the following February. The normalization of relations with China was symbolized by Gorbachev's visit to Peking in May 1989 and a further summit in Moscow in 1991.

The supreme test of the 'new thinking' came over the fate of eastern Europe. In 1989 the USSR accepted the electoral victory of Solidarity in Poland and the appointment of a non-Communist prime minister. The signals from Moscow emboldened anti-Communist protest in each of the Soviet Union's other satellites. And this time the embattled Communist regimes of eastern Europe were left to fend for themselves. In a series of almost peaceful revolutions, the old regimes were swept from power in Hungary, Czechoslovakia, Romania, Bulgaria and East Germany. The Berlin Wall, the prime symbol of the bi-polar world, was torn down and in September 1990 the USSR signed an international treaty recognizing the reunification of Germany. The following year the Warsaw Treaty Organization and Comecon were dissolved. The cornerstone of post-Stalin foreign policy was allowed to crumble away.

The Soviet Union's global retreat reflected Gorbachev's recognition of her steep relative economic decline. It held out the prospect of shifting resources from the military to the civilian economy, of negotiating more favourable trade agreements with the West, and of applying to join the IMF with a view to receiving low-interest credits. And from the outset, the economy was the central preoccupation of the Gorbachev leadership. The reforms undertaken here, however, proved much less consistent and internally coherent than those in foreign affairs. In part this reflected the fact that, as we have seen, the General Secretary's control over domestic policy had come to be much more narrowly constrained than in the case of foreign policy. Gorbachev, of course, made full use of his position – and of the advanced age of many of his colleagues – to remove those who had opposed his election and to promote more sympathetic figures to the leadership. By the end of 1988 he had replaced seven of his nine colleagues on the Politburo of 1985. Yet the sternly conservative Ukrainian party leader, V. V. Shcherbitsky, survived until 1989, while the new members promoted were by no means all of one mind. Both Y. K. Ligachev, who ranked second and was responsible for ideology, and the new KGB chief, V. M. Chebrikov, made increasingly plain their reservations about the scope of reforms. In September 1988 Ligachev was demoted and given responsibility for agriculture, while Chebrikov was replaced by V. A. Kriuchkov, but more than once Gorbachev was driven to threaten resignation. Throughout it was clear that he had less than a free hand, and divisions within the leadership were responsible for some of the ambiguities and changes of course. Of greater significance, however, was the manner in which Gorbachev's efforts at reform, like those of his predecessors, ran up against entrenched interests within the machinery of State – both in the central planning agencies and economic ministries and at the local level. It was this that led him not only to veer from one economic initiative to another, but also to seek solutions outside the traditional framework, to mobilize public opinion and ultimately to recast the political system.

The initial catchword of economic reform, inherited from Andropov, was *uskorenie* or 'acceleration' and the Party adopted the highly ambitious goal of doubling national income by the end of the century. The commitment to an immediate improvement in the quality of life saw a sharp rise in pensions and social benefits and major new programmes undertaken in housing and health care. In 1985 and 1986 a wide variety of measures were taken in an attempt to raise output and efficiency. Although they were pursued with a new vigour and sense of urgency, these measures represented a bolder application of the reforms and experiments of the early 1980s, rather than a fundamental overhaul of the economic system. Besides a stream of administrative reorganizations, half a dozen palliatives were adopted. To expand the economy's capacity, investment was to be increased and rationalized: there was to be a drastic pruning of major construction projects in order to speed up the desperately slow rate of completion, and overriding priority was to be given to modernizing the machine-building sector on which productivity throughout the economy depended. To achieve an immediate improvement in the quality of production, a new system of quality control was introduced on the principles long used to vet armaments production. Teams of inspectors were appointed to sample the output of key enterprises (including the majority of those responsible for machine building) and ruthlessly to reject defective products. The objectivity of the new inspectors was to be ensured by making them independent of enterprise management, unlike those inherited from the Brezhnev era; to attract high quality personnel and limit the scope for bribery, they were paid generously. To renew incentives for hard work and the acquisition of skills and education, wage differentials were stretched in favour of the intelligentsia and managers were given fresh powers to dismiss surplus labour and reward productivity increases with the savings made. To cut absenteeism, slipshod work practices, and the burden that very high rates of alcoholism placed on the health services, drastic restrictions were placed on the sale of alcohol – earning Gorbachev a variety of caustic nicknames. To reduce bribery, corruption and embezzlement, major scandals, notably that in Kazakhstan, were exposed to public scrutiny and there was a highly publicized campaign against all 'unearned incomes'. Finally, to inject fresh vigour into the Party, State and management, there was a rapid turnover of personnel as the Gorbachev leadership promoted men and women believed to share their commitment to bringing dynamism and legal rectitude to the Soviet economy.

The upshot of each of these initiatives was intensely frustrating for the new leadership and exposed the intractable problems of the command economy. Where investment policy was concerned, the leadership proved unable to overcome powerful ministerial pressure which diverted funds into what seemed the bottomless pit of agriculture and rural infrastructure, into reversing a sharp decline in oil production, and into countless fresh construction projects. The new quality inspectors, precisely because they rejected so much output as substandard, aroused furious hostility from officials and managers whose plan fulfilment was imperilled and from workers whose bonuses were placed in jeopardy. The revision of wage scales made no dramatic impact on productivity and in few sectors did managers take the risk of drastic cuts in labour for uncertain reward. The anti-alcohol campaign proved deeply unpopular and resulted in an alarming fall in indirect tax revenue. In any case, its initial impact was quickly undermined by a massive increase in illicit distilling. The anti-corruption drive rapidly became bogged down in the multi-layered, interdependent and seemingly pervasive morass of illegal payments, from petty bribery to spectacular embezzlement. 'We dig and dig', complained Boris Yeltsin (b. 1931), the outspoken reformer brought in by Gorbachev from Sverdlovsk to head the drive in Moscow, 'but there is no end to the filth we find...'.[3] And it became increasingly evident that changes in personnel had little effect in the absence of deeper structural reform.

From 1987 a more radical approach was adopted, drawing upon a host of different programmes devised by rival groups of Soviet economists to combine planning and the market. Emphasis on *uskorenie* faded before the catchword which came to label the entire revolution which Gorbachev proclaimed was under way: *perestroika*. Earlier attempts at decentralizing control of the economy were to be taken much further by giving individual enterprises – and, in time, each Republic – responsibility for balancing their own budgets. By the Law on State Enterprises which came into effect on 1 January 1988, enterprises were to be given a qualitatively new degree of autonomy while being constrained to operate on a strict cost-accounting basis. After satisfying the orders of their respective ministries, they were to

---

[3] *Détente*, 7 (1987), p.3.

be free to employ their remaining capacity according to market principles, alter their product mix as they thought best, reward increased productivity with wage increases, and within limits decide for themselves the prices to be charged for new products. If they competed successfully, securing and fulfilling profitable contracts, managers and workers alike would benefit directly; if they failed to do so and went into deficit, they would be declared bankrupt and closed. In principle, the leadership intended at the same time to undertake drastic price reform. Subsidies would gradually be cut and prices brought into line with production costs and demand. Managers would thereby be encouraged to move away from measuring output in traditional volume terms and reorientate themselves instead to respond to the market, to satisfy their customers and produce high quality products. Further stimulus was to be introduced by empowering both ministries and enterprises to engage directly in foreign trade: foreign competition and the lure of hard currency earnings would drive Soviet industry to raise quality and cut costs. To arouse the enthusiasm and engage the commitment of workers, they were to be given the power to elect both their managers and a new Council of the Labour Collective which was to organize regular factory meetings to consider management's plans.

The results were desperately disappointing. For one thing, the ambitious plans of *uskorenie* left enterprises little spare capacity with which to develop either domestic or foreign market-orientated production strategies. The great bulk of their output continued to be monopolized by the ministries. Moreover, since the ministries continued to control most material supplies, managerial autonomy was in fact far more restricted than official propaganda implied. Where managers made most use of that autonomy was not in cutting costs, purchasing new machinery or introducing new products but in raising prices and inflating wage packets. In any case, unprofitable enterprises continued in practice to be subsidized rather than closed so that, in reality, they were not subjected to firm budgetary constraints. Moreover, there were repeated postponements of the comprehensive price reform which was essential to bring about the shift from targets handed down from above to a flexible market response. It was not until the first half of 1991 that both wholesale and retail prices were substantially raised across-the-board. But even this long-postponed measure, which saw the average cost of consumer goods and services double, was qualified by continuing attempts to control prices. With production falling steeply by then, while nominal wages rose, prices did not reflect the balance between supply and demand and shortages abounded. In these conditions, the new regulations on factory meetings and the election of management (closely monitored by party and state officials) aroused little enthusiasm. It seems that, in those cases where competitive elections were held, it was cautious candidates promising to protect workers from the uncertainties of the new experiments and to raise wages who tended to be favoured.

317

As a result, *perestroika* was accompanied not by an increase in national income but by stagnation up to 1989, contraction in 1990, and precipitate decline thereafter. The waning authority of orders from above was not compensated for by the expected new vigour of the 'socialist market'. Instead of a smooth progression to the new system, the existing flow of supplies was interrupted. Enterprises sought to shore up their position by producing only what they could be assured of being paid for, and cut back on low revenue consumer items. At the same time, with state authority undermined and money losing its value, internal trade declined. Individual republics, regions, cities and even factories and state and collective farms tended to resist parting with their produce except for direct barter. The central ministries found their instructions ignored, and vital links between interdependent enterprises were ruptured by growing internal balkanization of the economy. And on top of everything else, the terms of international trade turned sharply against the Soviet Union from the mid-1980s, and with the output of oil and gas declining, foreign earnings fell sharply. As a result, instead of the country being able to rely on foreign goods to make up for the decline in domestic production, imports shrank precipitately – by no less than 50 per cent in the first half of 1991. Shortages in basic consumer goods – from meat and fruit to soap, washing powder and children's goods – became more and more severe. As life became harder and individuals devised increasingly desperate survival strategies, absenteeism spread and productivity fell. According to official estimates, national income declined by 4 per cent in 1990 and by as much as 15 per cent in 1991. Gorbachev presided over economic dislocation and depression of classic proportions.

The growing helplessness of the leadership was both reflected in and aggravated by a ballooning budget deficit. It was not until the end of the decade that any significant cuts were made in military expenditure or the massive and rising cost of subsidizing food prices, and repeated calls for cuts in the bureaucracy produced minimal results. Yet the government had taken on enormous new commitments, from the initial investment programme, through sharp rises in the wages of white-collar workers, to substantial increases in pensions and various social benefits. Moreover, in the attempt to increase the autonomy of enterprises, the government had loosened its grip on the funds they spent on both investment and wages. The wage bill had been further inflated in the summer of 1989 when the government acceded to the demands of an alarming miners' strike. On top of all this was large-scale emergency expenditure following the nuclear disaster at Chernobyl in April 1986 and the tragic earthquake in Armenia in December 1988. At the same time, government revenue had fallen sharply. The anti-alcohol campaign imposed a drastic cut on indirect tax revenue. A steep decline in the price of oil exports in 1985 and 1986, together with the rupture of Comecon and trade with the ex-satellites at the end of the decade, saw receipts from foreign trade shrivel. The budget deficit of 1990 was some ten times that of 1985 and yet the worst was still to come. From 1990 the republics, exercising their growing autonomy, began to withhold the bulk of the revenue on which the central government depended. The result of the swelling budget deficit was government borrowing from the state bank on a scale which threatened to spiral out of control and undermine the value of the rouble altogether.

The manifest failure of successive versions of *perestroika* gradually eroded the confidence of Gorbachev and his colleagues that it was possible to reinvigorate the existing economic system. Every lever, it seemed, had been pulled and all to no avail. A measure of the government's growing frustration was the dramatic change that overcame its attitude towards non-state economic activity. In 1986 a Law on Individual Labour Activity marked a sharp break from Soviet tradition by legalizing private enterprise in a wide range of consumer services and handicrafts. At that stage, however, the legislation was almost grudging in tone and individuals or families who wished to engage in private economic activity required a special licence, faced heavy taxes, and were strictly forbidden to hire labour. In 1988 a Law on Cooperatives went much further in opening the door to non-state enterprise. In the urban economy, the formation of cooperatives was to be positively encouraged in numerous notoriously poorly-served fields and there was a marked response by new cooperatives involved in domestic services, catering and certain consumer goods. In agriculture, the law freed collective farms from plan targets and encouraged, albeit with little success, the formation of cooperatives within state and collective farms. Further moves in this direction were taken the following year, when it became legal for groups of farmers to arrange long-term leases of state and collective farm land.

The government's voyage from toleration to encouragement of private enterprise was not accompanied by a commensurate blossoming of the private sector. Decades of Soviet hostility to private enterprise had left an imprint – stronger in Russia and the other Slav republics than in Georgia, Armenia and the Baltic trio – which could not be erased overnight and much of the necessary infrastructure was simply nonexistent. Elements of the 'second economy' were able to emerge from the shadows but there were grave obstacles in the way of would-be entrepreneurs and independent peasant farmers: political and legal uncertainty, spiralling inflation, the difficulty of obtaining supplies and equipment, abrupt changes in licensing fees and taxation, and, not least, studied hostility from local officialdom. In this situation, most workers, managers and officials in both agriculture and industry preferred the relative security of state employment. Popular hostility to the high prices charged by cooperatives, which helped prompt a steep increase in taxation in 1990, served to stem an initial surge in cooperative activity, and the number engaged in industrial production was minimal. But by 1990 sections of the leadership were openly and enthusiastically embracing the notion not merely that state and cooperatively-owned enterprises should submit to the discipline and stimulus of market relations, but that large parts of the economy should be privatized. Rival plans by radical economists were entertained, the most drastic being the so-called '500-day Plan' developed by a team of economists headed by S. Shatalin and G. Yavlinsky in August 1990. By then, as we shall see, the ability of the All-Union government to implement its will had been reduced to a shadow, and, in any case, Gorbachev abruptly drew back at the end of the year and adopted a much more cautious version of the plan. Nevertheless, the failure of *perestroika* had undermined faith even among the leaders of the Communist Party itself in the very principles of central planning and public ownership.

The economic impasse conditioned the outcome of Gorbachev's other major domestic reforms: the promotion of *glasnost* and democratization of the State. The constraints upon open criticism and free political expression were gradually lifted at the very moment that the cost of economic mismanagement was most manifest. As we have seen, cynicism towards the Party's claims to legitimacy, ideological infallibility, and economic wisdom and justice had grown steadily in the late Brezhnev period. The rapid deterioration in living standards and the material quality of life now ensured that, far from being overcome as Gorbachev had envisaged, such cynicism would reach new depths. Instead of being rejuvenated and invigorated by the liberalization of public life, the Soviet system was engulfed by simultaneous and uncontrollable ideological and political crisis.

Several motives lay behind Gorbachev's curtailment of censorship. For one thing, he was conscious that increasing public access to foreign radio and other Western sources of information was rendering Soviet censorship futile and even counterproductive. This was graphically demonstrated by the failure of initial attempts to play down the scale of the Chernobyl disaster in April 1986. He was conscious, too, that freer intellectual, cultural and travel interchange with the outside world would help to consolidate the new relationship he sought to forge with the West. Even more urgently, he saw in the excessive secrecy and inadequate flow of information of the traditional Soviet order a major cause of economic *malaise*, shielding incompetence and corruption and leaving even the best motivated officials, economists and managers operating in the dark. By broadening the scope for public discussion he sought to rationalize economic decision-making and stimulate constructive criticism. Equally, he hoped that more open, albeit guided, airing of the country's problems would arouse public enthusiasm for and commitment to economic reform. Above all, as he made plain in a passionate appeal to a meeting of leading writers in June 1986, he aimed to mobilize reformist opinion against those officials, from the most lowly to the Politburo itself, who were opposed to his efforts at *perestroika*. A powerful signal of his determination to do so was the release from internal exile and rehabilitation of the best-known dissident, Andrei Sakharov, in December 1986.

The effect of the new dispensation was electrifying. While the authorities themselves published long-suppressed social and economic data, sponsored increasingly ambitious public opinion surveys and liberalized access to archives, newspaper editors, investigative journalists, academics and writers seized the opportunity and, with dizzying speed, pushed far beyond the limits of what the leadership regarded as permissible. Press circulation soared as drab, uniform, orthodox commentary gave way to riveting exposure of the corruption surrounding Brezhnev, to open criticism and fierce political, social and economic controversy. The weekly magazine *Ogonyok* attracted a huge following with a 'Letters to the Editors' column which broke taboo after taboo and was quickly imitated by its rivals. Existing journals and newspapers were transformed and hundreds of new ones appeared both in Russia and in the other republics, many concentrating on 'new' issues from business, religion and feminism to homosexuality and conservation. Television audiences were fascinated by 'telelink' dialogues between Soviet and Western citizens and frank interviews with visiting Western statesmen, and coverage of the quickening pace of public life was followed with rapt attention.

Glasnost witnessed a quantum leap in popular consciousness. Glaring light was thrown on the disjuncture between the traditional claims, the pretensions and the very language of the regime, on the one hand, and individual experience on the other. Before their very eyes the Soviet public saw the rosy portrait of Soviet life bequeathed by Brezhnevite orthodoxy blown apart. Led by daring sections of the media, notably *Moscow News* and *Argumenty i fakty*, the country engaged in a process of public breast-beating without precedent in history. Myriad social problems, long treated as peripheral or nonexistent, were not only brought to light but pronounced more grave than anywhere in the developed world. Damning statistics and commentary poured forth on everything from alcoholism and drug abuse, prostitution and abortion, to infant mortality, life expectancy and health care. Even in areas where the malaise did not seem to match that in the West, such as crime and the incidence of AIDS, the picture appeared to be deteriorating rapidly. Much attention focused on the specific burden borne by women: their concentration in poorly paid, strenuous and subordinate jobs; the strain, after hours, of rearing children and running a home in a society of chronic shortages with minimal male assistance; the prevalence of traditional male chauvinist attitudes and women's drastic under-representation in key institutions. Even on issues where officialdom did most to discourage unpalatable revelations, notably environmental degradation and the special privileges enjoyed by the *nomenklatura*, protest became increasingly open and impassioned.

Until the latter part of 1988, the torrent of public criticism was couched in terms of the deterioration of Soviet life that had set in under Brezhnev, together with support for *perestroika* and reform of the Soviet system. From the start, however, it threatened to go much further and to call into question the very bases of that system. Crucial was the reappraisal of the past. Although most professional historians moved cautiously, the flood was fed by the publication of a host both of Western works and of long-suppressed Soviet and *émigré* novels and memoirs. Especially influential were Pasternak's *Doctor Zhivago* in 1988, Solzhenitsyn's *Gulag Archipelago* in 1989 and his *Cancer Ward* and *First Circle* in 1990, and Anatolii Rybakov's *Children of the Arbat* in 1987. Powerful anti-Stalinist masterpieces such as Tengiv Abuladze's film *Repentance* had enormous impact, as did ground-breaking historical dramas such as those of Mikhail Shatrov, which questioned received wisdom about the earliest days of Communist rule and humanized the hitherto virtually unmentionable Trotsky. Drawing ever more openly on Western historiography, journalists and writers brought home the full horrors of collectivization and the Great Terror, the price of Stalin's pre-war and wartime misjudgements, and the awesome scale of Stalinist repression. The press was filled with the painful memories of individuals, the tragedy suffered by families, the exposure of mass graves as countless villages, cities and regions relived the past. And for each national minority, alongside the common tragedy openly confronted at last, were specific abuses committed against its own political, religious or cultural leaders, its own traditions, its own identity. The intensity of public attention reflected more than natural interest at sensational revelations: it was as if vast sections of society were passing through a virtual catharsis as they were able at last to give vent to pent-up emotion.

The authorities could endorse parts of this process, rehabilitate Bukharin and other opposition figures from the past, and support the construction of a public monument to the victims of repression. But Gorbachev and his colleagues sought to balance their attacks on the 'stagnation' of the Brezhnev years and condemnation of Stalin's crimes with sympathetic references to Khrushchev and a search for precedents for *perestroika* under NEP and in Lenin's last works. Gorbachev himself warned against the excessively negative tone of public discussion, and provincial officials tended to keep a much tighter rein on the media than that exercised in the major cities. In March 1988, alarm among more conservative elements in the leadership that public discussion was getting out of hand was expressed by the publication of a strident defence of traditional Soviet orthodoxy in *Sovetskaia Rossiia*. Momentarily, it seemed possible that this open letter, written by Nina Andreeva, a Leningrad chemistry teacher, but evidently sponsored by Ligachev, would signal a sharp tightening of censorship. Three weeks later, however, *Pravda* issued an authoritative rebuttal and thereafter the bounds of *glasnost* rapidly swept far beyond anything Gorbachev had envisaged.

The number of independent newspapers and journals proliferated, reaching 500 in Russia alone by 1990, and radical commentators moved ever closer to a comprehensive repudiation of the entire Soviet period. Had it not involved generations in fruitless suffering? Had it not installed a corrupt and incompetent elite enjoying untold power, patronage and privileges? Had it not delivered a wretched quality of life which bore no relation to its bogus claims, insulted the aspirations of an educated society, failed on every score to match Western standards, and was now visibly deteriorating further? Given the West's ready response to Gorbachev's overtures, was it not clear that the regime had long alienated potentially friendly Western powers and distorted international reality to justify the monstrous waste of the military-industrial complex? By 1990 it was not merely Brezhnevite corruption, Stalinist oppression and deviations from a supposedly ideal Soviet norm that were at issue. The waves of *glasnost* had reached the pedestal of Lenin himself. It was openly argued that the October Revolution, the historical linchpin of Marxism-Leninism and the Communist claim to legitimacy, had been a disaster, the first step on seven decades to nowhere.

It was in this context that Gorbachev's political and legal reforms unfolded. The leadership's motives for these reforms closely paralleled those for promoting *glasnost*. Here, too, the primary impetus was the conviction that democratization was a necessary condition for economic regeneration. On the one hand, improvements in productivity and efficiency ultimately depended upon bringing into play what reformists dubbed the 'human factor'. Apathy had to be overcome and motivation and enthusiasm rediscovered – in factories and on farms, in offices and hospitals, in schools and homes. The morale and the whole tone of Soviet life had to be raised. This implied broadening the legal scope for citizens' initiatives in social, intellectual and cultural as well as economic life by reducing the role of the State. It implied, too, giving individual citizens a genuine sense of involvement in the moulding of public policy by democratizing the political process from the local to the national level. On the other, Gorbachev and his advisers looked to democratization to raise the quality of state and party officials in terms of their competence, integrity and above all commitment to reform and 'new thinking'. They looked to rank-and-file party members and ordinary citizens to bring pressure to bear against what they regarded as the prime obstacle to *perestroika*: conservative resistance within the party and state apparatus.

Like *perestroika* and *glasnost*, democratization developed in a manner unforeseen by the leadership. In part this was because here, too, Gorbachev and his advisers embarked on reform with a general sense of the direction in which they wished to move rather than with a clearly defined programme and, in the drive to overcome more conservative colleagues, they were led to radicalize their programme. In part, too, it was because even when they began to be alarmed at the speed with which the process was getting out of hand, the international penalty if they resorted to repression inhibited a change of direction. Above all, the process of democratization took on a momentum of its own.

The upshot was a rolling and multilayered political revolution. In the first phase, between 1986 and 1988, there was an upsurge in public activity unsupervised by the Party and State. The legal basis for such activity was initially ill-defined but was encouraged by Gorbachev's own public commitment to the principle that 'Everything which is not prohibited by law is allowed'. Institutions which had long maintained a twilight existence found the restrictions on their activity falling away. The minority churches enjoyed a resurgence, while the profile of the Orthodox Church was transformed amidst flamboyant public celebrations in 1988 of the millennium of Russia's conversion to Christianity. At the same time a vast range of small discussion groups and clubs came into being. Many of these 'informals', which were concentrated in the major cities, formed around leisure, sporting and artistic interests. The prominence of new youth groups exposed the moribund condition of Komsomol, which had long claimed to cater for these concerns, and like other party organizations it suffered acute internal division and a haemorrhage of support. Many groups, too, took up the more contentious issues championed earlier by dissidents – from the preservation of historic monuments and the protection of the environment to the status of women and the inviolability of human rights. The level of tolerance for autonomous organizations varied widely according to the attitude of party and police officials in each republic and locality. But even the most conservative apparatchiks were placed on the defensive by the leadership's insistence that public officials and the police were to be fully bound by the law; that the citizen was to be empowered to press charges against the abuse of power; that the judiciary's independence was to be strengthened, trial by jury introduced for many crimes, the rights of defence lawyers enhanced, and the principle established that the accused be presumed innocent until proved guilty. In these conditions the 'informals' – whose number exceeded 30,000 by the end of 1987 – became progressively more assertive in drawing up petitions, organizing meetings and forging links under broader umbrella federations. While virtually all proclaimed support for *perestroika*, they ranged from a Club for Social Initiatives established in Moscow to bring together socialist-inclined groups whose goals were much more radical than those of the party leadership, to *Pamyat* ('Memory'), which developed from its initial focus on the protection of Russia's cultural heritage to an increasingly strident anti-Westernism and rabid rejection of Soviet socialism as the product of Jewish intrigue. And in the course of 1987, they began to impinge directly on the political process.

At the Central Committee Plenum in January of that year, Gorbachev forced the question of internal party democratization onto the agenda with a devastating attack on the inadequacies of party officials. In June notice was given that a special Party Conference would be convened the following summer to undertake a far-reaching reappraisal of the role and structure of the Party. Across the country, tension within the Party over the pace and scale of reform became increasingly overt. It was epitomized by the furore over Yeltsin, the aggressive reformer brought from Sverdlovsk to Moscow in 1985. His outspoken and unqualified denunciation of the corruption, conservatism, incompetence and unearned privileges of the apparatus made him the prime target of more cautious figures in the leadership including Ligachev and Chebrikov. They appeared to achieve a major victory when in November 1987 Yeltsin was ousted from his party posts and publicly humiliated. But Gorbachev's willingness to see him fall reflected not so much a retreat from reform as caution and personal antipathy for an abrasive and independently-minded figure who did not mince his words in criticizing the leader himself. And as preparations for the forthcoming Conference got under way, evident conflict within the leadership, combined with the popular expectations that had been aroused over the impending political reforms, opened the way to unprecedented public involvement.

It was thus in the spring and summer of 1988, amidst vigorous public discussion in the media of the theses prepared by the leadership, that activists in various 'informals' moved to create overtly political organizations. Small-scale public meetings and demonstrations were organized in various cities to protest against the election of conservative delegates and to support leading reformist intellectuals who had sprung to prominence under *glasnost*. Political activity was particularly marked in the three Baltic republics where many party officials reacted sympathetically to emergent national 'Popular Fronts'. For the most part, Gorbachev's efforts to ensure the election of reform-minded delegates were frustrated as local officials used traditional means to minimize competitive elections and screen out more radical candidates. But reformist pressure succeeded in securing the election of a minority of radicals, including Yeltsin, while the decision to broadcast parts of the proceedings on television – notably a furious clash between Ligachev and Yeltsin over the issue of *nomenklatura* privileges – provided further impetus to public debate and involvement. The effect was to subject conservative delegates to powerful pressure to accept the dramatic programme of democratization sponsored by Gorbachev from the chair.

The guiding principle of the party reforms endorsed by the Conference in June, and the constitutional package subsequently enacted by the Supreme Soviet, was that the Party was to withdraw from its administrative control over the State. At all levels power was to be shifted from the party apparatus to the soviets. The Party Secretariat was drastically reduced and reorganized, thereby sharply curtailing its ability to supervise state and economic bodies. At the same time, to reinvigorate the soviets and stimulate popular participation, the electoral process in future was to allow for competitive ballots. And at the summit, the traditional, politically moribund Supreme Soviet was to be replaced by an entirely new Congress of People's Deputies responsible for the constitution and broad policy guidelines. Its members would elect from their number a smaller working Supreme Soviet which, unlike its rubber-stamp predecessor, would sit for much of the year and be responsible for detailed legislation.

The Gorbachev leadership by no means intended the Party to abdicate its leading role in society. Despite the general principle of competitive elections, one third of the 2,250 Congress seats were to be reserved for 'social organizations' including the Party itself and other Party-dominated public institutions. Equally, the assumption was that the General Secretary would chair the Congress and Supreme Soviet and that local party secretaries would chair their local soviets. Nevertheless, the Party's continuing political domination would depend as it had not done since the revolution upon its success in securing popular trust. Accordingly, at the same time as the constitutional structure was erected, Gorbachev pressed for democratization and *glasnost* within the Party; the Central Committee was to take the lead by issuing a new journal with unprecedented coverage of its own proceedings. To advance members most sympathetic to reform and most likely to command wide support among both rank-and-file party members and the electorate, Gorbachev urged competitive elections for internal party posts. Not surprisingly, conservative elements within the apparatus became increasingly alarmed at the scope of the changes under way, at the erosion of the *nomenklatura* system, and at the threat to their own positions. They succeeded in blunting the leadership's efforts at internal party reform and resisting the notion of mandatory competitive elections for their posts. Likewise, rather than entrust their fate to the electorate, those running for the Congress did their best to avoid competitive ballots for seats, to exploit the requirement that candidates be nominated by pre-election assemblies, and to obstruct the nomination of radical and non-party candidates. In many rural areas, most of the Ukraine and virtually throughout the Central Asian republics, traditional methods succeeded and local party leaders were returned unopposed.

Yet the election of the Congress in March 1989 marked a critical turning point. The campaign itself enormously broadened the scope for autonomous political activity, publicity and organization. Media coverage aroused intense interest, and public meetings in support of radical candidates dwarfed those preceding the Party Conference the previous year. Under fierce rank-and-file pressure, the 'social organizations' returned a significant minority of prominent radicals, including Sakharov who was among those chosen by the Academy of Sciences. Of the 1,500 constituency seats (half of which were allocated according to population size and half to represent the national territorial units regardless of population size) three-quarters were contested. Despite obstruction from local officials, dramatic defeats were inflicted on a number of candidates seen as traditional party apparatchiks. In Leningrad voters rejected virtually all the Party's top local office holders. In Moscow Yeltsin scored a remarkable victory, securing almost 90 per cent of the vote in his constituency in the teeth of desperate

13.2 Sakharov, observed by Gorbachev, addresses the Congress of People's Deputies in May 1989. He proposed that the constitutional guarantee of the Communist Party's leading role should be abolished.

efforts by the party apparatus to discredit him. Scarcely less sensational were the results in the Baltic republics where candidates sponsored by the burgeoning national Popular Fronts swept the board.

As a result, when the Congress met for the first time in May it was not at all the harmonious, supportive body Gorbachev had envisaged. Instead of demonstrating popular approval of the leadership, its proceedings – broadcast live on television to a huge audience estimated at over 80 per cent of the adult population in some areas – were marked by furious debate and withering criticism not only of the Stalinist and Brezhnevite legacy but of the failures of *perestroika*, the limitations of *glasnost* and democratization, and the current economic, social, cultural and political malaise. Radical deputies denounced the privileges enjoyed by the *nomenklatura*; they lambasted the regime for damaging the environment; voices were heard calling for far more drastic economic reform including wholesale privatization; Sakharov urged the removal from the Constitution of Article 6 which guaranteed the leading role of the Party. Gorbachev could point to the rigorous cross-questioning of the ministers proposed by the Prime Minister, N. I. Ryzhkov, as evidence of genuine democratic practice and constructive

327

relations between the legislature and executive. And, although he was sub-jected to personal criticism unthinkable even a year earlier, he was himself duly elected to the Chair of the Supreme Soviet established by the Congress. In both bodies, and in the commission set up to prepare a new constitution, he generally commanded a comfortable majority. Legislation to underpin his earlier commitment to the 'socialist law-governed State' was duly passed. Officaldom's right to circumscribe individual liberty was drastically reduced by a whole series of laws, notably those covering the right to strike (October 1989), press freedom (June 1990), freedom of conscience and religious organization (October 1990), and freedom to form public associations (October 1990). Nevertheless, in the course of 1989 and 1990, the authority of the Congress, the Supreme Soviet, and Gorbachev himself was under-mined with bewildering speed.

The process was most clearly registered in the breakdown of party dis-cipline. Some 88 per cent of the deputies elected to the Congress were still formally party members. But instead of deferring to the official line enunci-ated by Gorbachev, members responded more and more to the pressure and demands of their own constituents. This fragmentation was implicit in the elections which had pitted party members against each other on increasingly divergent programmes. Yeltsin's election manifesto, for example, featured attacks on the privileges of the *nomenklatura* and the cost of the defence sector as well as calls for a degree of political, economic and cultural decen-tralization that was wholly unacceptable to party traditionalists. In the Congress itself, the fragmentation was made manifest. On the one hand, a minority of radical deputies, including Yeltsin and Sakharov, formed an 'Interregional Group' to coordinate pursuit of an independent line. On the other, many of the deputies elected to represent the 'national territorial' constituencies were outspoken in championing the specific rights and griev-ances of their own republics. The Baltic deputies took the lead and created such a stir over the illegality of their republics' incorporation into the USSR and the secret protocols of the Nazi-Soviet Pact that the Congress agreed to establish an official commission to examine it. And in the aftermath of the Congress it was opposition forged around the issue of national sovereignty that seized the initiative.

The explosive potential of nationalist protest had become increasingly plain – to the bewilderment of Gorbachev and the party leadership – during the early years of *perestroika*. In December 1986 the appointment of a Russian to replace the Kazakh First Secretary (a close friend of the dis-credited Brezhnev) sparked demonstrations, in which a prominent part was played by Kazakh students who feared the change would put Russians at an advantage in competition for access to higher education and prestige posts. In the winter of 1987–88 nationalist passions in Armenia and Azerbaijan flared over the issue of Nagorno-Karabakh, the predominantly Armenian 'Autonomous Region' within Azerbaijan. Local demands for Nagorno-

Karabakh to be transferred to Armenia triggered mass demonstrations in both Armenia and Azerbaijan and outbreaks of violent communal strife. The following spring saw large-scale demonstrations in favour of independence in the Georgian capital, Tbilisi. By then, as we have seen, national Popular Fronts had been formed in the three Baltic states and during 1989 equivalent movements emerged in each of the European Republics of the USSR. Although in one sense rival nationalist movements were divisive – acutely so in the many cases where borders were disputed – in another they were mutually supportive. Activists in each republic took courage from the spectacle of nationalist resurgence elsewhere, not least in eastern Europe where, as we have seen, 1989 saw the dramatic reassertion of sovereignty against Moscow-backed communist parties in each of the satellite states.

The speed with which these movements gathered momentum reflected, in the first place, the ethno-territorial structure of the USSR. This provided the political and cultural preconditions for nationalist mobilization among the largest minorities. Each Union Republic had its own clearly defined boundaries, political institutions, and the symbols, flags and public rhetoric of sovereignty. Taken together with the availability of at least primary education in the native tongue of the titular nationality of each republic and the explicit ethnic definition of each citizen in the Soviet passport, this structure sustained national self-consciousness, despite the Party's protracted efforts to foster a 'higher' Soviet identity and patriotism. *Glasnost* dramatically intensified national self-consciousness as the cultural intelligentsia of each minority found itself free to recapture and glorify the nation's past; to denounce the conditions under which it was incorporated or forced into the USSR; to draw attention to the environmental damage the homeland had suffered under Soviet rule; to expose at once the cultural and demographic encroachment of Russian language and migration; and to assist in a rehabilitation of religious institutions which in some cases, notably that of the Armenian Church and Catholicism in Lithuania, were closely identified with national identity. The second feature of the Soviet system that heightened the potential appeal of nationalism was the pervasive role of the State in the economy, in the allocation of investment funds, employment opportunities and welfare provision. As we have seen, so long as Moscow had been able both gradually to increase these resources and to enforce its control over them, the system had served to underpin the subordination of each republic and each minority elite to centralized Communist rule. But the Gorbachev reforms made plain Moscow's failing ability to do either. On the one hand, manifest economic deterioration under *perestroika* created an almost universal conviction in each republic that it suffered from the Union, and that it was unfairly subsidizing or being exploited by other republics. On the other, the central government's declining economic authority, demonstrated by economic balkanization and the collapse in the value of the rouble, rendered subservience to Moscow increasingly unrewarding. In this situation, members

Map 13   The fifteen Union Republics of the USSR

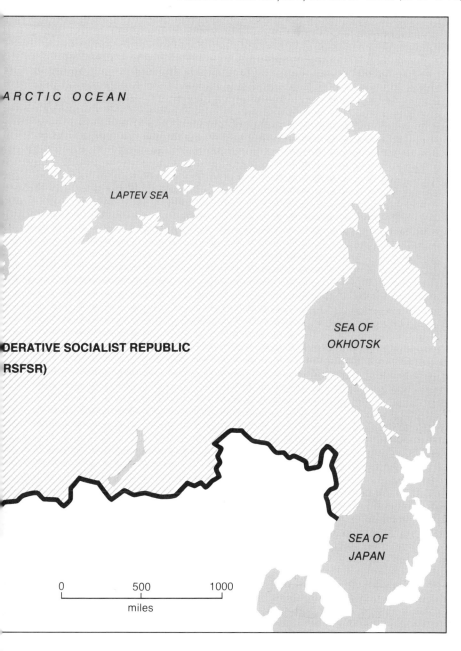

ARCTIC OCEAN

LAPTEV SEA

SEA OF
OKHOTSK

DERATIVE SOCIALIST REPUBLIC

RSFSR)

SEA OF
JAPAN

0   500   1000

miles

of the titular nationality of each republic could hardly fail to welcome the prospect of shifting control over local resources away from Moscow and into the hands of politicians who could be counted upon to favour them.

Pitted against a discredited regime rapidly forfeiting all legitimacy, therefore, the nationalist Popular Fronts exercised an appeal that was at once political, cultural and economic. Like equivalent movements across the globe ever since the emergence of modern nationalism in the French revolution, each Popular Front projected an ideal image, decked out in highly-charged rhetoric, of the untold benefits of national sovereignty. The promise of a freely-elected democratic government devoted to the cultural and material well-being of the nation attracted support from virtually every social stratum and from an array of differing interest groups with divergent or even contradictory aspirations. The effect was to overwhelm efforts to forge all-union movements of protest. Expectations that Yeltsin and the 'Interregional Group' of Congress deputies would form an all-union Popular Front were quickly disappointed and the Group's own members became caught up in asserting the rights of their own particular republics. Organizations formed to press transnational issues – be it for the protection of the environment or the assertion of the rights of women – found their agenda too restricted to compete with that of nationalism. Scarcely more successful were attempts to forge movements and parties based upon specific socio-economic constituencies – whether on an all-union basis or within individual republics.

On the face of it, potentially the most powerful such constituency in terms of numbers and economic leverage was the Soviet working class. Manual labourers in industry, mining, transport and services, as well as on state farms, constituted 63 per cent of the working population in 1987. And efforts were made both by socialist activists who aspired to an all-union role, such as those within the Club for Social Initiatives, and by socialist groups within individual republics to forge independent workers' movements against the status quo. But the difficulties they encountered were insuperable. Decades of Communist rhetoric and propaganda, accompanied by repression, had debased the currency of appeals to proletarian class-consciousness. The manifest failures of Soviet-style public ownership and 'planning' tarnished alternative socialist strategies. Soviet stratification of the working class, both between more and less privileged sectors and within each enterprise, militated strongly against class solidarity. Besides, workers' economic leverage was sharply reduced by the economic deterioration of the Gorbachev years. Steep inflation, consumer shortages and the threat of unemployment rendered workers more rather than less dependent upon the welfare provision dispensed by official trade unions. The patronage at the disposal of the official trade unions severely handicapped the numerous but small independent unions that were created. Moreover, given the potential insolvency of most enterprises in the absence of continuing state subsidies and orders, workers and unions alike were under heavy inducement to support rather than challenge management. The most strongly placed workers, coal miners, did stage major strikes in the summer of 1989 and again in the spring of 1991. Although the devastating implications for the whole economy were skilfully exploited by local managers and republican leaders seeking more autonomy from Moscow, the motive behind the strikes was primarily economic rather than political. They duly forced quick concessions from the Gorbachev government, but these provoked resentment amongst other workers and highlighted the division between workers in different branches rather than generating support for broader mobilization. Fear of provoking mass working-class protest undoubtedly played a key role in persuading the government repeatedly to delay and moderate proposed price increases. And election platforms and manifestos across virtually the whole political spectrum included calls to improve the lot of workers. But it proved impossible to channel their discontent into an effective independent workers' movement within individual republics, let alone across the Union as a whole. Even less well-placed to forge such a movement were collective farmers among whom the proportion of young workers was much lower, whose education level was markedly inferior, and who by 1986 constituted only 9 per cent of the employed population. The best-educated stratum, of course, and the best-equipped in terms of organizational and communication skills, were the 28 per cent of the working population categorized as non-manual workers. But it was precisely here – among intellectuals, professionals, teachers and a high proportion of managers and officials belonging to the titular nationality of each Union Republic – that the promise of national sovereignty exercised the strongest appeal.

Paradoxically enough, the further steps towards democratization which Gorbachev steered through the Congress and Supreme Soviet in the course of 1989 provided the ideal framework for nationalist self-assertion. Moscow's commitment to revitalize the soviets at all levels played directly into nationalist hands. Each republic was to hold competitive elections, not only to local soviets but also to its own Supreme Soviet – in the case of the RSFSR, the direct elections were to a new Russian Congress of People's Deputies which, on the All-Union model, would then elect a smaller Supreme Soviet from among its members. Between January and March 1990, national elections were held for twelve of the Union Republics, with those for Armenia, Azerbaijan and Georgia following later in the year. The fact that party members dominated the new parliaments numerically proved of even less significance than it had in the case of the All-Union Congress. The majority of deputies moved swiftly to assert and extend the authority of the newly elected bodies. In the three Baltic states, where candidates sponsored by or supportive of the Popular Fronts won overall majorities, newly installed republican leaders no longer at the beck and call of Moscow took the lead in pressing their rights. They repudiated the legitimacy of All-Union legislation which ran counter to local laws and they asserted control over the local economy, resources and tax revenue in a manner which went far beyond the limited economic decentralization envisaged by Gorbachev. The Soviet government found itself engaged in a 'war of laws', a battle for sovereignty in every republic.

What broke the back of All-Union authority was the assertion of national sovereignty by the giant RSFSR, containing as it did over half the population of the USSR and over three-quarters of the territory. In the Russian case, there was no exact counterpart to the national popular fronts elsewhere. The Moscow Popular Front founded in May 1989 aspired to this role but failed to gather momentum or to provide an umbrella bringing together the host of minuscule anti-communist parties – 'Socialist', 'Social Democratic', 'Christian Democratic', 'Liberal Democratic', 'Constitutional Democratic', even 'Bourgeois-Democratic' – which emerged in Russia between 1989 and 1991. No doubt this was in part because of the difficulties of communication and coordination presented by the sheer size of the RSFSR. But it was also because here the role of nationalism was more ambiguous and its appeal markedly more muted than that of minority nationalism. For one thing opinion surveys indicated that, until the very end of the 1980s, an overwhelming majority of Russians regarded the USSR rather than the RSFSR as their homeland. The presence of 25 million Russians in the smaller republics, as well as the predominance of Russians (and the Russian language) in all-union organizations of every description, provided a powerful incentive to support the integrity of the Union. Moreover, Russian nationalist motifs had been exploited by elements within the Soviet establishment since Stalin's time and the rabid Russian chauvinism of *Pamyat* served as a vivid reminder of its authoritarian and imperialist connotations. Party traditionalists in Russia, in contrast to those in other republics, found it possible to combine defence of the status quo with appeals to nationalism. By the same token, Russian domination of the USSR made it difficult for Russian reformers to regard or to portray the problems bequeathed by the Soviet system as the product of alien rule. Unlike their counterparts in the other republics, therefore, they were inhibited about identifying the cause of democracy, civil rights and the challenge to the Party with resurgent nationalism. Greater emphasis was placed instead on decentralization within the vast RSFSR, on shifting power from Moscow to the localities, on the right to relative autonomy of regions, cities and towns.

Nevertheless, Russian national consciousness was fed by ingredients similar to those inflaming minority nationalism – concern to recapture a buried past and to revive long-suppressed traditions and institutions, including the Orthodox Church; outrage against environmental damage to the beloved Russian land; resentment against migrants from other republics and the conviction that Russia was being bled dry by those republics. It was fed, too, by the spectacle of dynamic nationalist movements around the periphery. The prospect of power moving from all-union to republican organs generated mounting pressure for Russia to stake her claim and establish the autonomy of specifically Russian institutions – and indeed for their creation where traditionally Russian affairs had been subsumed under institutions responsible for the Union, as in the case of the Party, the KGB, the Ministry of Internal Affairs and the Academy of Sciences. The summoning of competitive elections for a Russian supreme legislature in March 1990 brought the national question into sharper focus. The elections pitted party traditionalists against a newly formed 'Democratic Russia' bloc of reformist communist and anti-communist candidates. The former were implicitly critical of the disruption caused by Gorbachev's reforms; the latter pressed for those reforms to be taken much further. And both sides tried to play the national card. Conservative elements within the CPSU agitated for the creation of a specifically Russian Communist Party to engage in the Russian struggle for power, while relatively mild but distinct nationalist strains began to appear in the rhetoric and electoral appeal of 'Democratic Russia' candidates. The latter won a third of the seats and did particularly well in Moscow and Leningrad where in parallel local elections they also gained control of the city soviets. When the Congress met in May the 'democrats' carried with them just enough wavering deputies to secure the election of their leader, Yeltsin, to the Chair with R. Khasbulatov as his deputy. On 12 June the gauntlet was thrown down when the Russian Congress declared the sovereignty of the RSFSR in defiance of the all-union Congress, the Supreme Soviet and the Gorbachev government.

Desperately Gorbachev tried to stem the flow of power from the centre. He sought to rally support from those republics which had elected relatively conservative Supreme Soviets, notably in Central Asia. He played upon divisions within each Union Republic: upon 'Autonomous Republics' and 'Autonomous Regions' seeking to enhance their status against that of the Union Republic to which they were nominally subordinate; upon regional soviets which in many cases returned much more conservative deputies than those elected to urban soviets and to the Supreme Soviets of the Union Republics; and upon the anxieties of Russian settlers fearful of being reduced to second-class citizenship should republican independence become reality. When Lithuania broke new ground and declared outright independence in March 1990, he imposed an economic blockade. In April the All-Union Congress passed a new law on secession, designed to place all but insuperable constitutional obstacles in the way of republics seeking independence. He attempted to reimpose restrictions on the media and banned strikes in key industries. In the winter of 1990 he replaced several relatively liberal ministers with much more conservative figures – prompting Shevardnadze to resign as Foreign Minister and warn of an impending reactionary *coup*. In January 1991 force was used to reimpose the Kremlin's

authority in both Lithuania and Latvia. At the same time, a battery of legislation was passed by the All-Union Congress and Supreme Soviet to shore up Gorbachev's authority. In March 1990 a new post of President of the USSR was established, elected by the All-Union Congress and entrusted with a panoply of executive and legislative powers. In May further laws were passed to enhance the prestige of Gorbachev's new office; in September he was voted temporary emergency powers; the following December additional steps were taken to tighten his grip on decision-making and executive power.

All to no avail. The necessary apparatus to make effective his nominal authority crumbled in his hands. He had himself weakened the traditional backbone of that apparatus, the Party, by slackening its internal discipline and reducing the influence of the Politburo, the Secretariat, and local committees. Indeed, the creation of a Presidency deriving its legitimacy from the Congress epitomized the Party's demotion: the key decision-making body had become the Presidential Council (and later the Council of the Federation) rather than the Politburo. Moreover, the option of restoring the Party to its traditional role, urged on him by leading conservatives, disappeared as wider democratization sent the Party into a dizzying decline. Several of its republican organizations, led by those in the Baltic, severed their links with the CPSU in an attempt to place themselves at the head of nationalist protest. Elsewhere, the Party rapidly found itself marginalized by the governments chosen by the newly-elected Supreme Soviets. Even at the regional level, where the party apparatus often retained control of the local soviet, party discipline and obedience to Moscow broke down. The Party's prestige suffered a devastating blow when in March 1990 the leadership gave way in the face of massive popular pressure – and the fate that had met unreconstructed Communist Parties in eastern Europe – and Article 6 of the Constitution was amended to remove the guarantee of the Party's 'leading role'. In July there was an exodus of prominent radical members, headed by Yeltsin. Mounting electoral defeats and cumulative loss of authority undermined party morale; membership began to contract at an alarming rate; the payment of membership fees and demand for party newspapers fell even more sharply, the Party's total income declining by no less than 60 per cent between 1989 and 1990 – and by then soviets in anti-communist hands had begun to confiscate party property. By 1991 the Party faced bankruptcy. Nor did the traditional bastions of the Kremlin's economic power, the central ministries, any longer provide an alternative instrument through which

---

13.3 Demonstration in Moscow, July 1990. The later Gorbachev years witnessed wave upon wave of mass political demonstrations. Here a huge crowd marches through central Moscow brandishing slogans denouncing the party, banners protesting the degradation of the environment, and a sea of national flags proclaiming Russian sovereignty.

13.4 Moscow, 1990. The traditionally orderly, ritualized celebrations on the anniversary of the October Revolution turned to chaos in 1990. The symbols of Soviet and Communist power were lampooned and Gorbachev and the leadership were driven from their place on Lenin's mausoleum by jeering crowds.

to shore up Gorbachev's authority. As we have seen, the effect of *perestroika* and economic balkanization had been to erode their control over the flow of resources.

Gorbachev appears to have been deterred from tentative moves to resort to force by the vigour of both Western protests and mass Soviet demonstrations against its use in Lithuania, as well as by the horror expressed by radicals and former allies such as Shevardnadze. To restore the KGB's repressive function would fly in the face of commitment to 'the socialist law-governed state'. In any case, under the impact of *glasnost* the KGB was experiencing acute internal friction and a severe crisis of identity. And by the end of 1990, it was itself showing signs of fragmenting along national lines as republican leaders, beginning with those in Georgia, defied Moscow and appointed their own local KGB chieftains. Where the army was concerned, both the High Command and rank-and-file soldiers made clear their reluctance to see it used to resolve the conflict of authority or to intervene in the growing number of ethnic clashes. The reliability of many units seemed increasingly doubtful as soldiers' morale was sapped by the steep deterioration in their conditions. Evasion of conscription became the norm; one republican government after another issued orders forbidding their nationals to serve outside their own republics; and, more ominously still, some began to form their own military units and 'national guards'. At the most basic level, the regular police force was demoralized by declining pay and conditions and disrupted and disorientated by the clash between the central government and Union Republics, between republican governments and regional soviets, and between regional and urban authorities. Violent crime and theft became increasingly common in the streets and suburbs of once relatively safe Soviet cities.

Each of the All-Union authorities underwent a catastrophic fall in public esteem between 1989 and 1991 – and none more so than Gorbachev himself. He was ideologically discredited and held responsible for economic deterioriation; his credibility was destroyed by the cumulative effect of his orders and decrees being openly flouted – in the continuing conflict in Nagorno-Karabakh, in increasingly frequent outbreaks of inter-ethnic violence in Central Asia, in the 'war of laws' in every republic. The prospect of shoring up the power of the central government by implementing a new union treaty, on which the Congress's constitutional commission had been working since 1989, became ever more fragile. In March 1991, having failed to submit himself to a popular vote before the collapse in his prestige, Gorbachev made a belated effort to secure a form of democratic mandate by calling a referendum on the issue of the unity of the USSR. Although 76 per cent of those who voted expressed approval for preserving a 'renewed federation' in some form, the referendum did little to buttress his position. Moldavia, Armenia, Georgia and the Baltic republics refused even to take part, and the last four of these staged separate referenda on independence which, in every case, was endorsed by overwhelming majorities. In the nine republics where Gorbachev's referendum was held, support was much lower in the cities than the countryside and six of these republics posed additional questions which elicited responses pointing in the direction of autonomy rather than unity. In the Russian Republic, most notably, 70 per cent voted in favour of establishing a directly elected Russian presidency.

Immediately after the referendum, Gorbachev was further enfeebled when sharp price increases turned rumbling discontent in the coalfields into a massive strike wave. Encouraged by Yeltsin's public show of sympathy, miners' leaders in Russia demanded that responsibility for the coalfields be transferred from the central to the republican government. Gorbachev bowed to the pressure and the transfer of a wide range of economic powers was one element in the so-called 'nine-plus one' agreement in April in which he and the leaders of Russia, Ukraine, Belorussia, Azerbaijan and the five Central Asian republics undertook to draw up a treaty for a new 'Union of Soviet Sovereign Republics'. Moreover, with each successive draft, the erosion of the centre's role became more plain. The shift in authority was underlined in June when Yeltsin and his running-mate, A. Rutskoi, inflicted a crushing defeat on the candidates favoured by Gorbachev in the elections to the new Russian Presidency. Yeltsin received 57 per cent of the vote, with Gorbachev's former Prime Minister, Ryzhkov, securing under 17 per cent, and the outspokenly nationalist and authoritarian V. Zhirinovsky finishing an ominous third with 6 million votes. Yeltsin immediately moved to attack the Party's waning influence at its roots by banning its activity in all state bodies and state enterprises in Russia. At the same time, Gorbachev's concessions created mounting tension between him and his increasingly frustrated ministers. In late July, it appears, they learned that he had agreed with Yeltsin that, following the signing of the new union treaty, he would remove Kriuchkov, the KGB chief, V. Pavlov, the prime minister and General D. Yazov, the defence minister. It was at this point, on 19 August 1991, the very eve of the scheduled signing of the new union treaty, that a group of conservative officials within the government attempted to halt the dissolution of central power and Soviet unity by force. Declaring Gorbachev too ill to perform his functions, and placing him under house arrest in the Crimea, where he was on holiday, they proclaimed a state of emergency and promised to deliver the motherland from what they saw as political, social and economic chaos. The eight-man State Emergency Committee, headed by G. Yanaev, the undistinguished official Gorbachev had chosen for the new post of Vice-President the previous winter, and including Kriuchkov, Yazov, Pavlov and the Interior Minister, B. Pugo, moved to silence the media, ban public meetings and strikes, and restore at least some measure of central control over the economy.

The August putsch proved a fiasco. Its leaders inspired little confidence even amongst those who shared their horror at the bewildering speed with which the system was unravelling. Although their general goal was clearly to stem the tide of change, the erosion of the Party's legitimacy and of faith in the command economy had proceeded too far for them to couch their appeal in terms of either. It quickly became plain that they could count on the loyalty neither of the army nor of much of the state apparatus. The fierce opposition of the air-force commander, Y. Shaposhnikov, heightened General Yazov's evident inhibitions about spilling blood. And Kriuchkov, the most resolute among them, found his orders to the KGB to arrest prominent radicals unheeded. Moreover, while more conservative republican leaders – notably those in Belorussia, Azerbaijan, Tadjikistan and Uzbekhistan – signalled support, elsewhere there was bold defiance. Its supreme symbol became the White House in Moscow, the seat of the Russian Parliament. Not only was the building quickly surrounded by a large crowd, who ignored the curfew, but a number of armed divisions moved to defend it from any military assault. Headed by Yeltsin, whose heroic pose astride one of the tanks drawn up outside the White House was flashed across the world, the parliamentary leadership frantically lobbied support, both in the West and among military and civilian officials, and appealed for mass resistance and a general strike. Workers' response was

13.5 Yeltsin defies the attempted *coup* of August 1991. Standing astride a tank drawn up outside the Russian Parliament building in Moscow, Yeltsin made a dramatic appeal for resistance across the USSR. Two years later he was to order the bombardment of the same building when his former allies, Khasbulatov and Rutskoi, led defiance of his presidential order for the parliament to dissolve.

patchy and protesters in Russia bemoaned the apparent extent of popular indifference. Yet Yanaev and his colleagues were faced by hostile demonstrations and declarations which dwarfed expressions of support for them, and by 21 August they were in disarray, Pugo committed suicide, and the putsch collapsed.

The leaders fled to the Crimea to make their peace with Gorbachev before being arrested. Gorbachev himself headed back to Moscow, but far from returning in triumph he was subjected to public humiliation by Yeltsin in the Russian Parliament. Were not the members of the 'Emergency

Committee' his own protégés and was not the Party itself deeply implicated? Before Gorbachev's very eyes Yeltsin signed a decree banning the Party's activities throughout Russia. On 24 August Gorbachev resigned as General Secretary, urging the Central Committee to dissolve itself, and the all-union Supreme Soviet subsequently extended the ban throughout the USSR. The failed putsch delivered the *coup de grâce* not only to the Party but to the tattered authority of the central apparatus as a whole – including the KGB, which was abolished in its existing form and its functions transferred to the republics or discontinued. Hard though Gorbachev strove to preserve some form of union, however shadowy, the dissolution of the USSR now proved irresistible. By the end of the year, all fourteen of Russia's partners had declared independence and quickly secured diplomatic recognition. In an effort to smooth the process of transition, Yeltsin and the leaders of Ukraine and Belorussia agreed on 8 December to establish a loose and ill-defined 'Commonwealth of Independent States' to which Armenia, Azerbaijan, Moldavia and the five Central Asian republics adhered a fortnight later. Gorbachev resigned the Soviet Presidency on 25 December and the lowering of the Red Flag over the Kremlin for the last time on 31 December 1991 marked the dissolution of the USSR. It was from the ruins of the Soviet Union that today's Russia, renamed the Russian Federation, emerged.

Chapter 14 ....

Epilogue

This historical background throws into sharp relief the momentous drama now unfolding in Russia. It brings home the scale and depth of the discontinuity marked by the passing of the USSR and the CPSU. At the same time, it illuminates the legacy bequeathed to the post-Soviet era, the imprint from the past upon every facet of contemporary Russia: her political fragility, economic disarray, social tension, international predicament, and cultural and ideological turmoil. It thereby provides a salutary warning against regarding the 'new Russia' as a virtual *tabula rasa*. As the USSR collapsed, the tendency to do so was especially pronounced among champions of the free market, whose view of Russia's prospects became dominant in the West. For them, the denouement to the Cold War represented the historic triumph of the principles of capitalism, not only over Marxism-Leninism but over the entire socialist critique. The path was now clear for Russia, along with the rest of the ex-Communist world, to recast economic life on free-market principles. Moreover, they took it for granted that this economic transition would be accompanied by political democratization. Indeed, in their eyes economic transition to capitalism and political transition to pluralist democracy were two sides of one 'reformist' coin. Free markets breed democracy. State intervention breeds dictatorship. Just as Communist rule had involved both political repression and state control of the economy, so its elimination promised the reverse of both. The economic role of the State would be beaten back to the bare minimum at the same time as a reborn civil society re-established effective control over it. The surest way to create a democratic Russia was to privatize, cut the role of the State, and unleash free-market economic individualism.

An almost identical view was taken by the 'reformist' ministry appointed by Yeltsin and most closely identified with the name of Yegor Gaidar, the young economist responsible for economic policy during most of 1992 and 1993. After the frustration of *perestroika*, Gaidar and his colleagues saw price liberation and privatization as the battering ram to demolish the overmighty State on which Communist oppression had arisen, destroy the ethos and the institutional structure of the command economy, and break the cycle of economic decline. They were enthralled by the dynamism of the free market which seemed at once the very antithesis of the Soviet system and the source of all Western progress and affluence. Moreover, the economic prescriptions of the West's 'new right' carried all the authority of those Western leaders, foremost among them President Reagan and Mrs Thatcher, who had proved the staunchest foes of the 'evil empire'. Egged on by Western economists of the Chicago school, by the advice of the IMF (to which Russia was admitted in April 1992), and by great swathes of the Western press, Gaidar and his colleagues saw commitment to the free market as the touchstone of their democratic credentials.

Accordingly, taking full advantage of emergency powers granted the President in November 1991, they moved swiftly to administer what was known as 'shock therapy' to the Russian economy. Between January and March 1992 prices of virtually all goods and services were freed. Later that year, an elaborate programme of privatization was developed. Local authorities were encouraged to sell municipal enterprises and transfer residential property into private hands; each citizen was granted vouchers worth 10,000 roubles to secure shares in industrial enterprises; steps were taken to encourage the break-up of state and collective farms, the conversion of parts of them into joint-stock companies, and the establishment of a mosaic of small private farms. At the same time, the government committed itself to pursue drastic cuts in public expenditure and in the huge budget deficit inherited from Gorbachev. With the help of the IMF and bilateral assistance from the West, the domestic currency was to be stabilized and rapid strides made towards the convertibility of the rouble. The structure was thus to be put in place for the blossoming of private enterprise, the attraction of foreign investment, and the integration of Russia into the world economy.

What underpinned the confidence of free-market enthusiasts in both Russia and the West that this programme could proceed hand-in-hand with democratization was the depth of public revulsion against the CPSU and the Soviet regime and the popular support for Yeltsin's assault upon it. Diehard Communists, nostalgic generals and reactionary bureaucrats would naturally oppose the destruction of the old system. But in the eyes of the electorate the whole Communist enterprise had been totally discredited. Indeed, the ideological, political and diplomatic break with the past appeared so profound that free marketeers favoured the analogy between post-war Federal Germany and post-Soviet Russia. Like Adenauer's fledgling democracy, Yeltsin's Russia had abandoned traditional Tsarist and Soviet territorial ambitions and would be free to slash defence expenditure without fear for her security. Equally, as in post-Nazi Germany, the entire ideological framework which had informed Soviet society had collapsed.

The CPSU had been destroyed and with it had collapsed the central organizing principle of Marxism-Leninism, of Soviet historical and cultural orthodoxy, and the whole notion of the USSR as the harbinger of a world destined for socialist transformation.

The reformers set about erasing as many relics of the Soviet regime as possible. They demolished its symbols, its monuments, its nomenclature, they repudiated its textbooks, its novels, its films, its very language. The hammer and sickle gave way to the crowned twin-headed eagle inherited from Tsarism. The Supreme Soviet was to be replaced by the 'State Duma' in memory of Nicholas II's ill-fated lower house. The names of cities, towns, streets and squares reverted to their pre-revolutionary form. Even Leningrad, following a referendum on the issue in the last months before the collapse of the USSR, was re-christened St Petersburg at a ceremony attended by Grand Duke Vladimir, the Romanov heir. The Soviet regime was treated as the totalitarian twin of the Third Reich, responsible for 74 years of tragedy and destruction over which a veil must now be drawn. And the assumption was that public disavowal would be matched by private reorientation. The very socialization process, the handing on of received values from parents to children, would be ruptured as those among the older generation who could not adapt found their authority repudiated by the younger. Soviet indoctrination would evaporate and society would embrace liberal values. The social sciences would be 're-tooled' with Western texts and techniques, teachers would be retrained, the bureaucracy remoulded to implement the will of a democratic government in strict accordance with the law. Thus the cultural obstacles to pluralism and private enterprise would melt away. The process would be sustained by the rewards which would rapidly become apparent. Given the vast domestic market and economic potential of an educated, largely urbanized society 150-million strong and possessed of untold natural resources, the stimulus of capitalism promised an economic miracle. Those with an immediate interest in entrenching the free market would grow inexorably in number and in economic and political weight. Despite the hardships inevitably involved in the 'transition period', popular revulsion against one-party dictatorship and the command economy would ensure democratic legitimization of shock therapy.

By contrast, the historical approach to post-Soviet Russia draws attention to the massive obstacles in the way of combining shock therapy and democracy. The difficulty of retaining public support for shock therapy had already been demonstrated in the ex-Communist countries of eastern Europe, where protest quickly found political expression. But nowhere were the grounds for scepticism about the 'reformers'' optimism stronger than in Russia. Not the least of these was the sheer scale of the hardship involved in the 'transition'. During 1992 and 1993 the cost of Gaidar's policies was already becoming painfully apparent. Budgetary constraints entailed a drastic fall in pensions, in social security payments, in provision for students.

The funding of health and education went into steep decline. The freeing of prices saw those for consumer goods rise by some 2,600 per cent in 1992, and with inflation rampant real wages amongst white- and blue-collar workers alike continued in most sectors to fall precipitately. Outright unemployment grew steadily, while the proportion of employees left unpaid for weeks and months on end, temporarily laid off, or threatened with redundancy grew much faster. The number of enterprises, farms and state institutions unable to meet the bill both for goods purchased and for wages soared. Alongside the *nouveaux riches* arose the spectacle of abject poverty, dilapidated housing and public services, beggars on unkempt and poorly-lit streets, malnutrition and a decline in the birth-rate which saw it fall below that of mortality. To make matters worse, the State had grave difficulty performing even the 'nightwatchman' role prescribed for it by free-market theorists. The growth of crime visible during the period of *perestroika* accelerated and became increasingly organized. The incidence of theft and violence multiplied in the countryside; rival armed 'mafia' groups vied for control over different urban areas and both legal and illicit commercial enterprises; respectable businesses found it impossible to rely for protection upon the demoralized and ill-paid police force.

The rate of economic decline appeared to be even greater in 1993 than in 1992, although the scale of structural change makes statistical precision impossible and some indicators pointed in a more positive direction. In the latter part of 1993 inflation briefly slowed and, although independent manufacturers and farmers remained few and far between, there was rapid growth in the ranks of entrepreneurs and petty-traders who began to change the face of the commercial centre of the major cities. But more striking was the continued drop in industrial output and the speed with which the gap grew between the new rich and poor. Conditions could hardly have been more conducive to disillusionment and cynicism. Instead of competition delivering the promised fall in prices, major sectors retained virtual monopolies: goods might reappear on shop shelves but few could afford them. Repeated official assurances of assistance to those most vulnerable carried ever less conviction. All too easily, privatization appeared to mean little more than the transfer of ownership into the hands of the old *nomenklatura* and the new '*biznesmen*' best placed by virtue of wealth, contacts and political influence. Opinion polls showed a catastrophic fall in public optimism, morale and respect for the government.

The new leadership's prospects of retaining popular support would have been much greater had it been in a position to engage popular enthusiasm, to instil a sense of democratic empowerment and common purpose.

14.1 Leningrad is renamed St Petersburg. There was no more emotional name-change, not least because for the older generation 'Leningrad' evoked the ordeal and the heroism of the city's 900-day siege during the Great Patriotic War.

14.2 Street markets revive. As the command economy was dismantled, the range of goods available from small-scale traders in the cities rapidly expanded – but price rises placed them out of the reach of many.

But its commitment to shock therapy ran against the grain of each of these. A programme of budget cutting, privatization and economic individualism was inherently at odds with collective endeavour and social solidarity. The message that it was to be left to private enterprise to remedy the appalling social, economic and environmental legacy of the command economy was difficult to reconcile with an appeal for active citizenship and energetic involvement in rebuilding democratic institutions. Efforts to raise the standards and transform the ethos of state officials were severely handicapped by drastic deterioration in the conditions and wages of public servants. The drive to reorientate and 're-tool' education and the academic world was bedevilled by the disastrous impact of sharp reductions in state subsidies, soaring inflation and an acute paper shortage upon academic institutes, colleges, schools, publishing houses, libraries, journals and many newspapers. More generally, shock therapy set the government at odds with all those whose security, livelihood and sense of dignity was placed in jeopardy. The fabulous wealth swiftly accumulated by a few rendered the squalor and impoverishment of most even more objectionable. The harsh conditions of 'transition' seemed to belie government assurances that the market's 'hidden hand' would ensure that the private effort of each would be to the common benefit of all.

Nor did the advocates of the free market find it easy to identify their drive to re-establish capitalism with resonant themes in Russia's heritage and history, with a 'usable past'. There was no doubt about the widespread appeal of much of what Western capitalism promised to deliver – its living standards, consumer goods and, among the younger generation, its popular culture, television programmes and sexual liberation. But this distant dream could not in itself fill the ideological vacuum or overcome the virtual crisis of identity induced by social dislocation, economic insecurity, the collapse of the USSR, and the precipitate decline in Russian prestige. And as the chief prosecutors against all things Soviet, the 'reformers' were easily depicted as repudiating not only the economic waste, intellectual arrogance and brutal repression identified with the Soviet regime, but also the endeavour of three Russian generations, their cultural and economic achievements, and even Russian victory in the Great Patriotic War. Moreover, even for those of the younger generation willing to draw a veil over the entire Soviet period, the pre-revolutionary era to which the 'reformers' turned for symbols and precedents offered singularly barren ground for champions of the free market and economic individualism. Few late twentieth-century Russians could find an inspiring model in the era of Witte and Stolypin with its grinding poverty, acute social polarization and minimal civil rights. Nor by stripping away the Soviet cultural heritage did the advocates of shock therapy bring to light some alternative rich seam of native bourgeois individualism. On the contrary, virtually every major current of Russian thought and literature had exhibited a powerful anti-bourgeois character. This was no mere artificial imposition of the Soviet regime. It had permeated much of the dissident tradition and was deeply rooted in both high and popular culture – in the works of Tolstoy and Dostoevsky, of Herzen and the revolutionary tradition, in the collectivism of the peasant commune, in the ethos of the Russian Orthodox Church.

No less severe a handicap suffered by the 'reformers' was their difficulty in associating the requisites of shock therapy with an appeal to patriotic and nationalist sentiment. Here the problem lay not in the fact that for so long capitalism had been identified as an alien Western system, but rather in the government's approach to foreign affairs. To maximize the chances of shock therapy taking effect and the Russian economy being integrated with all speed into that of the West, it was essential to minimize friction with the other ex-Soviet republics and the major industrial powers, to reduce the arms burden, and to draw upon western loans and assistance. Accordingly, the government adopted a highly conciliatory international stance. Further arms reduction agreements were made with the USA. A timetable was drawn up for the withdrawal of Russian troops from other parts of the former Soviet Union and a compromise reached with Ukraine over the division of the Black Sea fleet. Despite popular sympathy for Serbia, Russia joined in condemning her aggression in the Bosnian conflict. For a moment there was

349

even talk of placating Japan by handing back the islands annexed in 1945. Most emotive of all was the issue of the 25 million ethnic Russians who, as the Soviet Union disintegrated, found themselves subject to foreign governments. With the titular nationality of each of the other successor republics hastening to entrench their control and tending to favour their members over minorities, the flow of Russians returning to the motherland threatened to become a torrent. There were mounting calls for Moscow to exert its influence in defence of embattled compatriots in what became known as the 'near abroad'. All too easily the government's extreme caution in doing so was portrayed as a failure to uphold Russian interests, as humiliating subservience to the West, as betrayal. The analogy brought to mind was less that of Federal Germany than of the ill-fated Weimar Republic.

In this situation, the resistance to shock therapy proved much more potent than free market enthusiasts had anticipated. Military leaders made clear their grave disquiet at the decline in Russia's international status and planned defence cuts, as well as at soldiers' deteriorating living conditions. Managers of leading industrial enterprises protested vigorously at the government's proclaimed determination to whittle down subsidies and force them to adapt swiftly to market conditions and international competition. In many areas, municipal and local governments proved exasperatingly slow to implement the stream of decrees pouring from Moscow. Friction over shock therapy was among the issues inflaming relations between the central government and the autonomous units within the Russian Federation. A new Federal Treaty signed in March 1992 attempted to regulate these relations. It spelled out the overriding authority of the federal government and legislature while at the same time endowing each of the 'sovereign' republics (raised from sixteen to twenty and later to twenty-one) with its own constitution and parliament and placing them in other respects on the same formal footing as the all-Russian administrative regions. Only 12 per cent of the total population belonged to nationalities with their own national territories; of these 17.7 million people only some 10 million lived within their designated national territory; and in only four of the territories with republican status did the titular majority constitute a majority. Despite the ominous analogy with the Union Republics of the USSR, the threat posed to the integrity of the Federation by minority nationalism was of a lesser order. Nevertheless, pressure for increased autonomy grew markedly, and the leadership of two republics, those of Chechen and Tatarstan, refused to sign the Treaty, claimed independence, and directly challenged the authority of the federal government. In seeking to assert that authority, both over the national-territorial units and over recalcitrant Russian regional officials opposed to shock therapy, Yeltsin was driven to rely on specially appointed Presidential Representatives – and in the Chechen case on an abortive show of force.

The President's use of 'undemocratic' measures in pursuit of shock therapy was fiercely denounced in the Russian Congress and Supreme Soviet (elected, as we have seen, in March 1990). While a minority of deputies remained supportive of the government and its critics were divided into ill-coordinated factions, increasingly vitriolic attacks upon it were spearheaded by Yeltsin's former allies, the Speaker, Khasbulatov, and Vice-President, Rutskoi. In December 1992 Yeltsin was compelled to replace Gaidar, then Acting Prime Minister, with V. Chernomyrdin who favoured a more cautious form of market reform. The following March saw the Congress strip Yeltsin of his emergency powers. In April Yeltsin responded by holding a referendum to fortify his position and secured a vote of confidence both in himself (58.7 per cent) and in his government's socioeconomic policies (53 per cent). In the course of 1993, however, tension over these polices grew within the government itself as the ministries of finance and privatization remained committed to shock therapy, while those responsible for industry, agriculture and energy pressed the State Bank to loosen monetary policy and continue to subsidize embattled enterprises. At the same time, friction between President and parliament – over the pace of market reform, over the government's 'pro-Western' foreign policy, and over the distribution of power in the proposed new constitution – became ever more bitter.

By September 1993 Yeltsin's patience was exhausted and, in a move which he admitted was unconstitutional, he dismissed the parliament. A substantial proportion of the deputies defied his decree and barricaded themselves into the White House. The following month, after a tense siege, Rutskoi and Khasbulatov mistakenly took a riot by a few thousand supporters as evidence of popular support and called for the overthrow of the government. Yeltsin succeeded in mobilizing special military units to bombard the White House and arrest his critics. This victory emboldened the 'reformers'. They promptly amended the proposed constitution in order to enhance dramatically the powers of the presidency. The new parliament was to consist of two chambers, the Council of the Federation, representing the regions and republics, and a lower house, the State Duma, half of whose members were to be elected by proportional representation (PR) and half on a first-past-the-post constituency basis. But these bodies were placed in a clearly subordinate position. At the same time, the autonomy of the republics was reduced and reference to their 'sovereign' status was dropped. A referendum on the constitution together with fresh parliamentary elections was called for 12 December.

Gaidar and the 'reformers' anticipated the elections with confidence. It was true that divisions among those who had initially been broadly supportive of the government's economic policy led to the formation of rival electoral blocs, the most prominent being 'Russia's Choice' headed by Gaidar, the Yavlinsky-Boldyrev-Lukin Bloc, and the Party of Russian Unity and Accord. It was true, too, that Yeltsin declined to identify himself directly with any bloc. But it was clear where his sympathies lay and the 'reformers' were confident that the enormous prestige he had acquired in the

Map 14   The Republics of the Russian Federation, 1993

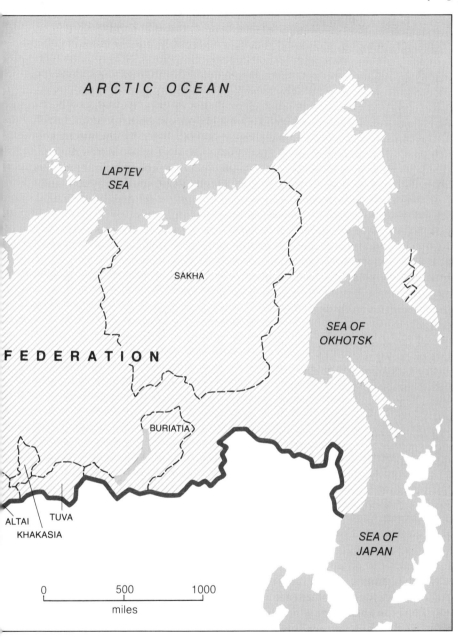

ARCTIC OCEAN

LAPTEV
SEA

SAKHA

SEA OF
OKHOTSK

F E D E R A T I O N

BURIATIA

ALTAI   TUVA
KHAKASIA

SEA OF
JAPAN

0   500   1000
miles

course of his struggle against Gorbachev and his resistance to the *putsch* of August 1991 remained intact. Moreover, even if the new parliament proved less easy to manage than they expected, they anticipated being able to rely upon the panoply of powers which the new constitution would entrust to the president. Their confidence was further bolstered by the low public esteem for their most strident opponents in the parliament that had been abolished. The government line that its critics were die-hard Communists, neo-fascists and irresponsible chauvinists terrified of facing the electorate might be a caricature. But from the outset, the democratic legitimacy of deputies in the Russian Congress and Supreme Soviet was compromised by the fact that they had won their seats in March 1990, under a system still heavily under the influence of the CPSU. The opposition presented by the many deputies intimately associated with the management of major state enterprises smacked of reactionary defence of their own interests and the discredited command economy. Both Khasbulatov and Rutskoi were widely regarded as opportunistic and inconsistent. Furthermore, television, radio and most of the press were in the hands of supporters of 'reform' and heavy pressure was brought to bear against dissenting voices. In the course of the election campaign, although opposition parties were given air-time, government spokesmen threatened to disqualify any candidate who criticized the proposed constitution and Yeltsin warned that its rejection would raise the spectre of civil war.

Yet by late 1993 the obstacles to sustaining democratic support for a government identified with shock therapy were becoming increasingly apparent. The popular enthusiasm and political involvement of the Gorbachev years had long faded. Since the heady days of 1989, the proportion of the electorate casting their votes in successive elections and referenda had steadily declined. Evidence of apathy and cynicism towards all politicians was clearly revealed in opinion polls, in a drastic fall in demand for newspapers (explained only in part by paper shortage and inflation), and in widespread expression of distaste at both sides for shedding blood in the struggle for the White House in October. A record of bold resistance to the CPSU, communism and Gorbachev was no longer sufficient to ensure support. However much 'reformers' might protest that the economic whirlwind was the inevitable product of Stalinism's appalling legacy, it was they who now ran the gauntlet of the 'protest vote'. It was by no means clear what form political expression of disenchantment with the 'reformers' would take. On the Left, the handicaps which had prevented the emergence of an independent workers' movement during *perestroika* remained. Advocates of a social-democratic programme combining a mixed economy with an active economic role for a democratic State were still unable to project a distinctive image. So negative was the image of state intervention bequeathed by Stalin that they found themselves denounced by 'reformers' as surrogate Communists. So gruelling was the impact of Gaidar's version of market reform that they were scorned by latter-day Communists as softly spoken shock therapists. The refounded Russian Federation Communist Party, whose own programme read at face value very like a variant of the social-democratic mixed economy, carried the odour of its reviled predecessor. The electoral appeal of the Agrarian Party was largely directed towards rural voters and especially collective and state farm workers. The Democratic Party, headed by N. Travkin, was vulnerable to the charge that, despite its fierce disclaimers, it represented the vested interests of leading industrial managers and the ex-*nomenklatura*. The formation and vigorous campaign of the Women of Russia bloc pointed to new assertiveness over the specific burden borne by women, and the Constructive Ecology Movement reflected the depth of environmental concern. But neither appeared likely to make a major impact on the electorate as a whole. Of the thirteen electoral blocs, the least clear in its economic prescriptions, but the most strident in its attacks on 'reformers' and Communists alike, in its militarist and authoritarian tone, in its anti-Semitism and xenophobic assertion of Russian nationalism, was that of the ill-named Liberal Democrats headed by Zhirinovsky.

The election results duly dealt the 'reformers' a severe blow. A bare 55 per cent of the electorate population bothered to vote at all – compared to 80 per cent in Gorbachev's referendum of March 1991 and 64.5 per cent in Yeltsin's referendum of April 1993. Just over half – little more than a quarter of the electorate as a whole – endorsed the constitution. The Duma vote was widely scattered across the contending blocs, with 8 reaching the threshold of 5 per cent necessary to gain a share of the seats allotted according to PR. Gaidar's party scraped only 15.4 per cent (less than 9 per cent of the electorate as a whole) and, even more humiliating, was clearly beaten by Zhirinovsky's party. Although the Liberal Democrats won only a handful of the constituency seats elected according to first-past-the-post rules — many of which went to independents who subsequently formed a New Regional Politics faction — it was clear that the 'reformers' would be outnumbered in the new parliament. Moreover, Zhirinovsky's startling success catapulted him to centre stage and raised the spectre of an abrasive nationalist of his ilk challenging for the presidency when Yeltsin submits himself for re-election or comes to the end of his term (1996). The effect was dramatic. Abroad, Western governments became more wary of Russia, eastern European governments intensified their pressure to join NATO, and the ex-Soviet republics expressed alarm that Zhirinovsky's rise signalled an imminent threat to their independence. Yeltsin showed signs of becoming much more assertive, both in the 'near abroad' and towards the West in an attempt to assuage the apparent upsurge in Russian nationalism. In domestic affairs, the 'reformers' were thrown onto the defensive. The narrow margin by which the new constitution had been endorsed suggested that Yeltsin's identification with their policies had gravely eroded his own stature and popularity. Far from delivering a mandate for accelerated free-market reform, the election had demonstrated the depth of popular disenchantment. To sustain shock therapy would be to disregard the verdict. Gaidar resigned from the government and those sympathetic to the policies he had pursued were reduced to a small minority in the new administration headed by Chernomyrdin.

Table 14.1   The Duma Elections

Party/Bloc	% of PR votes	Seats: PR + constituency
Liberal Democrats	22.8	63
Russia's Choice	15.4	76
Communist Party	12.4	45
Women of Russia	8.1	23
Agrarian Party	7.9	55
Yavlinsky Bloc	7.8	25
Russian Unity & Accord	6.8	30
Democratic Party	5.5	15
New Regional Politics	–	65
Independents/Unresolved/others		53
Total		450

Pursuit of the free market dream appeared to have led the 'reformers' to an impasse. They had been unable to administer in full their chosen course of therapy, to balance the budget, stabilize the currency, dismantle the major monopolies or achieve the scale of privatization they had envisaged. Nor had they entrenched either the democratic institutions or the democratic ethos they espoused. On the contrary, in seeking to minimize parliamentary and social pressure upon the executive they had installed a constitution which, on paper, concentrated formidable power in the hands of the presidency. At the same time they had presided over a precipitate decline in democratic participation and provoked an electoral backlash with incalculable consequences. Over much of western Europe there had been a close correlation between democratization and the extension of state intervention, regulation of the market, and welfare provision. Russia's 'reformers', by contrast, had expected to establish democracy and secure popular support at the very moment they were drastically reducing the economic role of the State. They had expected to win popular endorsement for a programme which, in the short term at least, was bound to be associated with severe economic and social disruption. They had expected this endorsement from an urbanized, educated population, whose cultural heritage was steeped in hostility to bourgeois values and who had long been accustomed to guaranteed employment and welfare provision – albeit at a level which, by Western standards, had been spartan. And they had expected it from a nation reeling from blows to its status and very identity for which it is difficult to find a peacetime precedent. Their débâcle reflected both the acute tension between shock therapy and democratization and the grandeur and tragedy inherent in Russia's imperial and Soviet legacy.

Bibliography

This highly selective bibliographical essay draws attention to the works which I have found most illuminating as well as several of those I have found most provocative. The vast bulk of work on Russian history is, of course, not available in English. However, since the best Western studies constructively criticize Soviet findings, and since the torrent of recent publications places a high premium on space, in this edition I have excluded reference to those available only in Russian. A sample of significant Soviet and post-Soviet articles and book-extracts is published in *Soviet Studies in History* (from 1992 *Russian Studies in History*). On the Western side, I have concentrated on books at the expense of articles, but much of the most fresh research is to be found in the pages of the major journals: *Slavic Review*, *Slavonic and East European Review*, *Cahiers du Monde Russe et Soviétique* and *Russian Review*. For the pre-revolutionary period see in particular *Russian History* and *Canadian-American Slavic Studies*; for the post-revolutionary period see in particular *Problems of Communism* (ceased publication 1992), *Soviet Studies* (from 1993 *Europe-Asia Studies*) and *Post-Soviet Affairs*.

Chapters 1 and 2: The origins of the Russian Empire; The genesis of Russian 'absolutism'

There is no better foundation for an understanding of Russian history than mastery of the map. M. Gilbert, *Russian History Atlas* (London 1972) is invaluable for this purpose. Basic information on the territory and peoples long ruled from Moscow is presented in very digestible form in A. Brown *et al.*, eds, *Cambridge Encyclopedia of Russia and the Former Soviet Union* (2nd edn, Cambridge 1993).

The most judicious general survey is N. V. Riasanovsky, *A History of Russia* (Oxford 1984). Stimulating interpretations at variance with my own are: T. Szamuely, *The Russian Tradition* (London 1972); R. Pipes, *Russia Under the Old Regime* (New York 1974); and A. Yanov, *The Origins of Autocracy. Ivan the Terrible in Russian History* (Berkeley 1981), a polemic against both the Western and Soviet historiographical traditions written with verve and passion reminiscent of the nineteenth-century intelligentsia. The most valuable volume in V. O. Kliuchevsky's great nineteenth-century *History* is probably *The Rise of the Romanovs* (London 1970).

The main contours of Kievan, appanage, and Muscovite Russia are succinctly drawn by A. D. Stokes & N. Andreyev in R. Auty & D. Obolensky, eds, *Companion to Russian Studies 1: An Introduction to Russian History* (Cambridge 1976), 49–77, 78–120. A learned study of the ninth-thirteenth centuries is B. Rybakov, *Kievan Rus* (Moscow 1984). The best treatment of the thirteenth century is J. L. I. Fennell, *The Crisis of Medieval Russia, 1200–1304* (London 1983), while the same author provides a lucid account of the political and diplomatic history of Muscovy's rise in *The Emergence of Moscow, 1304–1359* (London 1968) and *Ivan the Great of Moscow* (London 1963). A more recent and extremely skilful synthesis is R. O. Crummey, *The Formation of Muscovy, 1304–1613* (London 1987). For the reigns of Alexis and the regency of Sophia, see P. Longworth, *Alexis: Tsar of All the Russias* (London 1984) and L. A. J. Hughes, *Sophia: Regent of Russia, 1657–1704* (New Haven & London 1990). P. Dukes's synthesis, *The Making of Russian Absolutism, 1613–1801* (2nd edn, London 1990), is enriched by emphasis on those features of Russian development common to western Europe. Muscovy's expansion at the expense of more primitive peoples is examined in W. H. McNeill, *Europe's Steppe Frontier, 1550–1800* (Chicago 1964) and G. L. Lantzeff and R. A. Pierce, *Eastward to Empire. Exploration and Conquest of the Russian Open Frontier to 1750* (Montreal 1973). W. Kirchner, *The Rise of the Baltic Question* (Newark, Del. 1954) focuses on a crucial dimension of Russia's Western involvement.

The essays by B. Plavsic and R. O. Crummey in W. M. Pintner & D. K. Rowney, eds, *Russian Officialdom: The Bureaucratization of Russian Society from the Seventeenth to the Twentieth Century* (London & Chapel Hill, N. C. 1980), 19–45, 46–75 are important contributions on Muscovite administration. Much light is thrown on court politics in Muscovy by G. Alef, *Rulers and Nobles in Fifteenth-Century Muscovy* (London 1983), N. Shields Kollman, *Kinship and Politics: The Making of the Muscovite Political System, 1345–1547* (Stanford 1987), and R. O. Crummey, *Aristocrats and Servitors: The Boyar Elite in Russia, 1613–1689* (Princeton, N.J. 1983).

On socioeconomic development in the countryside, the classic Western work is J. Blum, *Lord and Peasant in Russia from the Ninth to the*

Nineteenth Century (Princeton 1961). The debate over enserfment is reviewed in R. Hellie *Enserfment and Military Change in Muscovy* (Chicago 1971), where the emphasis is placed on the role of the State. The essays in R. Bartlett, ed., *Land Commune and Peasant Community in Russia: Communal Forms in Imperial and Early Soviet Society* (London 1990) provide much insight into the continuities and discontinuities in village society. Peasant life is illuminated by R. E. F. Smith, *The Origins of Farming in Russia* (Paris & The Hague 1959) and *Peasant Farming in Muscovy* (Cambridge 1977), while Part I of B. E. Clements *et al.* eds, *Russia's Women: Accommodation, Resistance, Transformation* (Berkeley, Los Angeles & Oxford 1991) brings together contributions from several of the leading scholars on the experience of women in pre-Petrine Russia.

On Russia's urban and commercial development, special mention should be made of J. M. Hittle, *The Service City. State and Townsmen in Russia, 1600–1800* (Cambridge, Mass. 1979), the essays in M. F. Hamm, ed., *The City in Russian History* (Lexington, Ky 1976), and S. H. Baron, *Muscovite Russia. Collected Essays* (London 1980). The development of large-scale production is examined in J. T. Fuhrmann's rather grandiosely titled *The Origins of Capitalism in Russia. Industry and Progress in the Sixteenth and Seventeenth Centuries* (Chicago 1972).

Attendance at an Orthodox service can offer more insight into the Church than many pages in a book. Differing views of the role and development of the Church and secularization are advanced by: A. P. Vlasto, *The Entry of the Slavs into Christendom. An Introduction to the Medieval History of the Slavs* (Cambridge 1970); D. W. Treadgold, *The West in Russia and China. Religious and Secular Thought in Modern Times. Volume 1, Russia, 1472–1917* (Cambridge 1973); D. Obolensky, *Byzantium and the Slavs. Collected Studies* (London 1971). *The Life of the Archpriest Avvakum by Himself* (London 1963) is an extraordinary monument to the ordeal of the Old Believers.

Although there are fewer collections of documents in translation for Muscovy than for subsequent periods, several are available, perhaps the most useful being R. Hellie, *Introduction to Russian Civilization: Muscovite Society* (Chicago 1967). The reactions of foreign visitors to Russia are introduced by A. G. Cross, *Russia Under Western Eyes, 1553–1825* (London 1971).

Chapter 3: The prime of the Empire

The lively theoretical debate over this period can be approached through P. Anderson, *Lineages of the Absolutist State* (London 1974), R. Hellie, 'The Structure of Modern Russian History: Towards a Dynamic Model', *Russian*

History, IV (1977), 1–22, and the works of the most prolific Western scholar on the period, M. Raeff, *Understanding Imperial Russia: State and Society in the Old Regime* (New York 1981) and *The Well-Ordered Police State: Social and Institutional Change in the Germanies and Russia, 1600–1800* (New Haven, CT 1983).

M. Raeff, *Imperial Russia 1682-1825: The Coming of Age of Modern Russia* (New York 1971) provides a succinct survey, though the latter part has now been superseded by D. Saunders's lively synthesis, *Russia in the Era of Reaction and Reform, 1801–1881* (London 1992). Valuable treatments covering both domestic and foreign affairs of the major reigns are: M. S. Anderson, *Peter the Great* (London 1978); L. Jay Oliva, *Russia in the Era of Peter the Great* (Englewood Cliffs, N.J. 1969); Isabel de Madariaga, *Russia in the Age of Catherine the Great* (London 1981); A. McConnell, *Tsar Alexander I – Paternalistic Reformer* (Arlington Heights, Ill. 1970); W. Bruce Lincoln, *Nicholas I: Emperor and Autocrat of All the Russias* (London 1978).

On the development of the military, two recent key works are J. L. H. Keep, *Soldiers of the Tsar: Army and Society in Russia, 1462–1874* (Oxford 1985) and E. K. Wirtschafter *From Serf to Russian Soldier* (Princeton, N. J. 1990), while J. S. Curtiss, *The Russian Army under Nicholas I, 1825–1855* (Durham, NC 1965) provides a detailed study of the later period. S. P. Oakley, *War and Peace in the Baltic 1560–1790* (London & New York 1992) throws much light on Russia's north-western expansion while C. Duffy, *Russia's Military Way to the West: Origins and Nature of Russian Military Power 1700–1800* (London 1981) offers a colourful essay on the eighteenth century. An interesting and broader study spanning three centuries is W. C. Fuller, *Strategy and Power in Russia, 1600–1914* (New York 1992).

For the political structure of the Imperial regime, and the relationship between State and nobility, see: M. Raeff, *Plans for Political Reform in Russia, 1730–1905* (Englewood Cliffs, N. J. 1969); B. Meehan-Waters, *Autocracy and Aristocracy: The Russian Service Elite of 1730* (New Brunswick, N.J. 1982); R. E. Jones, *The Emancipation of the Russian Nobility, 1762–1785* (Princeton 1973); D. L. Ransel, *The Politics of Catherinian Russia – the Panin Party* (New Haven, Conn. 1975); P. Dukes, *Catherine the Great and the Russian Nobility* (Cambridge 1967); J. T. Alexander, *Autocratic Politics in a National Crisis. The Imperial Russian Government and Pugachev's Revolt, 1773–1775* (Indiana 1969); M. Raeff, *Michael Speransky – Statesman of Imperial Russia, 1772–1839* (The Hague 1969).

On bureaucratic development, in addition to W. M. Pintner & D. K. Rowney, eds, *Russian Officialdom: the Bureaucratization of Russian Society from the Seventeenth to the Twentieth Century* (London & Chapel Hill, N. C. 1980), see H. J. Torke, 'Continuity and Change in the Relations Between

Bureaucracy and Society in Russia, 1613-1861', *Canadian Slavic Studies*, 5 (1971), 457–76; F. Starr, *Decentralization and Self-Government in Russia, 1830–1870* (Princeton 1972); and the idiosyncratic *tour de force* by G. L. Yaney, *The Systematization of Russian Government – Social Evolution in the Domestic Administration of Imperial Russia, 1711–1905* (Urbana, Ill. 1973).

On economic development, see the collection of essays edited by W. L. Blackwell, *Russian Economic Development from Peter the Great to Stalin* (New York 1974); A. Kahan, *The Plow, the Hammer and the Knout: An Economic History of Eighteenth-Century Russia* (Chicago & London 1985); W. L. Blackwell, *The Beginnings of Russian Industrialization 1800–1860* (Princeton 1968); the essays by A. Kahan in M. Cherniavsky, ed., *The Structure of Russian History: Interpretative Essays* (New York 1970), 191–211, 224–50; and W. M. Pintner, *Russian Economic Policy under Nicholas I* (New York 1967). Much additional information is presented in A. J. Rieber, *Merchants and Entrepreneurs in Imperial Russia* (Chapel Hill, N. C. 1982) which, together with J. M. Hittle, *The Service City. State and Townsmen in Russia, 1600–1800* (Cambridge, Mass. 1979), provides stimulating discussion of the problems of the urban elite.

On the peasantry, besides J. Blum, *Lord and Peasant in Russia from the Ninth to the Nineteenth Century* (Princeton 1961), see W. S. Vucinich, ed., *The Peasant in Nineteenth-Century Russia* (Stanford, Calif. 1968); M. Confino, *Domaines et seigneurs en Russie vers la fin du XVIIIe siècle* (Paris 1963), which recreates the outlook of the serf-owner; and two skilful case-studies, S. L. Hoch, *Serfdom and Social Control in Russia: Petrovskoe, a village in Tambov* (Chicago 1986) and R. Bohac's essay in E. Kingston-Mann & T. Mixter, eds, *Peasant Economy, Culture, and Politics of European Russia, 1800–1921* (Princeton, N. J. 1991), 236–260.

An excellent work on the blow dealt the Church by Peter is J. Cracraft, *The Church Reform of Peter the Great* (London 1971); there is a useful collection of essays in R. L. Nicholas & T. G. Stavrou, eds, *Russian Orthodoxy under the Old Regime* (New York 1981); while the Church at the local level in the nineteenth century is brought to life by G. L. Freeze, *The Parish Clergy in Nineteenth-Century Russia: Crisis, Reform, Counter-Reform* (Princeton, N. J. 1983). H. Rogger, *National Consciousness in Eighteenth-Century Russia* (Cambridge, Mass. 1960) brings out an interesting dimension of cultural development which is also examined in E. C. Thaden's older but still useful article on early Russian romantic nationalism in *Interpreting History: Collective Essays on Russia's Relations with Europe* (New York 1990), 179–201. N. V. Riasanovsky explores the growing tension between the regime and its critics in *A Parting of Ways. Government and the Educated Public in Russia, 1801–1855* (Oxford, 1976) and *Nicholas I and Official Nationality in Russia, 1825–1855* (Berkeley, Calif. 1959).

Of the wealth of material on the early intelligentsia, see in particular: M. Raeff, *Origins of the Russian Intelligentsia. The Eighteenth-Century Nobility* (New York 1966); I. Berlin, *Russian Thinkers* (London 1978); E. Lampert, *Studies in Rebellion* (London 1957); M. Malia, *Alexander Herzen and the Birth of Russian Socialism, 1812–1855* (Cambridge, Mass. 1961); E. D. J. Acton, *Alexander Herzen and the role of the intellectual revolutionary* (Cambridge 1979); A. Kelly, *Mikhail Bakunin: A Study in the Psychology and Politics of Utopianism* (New Haven, Conn. and London 1987); D. Offord, *Portraits of Early Russian Liberals* (Cambridge 1985); A Walicki, *The Slavophile Controversy. History of a Conservative Utopia in Nineteenth-Century Russian Thought* (Oxford 1975), and the same author's *History of Russian Thought from the Enlightenment to Marxism* (Oxford 1980).

Chapter 4: The Great Reforms and the development of the revolutionary intelligentsia (1855–1881)

Students of this period owe their greatest debt to P. A. Zaionchkovsky, the late doyen of Soviet specialists on the pre-revolutionary era. Two particularly valuable monographs, available in translation, are *The Abolition of Serfdom in Russia* and *The Russian Autocracy in Crisis* (Gulf Breeze, Fla. 1978, 1979). D. Saunders, *Russia in the Age of Reaction and Reform, 1801–1881* (London 1992) provides the best synthesis and there is a useful introduction and collection of documents in M. McCauley & P. Waldron, *The Emergence of the Modern Russian State, 1856–1881* (London 1988).

For differing interpretations of the political process of Emancipation, see: D. Field, *The End of Serfdom. Nobility and Bureaucracy in Russia, 1855–1861* (Cambridge, Mass. 1976); A. J. Rieber, ed., *The Politics of Autocracy. Letters of Alexander II to Prince A. I. Bariatinskii, 1857–1864* (Paris 1966); T. Emmons, *The Russian Landed Gentry and the Peasant Emancipation of 1861* (Cambridge 1968). The growing number of monographs on various aspects of the reform era include R. S. Wortman, *The Development of a Russian Legal Consciousness* (Chicago 1976), C. A. Ruud, *Fighting Words: Imperial Censorship and the Press, 1804–1906* (Toronto 1982), F. A. Miller, *Dmitrii Miliutin and the Reform Era in Russia* (Vanderbilt 1968), W. B. Lincoln, *Nikolai Miliutin. An Enlightened Bureaucrat of the Nineteenth Century* (Newtonville, Mass. 1977), the same author's *In the Vanguard of Reform: Russia's Enlightened Bureaucrats, 1825–1861* (DeKab, Ill. 1982), and D. T. Orlovsky, *The Limits of Reform: The Ministry of Internal Affairs in Imperial Russia, 1801–1881* (Cambridge, Mass. 1981). See also the relevant essays in T. Emmons & W. S. Vucinich, eds, *The Zemstvo in Russia: An Experiment in Local Self-government* (Cambridge 1982).

Lucid treatment of the economic implications of Emancipation can be found in L. Volin, *A Century of Russian Agriculture* (Cambridge, Mass. 1970) and A. Gerschenkron, *Continuity in History and Other Essays* (Cambridge, Mass. 1965). An invaluable guide, both to the extended debate over late-imperial economic development and to recent research in the field, is P. Gatrell, *The Tsarist Economy 1850–1917* (London 1986). On the formative stages of the Russian working class, see R. E. Zelnik, *Labor and Society in Tsarist Russia. The Factory Workers of St Petersburg 1855–1870* (Stanford, Calif. 1971). A. J. Rieber, *Merchants and Entrepreneurs in Imperial Russia* (London and Chapel Hill, N. C. 1982) provides treatment of developments on the employers' side. The quantity of innovative work on peasant society in late imperial Russia, some of it cited in the following sections, may be sampled in B. Eklof & S. P. Frank, eds, *The World of the Russian Peasant: Post-Emancipation Culture and Society* (Boston, Mass. 1990) and C. D. Worobec, *Peasant Russia: Family and Community in the Post-Emancipation Period* (Princeton, N.J. 1991). D. Field, *Rebels in the Name of the Tsar* (Boston, Mass. 1976) casts much light on peasant consciousness as well as on the problems of revolutionaries.

A useful starting-point on the revolutionary intelligentsia itself is the article by M. Malia in R. Pipes, ed., *The Russian Intelligentsia* (New York 1961), together with P. Pomper, *The Russian Revolutionary Intelligentsia* (Arlington Heights, Ill. 1970). A Soviet commentary written just as Soviet historiography was beginning to free itself from the hagiographic approach of Marxism-Leninism is V. Khoros, I. Pantin, Ye. Plimak, *The Russian Revolutionary Tradition* (Moscow 1988). Two distinctly hostile accounts are V. Nahirny, *The Russian Intelligentsia: From Torment to Silence* (New Brunswick, N.J. 1983) and A. Ulam, *In the Name of the People* (New York 1977). The best analysis of recruitment to 'the cause' is D. Brower, *Training the Nihilists. Education and Radicalism in Tsarist Russia* (Ithaca, N. Y. & London 1975). Much can be learned about the mentality of the young radicals from N. Chernyshevsky's influential novel, *What Is To Be Done?*, ed. and tr. M. R. Katz & W. G. Wagner (Ithaca, N. Y. & London 1989). Sparkling portraits of Chernyshevsky, Dobroliubov and Pisarev are provided by E. Lampert, *Sons Against Fathers: Studies in Russian Radicalism and Revolution* (Oxford 1965), while P. Pomper, *Peter Lavrov and the Russian Revolutionary Movement* (Chicago and London 1972) is a valuable biography. A useful essay on the intellectual history of the period is A. Walicki, *The Controversy over Capitalism: Studies in the Social Philosophy of the Russian Populists* (Oxford 1969). B. A. Engel, *Mothers and Daughters: Women of the Intelligentsia in Nineteenth-Century Russia* (Cambridge 1983) is one of several recent studies of female radicals. D. Hardy, *Land and Freedom: The Origins of Russian Terrorism, 1876–1879* (Westport, Conn. 1987) examines a key phase in the development of the underground while the major survey of the revolutionary movement in the period as a whole remains F. Venturi, *Roots of Revolution. A History of the Populist and Socialist Movements in Nineteenth-Century Russia* (London 1960).

To savour the cultural richness of the period there is no substitute for reading the great classics themselves. *War and Peace* appeared in 1869, *Anna Karenina* in 1877, *The Brothers Karamazov* in 1880, and Turgenev's six novels between 1856 and 1877. Of comparable literary quality and more direct historical interest is Alexander Herzen's *My Past and Thoughts* (London 1968), perhaps the greatest nineteenth-century autobiography in any language.

Chapter 5: Industrialization and Revolution (1881–1905)

P. A. Zaionchkovsky, *The Russian Autocracy under Alexander III* (Gulf Breeze, Fla. 1978) provides a good starting-point for the period, while the best synthesis is H. Rogger, *Russia in the Age of Modernization and Revolution* (London 1983).

A succinct introduction to Russia's industrialization is M. Falkus, *The Industrialization of Russia 1700–1914* (London 1972). A. Gerschenkron's highly influential – and beautifully written – account of the State's role in overcoming economic backwardness is available in *Economic Backwardness in Historical Perspective* (Cambridge, Mass. 1962). It and the stimulating account by T. H. von Laue, *Sergei Witte and the Industrialization of Russia* should be read in conjunction with O. Crisp, *Studies in the Russian Economy Before 1914* (London 1976), and P. Gatrell, *The Tsarist Economy, 1850–1917* (London 1986).

On the nobility, see G. M. Hamburg, *The Politics of the Russian Nobility, 1881–1905* (New Brunswick, N.J. 1984). On the economic condition of the peasantry, see J. Y. Simms, 'The crisis in Russian agriculture at the end of the nineteenth century: a different view', *Slavic Review* 36 (1977), 377–98, and the essays by E. M. Wilbur and S. Wheatcroft in E. Kingston-Mann and T. Mixter, eds, *Peasant Economy, Culture, and Politics of European Russia, 1800–1921* (Princeton, N.J. 1991). Much light is thrown on peasant life and culture by J. Brooks, *When Russia Learned to Read. Literacy and Popular Literature, 1861–1917* (Princeton, N.J. 1985), B. Eklof, *Russian Peasant Schools: Officialdom, Village Culture and Popular Pedagogy, 1861–1914* (Berkeley, Calif. 1986), and the essays on the period in B. Farnsworth & L. Viola, eds, *Russian Peasant Women* (1992) and B. E. Clements, *et al.* eds, *Russia's Women. Accommodation, Resistance, Transformation* (Berkeley, Calif. & Oxford 1991). T. Shanin, *The Roots of Otherness: Russia's Turn of Century* (2 vols, London 1985, 1986) is the most heavyweight 'neo-populist' treatment of the peasantry.

For the social and political development of the middle classes, besides A. J. Rieber, *Merchants and Entrepreneurs in Imperial Russia* (Chapel Hill, N. C. 1982), see T. G. Owen, *Capitalism and Politics in Russia: A Social History of the Moscow Merchants 1855–1905* (Cambridge 1981). An excellent study of higher education and student protest is D. Kassow, *Students, Professors, and the State in Tsarist Russia* (Berkeley, Calif. 1989). A ground-breaking work on seven decades of feminism is R. Stites, *The Women's Liberation Movement in Russia. Feminism, Nihilism and Bolshevism, 1860–1930* (Princeton, N.J. 1978). There are useful discussions of the first intimations of the 'silver age' and guidance to further reading on cultural developments in the period in vols 2 and 3 of R. Auty & D. Obolensky, eds, *Companion to Russian Studies* (Cambridge 1977, 1980).

P. Waldron's consideration of religious toleration (or lack of it) and R. Pearson's treatment of the 'nationalities question' are among a valuable collection of essays in O. Crisp and L. Edmondson, *Civil Rights in Imperial Russia* (Oxford 1989).

Until recently, the great bulk of work on the period focused upon workers, the intelligentsia and relations between the two. Light is thrown on workers from three very different angles by R. E. Johnson, *Peasant and Proletarian. The Working Class of Moscow in the Late Nineteenth Century* (Leicester 1979), R. L. Glickman, *Russian Factory Women. Workplace and Society 1880–1914* (Berkeley, Calif. 1984), and J. H. Bater, *St. Petersburg: Industrialization and Change* (London 1976). For the radicals of the 1880s, see N. Naimark, *Terrorists and Social Democrats. The Russian Revolutionary Movement under Alexander III* (Cambridge, Mass. 1983) and D. Offord, *The Russian Revolutionary Movement in the 1880s* (Cambridge 1986). Sharply conflicting views are presented by R. E. Pipes, *Social Democracy and the St Petersburg Labor Movement* (Cambridge, Mass. 1963) and A. K. Wildman, *The Making of a Workers' Revolution. Russian Social Democracy, 1891–1903* (Chicago & London 1967). J. Frankel, *Prophecy and Politics: Socialism, Nationalism and the Russian Jews 1862–1917* (Cambridge 1981) and R. Brym, *The Jewish Intelligentsia and Russian Marxism* (London 1978) are two highly perceptive studies of left-wing reactions among the worst-treated minority. For the intellectual debate of the 1890s see A. P. Mendel, *Dilemmas of Progress in Tsarist Russia: Legal Marxism and Legal Populism* (Cambridge, Mass. 1961). A social profile of the activists is given in D. Lane, *The Roots of Russian Communism. A Social and Historical Study of Russian Social Democracy, 1898–1907* (Assen 1969). J. Frankel, ed., *Vladimir Akimov and the Dilemmas of Russian Marxism, 1895–1903* (Cambridge 1969) is a useful contribution. On Lenin in this period, see N. Harding, *Lenin's Political Thought* vol. 1 (London 1977), and R. Service, *Lenin: A Political Life. Vol. 1: The Strengths of Contradiction* (London 1985). The works of both Lenin and Trotsky are easily available, and among the growing quantity of documents in translation, see in particular N. Harding, ed., *Marxism in Russia: Key Documents 1897–1906* (Cambridge 1983). M. Perrie, *The Agrarian Policy of the Russian Socialist-Revolutionary Party from its Origins through the Revolution of 1905–1907* (Cambridge 1976) provides detailed treatment of the development of early SR policy.

Russia's first revolution has been the subject of much recent study. A major new synthesis is the two-volume work by A. Ascher, *The Revolution of 1905. Russia in Disarray; The Revolution of 1905. Authority Restored* (Stanford, Cal. 1988, 1992). D. Geyer, *Russian Imperialism: The Interactions of Domestic and Foreign Policy, 1860–1914* (Leamington Spa, 1987) includes a good analysis of the background to the war with Japan. For the role and personality of the Tsar, see A. M. Verner, *The Crisis of Russian Autocracy. Nicholas II and the 1905 Revolution* (Princeton, N. J. 1990), and D. C. B. Lieven, *Nicholas II, Emperor of All the Russias* (London 1993). The gravity of unrest in the army is brought home by J. Bushnell, *Mutiny Amid Repression. Russian Soldiers in the Revolution of 1905–1906* (Bloomington, Ind. 1985). On the role of the nobility, see the article by R. T. Manning in L. H. Haimson, ed., *The Politics of Rural Russia, 1905–14* (Bloomington, Ind. 1979), 30–66. For the emergent liberal movement, see R. Pipes, *Struve: Liberal on the Left, 1870–1905* (Cambridge, Mass. 1970) and S. Galai, *The Liberation Movement in Russia: 1900–1905* (Cambridge 1973). On the intelligentsia and workers' protest in 1905, see L. Engelstein, *Moscow 1905. Working-Class Organization and Political Conflict* (Stanford, Cal. 1982) and G. D. Surh, *1905 in St Petersburg: Labor, Society and Revolution* (Stanford, Calif. 1989). For the SRs, see C. J. Rice, *Russian Workers and the Socialist-Revolutionary Party through the Revolution of 1905–1907* (London 1988), while a monograph that throws much light on developments in the countryside is S. J. Seregny, *Russian Teachers and Peasant Revolution: Politics and Education in 1905* (Bloomington, Ind. 1989).

Chapter 6: The end of the Russian Empire (1906–1916)

G. A. Hosking, *The Russian Constitutional Experiment: Government and Duma, 1907–1914* (Cambridge 1973) provides an excellent general account of Duma politics, and can be supplemented with T. Emmons, *The Formation of Political Parties and the First National Elections in Russia* (Cambridge, Mass. 1983), B. Pinchuk, *The Octobrists in the Third Duma, 1907–1912* (Seattle & London 1974), R. Edelman, *Gentry Politics on the Eve of the Russian Revolution: The Nationalist Party 1907–1917* (New Brunswick, N.J. 1980), and R. Pearson, *The Russian Moderates and the Crisis of Tsarism, 1914–1917* (New York & London 1977). The Kadets, who have traditionally attracted the lion's share of attention in the West, not least because of the memoirs of Miliukov, Maklakov and other leaders, are treated in T. Riha, *A Russian European: Paul Miliukov in Russian Politics* (Notre Dame, Ind. & London 1969) and C. E. Timberlake, ed., *Essays on Russian Liberalism* (Columbia, Mo. 1972). M. Szeftel, *The Russian Constitution of April 23, 1906* (Brussels 1976) gives a thorough commentary on the theoretical structure of the constitution. D. C. B. Lieven, *Russia's Rulers Under the Old Regime* (London 1989) provides a lively and detailed study of the members of the State Council. The declining reliability of Tsarism's coercive apparatus is brought out in W. C. Fuller, *Civil-Military Conflict in Imperial Russia, 1881–1914* (Princeton, N.J. 1986) and R. McNeal, *Tsar and Cossack, 1855–1914* (New York). For a useful introduction to the mounting problems posed by the national minorities, see H. Rogger, *Russia in the Age of Modernization and Revolution 1881–1917* (London 1983), chapter 9.

The *Cambridge Economic History of Europe*, vol. VII (Cambridge 1978) has three valuable contributions on Russia. Rural Russia in the period has been closely studied in recent years. L. H. Haimson, ed., *The Politics of Rural Russia, 1905–1914* (Bloomington, Ind. 1979) and R. T. Manning, *The Crisis of the Old Order in Russia: Gentry and Government* (Princeton, N.J. 1982) opened new vistas while a different view is argued by S. Becker, *Nobility and Privilege in Late Imperial Russia* (Dekalb, Ill. 1985). *The Urge to Mobilize: Agrarian Reform in Russia, 1861–1930* (Urbana, Ill., Chicago & London 1982) is another perplexing book by G. Yaney which must be handled with care. A more accessible account of the impact of the Stolypin land reform can be found in D. Atkinson, *The End of the Russian Land Commune, 1905–1930* (Stanford, Calif. 1983), while T. Shanin, *The Roots of Otherness: Russia's Turn of the Century* (2 vols, London 1985, 1986) is of major importance for this period too. T. Emmons and W. S. Vucinich, eds, *The Zemstvo in Russia: An Experiment in Local Self-government* (Cambridge 1982) has several useful essays bringing out, among other things, peasant hostility towards the zemstvos.

A highly influential essay on urban society is L. Haimson, 'The Problem of Social Stability in Urban Russia, 1905–1917', *Slavic Review*, 23 (1964), 619–42, and 24 (1965), 1–22. The conflicting portents for the development of 'civil society' are brought out in several of the contributions to O. Crisp and L. Edmondson, *Civil Rights in Imperial Russia* (Oxford 1989) and E. Clowes & S. Kassow, eds, *Between Tsar and People* (Princeton, N.J. 1991). R. W. Thurston, *Liberal City, Conservative State: Moscow and Russia's Urban Crisis, 1906–1914* (Oxford 1987) provides a valuable case study. An excellent analysis of the commercial press is L. McReynolds, *The News Under Russia's Old Regime: The Development of a Mass-Circulation Press* (Princeton, N.J. 1991). On the feminist movement, see L. Edmondson, *Feminism in Russia, 1900–1917* (London 1984). On the universities, see D. Kassow, *Students, Professors, and the State in Tsarist Russia* (Berkeley, Cal. 1989).

There is an illuminating discussion of urban and working-class development in the two capitals in J. H. Bater, *St Petersburg: Industrialization and Change* (London 1976) and the first two chapters of D. Koenker, *Moscow Workers and the 1917 Revolution* (Princeton, N.J. 1981). On the labour movement, see in particular V. E. Bonnell, *The Roots of Rebellion: Workers' Politics and Organizations in St Petersburg and Moscow, 1900–1914* (Berkeley, Calif. 1983), R. C. Elwood, *Russian Social Democracy in the Underground. A Study of the RSDLP in the Ukraine, 1907–1914* (Assen 1974), R. McKean, *St Petersburg Between the Revolutions: Workers and Revolutionaries, June 1907–February 1917* (New Haven & London 1990), and T. McDaniel, *Autocracy, Capitalism and Revolution in Russia* (Berkeley, Calif. & London 1988). Of the host of works concentrating on Lenin and the Bolsheviks, see R. Service, *Lenin: A Political Life. I: The Strengths of Contradiction, II: Worlds in Collision* (London 1985, 1991), N. Harding, *Lenin's Political Thought*, vol. 1 (London 1977), and R. C. Williams, *The Other Bolsheviks. Lenin and his Critics, 1904–1914* (Bloomington, Ind. 1986). On Trotsky the place to start is still I. Deutscher's classic trilogy. Three useful biographies of leading Mensheviks are: S. Baron, *Plekhanov: The Father of Russian Marxism* (Stanford, Calif. 1963); A. Ascher, *Pavel Axelrod and the Development of Menshevism* (Cambridge, Mass. 1972); and I. Getzler, *Martov: A Political Biography of a Russian Social Democrat* (Cambridge 1967), which should be read alongside the material in L. Haimson, R. Wortman and Z. Galili y Garcia, *The Making of Three Russian Revolutionaries. Voices from the Menshevik Past* (Cambridge 1987). On the SRs in the period, see N. Schleifman, *Undercover Agents in the Russian Revolutionary Movement. The SR Party, 1902–1914* (Basingstoke & London 1988) and M. Melancon *The Socialist Revolutionaries and the Russian Anti-War Movement, 1914–1917* (Columbus, Ohio 1990). The rupture within the intelligentsia symbolized by the publication of *Landmarks* is examined by C. Read, *Religion, Revolution and the Russian Intelligentsia 1900–1912* (London 1979). E. Lampert gives a sensitive survey of the 'silver age' in M. Bradbury & J. McFarlane, eds, *Modernism* (Harmondsworth 1976), 134–50. A very different milieu is entertainingly recaptured in A. de Jonge, *The Life and Times of Grigorii Rasputin* (London 1982).

An admirably succinct and yet wide-ranging discussion of Russia's path to war in 1914 is D. C. B. Lieven, *Russia and the Origins of the First World War* (London 1983). N. Stone, *The Eastern Front, 1914–1917* (London 1975) is invaluable on the course of the war, while the early chapters of A. K. Wildman, *The End of the Russian Imperial Army: the Old Army and the Soldiers' Revolt (March–April 1917)* (Princeton, N.J. 1980) traces developments within the army.

Chapter 7: 1917

The wealth of specialist studies appearing in the last decade and a half, many of them concerned with the revolution 'from below', has done much to advance understanding of the revolution. A guide to the debate is E. D. J. Acton, *Rethinking the Russian Revolution* (London 1990). As yet there has been no weighty synthesis of this new material. L. Schapiro, *1917: The Russian Revolutions and the origins of present-day Communism* (Hounslow 1984) is an elegant but narrowly political resumé. R. Pipes, *The Russian Revolution, 1899–1918* (London 1990) ignores much of the best recent work. More useful though becoming dated is M. Ferro's two-volume study, *The Russian Revolution of February 1917* (London 1972) and *October 1917. A Social History of the Russian Revolution* (London 1980).

Three valuable essay collections with a strong emphasis on the revolution 'from below' are D. H. Kaiser, ed., *The Workers' Revolution in Russia, 1917. The View from Below* (Cambridge 1987); R. Service, ed., *Society and Politics in the Russian Revolution* (London 1992); and E. R. Frankel *et al.*, eds, *Revolution in Russia: Reassessments of 1917* (Cambridge 1992). For the breakdown of the army and the Baltic Fleet respectively, see A. K. Wildman, *The End of the Imperial Army. 1: The Old Army and the Soldiers' Revolt, March–April 1917, 2: The Road to Soviet Power* (Princeton, N.J. 1980, 1987); H. White, '1917 in the rear garrisons', in L. Edmondson & P. Waldron, eds, *Economy and Society in Russia and the Soviet Union, 1860–1930* (New York 1992), 152–68; and E. Mawdsley, *The Russian Revolution and the Baltic Fleet* (London 1978). On the working-class movement see D. Koenker, *Moscow Workers and the 1917 Revolution* (Princeton, N.J. 1981); D. Mandel, *The Petrograd Workers and the Fall of the Old Regime* and *The Petrograd Workers and the Soviet Seizure of Power* (London 1983, 1984); S. A. Smith, *Red Petrograd. Revolution in the Factories 1917–1918* (Cambridge 1983); R. A. Wade, *Red Guards and Workers' Militia in the Russian Revolution* (Stanford, Cal. 1984); D. Koenker and W. Rosenberg, *Strikes and Revolution in Russia, 1917* (Princeton, N. J. 1989). Fewer Western monographs have been devoted to the peasantry, but government policy is described by G. Gill, *Peasants and Government in the Russian Revolution* (London 1979), while D. Atkinson, *The End of the Russian Land Commune, 1905–1930* (Stanford Cal. 1983), Part III, and O. Figes, *Peasant Russia, Civil War. The Volga Countryside in Revolution (1917–1921)* (Oxford 1989), chapter 2, provide overviews of the revolution in the countryside.

J. L. H. Keep, *The Russian Revolution: A Study in Mass Mobilization* (London 1976) is a complex and wide-ranging study of mass organizations in 1917 and 1918. O. Anweiler, *The Soviets: The Russian Workers', Peasants' and Soldiers' Councils 1905–1921* (New York 1974) remains valuable.

T. Hasegawa, *The February Revolution: Petrograd 1917* (Seattle & London 1981) presents a richly detailed account of February in the capital. High politics and the ordeal of the Provisional Government can be followed in R. P. Browder & A. F. Kerensky, eds, *The Russian Provisional Government 1917: Documents*, 3 vols (Stanford, Calif. 1961). For the Kadets, see W. G. Rosenberg, *Liberals in the Russian Revolution: The Constitutional Democratic Party, 1917–1921* (Princeton, N.J. 1974). For the SRs, see O.H. Radkey, *The Agrarian Foes of Bolshevism* (New York 1958). W. H. Roobol, *Tsereteli: A Democrat in the Russian Revolution* (The Hague 1976) is a useful biography of a key Menshevik, though the major study of the Menshevik dilemma is Z. Galili, *The Menshevik Leaders in the Russian Revolution. Social Realities and Political Strategies* (Princeton, N.J. 1989). The problem of the war is lucidly explored in R. Wade, *The Russian Search for Peace: February–October 1917* (Stanford, Calif. 1969). A. Rabinowitch, *Prelude to Revolution. The Petrograd Bolsheviks and the July 1917 Uprising* (Bloomington, Ind. 1968) carefully analyses the July days. Kerensky receives balanced treatment by R. Abraham, *Alexander Kerensky. The First Love of the Revolution* (London 1987); G. Katkov, *Russia 1917: The Kornilov Affair. Kerensky and the Break-up of the Russian Army* (London 1980) gives a sympathetic account of Kornilov; while J. L. Munck, *The Kornilov Revolt: A Critical Examination of Sources Research* (Aarhus 1987) is a meticulous study of the contradictory evidence on the Kornilov Affair. The atmosphere in Petrograd in October is brilliantly captured in J. Reed, *Ten Days that Shook the World* (Harmondsworth 1977), while the best analysis of the seizure of power is provided by A. Rabinowitch, *The Bolsheviks Come to Power* (New York & London 1976).

Of the many accounts by leading participants, the most interesting are: N. N. Sukhanov, *The Russian Revolution 1917* (Oxford 1955); V. Chernov, *The Great Russian Revolution* (New Haven, Conn. 1936); A.F. Kerensky, *The Kerensky Memoirs* (London 1965); P. N. Miliukov, *Political Memoirs 1905–1917* (Ann Arbor, Mich. 1967); Trotsky's classic *History of the Russian Revolution*, 3 vols (New York 1932). Various accounts by Western witnesses are skilfully woven together by H. Pitcher, *Witnesses of the Russian Revolution* (forthcoming).

On Lenin, see R. Service, *Lenin: A Political Life. II. Worlds in Collision* (London 1991) and N. Harding, *Lenin's Political Thought* vol. 2 (London 1981). Lenin's approach to revolution is set in the wider European context of European Marxism by G. Lichtheim, *Marxism* (London 1961) and L. Kolakowski, *Main Currents of Marxism. 2: The Golden Age* (Oxford 1981).

R. Pethybridge, *The Spread of the Russian Revolution: Essays on 1917* (London 1972) treats several under-emphasized themes, while D. J. Raleigh, *Revolution on the Volga: 1917 in Saratov* (Ithaca 1985) provides a useful counterpoint to general concentration on Petrograd and Moscow. Three studies of the revolution in non-Russian areas are R. G. Suny, *The Baku Commune 1917–1918* (Princeton, N.J. 1972); J. S. Reshetar, *The Ukrainian Revolution 1917–1920: A Study in Nationalism* (New York 1952); and A. Ezergailis, *The 1917 Revolution in Latvia* (Boulder, Cal. 1974). A wealth of material on the revolution is made readily accessible in H. Shukman, ed., *The Blackwell Encyclopedia of the Russian Revolution* (Oxford 1988).

Chapter 8: Civil War and the consolidation of Bolshevik power (1918–1928)

The fundamental work here is E. H. Carr's fourteen-volume *History of Soviet Russia* (London 1950–78), two volumes of which were written in collaboration with R. W. Davies. After completing the work Carr provided a crisp one-volume introduction, *The Russian Revolution: From Lenin to Stalin (1917–1929)* (London 1979). An excellent synthesis, without Carr's treatment of the international dimension but incorporating more recent work on social history, is L. Siegelbaum, *Soviet State and Society Between Revolutions, 1918–1928* (Cambridge 1992).

On the formative first years of Soviet foreign policy, see R. Debbo, *Revolution and Survival: The Foreign Policy of Soviet Russia 1917–1918* (Liverpool 1979). The best account of the civil war is E. Mawdsley, *The Russian Civil War* (London 1987), while O. Radkey, *The Unknown Civil War in South Russia. A Study of the Green Movement in the Tambov region, 1920–21* (Stanford, Calif. 1976) underscores its complexity. Bolshevik policy towards the national minorities is dealt with by R. Pipes, *The Formation of the Soviet Union: Communism and Nationalism, 1917–1923* (rev. ed., New York 1968), and H. Carrère d'Encausse's work in the field informs her *Lenin: Revolution and Power* (London 1982).

Much of the best work on the period revolves around the explanation for the Bolsheviks' increasingly oppressive rule and reliance upon coercion of the masses in whose name they claimed to rule. For the fate of the Mensheviks, see V. Brovkin, *The Mensheviks After October: Socialist Opposition and the Rise of the Bolshevik Dictatorship* (Ithaca & London 1987); for that of the SRs, see O. Radkey, *The Sickle under the Hammer: The Russian Socialist Revolutionaries in the Early Months of Soviet Rule* (New York 1963); for that of opposition within the Party, R. V. Daniels, *The Conscience of the Revolution: Communist Opposition in Soviet Russia* (Cambridge, Mass. 1961).

The liberal view of post-revolutionary development can be approached through L. Schapiro, *The Origins of the Communist Autocracy* (2nd edn,

Cambridge, Mass. 1977), the same author's *The Communist Party of the Soviet Union*, (2nd edn London 1970), and J. L. H. Keep, *The Russian Revolution: A Study in Mass Mobilization* (London 1976). The role of ideology is stressed in P. C. Roberts, 'War Communism: A Reexamination', *Slavic Review* 29 (1970), 238–61. The major socialist schools of thought are represented by two French scholars, C. Bettelheim, *Class Struggles in the USSR, 1917–1923* (Brighton 1977), *Class Struggles in the USSR, 1923–1930* (Brighton 1978), and D. Rousset, *The Legacy of the Bolshevik Revolution* (London 1982); for the libertarian Left, see C. Sirianni, *Workers' Control and Socialist Democracy: The Soviet Experience*, (London 1982).

More specialist contributions to the debate are: S. A. Smith, *Red Petrograd. Revolution in the Factories 1917–1918* (Cambridge 1983); R. Service, *The Bolshevik Party in Revolution: A Study in Organizational Change* (London 1979); P. Corrigan and D. Sayers, *Socialist Construction and Marxist Theory: Bolshevism and Its Critique* (London 1978); R. Medvedev, *The October Revolution* (New York 1979). Four valuable institutional studies are: F. Benvenuti, *The Bolsheviks and the Red Army, 1918–1922* (Cambridge 1988); G. Leggett, *The Cheka: Lenin's Political Police* (Oxford 1981); T. H. Rigby, *Lenin's Government. Sovnarkom 1917–1922* (Cambridge 1979); and T. Remington, *Building Socialism in Bolshevik Russia. Ideology and Industrial Organization, 1917–1921* (Pittsburgh 1984). Important case studies are provided by I. Getzler, *Kronstadt, 1917–1921. The Fate of a Soviet Democracy* (Cambridge 1983); R. Sakwa, *Soviet Communists in Power. A Study of Moscow during the Civil War, 1918–1921* (New York 1988); and Mary McAuley, *Bread and Justice: State and Society in Petrograd, 1917–1922* (Oxford 1991).

The last of these is one of the growing number of studies which focus on the social history of the civil war and NEP periods. An early contribution was R. Pethybridge, *The Social Prelude to Stalinism* (London 1974). M. Lewin, *The Making of the Soviet System. Essays in the Social History of Interwar Russia* (London 1985) brings together the essays of one of the major authorities on the period. Two valuable collections are D. Koenker *et al.*, eds, *Party, State and Society in the Russian Civil War* (Bloomington, Ind. 1989) and S. Fitzpatrick *et al.* eds, *Russia in the Era of NEP: Explorations in Soviet Society and Culture* (Bloomington, Ind. 1991). The experience of the working class under NEP is analysed by W. Chase, *Workers, Society and the Soviet State: Labor and Life in Moscow, 1918–1929* (Urbana & Chicago, Ill. 1987) and C. Ward, *Russia's Cotton Workers and the New Economic Policy* (Cambridge 1990). An interesting recent study is A. M. Ball, *Russia's Last Capitalists. The Nepmen, 1921–1929* (Berkeley, Calif. 1987). For the best study of the peasantry during the civil war, see O. Figes, *Peasant Russia, Civil War: The Volga Countryside in Revolution (1917–1921)* (Oxford 1989). For the 1920s, see

V. P. Danilov, *Rural Russia under the New Regime* (Bloomington, Ind. 1988), D. Atkinson, *The End of the Russian Land Commune, 1905–1930* (Stanford, Calif. 1983), and D. J. Malle, *Russian Peasant Organization before Collectivization: A Study of Commune and Gathering 1925–1930* (Cambridge 1971).

The most lucid economic history is A. Nove, *An Economic History of the USSR* (rev. edn London 1992). For government policy in the civil war period see S. Malle, *The Economic Organization of War Communism, 1918–1921* (Cambridge 1985), and L. Lih, *Bread and Authority in Russia, 1914–1921* (Berkeley, Calif. 1990) which provides a thoughtful study of continuity and discontinuity in the problems facing government before, during and after 1917. Rural developments under NEP are succinctly summarized in the first part of R. W. Davies, *The Socialist Offensive. The Collectivization of Soviet Agriculture 1929–1930* (London 1980). Several valuable articles are brought together in R. W. Davies, ed., *From Tsarism to New Economic Policy: Continuity and Change in the Economy of the USSR* (London 1990).

For the elaboration of the Soviet State in the 1920s, see O. A. Narkiewicz, *The Making of the Soviet State Apparatus* (Manchester 1970); G. Gill, *The Origins of the Stalinist Political System* (Cambridge 1990); and E. A. Rees, *State Control in Soviet Russia: The Rise and Fall of the Workers' and Peasants' Inspectorate, 1920–1934* (Basingstoke 1987). Of the large bibliography on the political struggles and economic debates of the 1920s, the following are particularly valuable: M. Lewin's very readable *Lenin's Last Struggle* (London 1975); A. Erlich, *The Soviet Industrialization Debate 1924–1928* (Harvard, Mass. 1960); S. Cohen, *Bukharin and the Bolshevik Revolution: A Political Biography, 1888–1938* (Princeton, N.J. 1974); R. C. Tucker, *Stalin as Revolutionary (1879–1929)* (New York 1973); M. Lewin, *Political Undercurrents in Soviet Economic Debates* (London 1975); R. Day, *Leon Trotsky and the Politics of Economic Isolation* (Cambridge 1973); B. Knei-Paz, *The Social and Political Thought of Leon Trotsky* (Oxford 1978); and, especially for the light it throws on Stalin's victory over the Right, C. Merridale, *Moscow Politics and the Rise of Stalin: The Communist Party in the Capital 1925–1932* (London 1990). A thoughtful discussion is provided in Mary McAuley, *Politics and the Soviet Union* (London 1977).

On cultural developments and Bolshevik relations with the cultural intelligentsia, see S. Fitzpatrick, *The Commissariat of the Enlightenment* (Cambridge 1970); C. Read, *Culture and Power in Revolutionary Russia. The Intelligentsia and the Transition from Tsarism to Communism* (Basingstoke 1990); J. Burbank, *Intelligentsia and Revolution: Russian Views of Bolshevism, 1917–1922* (Oxford 1986); R. Stites, *Revolutionary Dreams. Utopian Vision and Experimental Life in the Russian Revolution* (Oxford 1989); and A. Gleason *et al.*, eds, *Bolshevik Culture: Experiment and Order in the Russian Revolution* (Bloomington, Ind. 1985). For an introduction to the literature of the period see the collection of essays by Max Hayward, *Writers in Russia, 1917–1978* (London 1983).

Chapter 9: Stalin's revolution from above (1928–1941)

A crisp introduction to the debate here is C. Ward, *Stalin's Russia* (London 1993). On the concept of totalitarianism, see C. J. Friedrich and Z.K. Brzezinski, *Totalitarian Dictatorship and Autocracy* (2nd edn, Cambridge, Mass. 1965). Trotsky's classic analysis is *The Revolution Betrayed* (London 1937).

Among a spate of recent accounts focusing on Stalin himself, see in particular: W. Laqueur, *Stalin. The Glasnost Revelations* (London 1990); D. Volkogonov, *Stalin. Triumph and Tragedy* (London 1991); R. C. Tucker, *Stalin in Power: The Revolution from Above 1928–1941* (New York 1990).

The economic upheaval is skilfully traced in A. Nove, *An Economic History of the USSR* (rev. edn, London 1992). The debate over the mechanics of the First Five-Year Plan is summarized in M. Ellman, 'Did the Agricultural Surplus Provide the Resources for the Increase in Investment in the USSR during the First Five Year Plan?', *Economic Journal*, 85 (1975), 844–63. See also J. R. Millar, *The Soviet Economic Experiment* (ed. S. J. Linz) (Illinois, 1990). On the Second and Third Five-Year Plans, E. Zaleski, *Stalinist Planning for Economic Growth* (London 1980) is useful if unwieldy. There is an illuminating discussion by S. G. Wheatcroft, *et al.*, 'Soviet industrialization reconsidered: some preliminary conclusions about economic developments 1926–1941', *Economic History Review* 2 (1986).

For collectivization, see the two volumes by R. W. Davies, *The Socialist Offensive. The Collectivization of Soviet Agriculture, 1929–1930* (London 1980) and *The Soviet Collective Farm, 1929–1930* (London 1980), M. Lewin, *Russian Peasants and Soviet Power* (London 1968), and the essays in M. Lewin, *The Making of the Soviet System. Essays in the Social History of Interwar Russia* (London 1985). L. Viola, *The Best Sons of the Fatherland: Workers in the Vanguard of Soviet Collectivization* (Oxford 1987) examines sympathetically the role of the 25000ers. A thought-provoking discussion of the relationship between collectivization and labour mobilization, both forced and free, is S. Swianiewicz, *Forced Labour and Economic Development. An Enquiry into the Experience of Soviet Industrialization* (Oxford 1965).

For the experience of the Church, see D. V. Pospielovsky, *The Russian Church under the Soviet Regime, 1917–1982* (2 vols., Crestwood, N.Y. 1984) and for that of women, S. Bridger, ed., *Women in the Soviet*

Countryside: Women's Roles in Rural Development in the Soviet Union (Cambridge 1987). The horror of the famine is examined in R. Conquest, *The Harvest of Sorrow: Soviet Collectivization and the Terror-Famine* (New York 1986), while that of the camps can be glimpsed through R. Conquest, *Kolyma. The Arctic Death Camps* (London 1978), and of course the works of Alexander Solzhenitsyn, above all *The Gulag Archipelago* (London 1974–78). Key contributions to the grim debate over numbers can be found in *Soviet Studies* from 1981 to 1993.

There has been a flurry of new monographs on the working class in the period: V. Andrle, *Workers in Stalin's Russia: Industrialization and Social Change in a Planned Economy* (Hemel Hempstead 1988); D. Filtzer, *Soviet Workers and Stalinist Industrialization: The Formation of Modern Soviet Production Relations, 1928–1941* (London 1986); H. Kuromiya, *Stalin's Industrial Revolution: Politics and Workers, 1928–1932* (Cambridge 1988); and L. H. Siegelbaum, *Stakhanovism and the Politics of Productivity in the USSR, 1935–1941* (Cambridge 1988).

The process of upward social mobility is examined in S. Fitzpatrick, *Education and Social Mobility in the Soviet Union, 1921–1934* (Cambridge 1979). The experience of white-collar specialists and managers is treated in N. Lampert, *The Technical Intelligentsia and the Soviet State: A Study of Soviet Managers and Technicians 1928–1935* (London 1979) and K. E. Bailes, *Technology and Society under Lenin and Stalin: Origins of the Soviet Technical Intelligentsia 1917–1941* (Princeton, N.J. 1978).

The pioneering and still the best dissident work written in the Soviet period on the Terror is R. Medvedev, *Let History Judge. The Origins and Consequences of Stalinism* (rev. edn, New York 1988). The best-known account in the West (and recently translated into Russian) is R. Conquest, *The Great Terror: A Reassessment* (London 1990). Particularly good on the ordeal of minority nationalities is H. Carrère d'Encausse, *Stalin – Order Through Terror* (London 1981). A highly controversial contribution focusing on the mid-1930s is J. A. Getty, *Origins of the Great Purges: The Soviet Communist Party Reconsidered, 1933–1938* (Cambridge 1985). Interesting suggestions on the dynamics of the Great Terror of 1936–38 are contained in: Mary McAuley, *Politics and the Soviet Union* (London 1977); A. W. Gouldner, 'Stalinism: A Study of Internal Colonialism', *Telos*, 34 (1977–78), 5–48; G. T. Rittersporn, *Stalinist Simplifications and Soviet Complications. Social Tensions and Political Conflicts in the USSR, 1933–1953* (Chur 1991); N. Lampert and G. T. Rittersporn, eds, *Stalinism: Its Nature and Aftermath* (Basingstoke 1992); and J. A. Getty and R. T. Manning, eds, *Stalinist Terror* (Cambridge 1993).

For a fascinating collection of essays on the cultural revolution, see S. Fitzpatrick, ed., *Cultural Revolution in Russia, 1928–31* (Bloomington, Ind. 1978). For developments on the 'historical front', see J. Barber, *Soviet Historians in Crisis, 1928–32* (London 1981), on the 'literary front', A.

Kemp-Welch, *Stalin and the Literary Intelligentsia, 1928–1939* (London 1991). Two original treatments of cultural developments later in the decade are K. Clark, *The Soviet Novel. History as Ritual* (Chicago & London 1981) and V. Dunham, *In Stalin's Time: Middle Class Values in Soviet Fiction* (Cambridge 1976). On popular culture see the collection of essays in H. Gunther, ed., *The Culture of the Stalin Period* (London 1990).

On foreign policy, see E. H. Carr, *The Twilight of Comintern, 1930–1935* (London 1982), and the two volumes by J. Haslam, *Soviet Foreign Policy, 1930–1933: The Impact of the Depression*, and *The Soviet Union and the Struggle for Collective Security* (London 1983, 1984).

Chapter 10: World War and Cold War (1941–1953)

The most authoritative account is J. Erickson's two-volume history, *Stalin's War With Germany. The Road to Stalingrad* (London 1975) and *The Road to Berlin* (London 1983). The remarkable annotated bibliography is the starting-point for any detailed study of the military record. A less demanding introduction is the series of essays in J. F. Dunnigan, ed., *The Russian Front. Germany's War in the East, 1941–1945* (London 1978). The view handed down to successive generations of Soviet schoolchildren is presented in G. Lyons, *The Russian Version of the Second World War* (London 1976). A fascinating account of wartime Russia is A. Werth, *Russia at War, 1941–1945* (London 1964); W. Moskoff, *The Bread of Affliction: the Food Supply in the USSR During World War II* (Cambridge 1990) focuses on a crucial aspect of the war effort; while J. D. Barber and M. Harrison, *The Soviet Home Front 1941–1945: A Social and Economic History of the USSR in World War II* (London 1991) pulls together a mass of recent research. For a sympathetic account of Vlasov, see C. Andreyev, *Vlasov and the Russian Liberation Movement: Soviet Reality and Émigré Theories* (Cambridge 1987). On the mass deportation of minority nationalities, see A. M. Nekrich, *The Punished Peoples. The Deportation and Fate of Soviet Minorities at the End of the Second World War* (New York 1978).

Not surprisingly, studies of Soviet foreign policy in the 1940s and early 1950s are much less common than works contributing to the controversy over the degree of American responsibility for the Cold War. On wartime diplomacy, V. Mastny, *Russia's Road to the Cold War: Diplomacy, Warfare and the Politics of Communism 1941–1945* (New York 1979) is judicious. Z. A. B. Zeman, *Pursued by a Bear. The Making of Eastern Europe* (London 1989) includes a stimulating study of the immediate post-war years from the vantage point of eastern Europe. T. W. Wolfe, *Soviet Power and Europe 1945–1970* (Baltimore & London 1970) is particularly valuable on post-war military development. Four works which attempt to reconstruct post-war factional disputes and to relate them to foreign and domestic policy issues are: W. O. McCagg, Jr, *Stalin Embattled 1943–1948* (Detroit 1978); W. G. Hahn, *Postwar Soviet Politics. The Fall of Zhdanov and the Defeat of Moderation, 1946–1953* (Ithaca, N. Y. & London 1982); G. D. Ra'anan, *International Policy Formation in the USSR. Factional 'Debates' during the Zhdanovshchina* (Hamden, Conn. 1983); and T. Dunmore, *Soviet Politics 1945–1953* (London 1984). Though neither entirely convincing nor mutually compatible, they represent painstaking efforts to grapple with the inadequate evidence available. A recent and better documented account is contained in the new biography of Beria by A. Knight, *Beria: Stalin's First Lieutenant* (Princeton, N. J. 1993). Much of our knowledge of high politics in the period comes from the memoirs of Tito's envoy, M. Djilas, *Conversations with Stalin* (London 1962) and those of Khrushchev, *Khrushchev Remembers* (London 1971).

For the problems of economic mobilization see M. Harrison, *Soviet Planning in Peace and War, 1938–1945* (Cambridge 1985). For post-war reconstruction see E. Zaleski, *Stalinist Planning for Economic Growth* (London 1980), A. Nove, *An Economic History of the USSR* (rev. edn, London 1992), and R. Munting, *The Economic Development of the USSR* (London & Canberra 1982). T. Dunmore, *The Stalinist Command Economy. The Soviet State Apparatus and Economic Policy, 1945–1953* (London 1980) is a useful corrective to conventional images of the 'command economy'.

There has been relatively little work on the social history of Stalin's last years, but much can be learned from the collection of articles in S. J. Linz, ed., *The Impact of World War II on the Soviet Union* (Totowa, N.J. 1985). Both K. Clark, *The Soviet Novel. History as Ritual* (Chicago & London 1981) and V. S. Dunham, *In Stalin's Time: Middle Class Values in Soviet Fiction* (Cambridge 1976), examine the changing ethos of the upper echelons of Soviet society. The most absurd features of the post-war cultural atmosphere are brought out in D. T. Joravsky, *The Lysenko Affair* (Cambridge, Mass. 1970). Its tragic aspect is captured in E. Mossman, ed., *The Correspondence of Boris Pasternak and Olga Freidenberg, 1910–1954* (London 1982).

Chapters 11 and 12: Stabilization under Khrushchev and Brezhnev (1953–mid-1970s); Stagnation and Decline (mid-1970s–1985)

Study of the later Soviet period has suffered to some extent from the irresistible fascination exerted by the Gorbachev revolution, and much of the best work written before 1986 has yet to be superseded. For an annotated guide, see T. Konn, ed., *Soviet Studies Guide* (London 1992). A readable introduction to the post-Stalin period is A. Nove, *Stalinism and After* (3rd edn, London 1989). Two useful biographies of Khrushchev are E. Crankshaw, *Khrushchev: A Biography* (London 1968) and R. Medvedev, *Khrushchev* (Oxford 1982), while G. W. Breslauer, *Khrushchev and Brezhnev as Leaders: Building Authority in Soviet Politics* (London 1982) presents a suggestive comparison. On Andropov's rise to power, see Zh. Medvedev, *Andropov* (Oxford 1983).

On the economy, in addition to Nove's general history, see his *The Soviet Economic System* (London 1977), and M. I. Goldman, *USSR in Crisis. The Failure of an Economic System* (New York 1983). For a comparison between Soviet and Western productivity, see A. Bergson, *Productivity and the Social System: The USSR and the West* (Cambridge, Mass. 1978). There is a useful article on labour by D. Filtzer in M. McCauley, ed., *Khrushchev and Khrushchevism* (London 1987). T. Zaslavskaia's 'Novosibirsk Report' is available in *Survey* (Spring 1984), 88–108. H. G. Shaffer, ed., *Soviet Agriculture. An Assessment of its Contribution to Economic Development* (New York & London 1977) contains several stimulating pieces on the problems and achievements of Soviet agriculture. A major theme in A. Yanov, *The Drama of the Soviet 1960s: A Lost Reform* (Berkeley, Calif. 1984) is the effort at agricultural reform under Khrushchev. The best studies of late Soviet society are B. Kerblay, *Modern Soviet Society* (London 1983) and D. Lane, *Soviet Economy and Society* (Oxford 1985). The rise in living standards between the 1950s and 1970s is charted in V. George and N. Manning, *Socialism, Social Welfare and the Soviet Union* (London 1980). Two significant works on equality and social mobility are D. Lane, *The End of Social Inequality?* (London 1982), and W. D. Connor, *Socialism, Politics and Equality. Hierarchy and Change in Eastern Europe and the USSR* (Columbia, Mo. 1978). A good starting-place amidst the growing volume of work on the role of Soviet women is G. W. Lapidus, *Women in Soviet Society: Equality, Development and Social Change* (Berkeley, Calif. 1978). A more recent collection of articles is C. Green, *Soviet Women* (Ontario 1989). There is much colourful material on the privileged elite in M. Voslensky, *Nomenklatura: Anatomy of the Soviet Ruling Class* (London 1984), and on the 'second economy' in K. M. Simis, *USSR: Secrets of a Corrupt Society* (London 1982). N Lampert, *Whistle Blowing in the Soviet Union: Complaints and Abuses under State Socialism* (London 1985) provides insight both into popular attitudes and into the problems of law enforcement. The best of many accounts by Western journalists is M. Walker, *The Waking Giant: Gorbachev's Russia* (New York 1986). M. Lewin, *The Gorbachev Phenomenon. A Historical Interpretation* (Berkeley, Calif. 1988) brings home the scale and depth of social change in the pre-Gorbachev decades.

Sound bases for studying the questions of religion and nationality are

G. Smith, ed., *The Nationalities Question in the Soviet Union* (London 1990), and B. Nahaylo and V. Swoboda, *Soviet Disunion: A History of the Nationalities Problem in the USSR* (London 1990), while treatment of both questions is among the best features of G. Hosking's acclaimed *A History of the Soviet Union* (rev. edn, London 1992).

On foreign policy, a solid introduction is provided by J. L. Nogee and R. H. Donaldson, *Soviet Foreign Policy Since World War II* (New York 1981). There is an interesting exchange over Khrushchev's aims and the constraints upon him in the essays by W. Taubman, A. Yanov, and G. F. Minde II and M. Hennessey, in R. O Crummey, ed., *Reform in Russia and the USSR* (Urbana & Chicago, Ill. 1989). Two readable discussions of the later period are R. Edmonds, *Soviet Foreign Policy: The Brezhnev Years* (Oxford 1983) and J. Steele, *The Limits of Soviet Power. The Kremlin's Foreign Policy* (Harmondsworth 1983). On relations with eastern Europe before the emergence of Solidarity, see R. L. Hutchings, *Soviet-East European Relations: Consolidation and Conflict, 1968–80* (2nd edn, Madison, Wi. 1983). Two major essay collections are S. Bialer, ed., *The Domestic Context of Soviet Foreign Policy* (Boulder, Colo. & London 1981), and R. F. Laird and E. P. Hoffman, *Soviet Foreign Policy in a Changing World* (New York 1986), while S. Bialer, *The Soviet Paradox: External Expansion, Internal Decline* (London 1986) sets Gorbachev's early reforms and international initiatives in context. For discussion of the arms race, see D. Holloway, *The Soviet Union and the Arms Race* (New Haven, Conn. 1983), and C. J. Jacobsen, ed., *The Soviet Defence Enigma* (Oxford 1987). On the decline of détente, see F. Halliday, *The Making of the Second Cold War* (London 1983).

Among the interpretative studies of late Soviet politics, some of the most suggestive and original are: J. F. Hough and M. Fainsod, *How Russia is Governed* (Cambridge, Mass. 1979); J. F. Hough, *Soviet Leadership in Transition* (Washington 1980); S. Bialer, *Stalin's Successors: Leadership, Stability and Change in the Soviet Union* (Cambridge 1980); Mary McAuley, *Politics and the Soviet Union* (London 1977); and V. Zaslavsky, *The Neo-Stalinist State. Class, Ethnicity, and Consensus in Soviet Society* (New York 1982). Three useful collections of articles are N. Harding, ed., *The State in Socialist Society* (London 1984); T. H. Rigby, *et al.*, eds, *Authority, Power and Policy in the USSR* (London 1982), and A. Brown and M. Kaser, eds, *The Soviet Union Since the Fall of Khrushchev* (London 1978). R. J. Hill and P. Frank, *The Soviet Communist Party* (London 1980) offers a concise portrait of the Party, while the full text of the Brezhnev Constitution and its three predecessors, together with a lucid commentary, is provided by A. L. Unger, *Constitutional Development in the USSR* (London 1981).

A useful starting-point on Soviet culture since Stalin is M. Hayward, *Writers in Russia, 1917–1978* (London 1983), which includes a particularly valuable discussion of the decline of 'socialist realism'. B. Kagarlitsky, *The Thinking Reed: Intellectuals and the Soviet State* (London 1988) is a wide-ranging study by a Soviet dissident and committed socialist. On the dissident movement, see P. Reddaway, ed., *Uncensored Russia: The Human Rights Movement in the Soviet Union* (London 1982). The courage and dignity of many of the dissidents is powerfully conveyed in P. G. Grigorenko, *Memoirs* (London 1983), while the early novels of Solzhenitsyn represent the supreme expression of dissident moral fury.

Chapters 13 and 14: *Perestroika* and the fall of the Soviet Union (1985–1991); Epilogue

There is already a vast bibliography on the collapse of the USSR. Three wide-ranging studies of *perestroika* and the Gorbachev upheaval are S. White, *Gorbachev in Power* (Cambridge 1990) (superseded by *Gorbachev and After* (1992) and *After Gorbachev* (1993)); D. Lane, *Soviet Society under Perestroika* (London 1992); and R. Sakwa, *Gorbachev and his reforms 1985–1990* (Hemel Hempstead 1990). G. Hosking, *The Awakening of the Soviet Union* (London 1990) is an important discussion of the early Gorbachev years. The drama is placed in historical perspective by R. V. Daniels, *The End of the Communist Revolution* (London 1993) and C. Merridale and C. Ward, eds, *Perestroika: The Historical Perspective* (London 1991). A valuable essay collection is A. Brown, ed., *New Thinking in Soviet Politics* (London 1989).

The best guides to the economic reforms are A. Aslund, *Gorbachev's Struggle for Economic Reform* (2nd edn, London 1991) and M. I. Goldman, *What Went Wrong with Perestroika* (New York & London 1992). For a strident 'new right' view, see P. J. Boettke, *Why Perestroika Failed. The Politics and Economics of Socialist Transformation* (London 1993).

A good account of Gorbachev's rise is Z. Medvedev, *Gorbachev* (rev. edn, Oxford 1988). For Gorbachev's ideas, see M. S. Gorbachev, *Perestroika: New Thinking for Our Country and the World* (rev. edn, London 1988). On Yeltsin, see J. Morison, *Boris Yeltsin: From Bolshevik to Democrat* (London 1991). Yeltsin's apparently ghosted autobiography is *Against the Grain* (London 1990). Two of the most interesting accounts by leading figures are those of A. Sobchak, *For a New Russia: The Mayor of St Petersburg's Own Struggle for Justice and Democracy* (New York 1992) and Gorbachev's Foreign Minister, E. Shevardnadze, *The Future Belongs to Freedom* (New York 1991). Much light is thrown on the Soviet decision to withdraw from eastern Europe by T. Garton Ash, *In Europe's Name: Germany and the Divided Continent* (Oxford 1993).

For a view from the Left of events at the end of the 1980s, see the two works by B. Kagarlitsky, *Farewell Perestroika: A Soviet Chronicle* (London 1990) and *The Disintegration of the Monolith* (London 1992), and S. Clarke, *et al.*, *What About the Workers? Workers and the Transition to Capitalism in Russia* (London & New York 1993).

For the impact of *glasnost*, see A. Nove, *Glasnost in Action: Cultural Renaissance in Russia* (London 1989); R. W. Davies, *Soviet History in the Gorbachev Revolution* (London 1989); and C. Cerf & M. Albee, eds, *Voices of Glasnost: Letters from the Soviet People to Ogonyok Magazine 1987–1990* (London 1990). On religious revival, see M. Bourdeaux, *Gorbachev, Glasnost and the Gospel* (London 1991). On the role of women, see M. Buckley, ed., *Perestroika and Soviet Women* (Cambridge 1992). There is interesting material on the problems of youth in A. Wilson and N. Bachkatov, *Living with Glasnost. Youth and Society in a Changing Russia* (London 1988).

On the upsurge of nationalism, see G. W. Lapidus, *et al.*, eds, *From Union to Commonwealth: Nationalism and Separatism in the Soviet Republics* (Cambridge 1992), and G. Simon, *Nationalism and Policy Towards the Nationalities in the Soviet Union: From Totalitarian Dictatorship to Post-Stalinist Society* (Boulder, Co. 1991). On Russian nationalism, see S. K. Carter, *Russian Nationalism: Yesterday, Today, Tomorrow* (London 1990), and R. Szporluk, 'Dilemmas of Russian Nationalism', *Problems of Communism* (July–August 1989).

For an impressive study of post-Soviet Russia, with a valuable bibliography, see R. Sakwa, *Russian Politics and Society* (London 1993). An excellent collection of essays is S. White, *et al.*, *The Politics of Transition: shaping a post-Soviet future.* On the 1992 Federal Treaty and ethnic problems within the Russian Federation, see A. Barsenkov, *et al.*, 'Inter-Ethnic Relations in Russia in 1992', *Russia & the Successor States Briefing Service*, 1 (June 1993).

A good way to follow the unfolding drama is through the pages of *Current Digest of the Soviet Press* (from 1992 *Current Digest of the Post-Soviet Press*).

Index

Introductory note: readers should note that page references in italics indicate illustrations or maps and that subheadings are in chronological order.

Index

Fourth (1912–17) 128, 129, 133, 137, 147
  in 1917 150–1, 153, 171
  1993 345, 351–6
dumy (municipal dumas) 79, 121, 132, 154, 182
Durnovo, P.N. 127, 128, 141
Dzerzhinsky, F.E. 184

East Germany (GDR) 260, 285, 314
East Slavs 3
economy
  Muscovite 18, 22
  Imperial 45, 56
    and Emancipation 65, 66, 77–8
    and industrialization 93–4, 96–7
    1906–13 131
    World War I 143–5
    1917 160–1
  Soviet 182
    New Economic Policy 193–4, 201–4, 205, 206–8
    1928–41 211–12, 215, 219–20
    World War II 248
    post-war reconstruction 264
    post-Stalin 275–6, 278, 297, 299–302, 304–5, 309, 314
    uskorenie 315–16
    perestroika 316–20, 329, 332, 334, 339
    1992–93 343, 345–9, 351
  see also agriculture; industry and industrialization; planning, economic
education
  Imperial 54, 55, 60
    Great Reforms 75, 79, 81–2
    1881–1905 98, 99
    1905–16 126, 136
  Soviet
    post-Revolution 183
    under Stalin 211, 224, 227, 228, 231, 235, 236, 238
    post-Stalin 279, 281, 291, 298, 304, 305
    1992–93 347, 348
  see also culture; literacy; universities
Egypt 286

Eisenstein, S.M. 270
Elizabeth, Tsarina 38, 60
Emancipation of Labour Group 108
Emancipation, of serfs 65–6, 68–72, 85
  and redemption payments 89, 101, 118
Emergency Committee *see* State Emergency Committee
England 4, 30
  see also Britain
enserfment 26–9
  see also peasants; serfs and serfdom
environmental issues 327, 329, 334, 355
Estonia 38, 42, 241, 246, 268
  see also Baltic region
Ethiopia 286
ethnic minorities *see* nationalism
European Conference on Security and Cooperation (1975) 285

'500-day Plan' 320
factory committees, workers' control
  in 1917 155, 160, 161, 169, 177
  after October Revolution 188–90
famine 22
  1601–03 14, 26
  1891–92 98, 101, *102*
  1921–22 179, 194
  1932–33 218
farmers *see* peasants; state farms
Federal Treaty (1992) 350
Filaret, Patriarch 34, 35
Finance, Ministry of 95–6, 101, 106
Finland, Finns
  and Imperial Russia 38, 39, 106, 126, 165
  and 1917 174
  and USSR 181, 241, 256
First World War *see* World War I
Five-Year Plans 207, 210, 278, 281
  First (1928–32) 210–11, 224, 227
  Second (1933–37) 222
  Third (1938–41) 234
  Fourth (1946–50) 264
  Fifth (1951–55) 264, 278
  Ninth (1971–75) 278
  see also planning, economic

387